Family Learning

Also by William F. Russell, Ed.D.

The Gramma Game

The Parents' Handbook of Grammar and Usage

Classics to Read Aloud to Your Children

More Classics to Read Aloud to Your Children

Classic Myths to Read Aloud

family learning

How to help your children succeed in school by learning at home

William F. Russell, Ed.D.

FIRST WORD
Learning Systems, Inc.
ST. CHARLES, ILLINOIS

Published by First Word Learning Systems, Inc., Publishing Division, 37W222 Route 64, St. Charles, Illinois 60175.

Printed in the United States of America.

Cover design by Ann Gjeldum.

Illustrations by Paul Christenson.

The activities in this book have been tested and are safe when conducted as instructed. The author and the publisher accept no responsibility for any damages caused or sustained by the use or misuse of ideas or materials featured in this book.

Publisher's Cataloging-in-Publication *(provided by Quality Books, Inc.)*

Russell, William F., 1945–
    Family learning: how to help your children succeed in school by learning at home / William F. Russell.
    —1st ed.
    p. cm.
    Includes bibliographical references and index.
    Preassigned LCCN: 97-60548
    ISBN: 0-9657752-9-1

    1. Education—Parent participation.   2. Active learning.   3. Child rearing.   I. Title.

LB1048.5.R87 1997   649'.68
                       QBI97-40647

10 9 8 7 6 5 4 3 2

This book is for Kathy; in fact, this book wouldn't even be a book if it weren't for Kathy. You never allowed all the closed doors and the hardened hearts to be reason enough for me to give up. You always looked for, and found, that sure sign that an unseen hand was steering our course. You are my Barnabas, my joy, my love for ever and ever.

Acknowledgments

I am grateful for all the help and, especially, the encouragement I received from my parents, friends, and colleagues throughout the development of *Family Learning*, both as a practice and as a book.

Ann Gjeldum saw the fun and creativity of *Family Learning* right away, and she captured these aspects in a truly inspired cover design.

Paul Christenson wanted *Family Learning* to be not only useful, but used, and so he gave the book's pages and illustrations their open and friendly appearance.

Chuck Potts was, and always will be, my science advisor, my mentor, and my friend.

Tom Freking taught me just a narrow slice of what he knows, but in the process, turned words into type.

John Gjeldum graced the cover with his bright costume and even brighter smile.

I also want to express my gratitude to the following for permission to use their works in the production of *Family Learning*:

William Koechling for the photographs on the front and back covers.

Stephen Carr Reuben, Ph.D., for the extracts from *Children of Character* and *Raising Ethical Children*.

Eric Buehrer and Thomas Nelson Publishers for the extract from *Creating a Positive Public School Experience*, © 1994.

United Feature Syndicate for cartoon strip of "Nancy."

Universal Press Syndicate for cartoon strips of "Calvin and Hobbes" and "For Better or For Worse."

HarperCollins Publishers and Wayne Dosick for two excerpts from *Golden Rules*, by Wayne Dosick. Copyright © 1995 by Wayne Dosick. Reprinted by permission of HarperCollins Publishers, Inc.

HarperCollins Publishers and Dr. Robert Schuller for an excerpt from *Power Thoughts*, by Robert H. Schuller. Copyright © 1993 by Robert Schuller. Reprinted by permission of HarperCollins Publishers, Inc.

Contents

What Is Family Learning?

There is one fact that is absolutely essential for parents to know about their children's education, and for parents to think about when considering the kind of education they would like their children to receive, and it is this: **There is a difference between *learning* and *schooling*.**

We all know that this statement is true, and our experiences in everyday life confirm the fact for us again and again. But today we have reason to view this fact with new-found joy, for it may hold the secret to solving some of the most vexing problems in public education.

You see, if *learning* and *schooling* are not one and the same (as some educational bureaucrats insist they are), then we can actually do something about improving the former without solving all the myriad problems of the latter. After all, our children spend only about thirteen percent of their waking hours from birth to age eighteen in school, so what sense does it make to isolate all their opportunities for learning into that one, narrow sliver of their lives? The fact that we have done so, and that we have been told that we have no alternative, could explain very quickly how we as a nation could spend billions of dollars focusing on the *schooling* crisis without having much effect at all on the real problem that is plaguing our country's children, namely, the crisis in *learning*.

Family Learning is an attempt to change that focus.

Opportunities for learning are everywhere—all around, all the time. They are in everything we see and everything we hear, no matter where we live or where we go. Learning can happen in our homes, out under the stars, on a trip, even in a classroom. But the foundation for all these learning excursions should be the home and the family because that is where we spend the bulk of our time; that is also where we can acquire the learning attitudes and learning skills that will make all our outside learning opportunities—even those that occur in the classroom—valuable and rewarding educational experiences.

Then, too, the home and family should be seen as the primary educational setting because learning is not, cannot, and should not be confined to childhood alone. Solving all the problems of *schooling* would do nothing to feed the natural desire for learning that exists in adult human beings, such as parents, and so mothers and fathers would be no better at all in their roles as learning models or resource guides for their children.

What I call Family Learning describes a whole range of activities through which parents and children improve their knowledge of the world by learning and doing together as a family. It relies upon and takes advantage of the fact that families can be loving, caring, non-threatening environments where children can ask questions without fear of "sounding stupid," and where adults, too, can learn about, and think about, and talk about all the things they have ever wondered about, but couldn't explore in the presence of friends or co-workers. Family Learning makes use of learnings from school, learnings from experience, and learnings from books and other reference sources to broaden and deepen the understanding of adults and children so that they can begin to notice and take advantage of the many learning opportunities that exist all around them every day.

Family Learning is really a way of looking at the world—a life-style, if you will—that any family, no matter what its size or configuration, can practice at its own pace and can adapt to its own needs. In all honesty, I must say that the term Family Learning usually describes a result—a situation that takes some time to achieve. For it is usually the case that a parent, perhaps both parents, will adopt some of the learning habits and practices I suggest, then their children will begin to participate in a few Family Learning activities, then more, until the children adopt these learning habits for themselves. Family Learning will then describe the life-style through which that family grows together as a unit, while each of its members grows as an individual, autonomous, lifelong learner.

Parents do not have to spend vast sums to acquire the books and computer programs and laboratory equipment and all the other educational aids that are touted as "necessities" for parents who are interested in their children's education. They can, instead, learn to make use of all the free or inexpensive resources that are already present in their homes or are available to them through their own public library or through government agencies of all kinds. They can learn to see telephone books, newspapers, road maps, and dinner table conversations as valuable educational aids that can both stimulate and reinforce learning in the home.

Does this sound like "home-schooling" to you? Well, keep in mind that one of the main purposes of Family Learning is to help your children succeed *in school,* and so Family

Learning is not like the home-schooling that many parents have resorted to out of frustration over the public schooling their children were receiving.

But it is helpful, I think, for all of us—parents, teachers, school administrators—to keep in mind one vital point: **Every family home-schools its children.** That's right, **every** family—some more than others, to be sure—but **every** family is a home-schooling family because it is in their family life that children—**all** children—develop the attitudes and the behaviors and the understandings that they will carry with them into the classroom, into the workplace, into their adult lives, and into the families they themselves create. The term *home-schooling* actually covers a continuum that ranges from "I provide all my children's schooling at home" on one end, to "I didn't realize that I was actually teaching my children at home" on the other.

Do you as parents want and expect your children to apply themselves to their schoolwork with diligence and dedication? If you do, then you are teaching them a powerful lesson at home; and if you don't, then you are teaching them an equally powerful lesson at home. Does most of the language that you and your children hear in your home come from sitcoms, rock videos, and rap music, or do you read to each other—perhaps a newspaper article, a library book, a lesson from your child's textbook. In either case, you are teaching your children about language, and you are developing the attitudes they will have about language throughout their lives.

It is what you do in the course of your normal, everyday family life that determines and creates the attitudes that your children have both toward their schooling and toward learning in general. Is it okay to be curious in your home? Can children ask "why?" about things they see or hear or read without appearing silly or ignorant or meddlesome? Do your children ever hear you wonder aloud when something stimulates your own curiosity, and then watch or accompany you in a search for that missing piece of knowledge? This could be as simple as locating the place of a news event on your family globe, or looking up the spelling or pronunciation of a word in your family dictionary.

What? You don't have a family globe or a family dictionary? Well, that's home-schooling, too. You are teaching your children that *learning* and *schooling* are one and the same; you are teaching them that knowledge comes only from certified teachers and textbooks and an occasional filmstrip, not from resources that you can just summon up whenever you really need them. Even more important, though, is the accompanying lesson that serves to stifle whatever curiosity they still may have: Because they can't readily answer their own questions, it is best not to ask those questions in the first place and just wait for them to appear in a workbook exercise.

Now think of all the lessons that aren't taught in school, but are learned just the same—lessons about character, and conduct, and virtues, and what living a "good life" really means. You may not think you are providing instruction in your home about any matters like these, but when parents and teachers create a void in a child's knowledge and understanding of the world, the common culture will gladly rush in to fill it. MTV, Madonna, 90210, Ice T, Beavis and Butt-head, Roseanne, "Just do it!"—and all of their alluring messages about what to value in life and how to attain "success," these are part of the home-schooling curriculum, too. Here, again, you may not think you are teaching at home, but I guarantee that your children are learning at home.

You can't shut out these influences altogether, nor should you, because your children can benefit from seeing and hearing how the common culture thrives on people's weaknesses, and tries to take from them whatever respect they have for themselves. And this self-respect, which is so often praised by modern educators and hailed as the essential ingredient in all learning, is also a product of home-schooling. What you do—and what you don't do—as a family in your own home and in the course of normal family life will strengthen or weaken your children's self-respect, but just remember that it **will** do one or the other.

The attitudes that your children have about learning itself also come, in whole or in part, from their home-schooling. Do they think that the entire purpose of their school experience is to get a good-paying job? If so, there is little wonder that teachers find it so difficult to impress upon students the importance of lessons in spelling, or history, or algebra. But just think what wonders a knowledgeable and talented teacher could work with a classroom full of children who saw *all* learning as being self-improvement, and who saw self-improvement as being a guiding principle in their lives. Just think how a community, even a whole society, could benefit from children who looked upon their education as helping them to know not what they will do, but rather, who they will be.

Parents (as well as teachers and school administrators) need to understand that the research concerning learning in the home is both clear and consistent: The greatest single contributor to a child's academic success is not the quality of the school that the child attends, nor the number of parents in the home, nor their income, nor their education. Rather, it is the experiences that go on as part of everyday life in a family that are the truest predictor of a child's future success in learning. It is these home experiences that make it possible for some children to extract every educational benefit that their public schools have to offer, while their classmates slide further and further back each year, both in their learning and in their love of learning.

But in order for you to begin using these common home experiences in the pursuit of learning, you must first adopt a "learning attitude" and try to instill it in your children. Learning must become valued in your home, and learners must be respected; curiosity must be encouraged, and so must the tenacity to satisfy that curiosity. I find that some of the hardest words for parents (and teachers) to utter in response to a question from a child are "I don't know." In a Family Learning household they are common, but they are inevitably followed by "Let's find out!"

The focus of this book, therefore—and the focus of this entire practice that I call Family Learning—is upon helping parents to start adopting this learning attitude for themselves and to begin modeling it for their children. Ideally, this book should lead you and your children into looking for and recognizing the myriad chances to learn that are all around you—inside and outside your home. This is not a textbook or a reference book but an instruction manual for building your own learning machine, which will then be able to run by itself.

Family Learning is not *the* answer to all the problems in education today, nor is Family Learning right for everyone. But it is a way for concerned parents—single parents, low-income parents, college-educated parents, but *concerned* parents all—to help their children acquire the knowledge, the skills, and the attitudes that will help them succeed in school and continue their learning throughout the rest of their lives.

Nor is Family Learning any help to parents who want their children to have a good education, but are not willing to devote any time or energy to helping them acquire that education. If, however, you do want to apply whatever time you can afford to tapping the power that exists within your home and family, and use that power both to help your children succeed in school and, as the U. S. Army ads say, "be all that they can be," then Family Learning is for you.

Family Learning practices and activities are all designed to become part of your normal, everyday family life—not special, formalized, uncomfortable teaching or tutoring sessions that, except for the absence of a blackboard, would appear just like school. The regularity and frequency of these activities is left up to you, but even a little Family Learning is better than no Family Learning at all.

What Family Learning does require of all who practice it is a willingness to reacquire that sense of curiosity that was born into all of us—that inexhaustible need to know "why?" about everything we see and hear. And many of those who have adopted Family Learning as an identifying theme within their home say that one of the main benefits of learning as a family is that parents and children alike can feel the freedom to be curious again. Without peer pressure, without time pressure, we can all learn how to wonder again—how to marvel at sights and sounds that we cannot explain—without feeling any embarrassment for not knowing, or any shame for asking "why?"

This is why the family provides the ideal environment for our attempts at becoming independent, life-long learners, because we can make use of the existing bonds between family members to provide the acceptance and encouragement we need to wonder openly about the things we don't know, and then to take that first, all-important step toward satisfying our own curiosity. We won't find this acceptance or encouragement in the outside world—whether at school, in the workplace, or in any gathering of friends—because the simple and human act of wondering is generally taken as a sign and an admission of ignorance (and we'd *never* want anyone to think we're ignorant, would we?), and any personal attempts we make at satisfying our curiosity are seen as rejections of the group and its unspoken interest in uniformity and conformity.

So, the family is the perfect place—perhaps the only place—for us to find the strength we need to overcome the forces of complacency that are around us everywhere else in society. This strength does not come instantly or automatically when summoned up inside a family, either, but the power is at least available to us and to our children in this family setting, and we must learn how to structure that setting so that we can all take advantage of the benefits that can be derived from it.

I hope that wondering and investigating become "family themes" in your home— activities that identify your family and that your children can look back on years later as being characteristic of what home and family life was for them. It is these family themes and family traditions that can keep parents and children headed in the right direction even when the pressures and disruptions of modern life do their best to dissipate a family's power and weaken parental resolve.

Family Learning not only helps parents reinstill the curiosity that is so indispensable to learning, it also encourages adults and children to see applications in daily life for what they have already learned. The use or misuse of a word by a sportscaster on television can cause you to consider, and perhaps check in a dictionary, its spelling, its meaning, or its pronunciation. The date on a coin or on a gravestone or on the cornerstone of an old building may cause you to think about what events were going on at that time in your town, or in your country, or in the world at large. The simple pounding of a stake in your backyard on the equinox or the solstice can tell you the degree of Earth's latitude on which you live.

Reinforcements for everything you ever learned in school lie all around you—but outside the school. Our greatest failing as learners (and, perhaps, the greatest failing of our schools) is that we don't recognize all these opportunities that are staring us in the face. Robert Fulghum, in his best-selling book *All I Really Need to Know I Learned in Kindergarten*, makes the point this way:

> And then remember the Dick-and-Jane books and the first word you learned—the biggest word of all—LOOK.

Family Learning offers parents a way to help their children LOOK, and to LOOK for themselves as well. It does not, it cannot, tell you all there is to know or show you all the ways to reinforce your knowledge. But it can open your eyes to a new way of looking at all the things in your world, and in your children's world, and to the idea that if you want to be a learner, you must be a looker, too.

So the practice of Family Learning is much larger than this book, larger than any book. What I have collected here are examples of topics and activities, drawn from widely different fields, that are well suited to out-of-school learning. But these are examples only, and their purpose is to get you started looking for other examples and to get your children started on discovering how these out-of-school learnings can help them better understand their school lessons—and that those school lessons actually have some application in the real world.

Once you and your children start down this road to Family Learning, you will see that it can branch off into dozens of "learning paths" that you can choose to take as your interests lead. Unlike school learning, which is divided into subjects and classes and periods, these learning paths lead everywhere. Let's say that you and your child start out wondering why the winter sun never gets very high in the sky. Your learning about the sun's path leads you into creating a family sundial, which sparks an interest in learning about other methods of telling time, which acquaints you with the histories of ancient cultures and leads you to learn about where and when those cultures flourished on Earth.

Or perhaps you start out wondering why the tops of the ice cubes in the tray are higher than the lip of the tray itself, and this leads to some learning about density and buoyancy, and then about the great Archimedes, and an understanding of why the "forty-niners" who struck gold in California shouted "Eureka!" and then an investigation into the meaning of other state slogans as well. (But it just as easily could have branched off into a look at why icebergs float, and then into the sinking of the *Titanic*, and then into some stories of the Titans from Greek mythology.)

Unlike classroom teachers, who have only a single chance and a limited time to touch on a topic before they have to move the class along, you can come back again and again, from various directions and through widely different learning opportunities, and each time you will demonstrate an attitude that shows that learning is important in your life and that you want it to be important in your children's lives as well. They may not appear to be absorbing the particular lessons or the general attitude you are working so hard to convey; they may not appear to be listening at all. But don't be discouraged by their apparent lack of concern or your apparent failure as a teacher or a learning model. Often, very often, you will find that the lessons you thought had missed their mark entirely, because the only response you got was the glazed look of a "deer in the headlights," *did* sink in after all, and you'll hear the learnings you were trying to impart being repeated and applied to some new situation, perhaps days or weeks after you had written off the entire experience as a lost cause. Again, time is on your side.

Whenever I try to explain the concept of Family Learning to parents groups, or teachers groups, or church groups, or civic groups of various kinds, I always try to focus their attention and understanding upon four essential and defining ideas or principles, two of which I have already discussed: **There is a difference between *learning* and *schooling*, and *Every* family home-schools its children.** Here are the other two.

The principal beneficiary of Family Learning in your family may not have been born yet.

If you think about exactly who it is that will receive the benefit of your efforts to adopt Family Learning in your household, you will, I am sure, think first of all about your children. Indeed, it would be wonderful if those children took to the program right away and enjoyed every opportunity to share a learning activity with you whenever possible. But this will not always be the case. Teenagers, for example, are a tough lot to convince if you begin Family Learning when they are teenagers. (They are much more eager to retain the practice of making learning a family theme if they became accustomed to it as younger children.) Still, this difficulty alone does not mean that you shouldn't try. Maybe your teenagers are looking for "family ties," and the program will take root right away. Maybe a younger sibling will benefit from the experiences and activities that you are directing toward an older child. Maybe your own learning, the increase of your own understanding and excitement about knowing, will be such an important benefit that you will deem all your efforts worthwhile no matter what their effect on your children.

Ah, but now think of one more possibility. Whether you begin Family Learning when your children are teenagers or when they are in grade school, whether you have immediate success or whether your efforts all seem to be met with the stare of a "deer in the headlights," you are establishing *learning* as a family theme for **their** families. When they approach the time to choose how their own children will be raised and what kind of life they want for their own family, they will remember the learning activities that went on in your house and the efforts you made to show them how learning opportunities existed all around them. They will think fondly on these days because they know that you made all these efforts out of love, and they will make the same efforts for their children, out of love, and on and on.

The older we get, it seems, the less we think about planting grasses that grow quickly, but can wither and fade and die. What we are about, and the whole essence of Family Learning, is the planting of oak trees, with deep roots and the promise of continued growth in spite of temporary storms and changing winds.

**Even if our public schools were the best in the world,
Family Learning would still be the right thing to do.**

Family Learning is not an "anti-schooling" program; I believe very strongly that one of the beneficiaries of widespread Family Learning would be the schools themselves. But Family Learning can include topics and subjects and practices that the schools either do not or will not deal with at all. For example, I doubt if there are many elementary schools in the country that include in their standard lessons a study of the brightest stars and constellations. This is not because teachers think that knowing one's way around the night sky is unnecessary or worthless knowledge, but because the lessons from astronomy are difficult to absorb from books alone, and elementary schools simply don't hold classes at night. Family Learning, however, is not bound by this scheduling difficulty.

Then consider the whole area called "character development" or "moral education," which has been shunned by the school establishment out of the belief that such studies would inevitably lead to protests and unwinable legal battles over an apparent intrusion by the school into the area of religion. Promulgating these fears has become a common practice in teacher-training and administration classes in almost every university's college of education, and so most school districts don't even think about the possibility that their mission might properly include teaching children how to use their newly acquired knowledge and skills in the pursuit of a truly "good" life. School policy makers say that this goal should be left to parents or to churches or to anyone except the schools. Parents who practice Family Learning say, "Thank you. We accept."

Even in the supposed "school subjects," such as language, science, history, geography, and math, can you honestly say that focusing **all** of a child's learning in these subjects into the five or so hours of the 170 or so days each year that children spend in school is the best of all possible learning situations? Of course not. In order for children to become truly competent as learners, and in order for children to be prepared for the challenges of lifelong learning (not lifelong schooling), we must begin to incorporate into our educational system a means by which out-of-school learning is respected and used to inspire or reinforce learning in school. Family Learning provides that means. It provides us a way to have a nationwide education machine that is hitting on *all* cylinders, not just the few that are accepted and encouraged today.

Yes, we can have world-class schools *and* Family Learning; it is possible. But attaining the first will require a complete restructuring of our educational system and its philosophy. I can't even guess how long that will take or who will decide where to begin. But for you, the opportunity to make Family Learning part of your family, and part of your children's families, begins today and is right at your fingertips.

How to Use This Book

The driving principle behind this *Family Learning* book—and behind the whole idea of Family Learning in general—is that learning is a good and natural activity for **every** member of **every** family, not just for children alone. So, if you are a parent, you will find this book to be a valuable aid and resource in helping you catch that spark of curiosity and enlightenment that leads to learning, and in suggesting activities to share with your children so that they can catch that spark from you.

If you are a classroom teacher, *Family Learning* will suggest many activities and adventures that you can modify for in-class use or offer as enrichment or background lessons to individual students to meet their particular learning needs or interests. Indeed, *Family Learning* itself can be a worthwhile and ready suggestion to offer any parents who are interested enough in their children's education to ask "What can we do to help?"

No matter who the users may be, however, their use of this book will be directed by their particular interests and needs. This is not a book to read cover to cover, but topic by topic, instead.

Have you always harbored a secret fondness for word origins and stories about how things came to be known by the names we call them today? Then start with those essays in the language section and start passing on to your children your new-found knowledge and your reawakened enthusiasm for learning from that topic base. Do your children marvel at the wonders of the night sky and want to know "what . . . ?" "how . . . ?" and "why . . . ?" as they look up at the spectacle overhead on a clear night? Then let them spark your own curiosity and begin your use of *Family Learning* with the essays in the astronomy section, instead.

And always keep in mind that *Family Learning* is not subject based or even topic based; rather, it is driven by interest alone, so that you quickly and freely leap from one subject or topic to the next as your curiosity dictates, much in the way we use "hot links" on the computer to jump from place to place along the Internet.

The practice I call Family Learning can take you and your children anywhere and everywhere your curiosity dictates, but this *Family Learning* book is only an introduction to that journey. The book does not and cannot tell you *everything* about language or history or math or science. But it does show you how to set off on your learning journey, and it does offer you many points of departure. It also suggests other routes you can take and stopovers that will provide a more thorough understanding of where you are and where you have been. These features are part of the "Useful Family Resources" sections that can be found at the end of each essay. Here I have suggested some of the books and other materials that I have found useful in explaining the particular concepts I have focused upon in the essay. Many of these book also contain additional insights and learning activities that you can share with your children at home, and some contain lists of useful resources themselves, so that your learning path can continue to branch in the direction of your particular interests.

The very best way to avail yourself of these "Useful Family Resources" is by becoming familiar with your local public library. Your library may well have other, better resources that I have failed to list (in which case I would appreciate learning about these resources so that I can include them in subsequent editions). But the Dewey Decimal Classification numbers that I have listed in each section will guide you to the most fertile area for that particular topic, and from there you can browse your library's collection until you find the resources that fill your particular need.

Keep in mind that the letter *J* at the beginning of a Dewey classification number indicates that this book is likely to be found in the library's "Juvenile" or children's collection. Similarly, the letter *Y* (or *YA*) indicates a library section that is of special interest to teenagers or "**Young Adults**." The letter *R* means that the book is often classified as a reference book, and if it is, you will find it housed in the library's "**Reference**" collection; these books cannot usually be checked out for home use. When a Dewey number is given with no initial letter at all, the book is most likely part of the general or adult collection.

You must remember, however, that different libraries and different librarians use different criteria for cataloging materials, and so the same book that is found in the juvenile collection in one library resides on the adult shelves in another, and their Dewey numbers may differ only in that the first is preceded by the letter *J*.

Therefore, when you are browsing a particular area of Dewey numbers that you found listed in a "Useful Family Resources" section, browse those numbers in the adult collection, the children's collection, the young adult collection, and the reference collection, too. Who knows what you will stumble on to? Perhaps it will be the ideal explanation or the perfect learning adventure to share with your children. Perhaps it will suggest a wholly new area of inquiry that will excite your own curiosity and that of your children, as well.

So, use *Family Learning* as a way to begin your library explorations, get to know your library and librarians, and browse, browse, browse.

Still another way that parents and teachers can use *Family Learning* to start children thinking and wondering about various topics is to link those topics to particular days or times of the year. For example, by observing "special" occasions in your home or classroom—historic events, birthdays of famous people, celestial occurrences, etc.—you can create convenient lead-ins to help you introduce a topic or an activity to your children or your students. Most of the essays in this book can be tied (sometimes tenuously, I admit) to particular events or people that will provide parents with an "excuse" for bringing up the topic at home. It is very difficult, I know, to get children interested in joining any discussion, activity, or adventure that "seems like school," at least at first. But I also know that once children get used to the idea that learning activities can be inspired by events and topics rather than by subjects or clock hours, they begin to anticipate these "excuses," to look forward to them, and even to suggest some themselves.

I have, therefore, placed a notation at the top of each essay whose topic is directly linked with a certain event or date on the calendar. If you are looking for suggestions about learning topics that are especially appropriate for upcoming days or weeks in the year, I have cross-referenced these events and essays in a "Calendar of Family Learning," which appears on pages 360–61.

Another feature that I hope will be helpful to parents and others who are particularly interested in ways to share learning with their children is the placement in the outside margins of two symbols:　and　.

The first symbol suggests the idea of a family enjoying an activity together, in this case a learning activity. The symbol appears next to any section in the text that describes or suggests an activity that parents can do with their children to help stimulate their curiosity or improve their understanding of a particular topic. These activities, however, are not limited to improving children's learning alone, for they can be quite useful to parents who need a physical demonstration of some kind in order to cement a concept firmly in their own mind, or parents who wish to practice a certain procedure or activity before sharing it with their children.

The second symbol—the image of an open book—appears each time there is a story of some kind that you can read or tell to your children. The telling of stories and tales has been one of the most effective teaching devices throughout all of history, but we often don't recognize how powerful a tool it is—both in the home and the school. Stories have a way of sticking with the listener partly because their flow from beginning to middle to end provides a reliable memory aid. Then, too, stories say something about the storyteller. Children come to identify stories they heard from a parent, grandparent, or teacher as just that because each story, in order to be worth the telling, had to mean a lot to that particular parent, grandparent, or teacher.

Stories play an important role in any Family Learning home. Parents tell and read aloud character-building stories and instructive tales that happen to be about history and geography, even science and math, and children are encouraged to retell these stories to other family members. Even when the retelling is not perfect and the characters behave in ways somewhat different from the actions portrayed in the original version, learning has taken place. The child has, perhaps, talked about a historic event, pronounced a famous scientist's name, felt compassion for the plight of a character, even if no one before has ever heard the events of the story told in exactly that way.

Let these symbols also encourage you to make other notes and reminders in the wide outside margins as you study a particular section or prepare a particular activity to share with your children. These marks and notations can be easily seen, like the "activity" and "story" symbols I have included, as you thumb through the pages from either cover of the book.

Learning About the World of Words:
Language

Introduction

"Language is more caught than taught." Dr. Dolores Durkin made this observation more than twenty-five years ago following her study of the way children learn to read. I think this statement also applies to the way that children (and adults, too) develop their ability to use language in general—speaking, reading, and writing.

We know that our children are quick to adopt the vocabulary and the speech habits of their peer group, or of the rock stars, athletes, and actors they see on television. There is nothing new in this, and nothing particularly bad about it, either, provided that these are not our children's **only** language models and that our children come to realize that different situations demand different standards of usage.

Language development is ideally suited to Family Learning because language is so available for study. We hear it, read it, or speak it during practically all our waking hours, yet we don't see all these occasions as opportunities for learning.

Most parents think they must have vast vocabularies and refined language skills to be good models for their children's language education, but I would much rather that they concentrate on modeling an *attitude* about language for their children—a curious and playful attitude toward the language that is heard and seen and spoken in their homes every day.

This attitude toward language can be "caught" by children just as surely as language itself. Once children begin to see all the interesting paths that language investigations can follow and all the power and opportunity that language fluency puts at their disposal, they will no longer think it strange for their parents to consult the family dictionary during a television show, nor for themselves to be critical of a supposedly college-educated, star athlete who is unable to express clearly a simple thought.

And that's another attitude that can be developed and displayed during the course of normal, everyday family life—a respect for language skill. Parents can open a world of opportunity for their children just by showing a consistent respect and admiration for the skillful and artful use of Standard English. By listening and reading, by examining everything they hear and read, they can demonstrate that learning about language is a lifelong pursuit and that skill in speaking and writing is worth pursuing.

The main goal of this section of *Family Learning* is to have everyone—parents and children alike—come to see this wonderful English language as an engine or a force that you command, not as an impediment to the free expression of your thoughts. The rules of Standard English should not be seen as hurdles you have to jump over, but, instead, as the lanes in which you run. They keep you focused and centered along the clearest, most certain path to success. These rules can be broken—they are broken all the time, by even the best speakers and writers—but let that be **your** decision, **your** choice. Break the rules when they just won't allow you to convey an idea the way you want it to be conveyed, and break them with impunity and with swagger and with the confidence that you know which rules you are breaking.

Here, then, are some essays about various aspects of language, which are meant only to get you started on making your own investigations, developing your own usage standards, and modeling that curious and playful and respectful attitude about language in your home every day.

Children Have Fun With the Sounds of Punctuation

Ideas for Family Learning activities to share with your children can be found in places you wouldn't think were "educational" at all. But once you start to see **everything** as a resource for stimulating your curiosity or spurring you on to new understanding, you will discover that the world is just packed with learning adventures. Here's an example of what I mean, one that will also let you see right away how much fun you can have even with a subject that your children may not think of as "fun" at all: punctuation.

Do you remember Victor Borge? He was one of my favorite entertainers when I was growing up—a concert pianist who used classical music as a backdrop for his witty insights about music and about life in general. His thick Danish accent disguised a thorough understanding of the precision of the English language, and it seems to me now that what made his routines so special was his masterly feel for timing, to be sure, but also his careful attention to vocabulary: the perfect word in the perfect place—not a series of "ya know's" or a parade of gutter vulgarities that are so commonly employed by comedians of lesser skill today.

But the routine that most people identify with Victor Borge is one that is ideally suited to Family Learning. It requires no special skill either for adults or children to perform together; it can be used with children from grade school to high school; it can be performed with a single child or with a group of children; it teaches and reinforces worthwhile learnings; and, most of all, it is just plain fun!

Victor Borge called this routine "phonetic punctuation," and he would set it up for his audience by saying that he believed the reason most Americans frequently misunderstand what others say to them is that speech, unlike writing, has no marks of punctuation. However, if we could just put all the commas and periods and quotation marks into our speech that we use in our writing, all this confusion would be eliminated. Then he would proceed to suggest various sounds for each of the marks of punctuation, sounds that—owing again to Borge's sense of precision in vocabulary—seemed somehow to represent perfectly the shape of each particular mark.

It is, of course, virtually impossible to convey to you in writing the exact sounds that Borge made. But the whole point of this exercise is not for you to use his sounds, but sounds of your own instead. Remember, too, that in order for phonetic punctuation to be most effective as a Family Learning device, your children will have to be able to make some or all of these sounds by themselves (although this is rarely a problem for them). All right, here we go.

The period is the most common mark in this routine, and Borge made it sound like a point. It was a funny sound, rather like spitting out the letters *p-p-p-u-u-u-u-t-t-t*, ending very sharply. Go ahead; give it a try.

Now the reason that the period was so common in his act was that Borge used this same sound to form the "dot" portion of the question mark, the exclamation mark, the semicolon, and the colon. The question mark, for instance, began with a "curving" sound; the pitch changed as the letters seemed to squirm out of his mouth—*q-q-u-u-e-e-e-k-k*. Then the dot—the period sound—would go immediately below, and he would accentuate it by marking the dot with his finger in space (*p-p-p-u-u-u-u-t-t-t!*). The colon (:), of course, would sound like two periods, and his finger would position one right below the other as the sounds came forth.

The dash (—) was a marvelous sound, a *whooooosh* of constant pitch, which flew with his finger straight across from left to right. The same sound, but now with a rising pitch and an upward stroke of the hand, represented the top portion of an exclamation mark. And, of course, this mark was finished off by placing the period directly below (*p-p-p-u-u-u-u-t-t-t!*).

The comma was a quick, curved, little squelch that seemed to come from the side and back of his mouth, and when a semicolon (;) came along, the comma was sounded immediately after (and just below) the dot.

The sound needed to represent quotation marks seems to me to require the most practice and offer the most difficulty for a child to perform. Their sound was slightly different from the comma, and they always came in rapid-fire pairs: *quk-quk* at the beginning of the quotation, and *quk-quk* at the end, often with other marks and sounds preceding and following. Oh, and the quotation marks were always accompanied by two lofted fingers pointing inward from the left and then from the right.

Do you see what this exercise is doing? Your children may never have heard of, much less used, a colon in their lives. But now they will hear you using the word *colon*, they will even use it themselves as a natural part of this family activity, and they will look for every colon they can find just for the chance to spike the two dots with their fingers and say, "*p-p-p-u-u-u-t-t-t, p-p-p-u-u-u-t-t-t!*"

Now, in order to make this learning exercise go over as well as possible with your children on your very first try (which is an important consideration if you want to be able to return to the activity again and again), you must get the feel of the routine by practicing each of these sounds yourself. It may feel a little silly at first, but go off in a corner by yourself and try out several noises for each mark until you come up with sounds that are different enough from one another to be identifiable. I have rewritten the ending from "Little Red Riding Hood" for you so that it includes all the punctuation marks we have discussed, and so that you can use it right now for practice.

When you introduce this routine to your children, you might start out with this "Little Red Riding Hood" excerpt, too, but always be on the lookout for other simple stories that you can read aloud together using "phonetic punctuation." If the routine goes over as well as it usually does, you'll need every one of them.

Here are some other tips that I have found useful. First, use a pencil and notepad to show your child what each punctuation mark looks like, and write each name next to that mark. Your children may not encounter some of these marks for years in their "language arts" classes, but they can be familiar with the terms early on, and that familiarity will provide a convenient learning link and hook when their textbooks finally decide that the time has come.

Next, try to let your child make the sound of the period if at all possible. Whatever sound he or she uses to represent the period and the "dot" will be good enough as long as it is a fun sound to make. This gets children involved in the fun right away, gives them some success, and makes them want to try other sounds and other stories.

Last, remember to divvy up the work so that your children are participating as actively as possible. If there are several children involved, divide up the punctuation marks that each will be responsible for, and remember that older children can serve as narrators, too. (I have often done this routine with entire classes of thirty or more third graders or fourth graders, in which I have had students take turns sounding out a single punctuation mark, and have used different narrators for each paragraph.)

Are you ready? Here we go.

Little Red Riding Hood

the story continues...

The wolf put on the nightcap that Grandmother had been wearing.

Then he jumped into her bed, pulled up the covers, and waited for his supper to arrive.

In a little while, Red Riding Hood knocked at the door——tap, tap, tap.

"Who is there?" the wolf called out in a grandmotherly voice.

"It is Red Riding Hood, Grandmother, with some butter and sugar cookies for you," replied the girl.

"Oh, boy!" the wolf cried, barely able to contain his excitement. "The door is unlocked; come right on in."

The little girl was startled to see how the kindly appearance of her grandmother had changed.

"Why, Gramma: What big eyes you have!" she said in a tone filled with surprise.

"Well——, uh——," the wolf stammered; "That makes them all the better to see you with, my dear."

"Why, Gramma: What big teeth you have!" she exclaimed, not remembering her grandmother to have had fangs at all.

The wolf could restrain himself no longer.

"All the better to **eat** you with, my dear!"

And with that, the wicked wolf leaped from the bed; his mouth watered as he chased the girl around the room.

"Help——! Oh, help——! Won't someone help me?!" she cried. "Please hurry!——or I shall surely be eaten up by the . . . ."

The End.

Redesign Language Games to Fit Your Home and Family

Walk down the aisles of any toy store and you'll find quite a few games that are designed to bring spelling and vocabulary skills into the family living room. Parents may well wonder whether these games are useful in Family Learning, and whether the games actually make the learning of language concepts and skills more enjoyable for children.

The answer is, of course, that it is not the game but the family that makes the difference. The family that enjoys playing language games together as a regular feature of family life, not just as an infrequent learning aid to trot out when children are having trouble in English class, will experience multiple benefits from these games—benefits to their growth as a family as well as benefits to individual skill and learning.

But parents should realize that they can convey the same playful and creative attitude toward these games that they have about language in general. The standard rules for these boxed items may have been written for an "Ozzie and Harriet" family, or for one with skills and interests that are widely different from those shared by your family, and so you have to be willing and able to adjust the game to fit your children and your particular family situation. Let me show you what I mean.

Family Scrabble

The game of Scrabble has been the most popular word game on the market for decades; it is estimated that 27 percent of American homes today have at least one Scrabble set. But this game was not designed to be a teaching tool; rather, it was designed to put a premium on the knowledge that the players already have and on their skill in displaying that knowledge during the game. There is a measure of luck involved (as in the drawing of letters, for example), but Scrabble is still a very scary game to those who feel less than confident about their own vocabulary or spelling ability. And so when children, even teenage children, are asked to join a Scrabble game with their parents, they are intimidated by the likelihood that their comparative ignorance of words and spellings will be exposed during the play, and they will not only lose but also be embarrassed at the same time.

One way to include people of varying abilities in a single game of Scrabble is to give all players a pencil and notepad, so that they can write down various words and letter combinations before having to display their selection on the board. This levels the playing field somewhat by reducing the advantage of those who can "see" various words in their mind without having to write them out.

Now, don't make the mistake I did when I suggested that a fourteen-year-old boy, who was having some difficulty during a Scrabble game with his parents and me, use a tablet to aid him in seeing various letter combinations. Well, that idea fell so flat that it resulted in the boy's complete loss of interest in participating in any of our subsequent games. What I had thoughtlessly overlooked was the fourteen-year-old ego that didn't want to be seen as needing a handicap or special help of any kind. All I would have had to do, and what I do now every time I play Scrabble with children of any age, is to suggest that *all* the players in the game use notepads to aid them in seeing and spelling their words. This, then, is not a handicap or a sign that certain players are deficient in any way. Instead, it helps everyone contribute more creative words and makes it more likely that children and others of lesser language skill and experience will realize success in their play, even though they may not "win" the overall competition.

Another way to change the "rules" of Scrabble so that it becomes a better Family Learning game is to make a dictionary available for players to use during the game—not just for challenges. This practice not only encourages and builds dictionary skills, but it also helps the entire family become more familiar with their family dictionary. (This is just one of several reasons not to select a bigger-than-a-breadbox version for your home. A "desk-size or "collegiate" style is ideal for family use.) I also suggest that you eliminate the standard penalties that players incur for making unsuccessful challenges. And don't pile additional penalties on players who put down an incorrect word. Let's try to encourage dictionary use whenever possible, and to encourage people to take chances on words and spellings without fear of suffering harsh consequences if they are wrong.

A third technique for encouraging family Scrabble is to play in teams rather than as individuals. The weakest and strongest players can be paired as a team (on opposite sides of the table), and their scores combined. In this way, children can concentrate on contributing some points, even just a few, at each turn, rather than being solely responsible for their total score at the end of the game.

All these techniques can, of course, be employed at the same time, and other adaptations are possible as well. The whole point is to start tuning ourselves to our children's abilities and fears, and to start recognizing our own power to adapt this game, like all family games, in ways that will make everyone eager to participate.

There are many language benefits that can come from playing family Scrabble, including a knowledge of letter frequencies, common word endings, and letter combinations. But these benefits will not ever be realized by our children unless they participate in playing the game, and so it is incumbent upon us to use our imagination in devising ways to make the game interesting as well as challenging for everyone in the family.

Homemade Language Games

Language games don't all come in boxes. There are dozens of games, some hundreds of years old, that parents and children can play together and that feature spelling or vocabulary or word usage as part of the competition. These games are even better in some ways than the ones you find in the stores, because the only equipment they require is a pencil and paper, and some require no equipment at all. Therefore, they can be played during a long automobile ride or an airplane trip, or whenever a diversion is needed or some spark of interest happens to flare.

A good example is the very old game called Ghost, which can be played with or without pencil and paper. The object of Ghost is to trap an opponent into spelling a complete word. The first player thinks of a word and calls out its initial letter. (Let's say the letter *p*, as in *pole*.) The second player must now add a letter to the first, without having the two letters spell a complete word. If the second player added an *a*, for instance, thinking of the word *parrot*, he would lose because *p-a* spells a complete word (*pa*).

So the second player might choose an *r* instead, thinking of the word *praise*. The next player must continue the string, but again, without completing a word. He wouldn't add an *o*, as in *problem* (Why?), but he might try an *i*, thinking of the word *print*.

Each player must have a word in mind when adding a letter, and players can challenge one another to discover what that word is.

A variation of this game for more advanced players is called Superghost and allows the players to add their letters to either end of the string. So the initial letter *p* in our example might cause the next player in Superghost to place the letter *s* in front of that *p* (with the second player thinking of the word *spell*), and then subsequent players to offer the letter *i* (*spin*), then *a* (*aspire*), and so on.

In either version, when someone loses a challenge (that is, does not have a word in mind) or is trapped into spelling a complete word, he or she becomes "a third of a ghost," and so it takes three losses before you are eliminated.

When teaching the game of Ghost to your children, it's a good idea to use pencil and paper so that they can see the string of letters in front of them and try out various additions to it. Superghost almost demands this visual aid, and so the tablet can be passed around to all the players in the car or on the plane, each adding to the string of letters and indicating how much of a ghost each has become.

The 793.73 section of the children's books in your local library is the place to look for suggestions about language games to play with your family. Here you will find books that describe paper-and-pencil games like Ghost and Hangman and Word Squares and Mad Libs. (Mad Libs are stories in which certain words have been omitted. Children supply various nouns, adjectives, and other parts of speech to fill in the blanks before they know anything about the story, which takes on new and hilarious meanings when it is finally read with the suggested words in place.) Among my favorite collections of language games are A *Book of Puzzlements*, by Herbert Kohl, and A *Children's Almanac of Words at Play*, by Willard Espy.

Remember, too, that not all language games have to use paper and pencil, because much of the language we learn and use isn't written or even spoken. There is a whole world of body language, for example, all those physical gestures and signs that convey information—sometimes highly complex information—among people who are fluent in this form of language.

You may not think of gestures as making up a true language, but the Native American tribes developed a sign language that was rich with imagery and was used by many diverse groups speaking many different languages to carry on lengthy conversations. Just think for a minute how often and in how many ways you use nonverbal communication to transmit and receive information every day, and then ask yourself whether there is any real difference between this process and communicating through speaking or writing.

Nodding the head means "yes," and shaking it means "no"; we wave good-bye to people, but we reverse the action to beckon them to come here. We can show approval or disdain by a hand sign for "okay" or by holding our nose, by "thumbs up" or "thumbs down." We can add sounds to our messages—such as whistling for a cab, applauding a performance, "shushing" someone to keep quiet—and we still have communicated without words.

Understanding what nonverbal communication really is can help us use the word *verbal* more precisely, too. *Verbal* must, necessarily, mean using words, and so a verbal agreement could be one made in writing or made by "word of mouth." But if you want to describe a *spoken* agreement or commitment or promise, then the adjective you want is *oral*.

Children can profit from an early awakening to the many ways that people convey ideas without using words. Traffic signs, for example, have meanings that we understand and have agreed upon, as do the hand signals of umpires, referees, and orchestra conductors. And when children come to recognize symbols and gestures as forms of speech, they won't be surprised to find that these nonverbal messages can mean different things to people from different cultures. For example, our head shake for "no" means "yes" to Arabs and Bulgarians; our "good-bye" wave means "come here" in France and Italy; our hitchhiker's thumb sign would be taken as an insult by drivers in Scotland and Australia.

One of the best ways to introduce your children to the communication possibilities of gestures and body language is through the old parlor game known as Charades. We usually think of this game as requiring teams of players, but you and your child can have great fun, and a challenging learning experience at the same time, by acting out words, phrases, titles, and sayings just for each other to guess. You can even use Charades to reinforce other school subjects and topics by having players act out various words and names taken from categories like state capitals, foreign leaders, or famous scientists.

Children are especially keen to learn the codes and shortcuts that experienced Charades players use to convey nonverbal messages in the shortest possible time: A hand chop cuts the word into syllables, a beckoning hand says "you're warm," cupping or tugging the ear indicates "sounds like (a rhyming word)," a finger on the nose says "that's right."

Check the 792–794 section of the juvenile collection at your library for books about pantomimes and Charades, especially James Charlton's *Charades: The Complete Guide to America's Favorite Party Game*.

USEFUL FAMILY RESOURCES

An Almanac of Words at Play, by Willard R. Espy (New York: Clarkson N. Potter, 1975) [793.73 ESP or 828 ESP].

A Book of Puzzlements, by Herbert Kohl (New York: Schocken Books, 1981) [793.73 KOH or J 793.03 KOH].

A Children's Almanac of Words at Play, by Willard R. Espy (New York: Clarkson N. Potter, 1982) [J 793.73 ESP or J 818.5407 ESP].

The Oxford Guide To Word Games, by Tony Augarde (Oxford, England: Oxford University Press, 1986) [793.73 AUG].

The Whim-Wham Book, by Duncan Emrich (New York: Four Winds Press, 1975) [J 818.008 EMR].

JUNE 23: *First typewriter patented*
OCTOBER 30: *Birth of Richard Brinsley Sheridan*

Grouping Language Oddities Leads to Family Fun With Words

Many interesting and enjoyable language activities for the home are not really "games" at all. Rather, they involve the very normal desire among children and adults alike to see patterns and order in things. Learning is so much easier when we can put things in groups and see how they are similar, and why they are in this group and not in another. When a new item comes along, we might already have a group into which it fits perfectly, and a name to describe that group as well.

This need and desire to group things and to classify things is an especially good incentive to take advantage of when you work with your children on language activities in your home. You not only allow them to find order in what appears to them a most confusing and disorderly language, but you also provide the vocabulary that they will need to talk about language throughout their years in school.

I am not contending here that you must be scholars in the arcane terminology that is frequently used by dedicated students and teachers of language. I am, instead, suggesting that you—and your children, too—will find it a great advantage, both now and in the future, to learn some of the terms that are commonly used to describe special groups and arrangements of words or letters.

Palindromes
Take, for example, the word *eye*. This simple word is interesting in that it reads the same way both backward and forward. So do the words *mom* and *dad* and *bib*. This is an oddity of spelling that your children can see right away, yet how do we talk about all the words that are in this group? What do we call a word that is spelled the same backward as it is forward?

A palindrome [pronounced PAL-in-drome]. When you use the word *palindrome* to describe a word like *pop* or a name like *Nan* or *Bob*, your children will come to use it too, and they will have more ease and fun with finding words to add to this group simply because they can identify the group and describe it with a single word.

The most enjoyable and effective way to introduce palindromes to children (even to older children) is to start out with very short words, such as the three-letter palindromes above, and take turns coming up with other three-letter combinations. Now move on to four-letter palindromes such as *toot*, *noon*, *deed*, and *Anna*. Again, take turns, but realize that the possibilities are now more limited, and so the difficulty is increased.

Five-letter palindromes are even more rare, and from here on you may have to supply most or all of them yourself. But your children will take special interest in words like *radar*, *level*, *civic*, *madam*, *rotor*, *kayak*, and *refer* when they see what these words have in common, and when they know that all these words can be described by the name *palindrome*.

How long can a palindrome be? Well, once you've reached *redder* and *repaper*, you find yourself in the world of phrase and sentence palindromes. For example, when Adam introduced himself to Eve (her name is also a palindrome), he may have said, "Madam, I'm Adam." (Or, to carry it out a bit longer still: "Madam in Eden, I'm Adam.") Other extended palindromes include *A man, a plan, a canal—Panama!* and *Was it a car or a cat I saw?*

Another form of sentence palindrome that can be appreciated by children and adults alike is the sentence that is reversible when read word-by-word instead of letter-by-letter. Try reading the following sentence starting with the last word and ending with the first: *You can cage a swallow, can't you, but you can't swallow a cage, can you?*

Palindromes can be composed of numbers as well as letters. The year 1991, for example, was a palindrome. (When will the next palindromic year occur? Answer: 2002.) Palindromes make special numbers out of some zip codes (94049, for instance), telephone numbers (351-4153), times of day (12:21), airplanes (747), and calendar dates, such as July 9, 1997, which can be written 7-9-97.

Collecting palindromes with your children can be a long-term family activity that not only is fun but also benefits the children's language education by getting them to see early in life that there are all sorts of interesting patterns and similarities in the language they use, and that they can find other patterns and interesting combinations if they will just be curious about their own language and confident enough to try using it in new ways.

Did they, or did you, ever wonder about why the letters on the typewriter or computer keyboard are arranged the way they are? Why isn't the alphabet displayed in A-to-Z order from left to right or top to bottom? Well, it used to be. Back in 1868, when a printer named

Christopher Latham Sholes was issued a United States patent for the first practical typewriter, the letters on the keyboard were arranged alphabetically, but the machine kept jamming whenever two letters were typed in rapid succession. So Sholes decided to place the most commonly used letters as far apart as possible on the keyboard, and his arrangement (which is known as the "QWERTY" keyboard because those letters appear on the left side of the top row) survives today, even though other patterns have proved to be much faster and less tiring to use.

Sholes continued to develop and refine his invention, and in 1874 he signed a contract with the E. Remington & Sons Company (the gun manufacturers) to build and market his typing machine. Mark Twain was one of their early customers; in fact, he completed the first typed book manuscript in history, *The Adventures of Tom Sawyer,* on his Remington in 1875.

Pangrams

You may wonder what this discussion of typewriters has to do with language games or terminology, but I see the arrangement of the keyboard as a vehicle for introducing children to another from of word play and the name that describes it.

I remember a typing drill that had us practice our technique by pounding out *A quick brown fox jumps over the lazy dog,* because that sentence contained all twenty-six letters of the alphabet, and so it gave us practice in striking every letter key. A sentence or poem that includes all the letters from A to Z is called a *pangram,* which comes from two Greek roots meaning "all letters."

Our practice sentence actually used a few letters more than once, totaling thirty-three letters in all. A perfect pangram would have just twenty-six, but although people have tried for hundreds of years to create a sensible English pangram of just twenty-six letters, no one has yet succeeded. (If your children can succeed in creating this perfect pangram, they will achieve immediate fame among linguists throughout the world. They should know, however, that there are 403,290,000,000,000,000,000,000,000 possible combinations of the twenty-six letters for them to try!) Here are a couple of improvements on the "brown fox" example: *Pack my box with five dozen liquor jugs* (thirty-two letters), and *The five boxing wizards jump quickly* (thirty-one letters).

It's easier if you cheat a little by using proper names and initials in your pangrams, and I suggest that this is the variation you choose in introducing pangrams to your children. (For example, *Liz and JFK wove speech by quoting Marx.*)

There are other language and alphabet activities that you can spin off from this idea of pangrams, such as compiling a list of the names of twenty-six animals, each name beginning with a different letter. Or how about looking for words whose letters appear in alphabetical order; or words that contain all five vowels; all five vowels in order; all five vowels in reverse order; only one vowel, or one consonant, used several times; only letters from the first half of the alphabet; or the last half? Turn the technique around and give your children a sample word or two, and ask them what interesting patterns these words contain. Have them give you some words to see if you can find the pattern. The possibilities are almost endless, but you can find plenty of suggestions in such books as *The Abecedarian Book*, by Charles Ferguson [422 FER or J 422 FER]; *A Dictionary of Language Games, Puzzles, and Amusements*, by Harry Edwin Eiss [J 793.73 EIS]; *Word Works: Why the Alphabet Is a Kid's Best Friend*, by Cathryn Berger Kaye [J 372.6 KAY]; and almost any book by Willard Espy.

Let me show you one other classification of words that you can use to foster your children's language creativity and have some family fun at the same time. In order for your children to adopt a "playful" attitude about language that will encourage them to be curious about what they read and write and hear for the rest of their lives, they need to find out early on that language can be fun and that it can be played with and twisted about and turned inside out.

Malaprops

There is a language device called a *malaprop* [pronounced MAL-uh-prop], a name that comes from a character in a seventeenth-century play by Richard Brinsley Sheridan called *The Rivals*. In this comedy, Sheridan used a combination of the French words *mal à propos* (meaning "not appropriate") to create the name for Mrs. Malaprop, a character who took great pride in her use of big words, but who always seemed to confuse one for another. She described her niece as being "as headstrong as an 'allegory' on the banks of the Nile," and she urged her to "illiterate" a certain gentleman from her memory. Ever since, the often-humorous and unintentional misuse of one word for another has been called a malapropism or just a malaprop.

Malaprops abound in the written and spoken English of children and adults alike. Most are just simple cases of choosing the wrong word from the many pairs of English words that are similar and often confused (e.g., *censor/censure*, *flaunt/flout*). But occasionally the literal meaning of the malaprop can produce a very comical visual image, as when the politician said he "didn't want to cast asparagus" at his opponent, or when the science student wrote "The abominable cavity contains the bowels, of which there are five: *A, E, I, O,* and *U.*"

Malaprops, then, offer parents and teachers a way to combine learning and fun in children's language education. When children picture in their minds both what is actually being said and what the speaker or writer intended to say, the silly scenes not only stretch their imagination but also teach vocabulary and reinforce the importance of precise spelling as well.

You can get help in creating a list of comical malaprops from such library books as *A Children's Almanac of Words at Play*, by Willard Espy [J 793.73 ESP or J 818.5407 ESP], and from the routines of comedians who have built their careers on this type of wordplay (Norm Crosby comes quickly to mind). Have your children picture and describe what each sentence actually says, and then what the writer intended to say. Make sure you reveal (or have your child spell or write) the intended word after each sentence.

Even young children get a special pleasure from the silly scenes that result when words are misused or misinterpreted. The fact that so many common English words are identical in sound and sometimes in spelling to words with vastly different meanings creates an abundance of opportunities for having your children experience the many benefits of wordplay at an early age. Fred Gwynne (yes, he of television's "The Munsters" fame) wrote and illustrated several books (such as *The King Who Rained*) that picture for children the crazy ways that some words and phrases can be misinterpreted. Peggy Parish has also written a series of comical books about Amelia Bedelia, a maid who follows all directions literally and so, for example, takes out a sketch pad to "draw" the drapes.

It is only a very short literary distance from unintentional malaprops to intentional puns. Instead of discouraging children from repeating and creating "Knock-Knock" jokes and "How's Business?" jokes (for example, "I'm in the firecracker business." "How's business?" "Booming!"), parents should keep in mind that this type of wordplay allows children to see at an early age that their own language offers them a constant source of material to twist and shape for their own amusement. Soon the puns will grow into "Tom Swifties" ("'I can't find the oranges,' Tom said fruitlessly") and "Daffy Definitions" ("Boomerang: What you say when you frighten a meringue").

Other language classifications and rhetorical devices that you can find explained and demonstrated in the 793 section of both the children and adult collections of your library include anagrams, euphemisms, limericks, metaphors, oxymorons, similes, and spoonerisms. Each of these terms can be introduced to your children's vocabulary through interesting games and activities, and although the activities are more important than the rather strange-sounding terms used to describe them, you and your children will begin using the terms simply because they are the easiest, most understandable way for you to let each other know what you mean.

The Abecedarian Book, by Charles W. Ferguson (Boston: Little Brown & Co., 1964) [422 GER or J 422 FER].

Amelia Bedelia Goes Camping, by Peggy Parish (New York: Avon Books, 1985) and others in [JR PAR].

A Children's Almanac of Words at Play, by Willard R. Espy (New York: Clarkson N. Potter, 1982) [J 793.73 ESP or J 818.5407 ESP].

A Chocolate Moose for Dinner, by Fred Gwynne (New York: Prentice-Hall, 1976) [JE GWY].

A Dictionary of Language Games, Puzzles, and Amusements, by Harry Edwin Eiss (Westport, Conn.: Greenwood Press, 1986) [J 793.73 EIS].

The King Who Rained, by Fred Gwynne (New York: Prentice-Hall, 1970) [JE GWY].

Play Ball, Amelia Bedelia, by Peggy Parish (New York: Harper Collins, 1972) [JE PAR].

The Sixteen Hand Horse, by Fred Gwynne (New York: Simon & Schuster, 1980) [JE GWY].

Word Works: Why the Alphabet Is a Kid's Best Friend, by Cathryn Berger Kaye (Boston: Little Brown & Co., 1985) [J 372.6 KAY].

Proverbs Show That Big Things Come in Small Packages

September 28 is, by tradition, the birthdate of China's greatest philosopher and foremost teacher: Confucius [pronounced kun-FYOO-shus]. He was born to the K'ung family in 551 B.C., and the name by which he is known today is really a Latinized form of K'ung Fu-tzu, which means "K'ung the Grand Master."

I suppose that most people associate Confucius with the short, succinct observations and general truths that seem to have been designed to fit inside a fortune cookie. And, although Confucius's philosophy and teachings are elaborate and detailed, these pithy proverbs or adages or aphorisms do, indeed, reveal the virtues embodied in his beliefs and the wisdom in his teachings.

"Wise Sayings"

"Better a diamond with a flaw than a pebble without." This observation from Confucius has, of course, nothing to do with diamonds or pebbles. But can your children see that its wisdom lies in what it has to say about human beings and human aspirations?

The problem of getting children to see how one idea or object can stand for or represent another in a proverb (as the diamond in Confucius's adage can represent a person who strives for excellence or perfection) is just one of the problems we face in helping children to understand and profit from commonly known "wise sayings."

Another problem, one we overlook all too frequently, is that a lot of children have simply never heard many of the sayings that we use and hear and consider part of our common culture. These children may hear the phrase "a new broom sweeps clean" used in a political debate and not understand whether it is being said in support of the incumbent or

48

the challenger. What would they make of adages like "The early bird catches the worm," "One swallow does not a summer make," or "You can lead a horse to water, but you can't make him drink"?

Nothing, probably, and that's a shame, because proverbs like these **are**, in fact, part of our cultural heritage, and they do, in fact, provide us with some poetic generalizations about human experience that can help children better understand their world.

Parents need to explain both the literal and the metaphorical meaning of common adages for their children, and then have those children imagine other situations to which each saying can properly apply. For example, worms do come up to the surface in the cool damp morning, but not in the heat of the day. An "early bird" benefits from this knowledge, and so do many job seekers and ticket buyers who heed this advice.

One of my favorite ways to acquaint children with commonly used wise sayings (and to show them that they cannot live by proverbs alone), is to collect pairs of proverbs that contradict each other. I might advise, for example, that you "Look before you leap," but you could reply "He who hesitates is lost." "Nothing ventured, nothing gained"; but "It's better to be safe than sorry." "Don't look a gift horse in the mouth"; but "Beware of Greeks bearing gifts." "Above all, to thine own self be true"; but "When in Rome, do as the Romans do." "Actions speak louder than words"; but "The pen is mightier than the sword." "Silence is golden"; but "The squeaky wheel gets the grease."

You can find more examples of these contradictory proverbs listed in *An Almanac of Words at Play,* by Willard Espy [793.73 ESP or 828 ESP] (pp. 257–58), *The Hodgepodge Book,* by Duncan Emrich [398.20973 EMR] (pp. 192–99), and *The People's Almanac #2,* by David Wallechinsky and Irving Wallace [031 PEO] (p. 1121).

After your children are somewhat familiar with the most common proverbs and wise sayings in our culture, you might like to try two additional techniques to enhance their appreciation and understanding of these adages.

The first is to rewrite each maxim using very long words (polysyllabic and grandiloquent vocabulary) to replace the simple, common language that makes each proverb so easily understood. For example, you might rewrite the proverb that says "Never count your chickens before they are hatched" as "On no occasion enumerate your poultry prior to their incubation," and see whether your children can guess the common form of the saying that has been rewritten. How about these:

> *Avian species of identical plumage congregate.* (Birds of a feather flock together.)
> *The existence of visible vapors from ignited carbonaceous materials confirms con-*

flagration. (Where there's smoke, there's fire.)

Ululate not over precipitated lacteal secretions. (Don't cry over spilled milk.)

Other examples of these long-winded proverbs can be found in *A Book of Puzzlements*, by Herbert Kohl [793.73 KOH or J 793.73 KOH] (pp. 96–97).

So get out your dictionary and a thesaurus and have a go at writing a couple yourself. Then let your children try to stump you with one they have rephrased by themselves. (This, by the way, is an excellent language activity for the classroom, especially for small groups of children working together, each group trying to come up with a rephrased adage whose original form cannot be guessed by the other groups.)

 Another way to encourage children to see the wisdom in common proverbs, and to see the universal nature of these simple truths, is to let them learn that their culture is by no means alone in creating such sayings. The television detectives Charlie Chan and Banacek often spouted Chinese and Polish proverbs (of dubious origin) that always provided the necessary insight to solve the particular case on which they were working, but let's ignore the Hollywood versions of international proverbs for now.

Instead, try to find people from your community who came from another culture and who know that culture and language well. (Exchange students who are attending local high schools would be excellent resources for this knowledge, and they are generally delighted to have an opportunity to talk about their homelands.) Ask them to translate the proverbs and the sayings of common folk wisdom from the "old country" into English. You and your children will be amazed at the similarities between these proverbs and our own. For example, the Russian saying that "With seven nurses, the child goes blind," and the Japanese proverb that "Too many boatmen run the boat up to the top of a mountain," express the same sentiment we find in our own "Too many cooks spoil the soup." The same general rule of caution we express in our proverb "Don't put the cart before the horse" lies at the heart of the Finnish saying "Trees are climbed from the bottom, not from the top." We adopted the following proverb from the Romans: "In the land of the blind, a one-eyed man is king"; the Koreans, meanwhile, devised another saying that expresses the very same sentiment: "Where there are no tigers, a wildcat is very self-important."

We can also use adages or wise sayings to help our children develop an understanding of figurative language, and at the same time introduce them to the common literary devices known as the *simile* [pronounced SIM-uh-lee] and the *metaphor* [pronounced MET-uh-for].

Similes

There is an old weather adage, for example, that says "March comes in like a lion and out like a lamb." Now, children know the literal meaning of the word lion, of course, but learning that this word can be used "figuratively," as well, represents a major leap in their understanding and in their ability to use language. It requires them to see some similarities in things that appear to be quite different: the beginning of March and a lion, the end of March and a lamb.

A comparison between dissimilar objects or ideas that includes the word *like* or *as* is called a simile, which comes from a Latin word that means "similar." A simile is a common "figure of speech"; that is, it is one of the devices or turns of phrase that writers and speakers use to give added flavor and vividness to the words they use.

We hear and use similes every day; they are part of our culture and our linguistic heritage. But too often we just assume that our children understand the meaning of these rather strange comparisons, and so we're surprised to find that they often do not, and that they simply ignore the whole phrase rather than ask for any clarification. (When you start to think about some of our most familiar similes, you may be thankful that your children don't ask you, for example, why a "wet hen" is deemed to be so "mad," or a "hound's tooth" is so "clean," or what exactly is so "slick" about a "whistle.")

You can use these historic or common similes to help your children understand this particular figure of speech, and to help them create their own similes as well. You might start out, for example, by making a list of well-known comparisons that all feature characteristics of animals ("strong as an ox," "stubborn as a mule," "blind as a bat," "busy as a bee," etc.). If you start the phrase, can your child complete the comparison with an attribute that is characteristic of a certain animal? Don't be surprised if the animal your child chooses is different from the one that is usually featured in the simile. The whole point is to create meaningful comparisons, and to be able to understand and explain the figurative sense that ties the attributes of one thing to another.

But don't focus only on the similes that are part of our culture's proverbs and adages, for although the simile itself is a creative tool and can become a device that your children can use to add vitality to their speaking and writing, these time-worn similes are often dredged up to substitute for one's lack of creative ability. (A standard, off-the-rack expression is often called a "cliché" [pronounced klee-SHAY], which is a French word for a stereotype printing plate.)

Children need to be challenged into creating the unifying links between all sorts of objects and situations, and parents can help them develop this linguistic skill by offering up various situations that call for comparisons. "The traffic moved so slowly it looked from above like...," you might begin, and after they complete the comparison, they can start out a simile for you to complete.

Metaphors

Now, a metaphor is a bit different from a simile in that it doesn't make use of the words *like* or *as*, yet it calls upon the reader or listener to see a comparison—a similarity between the specific characteristics to which the writer or speaker wants to draw our attention. If we read that "cigarettes are time bombs," we immediately filter through all the distinctive features of "real" time bombs (such as shape, size, components, etc.) and come upon one (they cause injury or death after a period of delay) that puts meaning into the metaphor. It can be fairly said, in fact, that a metaphor says one thing and means another.

Have you ever heard someone referred to as being "a real snake in the grass" or as having "his head in the clouds"? The meaning of these phrases has almost nothing to do with the literal meaning (that is, the actual or exact meaning) of the words themselves. The writer is compressing a number of ideas into an image that uses only a few words and that depends upon you to extract the proper points of comparison. (Many adults, including almost all sports broadcasters, don't understand what the word *literal* means, and so it is quite common to hear such horrifying reports as the description of a runner who "literally exploded out of the starting blocks!")

Metaphor lets you use your imagination to see and communicate comparisons in things that don't seem similar at all. So politicians can speak of "the ship of state" and thereby use metaphor to create an image among their listeners about the care that is needed in steering a country's course through the dangerous waters of these troubled times. Or an environmentalist can invoke the phrase "spaceship Earth" and so, in just those two words, convey dozens of images and feelings and values and beliefs.

One of my favorite language writers and teachers, Theodore Bernstein, used to say that "metaphor is just about as close as the average writer gets to creating poetry." For this is just what poetry does: It evokes pictures and abstract ideas that would be impossible to express if just the literal meanings of words were used.

Yet metaphor abounds in the speech and writing of adults and children alike, and we should encourage our children to create these figurative usages for themselves because metaphor puts color and imagery into the way they write and speak and look upon their world.

Just think of all the metaphors that lie buried in the words we use every day—the "legs" or the "arms" of a chair, for example, or the "head" of a bed, or the "teeth" of a saw. How many other body parts can you and your children find in the names of common objects around the house?

You can find metaphors bubbling out of almost any classification of words—take "clothes," for example. You can be "too big for your britches," "hot under the collar," or "living on a shoestring." Colors? Try "once in a blue moon," "paint the town red," and "yellow journalism." Richard Lederer, in his book *The Play of Words* [793.73 LED or 422 LED], reveals hundreds of similar metaphors that you and your children can find in such categories as "ships and sailing," "weather terms," and "animals."

Many of these phrases, though, have lost their metaphorical punch and vibrancy over time and are now clichés that no longer summon up comparisons of any kind. Still, they are useful aids in alerting children to the world of figurative language and imagery and meaning that can be created by seeing some quality of one thing in another.

Herbert Kohl's *A Book of Puzzlements* [793.73 KOH or J 793.73 KOH] includes several games and activities designed to help your children create their own metaphors and to extend those metaphors into complete poems, as well.

USEFUL FAMILY RESOURCES

An Almanac of Words at Play, by Willard R. Espy (New York: Clarkson N. Potter, 1975) [793.73 ESP or 828 ESP].

A Book of Clichés, by Joseph W. Valentine (New York: The Vanguard Press, 1963) [808.88 VAL].

A Book of Puzzlements, by Herbert R. Kohl (New York: Schocken Books, 1981) [793.73 KOH or J 793.73 KOH].

Crazy English: The Ultimate Joy Ride Through Our Language, by Richard Lederer (New York: Pocket Books, 1990) [420 LED].

The Hodgepodge Book, by Duncan Emrich (New York: Four Winds Press, 1972) [398.20973 EMR].

The People's Almanac #2, edited by David Wallechinsky and Irving Wallace (New York: William Morrow and Co., 1978) [031 PEO].

SEPTEMBER 11: *Birth of O. Henry*

NOVEMBER 30: *Birth of Mark Twain*

Would a Rose by Any Other Name Smell as Sweet?

What do your children think about the name that they were given at birth? Do they know why you chose to give them the first name and the middle name you did? Do you, and they, know why you have the family name that you do? Do your children think they would seem more glamorous or exciting if they were known by another name?

The whole subject of names is a good one for Family Learning, not only because it involves family names—and can lead to studies in history, geography, cultures, and customs—but also because names are among the most common words we use every day and yet are almost never discussed in language classes or English classes at school.

Pseudonyms

Names are so important to us that some people change the name they were given at birth to another that is more to their liking. Many writers have become famous for works they wrote under a pen name rather than their birth name. Some well-known examples include Mark Twain, who was given the name Samuel Langhorn Clemens at birth, and O. Henry, the pen name of William Sidney Porter. Add to these the names Lewis Carroll, George Orwell, Ellery Queen, Mickey Spillane, and John Le Carrè—all of which are *pseudonyms* [pronounced SUE-doe-nymz], a combination of two Greek words meaning "false name."

Why each of these writers chose to be known by a pseudonym instead of his given name is a story in itself. (William Sidney Porter, for example, became O. Henry while serving time in prison for embezzlement.) But the thought that a change in name might improve one's chances for acceptance in the world has affected writers, movie stars, and musicians for many years. Would Charles Atlas have been as successful a body builder under his given name, Angelo Siciliano? Would Roy Rogers have projected the same heroic image if he had retained the name Leonard Slye? Do the names Elias McDaniel, Reginald Dwight, and Steveland Morris convey the same excitement as the names Bo Diddley, Elton John, and Stevie Wonder chose to replace them?

Teenagers, too, see in their names an opportunity for establishing individuality and identity, sometimes by making a small spelling change and sometimes by using a nickname. What I find unfortunate, however, is that so few teenagers today have any knowledge at all of how they acquired their own names in the first place.

A first name or a middle name may have some family history behind it, and if so, children can profit from knowing how and to whom their roots are attached. But it is one's family name, or surname, that can show us and our children how deep those roots run and how similar they are to those of other families around the world.

Given names and Family names

Take an imaginary journey with your children back to a time many centuries ago, before there were factories, stores, or cities at all. We humans are busy doing whatever we can to scratch out an existence, and it is an isolated existence for the most part. We tend our flocks or grow our crops without seeing many other people at all, and so we have little difficulty in identifying and labeling those few people we do see. One name will suffice. We may be acquainted with "Laura" (who lived near a laurel tree, as did "Lawrence"), and "Oliver" (this name was derived from the olive tree), and "Mark" (who had a distinctive birthmark). But none of them needs a second name, because they are the only Laura or Oliver or Mark in the area.

But soon we humans begin to cluster into small villages, not only for protection, but also so that we don't all have to be farmers or shepherds. Now we can make a living by performing various specialties such as baking or milling or weaving or carpentry. And as our village grows and we begin to come in contact with more and more people in our lives, we are faced with the problem of finding distinctive labels so that we are able to identify and differentiate all those people. There may be several Lauras or Olivers or Marks living near our village, and now church records have to be kept, and we find that we need a better way to identify people than just by saying, "No, not **that** Mark. I mean the Mark that lives over near Oliver. Not **that** Oliver, the one who...."

So the surname originated as a way to describe individual people for better identification, and this second name was frequently, at least among European families, derived from some distinctive feature of the land near where you lived. Perhaps your home was on a hill, or beside a river, or near a lake—can you see how those words could help identify your family, and how they could become part of your family name (Mark Hill, Laura Rivers, Oliver Lake)?

Family Names in Other Languages

The most important lesson for children to see in this, however, is that almost every village had people who lived near hills and rivers and lakes, but not every village called these features by the words *hills*, *rivers*, and *lakes*; that is, not every village spoke English. But there is something so universal about the creation of family names that we see these words even today in the surnames of people whose ancestors came from various countries across Europe. A family named Hill in England acquired its name in exactly the same way that a family named Dumont or Depew acquired its name in France. A family that was called Brooks or Rivers in England was called Rio or Rivera in Spain, Strom in Sweden, and Klink in Holland and Germany. Mr. Lake in England was called Mr. Loch in Scotland.

It is this international flavor of family names that I think makes the subject so interesting and gives children another opportunity to see that they are just like other people all over the world—even those with strange-sounding names.

Another way that family names were created was by identifying a person with the work that person performed. Every village needed someone to fashion objects out of metal, which is the work of a *smith* (or *blacksmith*), and so the surname Smith became common in villages wherever English was spoken. But remember that **every** village needed a smith, even those that didn't call the occupation by that name. The Germans referred to the family of the ironworker as the Schmidts; in Italy they were called the Ferraros; in Bulgaria they were the, Kovacs; in France they were known as Lefevres.

Think of all the common family names you know that identify and describe various occupations in those ancient villages: Carpenter, Miller, Weaver, Shepherd, Taylor, Baker, Butcher, Cook, Shoemaker, Carter, and so on and on. These names tell us about the kind of people we were; they not only tell us what we did, but also what we didn't do. You don't find occupational family names like Scientist or Engineer among our ancient ancestors. But every one of the occupations you do see represented by a family name has a counterpart in French, Spanish, Italian, Norwegian, and dozens of other languages as well, and so children with any of these names can begin to see how they are connected to names and families and countries that they previously thought of merely as "foreign."

One last example, and then I'll let you get on to investigating your own name and finding connections for it in history and geography.

All over the world, it was a common practice to refer to children by the name of their parent—usually their father, but occasionally mothers names were used—and so many family names were created in this way. The name Johnson, for example, originally meant "John's son" and referred to an offspring of a man who was called John. But the name John that was used in England has different forms in other countries—same name, just different forms—and so the family name Johnson is the same name that is known as Johanson in Sweden, Jantzen in Holland, Jansen in Denmark, and Ivanov in Russia.

There are many other ways that family names were created, of course, including the incorporation of identifying characteristics, such as a ruddy complexion or red hair (these families were called Rossi in Italy, Rousseau or Rouse in France, Roth in Germany, Flynn in Ireland, and Reid or even Russell in England). And while not all family names have their roots in European history, to be sure, the more children know about the way names were created—just as the more they know about word origins in general—the more they will feel connected to the people and to the history of the world in which they live.

You and your children can explore the history of names, given names as well as family  names, by looking in the 922 section of the shelves in your local library, especially the 922 area of the reference section. There you will find such books as *The New Dictionary of American Family Names*, by Elsdon C. Smith, and *Names*, by Paul Dickson, and you may be as surprised as I was to learn that the names of some of your neighbors and classmates— names that seem so foreign or unusual—are just translations of your own.

USEFUL FAMILY RESOURCES

The Book of Boys' Names, by Linwood Sleigh and Charles Johnson (New York: Thomas Y. Crowell, 1962) [929.4 SLE].

The Book of Girls' Names, by Linwood Sleigh and Charles Johnson (New York: Thomas Y. Crowell, 1962) [929.4 SLE].

A Collector's Compendium of Rare and Unusual, Bold and Beautiful, Odd and Whimsical Names, by Paul Dickson (New York: Delacorte Press, 1986) [428.1 DIC].

Last Names First, by Mary Price Lee and Richard S. Lee (Philadelphia: The Westminster Press, 1985) [929.4 LEE or J 929.4 LEE].

The New Dictionary of American Family Names, by Elsdon Coles Smith (New York: Gramercy Publishing Co., 1988) [929.4 SMI].

Our Names: Where They Came From and What They Mean, by Eloise Lambert and Mario Pei (New York: Lothrop, Lee & Shepard Co., 1966) [929.4 LAM or J 929.4 LAM].

Your Book of Surnames, by Pennethorne Hughes (London: Faber and Faber, 1967) [929.4 HUG or J 929.4 HUG].

For pen names and pseudonyms of famous people, see *Larousse Biographical Dictionary* (New York: Larousse Kingfisher Chambers, 1994) [R 921 LAR] and *The Almanac of Famous People* (Detroit: Gale Research, Inc., 1994) [R 920.02 ALM].

People and Products That Became Words

One technique for getting children interested in word origins and in the ways that words come into our language is to focus on the everyday words that are actually the names of real people. For example, November 3 would be a good day to introduce your children to the story behind the word *sandwich*, (perhaps while you are making or sharing a sandwich) because that is the birthday, in 1718, of John Montagu, the Earl of Sandwich. He once ordered his servant to bring him some sliced beef between two pieces of toasted bread so that he could eat with one hand and continue gambling at cards with the other.

It is strange how language occasionally enshrines forever the names of disreputable and decadent figures in words that have wholly admirable meanings and applications. The Earl of Sandwich's private life was characterized by intemperance and debauchery, and his years of public service as First Lord of the Admiralty (similar at that time to our secretary of defense) produced continual charges against him for graft, bribery, mismanagement, and general incompetence. He was, in fact, responsible for directing the rather pitiful performance of the British Navy during the entire American Revolution.

Yet he lives today in the name of our most popular meal and in the former name of our fiftieth state. The Hawaiian Islands, you see, used to be known as the Sandwich Islands because back in 1778, when Captain James Cook became the first European to explore the islands, he named them for the man who headed the British Navy at that time, the Earl of Sandwich.

Another example of a person's name that became a common word is the case of Dr. Joseph Guillotin [pronounced GILL-uh-teen], whose name today describes a most frightful device, which he did not invent, which did not cause his death, and with which he never wanted to be associated in any way. This is how it happened.

Dr. Guillotin was a French physician and a member of the National Assembly back in 1789, during the French Revolution. In an impassioned speech to that body he pleaded for a more humane and merciful method of execution "for all persons regardless of rank." Up until that time, the form of capital punishment used in France depended upon who was being punished: The upper classes were dispatched (although sometimes clumsily) with a sharp sword or ax, while commoners were by law required to hang for their crimes. Dr. Guillotin advocated the adoption of some unspecified "painless and infallible machine" that would not discriminate in dispensing its justice—it would cut across class lines, you might say.

Within three years, such a machine was in place, having been devised by a French surgeon, Dr. Antoine Louis. During its first years of use it was called a "Louisette," after its inventor, but soon the people began associating it with Dr. Guillotin's eloquent speech championing democratic executions, and they called it *la machine guillotine* and then just *guillotine*.

For the rest of his life Joseph Guillotin tried to dissociate his name from that of the machine, and for several years after his death his family petitioned the government to have the machine called something else. (The government refused, but it did allow them to change **their** name.)

Eponymous Words

Words like *guillotine*, that are created out of a person's name, are called *eponymous* [pronounced ih-PAH-nimm-us] words. This term comes from the Greek *epi-*, meaning "upon," and *onyma*, meaning "name." *Onyma* also is the root for several other words having to do with names, such as *anonymous* ("without" plus "name") and *pseudonym* ("false" plus "name").

Many children go through their entire language education thinking the words that name or describe things are somehow part of the things themselves. A *saxophone*, for instance, must be a saxophone; what else could it be called? They never experience the pleasure of discovering that there is a real human being residing in that word, the name of the inventor himself—Antoine Joseph Sax.

Human beings who became words are buried in our language, but they can be resurrected if we will just be curious enough to look for them. Out in the garden, for example, lie the linguistic remains we know as the *begonia, camellia, gardenia, magnolia, poinsettia,* and *zinnia*—humans all not so very long ago.

At least one animal, too, became a common word in our language: Jumbo. Today we frequently hear of things that are of unusually large size described as "jumbo": "jumbo jets," "jumbo-size" boxes of cereal, "jumbo shrimp" (a combination of seemingly contradictory terms). But just a little more than a century ago, *jumbo* meant nothing at all to Americans, for it was just the name given to a certain African elephant who lived at the London Zoological Gardens. But what an elephant this was! When the famous promoter and showman P. T. Barnum bought Jumbo in 1882, the elephant weighed almost seven tons, stood twelve feet tall at the shoulders, had a seven-foot trunk, and could nibble on leaves that were twenty-six feet above the ground. No elephant this size had ever been seen before, in or out of captivity.

Jumbo became the most popular attraction in the Barnum & Bailey Circus, and for three and a half years he led each circus parade waving a huge American flag with his trunk. Using his enormous strength, he helped load and unload tons of equipment from the circus flatcars, and he brought delight to countless children who were allowed to ride on a special platform that had been fitted with several benches and strapped on to the elephant's broad back like a saddle.

But after the last show of the season in 1885, in the Canadian town of St. Thomas, Ontario, while Jumbo was being led back to his private railroad car, he was struck and killed by a speeding freight train as he crossed the tracks in the darkness. The circus world, and the world in general, mourned Jumbo's passing, but his name lived on as a way to describe anything huge or of unusually large size.

The word *jumbo*, then, is an eponymous word, just like *sandwich* and *saxophone*, because it is based upon or created from a name. Eponymous words can also be derived from the names of places as well as people, and so we can get a geography lesson by looking up the origins of words like *bologna* sausage, *parmesan* cheese, *lima* beans, *frankfurter*, *hamburger*, and even *denim* and blue *jeans* (see pages 207–8).

Parents can help open up their children's world of language by displaying a curiosity about how various words came into being and by focusing on the many common words that take their form from the name of a real person, fictional character, or geographical place. A good desk-size or collegiate-size dictionary will include in the entry for each eponymous word the name of the person on whom that word is based. (Under *leotard*, for instance, will be a reference to "Jules Léotard, 19th-century French aerialist.") You can then consult an encyclopedia or a biographical dictionary to find the dates on which these people were born or died, and you can use those dates to introduce or feature those words in discussions and celebrations with your children.

Word Histories

Word histories appear frequently throughout this book and are featured in the discussions and the activities that involve science and geography and history, not just language alone. I try to focus parents' attention and study on etymology (not *entomology*, which is the study of insects) for two reasons. First, it is a subject that seems to become more interesting to people as they get older. There are countless adults today who are fascinated by word origins and histories but who, as children in school, displayed no similar interest whatsoever. Some of this early ambivalence was surely due to the lack of knowledge or enthusiasm that many teachers have about making word histories become a meaningful part of every subject and every grade. But, it may also be true that word histories often require some knowledge of the world—some experience with the world—before they can provide us those entertaining and sometimes illuminating connections between what we thought were unconnected parts of that world. Word histories, then, are a good example of how Family Learning can encourage learning in all family members—adults and children alike.

Second, there are many opportunities in family life for the passing on of word origins and histories from parent to child. The simple act of making a sandwich can also include a little unobtrusive history and geography. Yet, how many sandwiches will be made this week in how many homes across the country, with the only result of that effort being the sandwich itself?

As with every other subject or topic that is worth learning at all, parental interest in the origin of words will—sooner or later—show up in the knowledge and interest of their children. No one has to be a master of Latin or Greek to be intrigued by the connections that these languages provide to the spelling and use of thousands of English words. Nor is it necessary to know the stories behind the names of every plant in the garden and every food on the table. But there are numerous adventures and illuminations for adults and children alike to be found in the word history section (Dewey number 422) of your local library. Here you will find several very readable collections such as *Thereby Hangs a Tale*, by Charles Earle Funk; *The Story Behind the Word*, by Morton S. Freeman; and *Word Mysteries & Histories*, by the editors of The American Heritage Dictionaries.

With these books and your dictionary, you and your children will be able to bring to life the human beings who lie buried in the following words: *boycott, derrick, dunce, hooker, lynch, maverick, nicotine, sideburns, guppy, hooligan, dunce, czar,* and *silhouette*.

Capitalizing Product Names

Your children many wonder why these words aren't capitalized if they are based on the names of real people. Isn't the first letter in a person's name supposed to be capitalized?

Well, yes, it is—when it refers to the name of an individual person. But a *leotard*, for example, or a *sandwich* isn't the name of a **person**; that is, the word does not stand for and represent a human being. Instead, these words are names for a general class or group of objects, and so they are not spelled with a capital letter.

Aha! you say. But what about product names that **are** capitalized, like Levi's and Big Macs? How are these different from *leotards* and *sandwiches*? How are children ever to learn which words should be capitalized and which should not?

How indeed. The problem of capitalization flourishes well beyond the school walls, having become a daily concern for major corporations and the federal courts as well. Does the name Jell-O, for instance, stand for a specific product, or can it be written *jello* (with a small *j* and no hyphen) to mean "any gelatin dessert no matter what the brand might be"? (Answer: Jell-O is a protected trademark that names a particular gelatin dessert and distinguishes it from Royal gelatin, for example. There is no *jello*.)

Adults may find it interesting to learn that it is exactly this kind of question that the federal courts ask in determining whether a brand name has become so generic that it loses its right to be spelled with a capital letter. As soon as the name of a particular brand of product comes into general use as the name for all similar products, the original manufacturer loses the protection of its capitalized trademark, and the name becomes a common, and uncapitalized, word in the language.

Here is just a partial list of words that today describe whole classes of goods, but years ago each was the specific trademark of a specific company and was spelled with a capital letter: *aspirin, cellophane, dry ice, escalator, kerosene, nylon, shredded wheat, thermos, trampoline, yo-yo.*

The importance of that capital letter can be measured in the many millions of dollars that companies like Xerox and Coca-Cola and Band-Aid spend each year trying to keep their trademarks from slipping into the list above. Some brand names teeter so close to the brink that we are surprised to find that they are now, or ever were, spelled with a capital letter (e.g., Ping-Pong, Pogo Stick, and Laundromat).

One way that children can learn to separate trademarks and brand names—such as Coke and Kleenex—from the names of general classes of products—such as cola and facial tissue—is to have them be responsible for writing out the family's shopping list. The list should include brand names whenever possible so that children can face the problem—just as lawyers and judges do—of deciding whether or not to capitalize the initial letter. (If you wrote down *Coke*—with a capital *c*—and someone else did the shopping, would you be disappointed if that person interpreted Coke to mean "any cola," and brought home Pepsi? If you wrote down *coke*—with a small *c*—would you be disappointed if that person returned with a solid lump of coal that had been heated in a furnace? Yes, I guess you'd have reason to be.)

Having children be responsible for the actual writing of your shopping list, perhaps while you dictate the items to them, is a good practice to follow for several reasons, not the least of which is that the technical parts of writing (such as punctuation, spelling, and capitalization) become ingrained only through the process of writing itself. Therefore, any writing opportunities parents can find for children—including thank you notes, telephone messages, and shopping lists—should be employed with such frequency and regularity that they become routine in a child's life. Children can read about the spelling rules for forming the plurals of nouns, but it is when they use the words *potatoes* and *tomatoes* on the shopping list, time after time, that they acquire the ability and the confidence to spell these plurals correctly.

Then, too, just having children face the task of deciding how a word will be interpreted when it is capitalized, and what it can mean when it is not, encourages them to see meaning in matters that seemed so trivial and meaningless before, and in this way they grow to care a little more about the language they speak and write. Knowing word histories and word origins, seeing the names of dead people and dead trademarks in words that live today—these abilities do not ensure language fluency or wide vocabularies for our children. But they do open up the world of language so that our children can see how English was created and how it continues to be created by real people having to face the real problem of expressing themselves clearly to others.

I have always found that people who understand the workings of something and how that something was made, whether it is an automobile or a computer or an article of clothing, tend to take better care of it and are less sloppy about the way they put it to use. This applies to language, I think, as well.

USEFUL FAMILY RESOURCES

A Collector's Compendium of Rare and Unusual, Bold and Beautiful, Odd and Whimsical Names, by Paul Dickson (New York: Delacorte Press, 1986) [428.1 DIC].

The Dictionary of Eponyms: Names That Became Words, by Robert Hendrickson (Briarcliff Manor, N.Y.: Stein and Day, 1985) [423.1 HEN].

Heavens to Betsy! and Other Curious Sayings, by Charles Earle Funk, (New York: Harper & Row, Publishers, 1955) [423.1 FUN].

Horsefeathers and Other Curious Words, by Charles Earle Funk (New York: Harper & Row, Publishers, 1958) [422 FUN].

O Thou Improper, Thou Uncommon Noun, by Willard R. Espy (New York: Clarkson N. Potter, 1978) [422 ESP].

The Story Behind the Word, by Morton S. Freeman (Philadelphia: ISI Press, 1985) [422.03 FRE].

Thereby Hangs a Tale: Stories of Curious Word Origins, by Charles Earle Funk (New York: Harper & Row, Publishers, 1950) [422 FUN].

Word Mysteries & Histories: From Quiche to Humble Pie, by the editors of the American Heritage Dictionaries (Boston: Houghton Mifflin Company, 1986) [422.03 WOR].

Word Origins and Their Romantic Stories, by Wilfred Funk (New York: Bell Publishing Co., 1950) [422 FUN].

Word People, by Nancy Caldwell Sorel (New York: American Heritage Press, 1970) [422 SOR].

Words Can Be Created Right out of Thin Air

Words are created in all sorts of ways, and children need to know that their language isn't fixed or static by any means. New words are invented all the time, and they are invented by people—even by children. For example, some—very few, but still some—of the slang words adopted by every generation's teenagers find a home for themselves in general usage, eventually even becoming accepted into "polite" speech and writing when there is a need for them.

William Shakespeare created approximately two thousand words all by himself. He had such a precise sense and "feel" for language—especially for the sounds of words—that if he needed a particular word, with a particular sound, to express a particular idea, and no such word existed in the Elizabethan vocabulary, Shakespeare simply coined one, and presto! it became an accepted part of English speech and writing. That is just how our language acquired such words as *critical, leapfrog, monumental, majestic, obscene, frugal, radiance, dwindle, countless, submerged, excellent, gust, hint, hurry, lonely, summit, assassinate, bump, impartial, laughable, misplaced.*

Did you know that every time you use these words you are "quoting" Shakespeare?

It is more difficult for anybody to create words today, simply because there are so many English words already in existence—over 600,000 of them, and that doesn't include all the chemical compounds, molecular chains, animal and plant classifications, and other scientific designations that are "words," too, in every sense, and would run the total into the millions. Then consider that so many of our words have multiple meanings—should the word *key* that refers to the instrument used in opening a lock, and the *key* that means the finger lever on a typewriter, be counted as a single word in our vocabulary, even though the two words have nothing in common except their spelling?

Take your children to the reference room in the public library some day and show them the twenty-volume collection that is called the *Oxford English Dictionary*. Locate the volume that includes the word *set,* and let them see how many different meanings this simple word has acquired over the years. (The definitions go on for twenty-five pages, with three columns on each page!)

Still, new words are created every year, although in recent generations, many additions to our vocabulary have come from the names for new products, inventions, scientific discoveries, and technological innovations. Whenever and wherever a need for a word exists, one will be created, and not by scholars or by a government committee on language, but by people who actually use the language, and that means you and me, and our children, too.

When children are young, before we've succeeded in drumming out their natural curiosity and inquisitiveness, they wonder why a thing—anything—is called by the name it is, and often we are stumped or we don't want to go into the whole subject of word origins just then, and so we leave our children with the impression that words have no reason for being as they are. They just are, that's all. Well, here are two classes of words—words formed by combining other words, and words that imitate sounds—that you can use to show your children how words are created to fill various needs, and that your children can use to play with their own language by creating similar words.

A great era in aviation came to a tragic end on May 6, 1937, when the giant German airship *Hindenburg* burst into flames as it prepared to land at Lakehurst, New Jersey. The *Hindenburg* was the largest airship ever to fly—more than four times the size of today's Goodyear blimps!—with private staterooms for seventy passengers, an elegant dining room, a sumptuous lounge complete with a grand piano, a crew of twenty-seven, and space for thirteen tons of cargo.

But inside the framework of its huge hull were sixteen separate lifting cells filled with millions of cubic feet of flammable hydrogen, and when a spark of some kind—perhaps from static electricity—caused an explosion in one of those cells, the others quickly ignited, and in less than forty seconds the *Hindenburg* was reduced to a charred and smoldering skeleton.

This great ship was originally designed to be lifted by helium, which is an inert gas and would have been much safer, but Germany was in the firm control of Adolf Hitler and the Nazis at this time, and the United States refused to sell any helium to Germany for fear that it would be used for military purposes.

There are two common misunderstandings that people have about the *Hindenburg*. First, that when it burned and crashed to the ground, all on board the ship were killed. Not so. In fact, sixty-two of the ninety-seven passengers and crew miraculously survived.

People also mistakenly think of the *Hindenburg* as a blimp, which it was not. The *Hindenburg* like all the German zeppelins and a few large American airships of the time, had a rigid metal framework that formed its hull, and inside this framework were attached separate cells filled with gas. A blimp, on the other hand, has no framework at all, and so the entire hull is just one big gas bag.

Both types of airships, though, are known as *dirigibles* [pronounced DIH-ridge-uh-bulls], which means "steerable" (from the Latin word *dirigere*, meaning "to direct"). A hot-air balloon cannot be steered; it goes wherever the wind takes it, and so a hot-air balloon is not a dirigible. But both the rigid dirigible (like the *Hindenburg*) and the nonrigid (blimp) type have engines and propellers to travel wherever they choose.

Portmanteau Words

During World War I, the British began referring to these two types of dirigibles as "Type A-rigid" and "Type B-limp," the second designation being slurred into "Type Blimp" and finally just "blimp." This collapsing or "telescoping" of separate words or parts of words into a new word that combines the meanings of the others is one of the ways that English enriches its vocabulary. Lewis Carroll, the author of *Alice in Wonderland*, called such words "portmanteau [pronounced port-MAN-toe] words" after a type of leather traveling bag whose two hinged compartments could be folded together. As Carroll put it, "You see...there are two meanings packed into one word."

See if your children can identify the portmanteau words that come from the combinations given below.

> A meal between *breakfast* and *lunch* =
> A mixture of *smoke* and *fog* =
> A roadside *hotel* for *motorists* =
> A laugh that mixes a *chuckle* and a *snort* =
> The sound of a *splash* and a *sputter* =
> (Answers: *brunch, smog, motel, chortle, splutter*)

I'll bet, just by *happenstance*, you know some others, but that's just a *guesstimate*.

Onomatopoetic Words

Not everyone agrees, however, that the word *blimp* is a portmanteau word at all. The Goodyear company, for example, published a booklet titled *Aerial Ambassadors* some time ago, in which they credited the creation of the word *blimp* to a Lieutenant Cunningham of the British Naval Air Service. In 1915, according to this booklet, Lieutenant Cunningham was conducting a close inspection of one of the new British airships, and he happened to flick or snap his finger against the side of the balloon. "An odd noise echoed off the taut fabric," says this account, which Cunningham imitated orally: "Blimp!" Everyone within earshot began repeating the sound, and soon that sound came to stand for the airship itself. The word *blimp* was born.

It could be, although most authorities still say that the portmanteau origin is more likely to be the correct one. But you can imagine, can't you, the sound of that echo inside the huge gas bag, and the human compulsion to duplicate that sound with one's voice?

A whole host of words have been created in exactly this way. We imitate with our voices the sounds we hear in nature, and then discover that we have no words to describe those sounds, so our imitations become words, and they fill the need very well. We drop a stone into a pool of water: "PLOP!" That's how it sounds, and so *plop* becomes our word to describe that sound. A lightning bolt flashes overhead, and then a loud clap of thunder almost makes us jump: "CRACK!" What better word can there be to describe that sound?

Words like *plop* and *crack* and *fizz* and *boom* and *buzz* and *bang* and *hiss* are all examples of *onomatopoeia* [pronounced ah-nuh-mah-tuh-PEE-uh], from the Greek for "word making." It signifies the forming of words that sound like the action or thing described. All words that are created in this way are known as *onomatopoetic* [pronounced ah-nuh-mah-tuh-poh-ETT-ick] words. Now that seems to be a strange and obscure name for such a simple and easily understood classification of words, but we really don't have a better one. Some teachers call these words "sound words," or "imitative words," but that really doesn't do the trick. I think we should just get used to hearing ourselves say "onomatopoetic" and make sure that our children pay more attention to knowing what words are in this group than to knowing what the group is called.

Some words that were created to imitate sounds will surprise you, because over the course of years you have come to separate the word from the sound it was created to imitate. Take the word *murmur*, for example. Don't you have a completely new and different feeling for this word now that you know that it was a human effort to duplicate the sound of a murmur? You may associate the bird that is called the bobwhite with the sound it makes, but do you also see the names for the cuckoo and the whippoorwill as being created in this same way?

GALOSH
GALOSH
GALOSH

 You'll find onomatopoetic words all around you, once you start looking for them, and you'll also find that they enrich the spoken and written language more than you ever thought possible. Here is a sample of how they sound when they flow from the pen of a master—Mark Twain. Twain had a great ear for the English language, and this passage, in which Huckleberry Finn describes a gathering storm in his own distinctive dialect, demonstrates how truly vivid descriptions make use of words that appeal directly to the senses.

Pretty soon it darkened up and begun to thunder and lighten; so the birds was right about it. Directly it begun to rain and it rained like all fury, too, and I never see the wind blow so. It was one of these regular summer storms. It would get so dark that it looked all blue-black outside, and lovely; and the rain would thrash along by so thick that the trees off a little ways looked dim and spider-webby; and here would come a blast of wind that would bend the trees down and turn up the pale underside of the leaves; and then a perfect ripper of a gust would follow along and set the branches to tossing their arms as if they was just wild; and next, when it was just about the bluest and blackest— *fst!* it was as bright as glory and you'd have a little glimpse of tree-tops a-plunging about away off yonder in the storm, hundreds of yards further than you could see before; dark as sin again in a second, and now you'd hear the thunder let go with an awful crash and then go rumbling, grumbling, tumbling down the sky towards the under side of the world, like rolling empty barrels down-stairs—where it's long stairs and they bounce a good deal, you know.

Good Times to Celebrate the French in All of Us

When you and your children start to look at the English language with an inquiring mind, when you begin to wonder why certain words came to have the meaning or spelling they do, you will discover very quickly that English is truly a melting pot, for our vocabulary is really a collection of words from other countries and cultures, some of which died long ago and many that flourish today. Our language borrows and absorbs more words than any other language in the world, and it has enriched itself in this way for centuries. Whenever our linguistic ancestors conquered, or were conquered by, the people from another culture, they appropriated whatever words they found useful, made minor changes in spelling or pronunciation, and added them to their own word stock.

The Roots of English

It is quite surprising to most Americans, therefore, to learn that the root source of their English language is not Latin or Greek, but German. In fact, the modern language that most resembles ours today is Dutch, along with its Belgian variant, Flemish, and a South African variant called Afrikaans.

Our linguistic ancestors—the tribes known as the Angles, the Saxons, and the Jutes—came to England from their home in Northern Germany. (The name England comes from "Angle-land" or "Land of the Angles.") Here they encountered the Roman culture, which added many Latin and Greek words to the Anglo-Saxon vocabulary, and later the Vikings, who contributed a Danish stock of words. (The phrase "Take the knife and cut the steak" contains only two Anglo-Saxon words, *the* and *and*; the rest are pure Danish.)

The point here is that if you and your children become curious about origins of the words you use, you'll find history and geography and the story of human culture all bound up in your own vocabulary.

English Words of French Origin

A particularly good time to launch a family investigation into word origins would be October 14, because that date marks the anniversary of a time when history and geography, and even technology, came together in an event that changed the way we speak and write today.

When William, Duke of Normandy (look at a globe or a world map to see how close the peninsula in northwest France called Normandy is to England), invaded England in 1066, and when he defeated King Harold at the Battle of Hastings, he brought the French language and culture into the land of the Anglo-Saxons. For the next several centuries, the French language was spoken by the Norman conquerors, while Anglo-Saxon speech identified those who had been conquered. All the kings of England during this time (including Richard the Lion-Hearted) spoke French, as did all the noblemen and ladies, as well as everyone who dealt in politics, education, science, the arts, and all areas of refined living. Anglo-Saxon speech, on the other hand, was used among the lowest, the basest of occupations and workers.

We can see this division of cultures and languages in the words we use today. The language of the Saxons who worked in the fields and in the sheds with live animals is the basis for our words *ox, cow, bull, calf, steer, chicken, sheep, pig, sow, swine,* and *deer.* But the names for the meats that came from these animals and were served in the Norman castles are distinctly French in origin: *beef, veal, pork, bacon, sausage, mutton, venison,* and *poultry.*

During this Norman occupation of England, several hundred words that we commonly use today were co-opted from French into English. Most pertain to the affairs of the ruling Normans, who dominated such fields as religion (*prayer, friar, clergy, baptism, chaplain, miracle, sermon*); government (*court, crown, govern, reign, country, authority, baron, duke*); law (*justice, jury, plaintiff, defendant, attorney*); art (*beauty, image, tower, choir, design*).

The French language has continued to be a major contributor to our English vocabulary ever since. In fact, French is the source of more modern English words than is any other language except Latin (which is, itself, the source of most French words). Many of these words have undergone some changes in their spelling and pronunciation so that their French heritage is somewhat obscured today. The words *liberty, charity,* and *restaurant* are typical of the tens of thousands of common words that came to us from France but no longer appear or sound French. Some familiar place names, too, have a French origin but no longer any relationship to their original meaning: Baton Rouge ("red stick"), Terre Haute ("high ground"), Des Moines ("the place of the monks").

There are, however, hundreds of words that are part of our common American vocabulary but still retain much of their French spelling and pronunciation. Your children may already be familiar with the meanings of words like *ballot*, *cafe*, *morgue*, *gourmet*, *prestige*, *chauffeur*, *camouflage*, *routine*, *cuisine*, *connoisseur*, *debut*, *champagne*, *casserole*, *fondue*, *mayonnaise*, and *cologne*. But here are some French words and phrases that may not be as familiar to them, or to you. Each, however, is so much a part of the English language that its meaning and pronunciation can be easily found in any desk-size dictionary: *liaison*, *cliché*, *cachet*, *résumé*, *à la carte*, *à la mode*, *avant-garde*, *bon voyage*, *carte blanche*, *coup de grace*, *deja vu*, *esprit de corps*, *faux pas*, *par excellence*, *savoir-faire*.

Try to accustom your children to the meanings of these words and phrases by using them in your own speech and by pointing them out when you hear them used on television. It is not the strange spellings that are important here but that children hear these words in context and come to see English as a collection of languages from around the world.

There is one special time of year when a decidedly French pronunciation will be featured on television, and its decidedly French spelling will appear in newspapers: Mardi Gras. We think of Mardi Gras as being the lavish festival celebrated in New Orleans each year, but we almost never think about why we call the festival by this French name. What does *Mardi Gras* mean, anyway?

Mardi Gras actually refers to only the last day of the pre-Lenten festival that is called Carnival. This approximately two-week period of eating, drinking, and general merrymaking precedes the forty days of fasting and self-denial that begins on Ash Wednesday and is known as Lent.

So the day before the beginning of Lent—that Tuesday on which all the lard (animal fat) in the house was used in festive baking before the meatless days of Lent—that Tuesday came to be called "fat Tuesday" or, in French, *mardi gras*.

Place Names from Other Languages

Helping your children identify common words and place names that tie the English language to French is, of course, just an example of similar connections you can help them find between English and other languages, such as Italian or German or Spanish. Familiar names of cities, rivers, and mountains provide a good starting point, not only because we are often surprised to find that the names actually meant something and were applied to the city, river, or mountain for a reason, but also because these names can provide a link that helps us associate language and geography at the same time.

For example, your children may already see in the names of cities like St. Paul, Minnesota, and St. Joseph, Missouri, the names of revered religious figures (the Apostle Paul and Mary's husband), but do they see these same figures enshrined in the city names São Paulo, Brazil (Portuguese), and San Jose, California (Spanish)? Do they know that the English name James is Iago in Spanish? If not, then they'll miss the revelation of seeing that Saint James (brother of John) is the namesake for the capital of Chile: Saint Iago runs together to form Santiago.

USEFUL FAMILY RESOURCES

Success With Words: A Guide to the American Language (Pleasantville, N.Y.: Reader's Digest Association, 1983) [427.973 SUC].

What's in a Word? by Mario Pei (New York: Hawthorn Books, 1968) [412 PEI].

Words on the Map, by Isaac Asimov (Boston: Houghton Mifflin Co., 1962) [910.3 ASI or J 910.3 ASI].

WEDNESDAY AND THURSDAY AFTER MEMORIAL DAY: *National Spelling Bee finals*
JUNE 15: *Signing of the Magna Carta*
JULY 26: *Birth of George Bernard Shaw*

Confident Spellers Are Made, Not Born

Of all the wrong-headed and destructive attitudes about learning that children pick up in their homes, take with them to school, and suffer for as a result, none is more easily spotted, and less easily remedied (at least in the classroom), than the all-too-common belief among parents that accurate spelling is just too difficult for anyone to achieve, especially children.

It's not just a matter of whether parents are good spellers themselves; it is, instead, a matter of whether parents think that good spelling is important at all. If parents don't care about accurate spelling, if they convey the notion to their children that spelling is just a "little thing" or that English spelling is "impossible to learn," it will be highly unlikely that any teacher will be able to persuade those children otherwise. (And if any of a child's teachers happen to have similarly destructive attitudes, then the chances of that child's ever attaining any skill or confidence in spelling are reduced even more.)

Parents can improve their own ability to spell if they wish to do so; there are many good paperback books on the market today that are specifically designed to attack adult spelling problems. There are, in addition, a number of useful memory aids and techniques that adults can learn and master as a way of gaining confidence in spelling those words that offer them particular or frequent difficulty, one of which I'll show you later on.

Valuing Spelling in the Home

But what is most important is for parents to start letting their children know that good spelling is something to be valued, that it is important in life, and that it can be learned by everyone. Spelling can become a part of daily life in your home, part of contests back and forth, not to stump one another with spelling "demons," but to confirm one another's abilities and to stretch those abilities as well.

To do this, you and your children are going to have to let go of some widely held notions about English spelling, most of which seem on the surface to be true, but all of which are just plain wrong. For example, how many times have you heard people say that "English is the most irregular language on earth"? But in fact, English is—by comparison to other languages—very regular and systematic, especially in its consonant sounds. Sure, the sound of our vowels and combinations of vowels may jump around from word to word, but most of the spelling difficulties that this poses can be handled by knowing word families, patterns, and origins.

You may also have heard that "English spelling rules have more exceptions than those in any other language," and this, too, is just not borne out by the facts. Most of the people who parrot this line have little knowledge of what the "rules" of English spelling are to begin with, and besides, exceptions are easily remembered simply because they are exceptions. We would all do well to keep in mind what a wise teacher once told me about English: "Remember that the language was invented before the rules."

I am certainly not claiming that the English spelling system is as regular and orderly as, say, the number system we use, or our system for classifying earthly elements, or any other system we have devised with orderliness as its primary objective. But English spelling was not "devised" at all; it evolved, instead, and so it incorporates the changing ideas and beliefs and conditions that affected human beings throughout history, from cultures that thrive today and from those that died long ago.

The question we must ask is whether we would be better served with a completely regular system of spelling, or whether we can use the system we already have as a springboard for learning about history and geography and anthropology, and as a way to see ourselves as related to, and indebted to, the myriad, nameless and faceless humans throughout the history of the world who helped to shape the way we write and speak today.

Phonetic Spelling

As you can tell, I think that there are worlds of learning to be found in the study of English spelling, but let's look at the case for one often-proposed alternative: a phonetic system, in which the way that words are spelled conforms exactly to the way that they are pronounced. Even here we will find tools that parents can use in their homes to aid in the Family Learning of English spelling.

Perhaps the loudest and most persistent cry for spelling reform came from the British playwright, essayist, social critic, and vegetarian, George Bernard Shaw. Shaw was born in 1856 and is most widely known for *Pygmalion* [pronounced pig-MAIL-yun], a play he wrote in 1912. It dealt with the attempts of a language professor named Henry Higgins to turn a lowly street urchin into an elegant lady merely by changing her accent and her mannerisms. The play was adapted for the musical theater in 1956 and became the smash hit *My Fair Lady*.

Throughout his life, Shaw campaigned for the adoption of a system of phonetic spelling, and he even left the bulk of his sizable estate to the development of an English alphabet that would have at least forty letters. Shaw realized that in our twenty-six letter alphabet, we have only five written vowels, yet we have at least thirteen vowel sounds that we use in pronouncing our words. So we have to combine our few vowels in various ways to render those extra sounds, and over the years we have come up with about thirty various vowel combinations, many whose pronunciations overlap, and many having multiple pronunciations themselves.

Take the *ou* combination, for example, which has a distinctly different sound in each of the following words: *house, cough, cousin, through, dough,* and *could.* Even single vowels can be pronounced in a variety of ways, such as the four *e*'s in *reentered,* which have four different pronunciations, one of which is silent.

Perhaps two-thirds of all English words include a silent letter of some kind, and so you and your children might try making a list of words in which each of the letters from a to z appears as a silent letter. For example, *a: bread, b: debt, c: indict...x: faux pas, y: crayon, z: rendezvous.* (Just such a list appears in a wonderful book by Richard Lederer titled *Crazy English* [420 LED].)

Consider, too, the fact that there are only about forty-four sounds (vowel and consonant sounds combined) in all of English, yet we have over 200 ways of spelling those sounds. The *sh* sound alone can be spelled in about a dozen ways (*shape, sure, passion, fictitious, ocean, champagne,* etc.), and there are also a dozen ways to spell the sound of long *a,* and a dozen ways to spell long *o.*

In fact, one of George Bernard Shaw's most famous pronouncements was his observation that he had discovered a very "logical" way to spell the word *fish: ghoti.* He used the *gh* from enou*gh*, the *o* from w*o*men, and the *ti* from na*ti*on. Although Shaw intended this as a way to show the need for phonetic spelling, it might also suggest another good family spelling activity. Help your child create a new spelling for his or her name by using the sounds from other words, just as Shaw did with *fish.* Each of you can also come up with *ghotiy* (that is, "fishy") spellings for the other to decipher by listing the words from which the sounds were taken. For example, you might create the word *pphaumylei,* and tell your children that it was created from the sounds of letters in the words *sapphire, laugh, mystery, leisure.* What English word do you say when you pronounce *pphaumylei?* (Answer = *family*).

Well, what do you—and your children—think of this idea to have words spelled the way they are pronounced? It sounds so sensible, and so easy, but here are a couple of things that you may want to consider, and discuss. Just whose pronunciations should we use as our spelling models, anyway? Many people mispronounce the word *nuclear* as nuc-*you*-ler, and *athlete* as ath-*uh*-lete. But does that mean that we all should spell the words with those sounds? And how would we distinguish all the words that are pronounced the same but have different spellings and meanings, such as *seize* and *seas, aloud* and *allowed, to* and *too* and *two?*

In fact, spelling reform is going on all the time, all by itself, which is why we spell the words *catalog* and *dialog* without the letters *-ue* at the end, as was the "preferred" spelling only a generation ago. Benjamin Franklin was an ardent supporter of spelling reform, but in his time there were hundreds of English words that could be properly spelled in two distinctly different ways. Today, on the other hand, there are only a very few (*ax* and *axe, gray* and *grey,* for example, although *theatre* and *centre* are gaining a foothold), but there are still hundreds of words that are spelled differently in England than they are in the United States (*colour, travelled, programme,* and *judgement,* for instance, are British spellings).

Once parents accept the idea that good spelling **is** important and should be encouraged in their homes, and once they understand that **anyone** can become a confident speller— even an adult who always had difficulty with spelling in school—then the Family Learning and reinforcing of spelling can commence. In fact, once those conditions are satisfied, the learning will have already gotten under way.

Mnemonics

One of the "tricks" to becoming a confident speller—notice I didn't say a *perfect* speller, because what we want to achieve is a feeling of confidence in our own ability to spell the words we use every day, not all the 600,000 words in the language—is the use of memory aids that are called *mnemonics* [pronounced nee-MAH-nicks]. Do you see that silent *m* at the beginning of this word? The reason it is there is that the word *mnemonic* is derived from the name of the Greek goddess of memory—Mnemosyne [pronounced nee-MAH-sin-ee]. We see her name most often in words that combine the idea of "memory" with the Greek prefix *a-,* meaning "without," for example, *amnesia* and *amnesty.* Notice that the initial and silent *m* from Mnemosyne's name is pronounced in these words.

Mnemonics are used every day to help adults as well as children link various items one to another so that they can be remembered together. For example, "Thirty days hath September, April, June, and November..." helps us remember the rather odd and irregular lengths of the months on the calendar. The letters in the word *homes* correspond to the initial letters in the names of the five Great Lakes (**H**uron, **O**ntario, **M**ichigan, **E**rie, and **S**uperior). My father taught me a mnemonic that helped me make it through some tough times in my geometry courses. He said, "Just remember the wise leader of the tribe of Triangles, Chief *Sohcahtoa*." From the spelling of the chief's name, I can always remember that the **s**ine = **o**pposite over **h**ypotenuse; **c**osine = **a**djacent over **h**ypotenuse; **t**angent = **o**pposite over **a**djacent.

Mnemonics are also useful in recalling historical facts. I will always remember what year it was that the Magna Carta was signed because, a long time ago, a teacher told me to picture in my mind a billboard announcing the historic event outside the castle where King John was meeting with the wealthy barons who had forced him to meet their demands. In large letters the advertisement proclaimed: "Come one and all! See the Magna Carta signed today at 12:15. Lunch will be served." The idea of having lunch at this event reinforces the time mentioned on the sign (12:15), and 1215 is also the year that the Magna Carta was signed.

Let me show you how mnemonics can help you focus in on words that are troublesome for you to spell, and specifically on the precise parts or letters of those words that give you whatever trouble you are having.

The title of the highest official in a school district offers only one spelling problem and, consequently, is misspelled only one way. Virtually every child and adult has absolute confidence in beginning the word "s-u-p-e-r-i-n-t-e-n-d...," but now is it "a-n-t" or is it "e-n-t"? Even if you think you know, are you absolutely certain? Certain enough to address that envelope without checking the dictionary first?

A reliable memory aid would link that one troublesome syllable to a word that you already know how to spell. I teach and use the following mnemonic: "The superintend*ENT* is concerned about every stud*ENT*." (I always make sure to write the specifically troublesome letters larger than the other letters as a way of focusing attention precisely on those few problem letters that cause all the spelling difficulty in a particular word.) This is a useful memory aid because it makes sense and because very few people are likely to misspell the final word as "studant."

I can also expand this mnemonic to include several other words that I find difficult to spell. For example: "The superintend*ENT* is concerned about every stud*ENT*. He must be insist*ENT* and persist*ENT* about the education of all the stud*ENT*s because his job is depend*ENT* upon how well they do."

I can include other troublesome words ("correspond*ENT*," for example) by extending the story, and the mnemonic offers up several related words on its own, such as insist*Ence*, persist*Ence*, depend*Ence*, depend*Ency*, and correspond*Ence*. All I must do is design the story to meet my own spelling needs and then repeat that story to myself in exactly the same way each time.

Mnemonics let you attack your own, individual spelling problems by designing your own memory aids. First, of course, you have to examine exactly why certain words give you the difficulty they do; generally there will be just one troublesome letter, or perhaps two, even in the longest troublesome words. Then it is just a matter of devising a mnemonic that will link that particular word, and that particular letter, to something that recalls the correct spelling to your mind.

When you create these personalized spelling mnemonics, however, be careful that whatever images you create to help you spell one word don't confuse you into misspelling other words. Let me show you what I mean.

"The princi*pal* is your *pal*" is a mnemonic device that has been used by teachers and parents for generations now, yet every year it creates more *mis*spelling than it cures. Students who try to spell the word that means "a leading part in a play," or the word that means "the main body of money (as distinct from the interest)" will, with perfect surety, write *principle*—which is incorrect. They know the mnemonic, and so they think that any meaning other than "the head of a school" must be spelled *principle*.

We would all be far better off by retiring that old mnemonic altogether and replacing it with the words m*A*in and ru*LE*. Any meaning of *principal* that carries the idea of m*A*in (a m*A*in part in a play; the m*A*in part of your money; the m*A*in teacher at a school) is spelled princip*A*l. Any meaning that conveys a ru*LE* (a ru*LE* of etiquette; a moral ru*LE* or standard; the ru*LE* of relativity) is spelled princip*LE*.

Here are a few more mnemonic spelling aids, which may help you become more confident in your spelling of some frequently troublesome words, and which can also serve as models for you in creating your own mnemonics to use in conquering your own spelling demons.

SPELLING WORD	MNEMONIC
all right	How would you spell *ALL WRONG?*
	(prevents the misspellings *alright* and *allright*)
capitol	The capit*Ol* building has a d*Ome*.

inoculate	i*N*ject
parallel	*ALL* railroad tracks are par*ALL*el.
anoint	You a*N*oint someone with a*N* oil.
pursuit	I am in p*U*rsuit of the thief who snatched my p*U*rse.
separate	Se*PAR*ate means to move things a*PAR*t.

Mnemonics are just another tool to add to your spelling resources. Knowing how to sound out words and knowing the rules that govern English spelling are important, of course, but mnemonics can fill in all those exceptions and those areas that seem so perverse they can trap us into thinking that good spellers are born, not made. That's bunk, but this is not: Good spellers are made in homes that value good spelling.

USEFUL FAMILY RESOURCES

Crazy English, by Richard Lederer (New York: Pocket Books, 1989) [420 LED].

The Memory Book, by Harry Lorayne and Jerry Lucas (New York: Stein and Day, 1974) [153.14 LOR].

6 Minutes a Day to Perfect Spelling, by Harry Shefter (New York: Washington Square Press, 1954).

303 Dumb Spelling Mistakes and What You Can Do about Them, by David Downing (Lincolnwood, Ill.: National Textbook Co., 1990) [421.52 DOW].

20 Days to Better Spelling, by Norman Lewis (New York: Harper & Row, 1966).

A Perfect Month to Practice Precise Pronunciation

Not only do children adopt their parents' attitudes about spelling, they also form their attitudes about pronunciation in the home, and these attitudes are likely to stay with them for the rest of their lives. If parents don't know very much or care very much about precise pronunciation, then their children will almost certainly adopt a slovenly, "anything goes" style of speech, which schools find difficult to correct, especially when precise pronunciation is modeled and valued only in English classes, if then.

I am not talking about differences among regional dialects here, but rather a nationwide carelessness that leads people to take the easy path, resulting in fuzziness of expression and sloppiness of thought.

There are many reasons for parents and teachers to encourage, especially in older children and teenagers, an attitude that prizes language clarity and precision, instead of the attitude of sloppiness and carelessness that is promoted and modeled in advertising and in rock videos. Think, for example, how difficult it is for older children to learn precise spelling when their pronunciation is imprecise. How many times are the words *February* and *arctic* misspelled simply because they are mispronounced as feb-*yoo*-ary and *ar*-tic?

Yes, it is more difficult to include that first *r* when you pronounce the word feb-*roo*-ary, and it requires some effort, too, to say *ark*-tik instead of *ar*-tik, but if spelling and language precision in general are important to you, and if you want them to be important to your children, then you must adopt an attitude of caring about precise pronunciation, too.

Choosing Precise Pronunciations

Now, I can almost hear the angry scratching of pens and pounding of keyboards that a statement like this will generate among certain readers. Any mention of "should" or "preferred" or "standard" in reference to the spelling, pronunciation, or mechanics of English strikes some people as an invasion of their personal right to use English any way they choose.

And that is just the point: Our use of language—and our children's use of language as well—should be a matter of choice. If you choose not to pronounce the first *r* in February, fine, but you will be making your choice based on knowledge, not on ignorance or misinformation.

NANCY reprinted by permission of United Feature Syndicate, Inc.

But there is much more here than just accurate spelling. The whole idea of Family Learning, and of lifelong learning in general, is that the world around us is brimming with opportunities for learning and for knowing, and that knowing is better than not knowing. The desire for self-improvement is, I think, one of the finest traits a human being can possess, and it may be the single, most valuable habit we can instill or encourage in our children. It is, or should be, the habit our schools are trying to instill as well, for it is this desire for self-improvement that makes all the lessons of school worth knowing.

All this in the pronunciation of *February*, you ask? Oh yes, and more.

Children who see and hear their parents wrestle with the precise pronunciation of a word like *February*, are very privileged children because they see the modeling of self-improvement in action. They see adults creating standards for themselves rather than taking the easy path and excusing their actions by saying "everybody else does it."

Even though the entire month of February offers us an excellent opportunity to listen for and encourage the precise pronunciation feb-*roo*-ary in our children's speech and in our own, most parents are well aware that correcting their teenager's speech in midsentence is, in most cases, fruitless if not counterproductive. But we all have a third party available to us, a handy foil that we can interrupt and correct without regard to any feelings or consequences—the television.

Using the Television

When you and your children are watching television together, and when you hear an announcer, or a newscaster, or a meteorologist say feb-*yoo*-ary (as you often will during this month), get in the habit of interjecting aloud the precise pronunciation. ("No it isn't; it's feb-*ROO*-ary!") Children who hear this form of correction receive all the benefits without the hurt that comes from always being on the receiving end. And let them have a crack at it, too, so that they start supplying the correct syllable each time they hear a televised mispronunciation of *February*. No, you won't be teaching them that it's polite or permissible to criticize and correct the speech of their elders—this is television, after all. This is learning in the privacy of your own home. And most of all, this is supposed to be fun.

Now, although the month of February is a great time to concentrate on the pronunciation of the word *February*, it may also be an ideal time to launch a family attack on other pronunciation problems, especially those that lead directly to spelling errors in your children's written work. I mentioned the word *arctic* earlier, and during the month of February you are likely to hear this word used in weather reports about "an arctic blast from the north." Frequently, however, you will hear about "an *ar*-tic blast," or about "*ar*-tic air" instead of the precise pronunciation *ARK*-tic, and here again, you and your children can shout out the proper form, thereby fixing it in their own vocabulary, without hurting the reporter's feelings one bit. If you are watching a football game together, and you hear a coach talk about the performance of his ath-*uh*-letes or about ath-*uh*-let-ics in general, you can speak out right away and say, "It's pronounced *ATH*-lete!" (or, ath-*LET*-ics!), perhaps spelling the word aloud and asking the coach to locate that extra syllable he is pronouncing.

Parents should focus their corrections on the televised mispronunciations that are also common in their children's speech, and in their own speech as well. Don't waste your effort on problems that aren't problems. But the question will arise about which pronunciations *ought* to be considered problems; that is, which words—like *February, arctic, and athlete*—are frequently mispronounced by adults and children alike and should be the focus of your family's concern for precise pronunciation.

Words Frequently Mispronounced

I have found that the words that are most troublesome for most people can be grouped into three distinct categories, and you may want to attack each group separately. I happen to have difficulty with a few words in all three groups, but the groupings are helpful to me just the same because when I catch myself mispronouncing one word, that word reminds me of other words in that category, and so I get the benefit of reinforcing several troublesome words at a time.

The difficulty in pronouncing words like *February* and *arctic* is in articulating **all** the sounds that are in each word (feb-**ru**-ary, **arc**-tic). This is easily the most common type of pronunciation problem, and it accounts for a large part of the spelling errors that are made by children and adults alike. Here are some other common words that fall into this category (I have highlighted the letters that are most frequently left out of their pronunciations): gover**n**ment, reco**g**nize, qua**n**tity, choco**l**ate, proba**b**ly, resta**u**rant, valua**b**le, accidenta**l**ly, incidenta**l**ly, persona**l**ly, enviro**n**ment, minia**t**ure, cabi**n**et, sand**w**ich.

There are also a few other words in this category that have often-unpronounced letters, but these missing sounds are almost undetectable in normal speech even when they are pronounced. You just have to know that the letters are there, and hear them in your mind as you speak: di**a**mond, di**a**per, groc**e**ry, jewe**l**ry, temper**a**ture.

Now, the second category includes words that are commonly pronounced with sounds that are different from those represented by the letters in the word. When children hear the word *basketball* carelessly pronounced bas-**kuh**-ball so often by coaches and television commentators, it's little wonder that they adopt that pronunciation themselves. In the following words, I have highlighted the areas that we need to focus our attention upon in order to ensure that we are pronouncing each word as it is spelled: pro**nun**ciation, congratu**l**ations, kinder**g**arten, ni**n**ety, real**t**or, m**e**mento, pompo**n** (a "pom-pom" is a military weapon, and, so far at least, has not become standard issue for cheerleaders).

The last category includes words that are sometimes pronounced with syllables that aren't in the spelling of the word at all. We commonly study "silent" letters in school, but the words in this group are often pronounced with "invisible" letters! athlete/athletics (not ath-**uh**-lete/ath-**uh**-let-ics); mischievous (there are only three syllables, and the last one is spelled **vous**, not **vious** or **veous**, so the pronunciation must be MIS-chi-vus); disastrous/monstrous (not disasterous/monsterous); hindrance/remembrance (not hinderance/rememberance); laundry (not laundery); recur (not reoccur).

Well, that should be enough to hold you for a while. As you focus your attention, and perhaps your children's attention, on these words, concentrate on only one or two words at a time (especially if you're trying to instill these pronunciations in your children), and then later go on to another one or two. Once the proper pronunciations are cemented in your children's listening vocabulary and in their speaking vocabulary, they will remain intact for many years, and they will aid your children's spelling confidence and their speaking confidence, too.

"Fillers"

There is a related language problem that is very common among children, especially teenagers, which can be dealt with at home in just this same way. The problem I refer to is the frequent use of "fillers" in children's speech. Now, fillers are those meaningless words and phrases that we mindlessly toss into our spoken communications but almost never include in our writing. The most common (and annoying) fillers in vogue today, I think, are *like* and *ya know*.

The reason I say that the use of these fillers in our speech is related to the problem of mispronouncing words like *February* is that both problems are caused by the speaker's being unaware of what he or she is saying. Many teenagers, for example, simply do not hear themselves inserting the word *like* into every phrase and sentence they speak, and so one way to eliminate this filler problem is to help children become aware of what they are actually saying.

This is one area that is better suited to Family Learning than to classroom learning because the family can provide the nonthreatening, uncritical arena wherein speech habits can be examined without embarrassment.

If—**and only if**—you and your child agree that these fillers should be pointed out when they occur, and if you agree to make these observations only in your home as a private "game" between the two of you, then you can interrupt with the question "What was it like?" whenever you hear *like* used as a filler.

"Then Mrs. Henry called on Mike, and he was like sound asleep—"

"What was he like?"

"Huh?"

"Well, you said that Mike was '*like*' something, and I just asked what it was he was '*like*.'"

"I mean, he **was** sound asleep at his desk."

Here, again, the television set provides both parents and children with an ideal vehicle for listening to, and correcting, slovenly habits of speech. When a character in a situation comedy uses *like* as a filler, either the parent or the child can jump in with a hearty "What was it like?" and within a matter of just a few days, that particular filler will drop completely out of your children's speaking vocabulary.

You may want to work on *ya know* by following the same steps. In order to get your children to realize that they are including this filler in their speech, you may want to interject "No I don't; tell me about it" immediately upon each usage. Then, when either of you hears *ya know* used by someone on television (interviews with college or professional athletes should provide numerous examples of the repetitive use of this particular filler), it will seem like a race to see which of you can be first to shout out "No I don't; tell me about it!" and in so doing, cleanse the hated phrase from your own speech habits.

"He Goes/I Go"

This technique also works well in eliminating other speech habits besides mispronunciations and fillers. Take, for example, the case of "he goes and I go." Here is a usage that became popular in the "Valley-talk" of Southern California some years ago and has now become fixed in the speech habits of many children, college students, and even some teachers. Instead of using the verb *say*—and its related forms *says, said,* and *saying*—some speakers use the verb *go*—and its related forms *goes* and *going*.

Whenever Janet came up to me, ya know? and she *goes*, 'Like, whoa! What happened to you?' So I *go*, 'Whaddaya mean?' and she *goes...*"

Whenever I hear speech like this, I'm the one who feels like going, and just as quickly as I can.

Now, the reason I threw "ya know" and "like" into the example I just gave is that I think the "he goes/I go" problem and the fillers problem are related: Those people who use these constructions in their speech simply do not know or hear what they are saying, and so they cannot know how irritating their speech is to others. The assumption that is made by those who hear anyone use *go* to mean *say* is that the speaker is careless or scatterbrained at best, uneducated or illiterate at worst. You can argue all you want that this impression may be false and that people shouldn't make judgments about others on the basis of their speech, but the impression and assumption will exist just the same, unless, of course, you are "fortunate" enough to be heard only by those who speak Valley-talk themselves.

A Family Learning solution to this language problem is to use television, to use the relationship you have with your children, and to use the loving atmosphere that is within your home as aids in allowing your children to hear what other people are hearing them say. When the "he goes/I go" usage crops up in your children's speech, interrupt with the question "Where did he go?" or "Where did you go?" and continue to use those same interruptions with each subsequent usage until your children begin to anticipate them and start supplying them on their own.

"Well, if someone asked me to do that, I'd go—

"Where would you go?"

"I mean, I'd **say**, 'No way!' and if he goes...I know, 'Where did he go?'...Okay, if he **says**..."

"Very good; I'm proud of you."

Just as I cautioned you about not trying to correct all your children's mispronunciations at once, let me suggest here that you focus just on the "he goes/I go" problem and let the fillers slide for a while. Or focus just on the fillers and attack "he goes/I go" later on. Once you get the procedure down, and you start to watch television together with your language education in mind, you and your children can adapt your conversations and your television viewing to meet any language need you might choose. Just keep in mind that language improvement has no place in "heart-to-heart" talks or other private discussions. And remember that not every language problem has to be conquered during February.

Learning About the World of Numbers:
Mathematics

Introduction

Do you enjoy working with numbers? Do you have fun with numbers and number problems, and are you comfortable with tossing numbers around and then putting them together again in a new way? If so, you can probably skip this whole section because that's all I want parents and children to realize from mathematics: enjoyment. If parents already have a playful attitude about numbers and if they are comfortable with using numbers and talking about numbers at home, then their children will probably never be afflicted with the disease called "math anxiety," which is sweeping the country today.

Maybe your children will be blessed by having grade-school teachers who truly enjoy mathematics and have a playful spirit about numbers and are able to pass that enjoyment and spirit on to the students they teach. I only wish that this kind of attitude about mathematics and numbers were a requirement for all teachers and a goal for all teacher-training institutions, but I am realistic enough to know that such a hope is folly, pure folly. Still, there are teachers out there who have this quality in abundance, and they should be both praised and prized. But for the most part, your children's interest and excitement about mathematics will come from the attitudes and activities you provide them in your home.

What Family Learning offers to parents who aren't completely comfortable with numbers is a way to look at your own world, and your child's world, with an eye toward making numbers a more common and natural part of everyday living. This section gives you a start and shows you how to begin looking for ways to bring numbers into your home and family life, where you can examine them, play with them, and get some enjoyment from them without always having to get the "right" answer or being embarrassed by not even understanding the question.

For some additional suggestions about ways to create a "numbers atmosphere" in your home and to encourage a "math habit" in your children, I suggest you read the chapter titled "Math for the Real World" in Thomas Armstrong's book *Awakening Your Child's Natural Genius* (Los Angeles: Jeremy P. Tarcher, Inc., 1992) [649.68 ARM], and that you obtain a copy of *Family Math*, by Jean Kerr Stenmark, Virginia Thompson, and Ruth Cossey either through your local library [J 510 STE or J 793.74 STE] or through the address that appears on page 102.

Making Numbers Part of Your Home

The Family Learning of mathematics has little if anything to do with parents *teaching* math to their children. There—that ought to relieve a lot of your concern and reluctance right off the bat. Family Learning is **not** just schooling at home, and its success or failure is **not** dependent upon your own level of proficiency in mathematics or any other subject.

The aim of Family Learning is to create a "learning atmosphere" in your home and a "learning attitude" among your children, and so the Family Learning of mathematics must be focused primarily upon getting numbers into your home and into your children's everyday activities. This is how children can become comfortable with numbers, for they can work with numbers and talk about numbers without being pressured by their peers or graded by their teachers. Arithmetic and mathematics must become common features in their daily lives, and not through having them complete page after page of workbook problems at home, but through showing them the myriad ways that numbers can make life in the real world easier and more enjoyable as well.

Some parents think that only certain children—those who enjoy working with numbers—can ever become successful in their math classes at school. But maybe they are looking at this situation the wrong way around. Surely children will be much more likely to enjoy working with numbers when they achieve some success with numbers in school. Without these initial triumphs, however small, enjoyment wanes and anything to do with numbers becomes a struggle.

This is one of the reasons that it is so important for children to develop a high degree of competence in the simplest mathematics. Learning the number tables and combinations backward and forward not only ensures early success with number problems in school, it also provides a rock-solid foundation for all subsequent lessons in math and all applications of those lessons as well. But just how do parents go about the task of reinforcing their children's knowledge of simple number combinations and operations without resorting to workbook-type exercises and all the drudgery they bring to mind? Let me suggest one technique that you may find so useful and so enjoyable that it will become a feature of your home and family life for many years to come.

"Consider the Number..."

Many years ago, I was privileged to have a teacher who would begin each school day with a little game that would provide a mental exercise for his students, just as a gym teacher, for example, might start off a class with stretching and gentle physical exercises. This teacher would open the class by saying, "Consider the number 3 . . ." (or whatever number happened to be featured that day). "Now, multiply by 4, subtract 1, add 7, and divide by 2. Who knows the answer?" Some hands would shoot into the air; others would creep, with the reluctance of uncertainty, in that general direction; while a few other hands would be covering the faces of students who were still considering the number 3.

Another string would follow, and perhaps another—a little longer string now or one that had more difficult combinations in it—but the entire game took only a minute or two, and it always accomplished its two main objectives: (1) it focused our attention on the world of numbers, and (2) it was fun!

Some parents to whom I have suggested this game report that it has been such a success in their homes that it has become an accepted and expected ritual on school mornings. Just before their children leave for the bus, or while they are driving their children to school, their loving send-off always begins with the words, "Consider the number. . . ." Parents choose the numbers, the combinations, and the operations to focus upon in their strings by knowing which ones need the most work and practice and emphasis for their particular children. Here is an advantage that the home application of this game enjoys that is simply unavailable to a classroom teacher.

As you create numbers for your children to consider, remember that the Family Learning version of this game has a third objective: to encourage your children by having them experience success. Over the past several years, education research has demonstrated conclusively that children need massive amounts of success before being moved on to tasks at which they may, initially, fail. Our natural inclination is to jump right up to longer and more challenging strings, complete with difficult number combinations that will really put them to the test. But I hope you will resist this urge until your children come up with the correct answers several times in succession, until they are straining at the bit and eager for a new challenge. Then throw in a new operation or a number combination they have been working on at school or at home, and hammer at it in as many ways as you can (9 X 6 = 54 and 54 ÷ 9 = 6 and 54 ÷ 6 = 9) and have them be successful with it, over and over again.

Remember, too, that with "Consider the number . . . ," just as with practically every other Family Learning activity, there is a whole other world of enjoyment and enrichment awaiting those who will merely reverse the roles. Let your child have you "Consider the number . . . ," and you try to come up with the correct answer. Then, perhaps, take turns and make a contest out of it.

Oh, and just in case you think that "Consider the number . . ." is suited only to children who are in the primary or elementary grades, I should mention here that the teacher in whose class I played this game long ago was my high school physics teacher, who would awaken our class of seniors with his early morning strings that included squares and cubes and fractions and roots.

Games like this allow you to bring numbers into your home and to make them a common and natural part of your family life. The more common that numbers become in your home, the more natural your children will think them to be.

Multiplication Table

The home is an especially good place to reinforce those basic concepts (in every subject) that children are expected to commit to memory. For example, some children have no other opportunity to practice or use a multiplication table except during the portion of the school day devoted to arithmetic. (Other children are even more unfortunate, being prisoners of "modern" teaching fads that don't permit them to see or use a multiplication table at all, but that's another story.) These children are much more likely than their classmates to see multiplication and numbers in general as being "school things" and as having no usefulness or place outside the classroom.

 Parents need to be imaginative in finding ways to make numbers and arithmetic become common parts of their children's out-of-school experiences. For example, parents can increase the frequency of their children's contact with the multiplication table by, quite literally, making the multiplication table part of their home. The multiplication table can become a child's breakfast table or dinner table place mat. Here's how to do it.

First, recognize that your children will get much more use out of this place mat, and they will take much more pride in their place mat, if they are directly involved in constructing it. You can choose the materials, decide on the dimensions for the grid, and oversee the whole project, but your children should be responsible for actually writing the numbers in their proper spaces, and they can personalize their place mats in other ways as well.

Cut a sheet of construction paper to the dimensions you want your place mat to be (18 x 13 inches is a convenient size). Now, the number portion of the mat will occupy a square at the far left, leaving a narrow space at the right for a child's name, age, school photo, the date—the more personalized the better. Cut a sheet of white paper into a 13 x 13-inch square that will be the multiplication table itself. Using a ruler, draw a grid on this square with lines across and down, spaced one inch apart (there will be twelve lines across and twelve down). Have your child write the numbers 1 through 12 across the top row and down the far left-hand column, but be sure to leave the box at the upper left blank. Your child can then fill in the remaining squares so that the intersection of each row and column shows the product of the numbers written at the top and left.

Why use 1 through 12 instead of 1 through 10? Because 12's pop up so frequently (inches in a foot, months in a year, etc.) that memorizing these combination can have frequent, practical applications. If you use the standard version of the multiplication table (showing the products of 1 through 10) instead, you should cut the sheet into an 11 x 11-inch square.

Now paste or glue the number table onto the larger place mat paper, and also add the personal touches that will identify this as your child's own place mat. (A sample place mat, reduced in size, appears on page 98) This mat can now be plastic coated by a process called laminating, which is available at local copy centers and photo shops for just a couple of dollars (look under "laminations" in the classified section of your phone book).

"Concentration"

Another way to give your children an opportunity to work with number combinations without having the activity seem "like school" is to adapt the television game "Concentration" to whatever your learning and teaching goals happen to be.

Take thirty blank file cards (the standard 3 x 5-inch size works well), and write the individual combinations you want to focus upon on one side of fifteen cards—for example, 9 X 4 = _____ or 7 – 2 = _____. Now write the answers to each of those fifteen combinations on one side of fifteen other cards, so that all thirty cards will have one blank side. Shuffle the cards and arrange them in a rectangle on a table or floor, blank side up. You and your child now take turns turning over two cards (one at a time), trying to match the arithmetic problem on one card with its correct solution on another. If the two cards you choose do not match, you turn them over to their blank side again, but if they do match, you pick up the cards and you get another turn.

Meg's
Multiplication Table Mat

Created by: *Meg Arbiter*

Date: May 21, 1997

Age: 10 years, 3 months

Fractions and decimals:

½ = .500	1/8 = .125
¼ = .250	1/5 = .200
¾ = .750	1/3 = .333

	1	2	3	4	5	6	7	8	9	10	11	12
1	1	2	3	4	5	6	7	8	9	10	11	12
2	2	4	6	8	10	12	14	16	18	20	22	24
3	3	6	9	12	15	18	21	24	27	30	33	36
4	4	8	12	16	20	24	28	32	36	40	44	48
5	5	10	15	20	25	30	35	40	45	50	55	60
6	6	12	18	24	30	36	42	48	54	60	66	72
7	7	14	21	28	35	42	49	56	63	70	77	84
8	8	16	24	32	40	48	56	64	72	80	88	96
9	9	18	27	36	45	54	63	72	81	90	99	108
10	10	20	30	40	50	60	70	80	90	100	110	120
11	11	22	33	44	55	66	77	88	99	110	121	132
12	12	24	36	48	60	72	84	96	108	120	132	144

(Younger children and those who are struggling with number combinations might start out with a smaller set of cards, let's say sixteen, so that they can work on just a few combinations at a time and so that they can have success right away. Later, you can increase the number of cards in each set, but slowly, as their knowledge and ability increase. Thirty cards, however, seems to be a good upper limit.)

This activity allows you to focus on the particular combinations and operations that are most troublesome for your child by including only those particular cards in the set with which you are playing. You can then remove cards that no longer pose any difficulty and replace them with combinations that need more work. "Concentration" also permits you to reinforce all kinds of math and science facts—such as fractions and their decimal equivalents (the $\frac{2}{5}$ card would match one showing **40%**), English and metric conversions (the **1 kilogram** card would match the one showing **2.2 pounds**), or common amounts and measures that are wholly within the English system (the **1 mile** card would match the one showing **5,280 feet**). It is a family game that you can design and redesign to meet the specific learning needs of your own family.

Once you begin to look for them, you'll discover all sorts of home activities that you can create or modify to help your children actually **use** mathematics and to discover that mathematics can be a tool and a convenience instead of an obstacle to be avoided whenever possible. And these activities do not all focus on memorization or elementary arithmetic. Take, for example, the discoveries that your adolescent children can make about a mathematical concept that has concerned and fascinated human beings for several thousand years.

Discovering Pi

The ancient Babylonians, Egyptians, and Chinese all knew that there was some relationship between the distance around a circle and the distance across its center, and they knew that this relationship existed because they discovered it through a process very similar to the one you can design for your children.

All you need is a cloth or plastic tape measure (sometimes called a dressmaker's tape), some paper, a pencil, and a pocket calculator. Now look for a variety of circular objects around your house—dinner plates, drinking glasses, vegetable cans, lamp shades, tables, rugs—and have your children measure and record the distance around each circle (circumference) and the distance across its center (diameter).

You'll need to use decimal measures for any fractional parts of an inch, but this is really not a problem if you remember that each $\frac{1}{16}$ inch is .0625. So, $4\frac{3}{16}$ inches would be recorded as 4.1875 inches. (Yes, things would be much simpler with the metric system, but we'll save that discussion for another day.)

Now, use the calculator to divide each circle's circumference by its diameter, and record your findings. None of the results will be identical, but each will be a little larger than 3. Now your children can use this finding to predict the circumference of some other circular object. Have them measure the diameter, multiply by the average of their previous calculations, and then confirm their prediction by actually measuring the distance around the object's outer edge.

Ancient contractors and engineers noticed, too, that there was a constant relationship between the circumference and the diameter of every circle they built, and they kept trying to make increasingly accurate and precise measurements of these circles in order to determine exactly what this ratio was and how to express it in numbers. The Babylonians thought it was 3.1250; the Egyptians thought it was 3.1605; the great Archimedes, in 240 B.C., proved that the number was between 3.1408 and 3.1428; a hundred years later, Ptolemy said it was 3.14166.

The ratio they were seeking is one that we know as *pi* [pronounced PIE], the sixteenth letter of the Greek alphabet and the first letter in the Greek word *perimetron*, which means "the measurement around." (It is somewhat strange, I think, that we use this Greek root in discussing the perimeter of a triangle, a square, or any other polygon, but we use the Latin *circumferre*, meaning "to carry around," when referring to the circumference of a circle.) It was not until 1761 that a German physicist named Johann Lambert proved that pi could not be expressed exactly by **any** number because its digits were never ending.

Modern computers have carried pi out to billions of decimal places, but you and your children can remember the first eight numbers in the string by memorizing the phrase "May I have a large container of coffee?" The number of letters in each word corresponds to 3.1415926, which is an extremely close approximation of pi's true value. It is so close, in fact, that if the diameter of the earth were exactly 8,000 miles, and you used "May I have a large container of coffee?" for the value of pi in determining the circumference of the earth at the equator (pi X diameter), your answer would be within *two feet* of the distance you would have gotten had you used a value of pi that had a million decimal places!

In any event, the whole process of measuring dinner plates and vegetable cans and bicycle wheels gives you and your children a better understanding of what pi really is, and of how pi can be used and figured, than some of the lawmakers in the Indiana state legislature had in 1897. They proposed a bill that would have established the value of pi, throughout the state of Indiana, to be exactly 3! The bill was defeated, and so we can only wonder whether, if it had become law, all law-abiding circles in the state would have changed themselves into hexagons.

The Problem With Story Problems

This type of "discovery learning," and the other family activities that you can devise to encourage your children's use of numbers, and to have them investigate the myriad other mathematical relationships that lie hidden around the house, is quite different from just recreating typical workbook or textbook math problems for them to do at home.

I recently reread an article that Stephen S. Willoughby wrote sixteen years ago titled "Teaching Mathematics: What Is Basic?" and I noted with some dismay that the observations he made about the teaching of mathematics, and about math textbooks in particular, are still true and applicable today.

Among his criticisms was an attack upon the way that most school texts include "story problems" that have little or nothing to do with the mathematics that is used in the real world. For example: "An anthropologist uncovered seventeen bones on Monday and three times that may bones on Tuesday. How many bones did she uncover on Tuesday?" Well, don't you think that the anthropologist would simply count the bones she uncovered on Tuesday? And don't you think that children who are required to read and execute problems like this one will begin to think of mathematics as being a subject designed to make people work harder than they would otherwise have to work?

Here's another one: "Mary took $5 to the circus. She spent $3.85. How much money did she have left?" Now, I know that the whole idea of this problem is to get children to consider the meaning of subtraction, and to give them a supposedly "real" situation in which subtraction can be profitably employed. But again, if you were Mary, how would you determine how much money you had left? Of course, you'd take the money out of your pocket and count it.

Willoughby's point here is that these textbook problems, which look so harmless on the surface, condition children into seeing mathematics only as a useless and joyless enterprise. Parents, therefore, instead of trying to create similar problems for their children to figure out at home, should concentrate on looking for examples and instances in the real world, where mathematics is actually employed as a problem-solving device.

Most word problems or story problems in textbooks involve only one step, but most real-life math problems involve several steps, and they require us to decide which pieces of information are necessary and which are useless in solving the problem at hand.

Recently, as I was looking for potato chips in the grocery store, I saw that there was a sale on the "jumbo" size of my favorite brand, and though I didn't want to buy that large a bag, I thought that I might do so if the sale price generated a significant saving. That 14-ounce size was on sale for $2.99, while the 6-ounce bag cost $1.19. Now here is a multi-step problem that a grade school child can figure out without pencil or paper or calculator, and one that will demonstrate how mathematics can solve problems in the real world. (A quick glance at the price of the smaller bag shows that its contents cost almost exactly 20 cents per ounce. At that rate, the regular, non-sale price of the larger bag whould have been only $2.80. Some sale!)

In creating math aids for your children, keep in mind Willoughby's central theme: "The main purpose of teaching mathematics is to educate people to use mathematical thought to solve real world problems. . . . so that they will solve problems by thinking even when they are not required to do so in school."

USEFUL FAMILY RESOURCES

Asimov on Numbers, by Isaac Asimov (Garden City, N.Y.: Doubleday & Co., Inc., 1977) [512.7 ASI].

Family Math, by Jean Kerr Stenmark, Virginia Thompson, and Ruth Cossey (Berkeley, Cal.: University of California, 1986) [J 510 STE or J 793.74 STE]. For information about this book and about the "Family Math" programs for schools and communities, write to: Family Math, Lawrence Hall of Science, University of California, Berkeley, CA 94720.

More Joy of Mathematics: Exploring Mathematics All Around You, by Theoni Pappas (San Carlos, Cal.: Wide World Publishing, 1991) [510 PAP].

A New Answer Book, by Mary Elting and Rose Wyler (New York: Grosset & Dunlap, 1977) [J 793.73 ELT].

"Teaching Mathematics: What Is Basic?" by Stephen S. Willoughby (Washington, D.C.: Council for Basic Education, 1981).

Using Numbers Outside the Home

In order for children to understand and accept the idea that numbers and arithmetic are not just used in school, parents must seize every opportunity, both inside and outside the home, to encourage their children's use of their mathematical skills. Unfortunately, mathematics is a particularly difficult subject to apply to a child's out-of-school life, and the reason for this is that most parents don't have to apply much mathematics in their own lives, either. The cash register totals your grocery bill; the bank's computer tells you your checking account balance; all the sports statistics you could ever want are already calculated and appear every day in the newspaper.

Calculating Restaurant Tips

Still, there is one occasion on which adults frequently have to use simple mathematics, and this occasion provides all of us a good chance to allow our children the opportunity to use their mathematical knowledge in the real world. That occasion is the calculating of the tip after a meal in a restaurant.

Many people leave 10% of their bill as a tip because that is the custom in their area, but many also leave 10% because it is an easy percentage to figure: You just move the decimal point in the total bill one place to the left. A 15% tip, however, is almost as easy to calculate if you just add one extra step.

Let's say that the bill comes to $24.80, and you want to know what 15% of that amount would be. First, move the decimal point one place to the left to find out what 10% of $24.80 is: $2.48. Now, because 15% is the same as 10% plus 5%, and because you already know what 10% of the bill is, all you need to do is determine how much 5% would be.

Well, 5% is just half of 10%, and half of $2.48 would be $1.24. So, 15% of your $24.80 bill is just 10% ($2.48) plus 5% ($1.24): $3.72.

Once children learn this simple system for determining 15% of any amount, they should be the ones invested with the responsibility for calculating restaurant tips. You can also throw into their calculations your desire for them to round the amount to the nearest dime, or quarter, or dollar. Or have them move the decimal two places to see what 1% of the bill would be, and then increase or decrease the tip in 1% increments.

Estimating Sales Tax

When they understand how easy it is to figure out what 1% of an amount is, and then how simple multiplication allows them to quickly and easily ascertain what *any* percent would be, they can use this knowledge and ability to estimate the sales tax that will be applied to purchases in other stores besides restaurants. Make sure that your children know the applicable sales tax rate in your state, and have them figure the tax on the next single item you purchase in the store together. (Later on, you can have them add the prices of two or more items, and figure the tax on the total.) The cash register receipt will list the exact amount of tax paid, and so you will know right away whether your computation was accurate.

There are dozens of other simple and useful calculations that you and your children can perform on store receipts or other amounts that you and they encounter in the real world, and each offers you another way to bring numbers into your children's out-of-school life and to reinforce their knowledge and skills in mathematics as well.

Dividing Evenly

For example, let's say that you want to have each person in your party pay an equal share of the total restaurant bill. If there are only two of you, the answer is easy because all you need do is look at the last digit to see whether it is odd or even (all even numbers can be divided into two equal halves). But you may not know that it is almost as easy to tell whether a number can be evenly divided by three. Just add up the individual digits, and if that sum is divisible by three, so is the original number. For example, the number 72,156 can be evenly divided by three because the sum of the digits (7 + 2 + 1 + 5 + 6 = 21) is evenly divisible by three (21 = 7 ÷ 3). (Check it out: 72,156 ÷ 3 = 24,052.)

This same system also works for determining whether a number can be evenly divided by nine. Add up the digits, and if the total can be divided by nine, the original number can be, too. (For example, the sum of the digits in 513,846 is 5 + 1 + 3 + 8 + 4 + 6 = 27, which is evenly divisible by nine, and 513,846÷9 = 57,094.)

You can find many other math "tricks" and math activities like these in the 793.74 section of your local library, especially in books like *Number Games To Improve Your Child's Arithmetic,* by Abraham B. Hurwitz, Arthur Goddard, and David T. Epstein.

Using Numbers in the Car

Once you start looking for math opportunities outside the home, you'll find possibilities and suggestions no matter where you go and no matter how you get there. A short trip in the car—to the library, for example, or to the grocery store—can provide an opportunity to have your children become more aware of distances that are measured in miles and tenths of miles. How far is it to that next traffic light? Let's see who can come closer to guessing the distance from the Main Street Bridge to the parking lot at the mall.

Highway trips, especially long car trips for holidays or vacations, are particularly good for helping children understand the relationships among distance, time, and speed because these trips allow children to become actively involved in calculating such measures. If you happen to be traveling on a straight, flat, uncrowded stretch of interstate highway, you can have your children do a hands-on experiment that will help them experience numbers and measurements and mathematics for themselves. Just hold the speed of your car at a constant sixty miles per hour while your child times the interval between two of the green mile markers that are placed along the side of most interstate highways. How long should it take to travel exactly one mile at sixty miles per hour? Well, because there are just as many seconds in each minute as there are minutes in each hour—sixty—traveling at a speed of sixty miles per hour means that you are covering each mile in exactly one minute, hence you are going "a mile a minute."

This is one way that parents can take arithmetic problems out of the classroom and out of the textbook, and put them into the real world so that children can get a feeling for what various numbers and measures really mean. When the phrase "sixty miles per hour" begins to live in your children as "one mile every minute," and when they see "miles per hour" as saying to them "miles divided by hours," then they will be able to estimate and calculate and understand why any measure of speed (feet per second, kilometers per hour, etc.) is just a measure of distance divided by time.

Now, let's say that they don't know what speed you are going, but that you maintain that constant speed while they time the interval between two mile markers. (A stopwatch would be excellent for this activity, but any watch that measures seconds will do.) If that measured mile is covered in less than a minute, the car must be going faster than sixty miles per hour; if it takes longer than a minute, it is going slower than sixty miles per hour. But they can make an even better estimate than this; in fact, they can use their math skill to tell exactly how fast the car is traveling.

Let's say that their watch shows 65 seconds as the time between the two markers. They know they've gone one mile, but how many hours is 65 seconds? Well, there are 3,600 seconds in an hour (60 seconds x 60 minutes), and so 65 seconds is exactly $\frac{65}{3,600}$ hours. Our equation (miles ÷ hours = mph), therefore, is 1 mile divided by $\frac{65}{3,600}$ hours = _____ mph.

The procedure for dividing by a fraction is simply to invert that fraction and multiply, so 1 divided by $\frac{65}{3,600}$ = 1 x $\frac{3,600}{65}$ = 3,600 ÷ 65. Just divide 3,600 by 65 on your calculator and voila!—the result is 55.3846 miles per hour. (You don't have to use a calculator, of course; the division can be worked out with pencil and paper, but it takes a while and really doesn't teach children anything new. So, if children first understand what they are doing— that is, what the numbers mean and why they are performing various operations on them— then a calculator can actually improve their math skills by allowing them to work more problems and to use bigger numbers without tedium or frustration. Keeping an inexpensive calculator in the glove compartment, therefore, is a good idea because it allows you to take advantage of whatever Family Learning opportunities may pop up away from home.)

So, they determine the number of seconds it took to travel between two markers, then simply divide 3,600 by that number, and the result is your average speed in miles per hour over that distance. This, by the way, is precisely the method used by the police officer in the patrol plane that may be flying directly overhead as you are performing this activity.

Family Learning Solves a Math Problem

Let me show you how this experience with speeds and distances and watches and cars—and especially the "feeling" that your child can get for the meaning of "a mile a minute" and "goin' like sixty"—can be put to use in helping them solve math problems in school.

Here is a problem that I remember from my high school days, one that appeared on a college-entrance exam I was taking at the time, and one that I was able to solve only because my father had taught me and shown me the meaning of "a mile a minute."

You take your car to a racetrack that measures exactly one mile in circumference. Your goal is to make two complete laps of that track and average exactly sixty miles per hour for the two-mile test. During the first lap, you experience some trouble, and you average only thirty miles per hour for that first mile. Question: What speed must you average over the second lap in order to have your two-lap (that is, two-mile) average come out to exactly sixty miles per hour?

This is not a trick question, nor is it a simple problem whose answer is easily apparent. But it's a good problem to ponder—worth the effort, I think—and so you might want to take a few minutes and do just that. . . .

What was your answer? 90 miles per hour? 120 miles per hour? 180 miles per hour? All three of those were given as possible solutions on the multiple-choice test I remember. But none of them is correct.

The first question to ask yourself is, how long would it take you to accomplish what you originally set out to do, that is, how long would it take to go two miles at an average of sixty miles per hour? Well, sixty miles per hour is "a mile a minute," so two miles at that speed would take exactly two minutes. You could stop and start again, slow down, speed up, do anything you wanted; if you made the trip in two minutes, you would have averaged sixty miles per hour.

Now, how long did it take you to go the first mile at thirty miles per hour? Well, thirty miles in an hour is one mile every two minutes, so that first mile took you exactly two minutes.

Do you see what has happened? You have already used up your two minutes, and so no matter how fast you travel during that second mile, it is impossible for you to average sixty miles per hour for the entire two miles.

USEFUL FAMILY RESOURCES

Games for Math: Playful Ways to Help Your Child Learn Math, by Peggy Kaye (New York: Pantheon Books, 1987) [510.7 KAY].

Mathematical Puzzles, by Martin Gardner (New York: Thomas Y. Crowell C., 1961) [793.74 GAR].

Number Games to Improve Your Child's Arithmetic, by Abraham B. Hurwitz, Arthur Goddard, and David T. Epstein (New York: Funk & Wagnalls, 1975) [793.74 HUR].

Estimating Turns Guesses into Educated Guesses

When you try to think of ways to bring the world of numbers into your home, and ways to make mathematics a more common part of your family life, don't automatically discard all techniques that are used in schools. Don't think of a method as being applicable *either* to Family Learning *or* to school learning, but never to both. In fact, one of the things I find most fascinating about the techniques that work well in Family Learning is that most of these techniques can also work quite well in school settings too, and, conversely, the techniques that are worthless and boring and uninspiring in the classroom fare no better when applied in the home.

Estimating Vast Amounts

I remember a math teacher I had long ago whose techniques did not come from any teacher's manual, but whose classes were always exciting to attend—not "fun," necessarily, but interesting every day. I recall how he got our class accustomed to making estimates of amounts and distances and weights, and how we learned to use numbers and mathematics to refine and polish those estimates, and how we enjoyed every minute of it.

One day he opened up the class by asking, "About how many Ping-Pong balls do you think would fit inside this room?" There was a general murmur of disbelief, but the repetition of the words "impossible" and "zillions" helped them penetrate the whispered conclusions that our teacher had "lost it for sure this time."

"More than a hundred?" he asked. Of course. "More than a thousand?" Oh, yeah; way more than that. "More than ten thousand?" he went on. Certainly. "More than a million?" Well, probably—maybe a million, yeah. "Ten million? A hundred million? A billion?"

Little debates began breaking out among various factions in the class concerning the upper limit of the Ping-Pong ball capacity of our room, which was precisely what our teacher had wanted. What we needed, he said, was some plan by which we could estimate this "unknowable" number with enough precision to put us at least in the right numerical ballpark. He finally educed from us the idea that if we could just estimate the number of Ping-Pong balls that would fit along one wall, then the number along the adjoining wall, and the number from floor to ceiling, the volume of the room would be the product of our three estimates.

The ability to make reliable estimates is one that can benefit children in their schoolwork and throughout their adult lives as well. Exercises in estimating the magnitude of enormous distances or weights or volumes may seem to be wholly unrelated to a child's understanding of the real world, but these exercises require children to bring different pieces of outside information and knowledge to bear upon each different problem. Our Ping-Pong ball estimate, for example, would have been impossible without the knowledge that volume = length X width X height. This not only reinforces the meaning behind such an equation, but it also provides an immediate and useful application of the concept as well.

Would a stack of a million pennies reach to the top of the Empire State Building? Just look at the several pieces of information—the supposedly "common knowledge"—that children must put to use in making this estimate. A roll of pennies is about three inches long; there are fifty pennies in a roll; there are twelve inches in a foot; the Empire State Building is 1,250 feet tall. (A stack of a million pennies would reach four times the height of that building.)

Other fantastic problems (and the more fantastic the better, I think) can require children to call up, or look up, additional pieces of knowledge in order to make their estimates—the circumference of the earth, the number of feet in a mile, the distance to the moon, the length of a football field.

These exercises in estimating mammoth amounts are ideal for use in the home precisely because they have no "correct" answer. What parents should focus on is their children's plan for arriving at a reasonable estimate. "How should we go about figuring this out?" is much more important than "What is the answer?" You might have your children draw circles or boxes on a piece of paper to represent the information that they need, then have them map out what they would do with that information if they had it at hand. Last of all, where do they get that information to plug into their plan?

The real beauty of this technique as a Family Learning activity is that it can be suggested by something you read or hear together with your children, or it might be suggested by nothing at all and just pop up at some time or place for no reason other than it is just a fun thing to do together. And, of course, your children can be the ones who come up with the absurd or fantastic situation that calls for an estimate, and they can compare their estimates to yours.

For example, you might hear the current price for an ounce of gold given during the evening news, and this might cause you to wonder aloud what your children's dollar value would be if they were "worth their weight in gold." Do they think they'd be worth more than a thousand dollars? More than a million? More than a billion?

Or, let's say you're sharing a bowl of popcorn. Could your children estimate how far a line of a million popped kernels would stretch if the kernels were placed edge to edge? Across town, perhaps? Across the state? One of these is a better answer than the other, but how would your children go about the process of learning which is which? (Try lining up some kernels to see how many there are in one foot. There will probably be about fifteen.) So, 1 million divided by 15 gives you the length of a million kernels in feet—66,666.7—and since there are 5,280 feet in a mile, divide 66,666.7 by 5,280 and you get 12.6 miles. Now that is a useful estimate because, even though it may be off by a little or even a lot, you know with confidence that a million kernels will stretch several miles, but not a hundred miles.

Making a reliable estimate of large amounts and measures is really not just the stuff of fantasy, for we all have heard stories about huge military contracts, loan scandals, baseball salaries, government deficits, and we've tried to put the "fantastic" numbers in some sort of perspective that we can understand and discuss intelligently. In fact, the way your children go about estimating the Ping-Pong ball volume of your living room or the length of a million kernels of popcorn is exactly the same method that was used long ago by a Persian general to estimate the number of soldiers in his army.

Xerxes [pronounced ZERK-seez] was the ruler of Persia during the fifth century B.C., and he commanded the largest and best army of soldiers that the world had ever seen. The trouble was that Xerxes didn't know how many soldiers were in that army—many thousands, to be sure, but how many thousands? Unless he knew how many soldiers he had, he couldn't very well plan how to deploy them against an enemy. What he needed was a good, reliable estimate.

Xerxes accomplished this task by counting out individual soldiers, one by one, until he had a group of exactly 10,000 men. He ordered these men to stand as close as they could to one another, packed together into a tight bunch, and then he had a line drawn in the dirt completely around their entire group. When the men were dismissed, Xerxes had a wall constructed all the way around that line, with just a single entrance on one side of the wall.

Now he had his entire army line up outside the wall, and then had the soldiers cram themselves into the walled space until no more could fit inside. These soldiers were then sent away and another group was packed inside the wall, then another, and so on all day long. Xerxes knew that each such group would contain approximately 10,000 men, and because it required 170 different groups to account for all the soldiers in his army, he estimated their total number at 1,700,000.

But in addition to large numbers and fantastic amounts, we can use everyday, practical situations, as well, in helping our children improve their skill at making reasonable estimates. After all, this is precisely how most adults use math most frequently throughout most of their lives. They estimate how long it will take them to drive across town, or how far they can go without buying gas, or how much the groceries will cost. Why not use these opportunities to develop our children's estimating skill as well? Let them know how many gallons the gas tank holds, and have them estimate from the gauge how many gallons it will take to fill. About how much does this bunch of grapes weigh?

Rules of Thumb

The more experienced a person becomes with any activity, the more able that person is to make accurate estimates about it. We all employ little tricks we have learned to help us in making useful estimates, and these tricks are collectively known as "rules of thumb." (No one knows for certain how this name came about, but it probably has something to do with the fact that the width of the human thumb is a convenient approximation for one inch.)

For example, cooks know that the amount of uncooked spaghetti they can encircle with their thumb and forefinger will be enough for four modest servings. Or that they must prepare one and a half times the number of mashed potatoes that they would if they were serving baked potatoes instead. Typists and editors figure that a full page of double-spaced, pica type contains about 250 words. A handy rule of thumb to use for estimating how long it will take to double your money at a certain interest rate is to divide the number 72 by the interest rate (e.g., money invested at 6% will double in about 12 years). This "Rule of 72" works in reverse, too, so if you want to double your money in 10 years, for example, you divide 10 into 72 to learn that you'll need an interest rate of approximately 7.2%.

Can your children think of any rules of thumb that they use in making everyday estimates? How about the way they estimate how long it will take them to get ready in the morning? How long it will take them to get to school? Does it take longer in the winter? When it's raining?

Using Math in Estimates

There are certain mathematical relationships that, even though they are precise and absolute instead of general approximations, can be thought of and remembered as useful rules of thumb, in helping us to make reasonable estimates. For example, the surface of a sphere has four times the area of the greatest circle in it. So, to estimate the surface area of any sphere, find the area of a plane that passes through its center, and multiply by 4. Want to estimate the total surface area of the earth? Well, the radius of the earth at the equator is about 4,000 miles. So we find the area of a circle with that radius by taking 16 million (the radius squared) x 3 (a very rough approximation of pi) x 4 = 192,000,000 square miles. How accurate would this quick estimate be? Well, the actual area is 196,938,800 square miles.

Other mathematical tools we use to estimate and make sense out of extremely large numbers include fractions and percentages. We can read data from the latest U.S. census, for example, and discover that there are exactly 263,814,032 people living in our country. But a number like this is practically meaningless because any exact count of a large population is impossible to achieve. The number changes almost every second—a person dies, two more are born, some move in, others move away—and so even though the population numbers appear to be precise, they must be treated as estimates and generalizations.

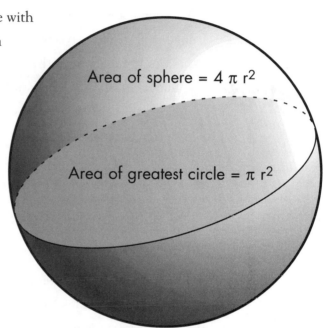

Area of sphere = $4 \pi r^2$

Area of greatest circle = πr^2

Finding the surface area of a sphere. All you need to know is the distance from the middle of the sphere to the surface (that is, 1/2 its diameter).

Perhaps even more important is the fact that no one can possibly grasp a number as large as 263 million; I'm not sure we can have any real understanding of even one million of anything—dollar bills, miles, or people. So to make large numbers more meaningful, we use mathematical concepts such as percentages and fractions. Here, then, is an opportunity for us to help our children understand percentages and fractions by applying them to real-world situations, not just in unconnected workbook problems. For example, how much more meaningful it will be to them, instead of learning that California alone has over 31 million residents, to see that number as being just about 12 percent of our total population, and that approximately one out of every eight people in the whole country lives in California today.

Another eye-opening way to look at census data and population statistics is to transform them into numbers and situations that we and our children actually can grasp, understand, and have a feeling for. We cannot comprehend the number 5.8 billion, which describes the current world population, but we can imagine a single village of 1,000 people, each of whom represents one one-thousandth of the world's people. In that village of 1,000 people, then, there would be 213 Chinese, and only 46 people from the United States. The village would have 330 children, and of the 670 adults, half are illiterate. Seven of these 1,000 people are teachers, five are soldiers, but there is only one doctor in the entire village. Donella H. Meadows has worked out many other interesting characteristics of this village in an article published in the 1992 *Old Farmer's Almanac* [031.02 OLD].

You can transform data from the U.S. census into a representative village of 1,000 Americans as well, by finding out what percentage of the U.S. population is composed of people from various occupations (from such sources as *The World Almanac and Book of Facts* [032.02 WOR]) and multiplying each percentage by 10. You'll find that only 19 of the 1,000 people in this village live on farms, 60 work for state or local governments, and 61 are unemployed.

Metric Conversions

Another way that estimates come into our children's lives is in the conversions that we all perform between the metric system and the English system of measurement. In spite of all the chidings from educators and legislators back in the 1970s, "metrification" has been a very slow process in the United States, but one that is occurring naturally instead of through government edict. Americans are becoming familiar with buying soft drinks in two-liter bottles, motorcycles and automobiles with engines measured in cubic centimeters, electricity in kilowatt hours, vitamins in milligrams, and on and on.

We have begun to get a feel for metric amounts without having to perform precise conversions between the systems. We do this by making instantaneous estimates—a liter is about a quart, so a two-liter bottle is about a half gallon. We don't have to know that a liter is equal to 1.06 quarts, but we do have to know that it is "about" one quart. The running track at your local high school measures 400 meters around, and it takes "about" four laps to run a mile on that track. From this information alone we know that a mile is about 1,600 meters long (actually 1,609 meters), and that a kilometer (1,000 meters) is quite a bit shorter than a mile (actually .62 of a mile).

You can help your children get a feel for metric measurements by focusing upon a few common reference points that will allow them to make thoughtful estimates of how amounts in one system compare with amounts in the other. For example, a nickel weighs about 5 grams; the wire in a paper clip is about 1 millimeter wide; a cubic centimeter is about the size of a sugar cube; a thimble holds about 3 milliliters (1 teaspoon = 5 milliliters); normal body temperature (98.6 degrees Fahrenheit) is exactly 37 degrees Celsius.

Let's look at this last measurement in particular to see how we can use Celsius readings of temperature in our Family Learning math activities. Where do you see those Celsius readings most often? Right: on the bank clock that flashes the time and the temperature, first in the English system of Fahrenheit degrees and then in the metric system of Celsius degrees or centigrade. Because both measures of temperature are given, you don't ever *have to* convert from one to the other, but you *can* view that clock as a learning tool that will pose a math problem to you and supply an accurate answer as well.

A quick way to estimate the Fahrenheit temperature when you are given the Celsius reading is to multiply by 2 and add 32. So, a Celsius temperature of 10 degrees, for example, would be "about" 52 degrees Fahrenheit. Can you and your children make this estimate before the bank's sign shows the correct answer? If not, then don't look at the sign until you have completed your calculations, and then let the flashing lights show you how good your estimate really was. (As you become more comfortable with this process, you might try multiplying by 1.8 instead of by 2, and that will give you the exact Fahrenheit reading. For example, 10 degrees Celsius $\times$ 1.8 = 18 + 32 = 50 degrees Fahrenheit.)

Probability

There is at least one other area in which we can help our children acquire the mathematical tools and understandings that will allow them to make reliable estimates about things they encounter in the real world, and that is the area known as *probability*.

Many children, and adults as well, use words like *chance, luck, odds,* and *coincidence* without any real thought about the likelihood that the event in question might occur. The easiest way to find out what pure chance is, or at least to see how it operates, is to do precisely what the mathematicians in the seventeenth century did when they began studying the theory of probability: They started tossing coins and throwing dice. These home learning aids allow us to observe, to learn, and to demonstrate some very difficult mathematical concepts without having to do some very difficult mathematics. The principles of probability are exactly the same in simple problems as in complicated ones.

Now instead of just tossing the coin a hundred times and seeing how many heads and tails result, let's have our children think about various possible outcomes first, and then use a pencil and a notepad to help them visualize those outcomes.

For example, tossing a single coin will result in one of two equally likely outcomes: heads or tails. Mathematicians would say that the probability of heads is $\frac{1}{2}$ —that is, there is one "favorable" outcome, and there are two "possible" outcomes.

Toss #1	Toss #2
T	H
T	T
H	T
H	H

Now, what is the probability (or chance) of getting two heads in two tosses? Here you will use the notepad to make a small grid, labeling one column "Toss No. 1" and the other "Toss No. 2." How many possible outcomes are there? Well, your grid should show four pairs: T–H, T–T, H–T, H–H. Since each of these pairs is equally likely to occur, and since only one of those four possible outcomes is the "favorable" combination of two successive heads (H–H), the probability is one chance in four or $\frac{1}{4}$.

Now use the coins and the notepad to show your child that tossing one coin twice is just the same as tossing two coins once. The columns will now read "Coin No. 1" and "Coin No. 2," but the outcomes will be identical.

What are the chances of tossing three coins and having them all come up tails? When you draw it out or lay the coins out on a table, you'll see the answer: 1 chance in 8.

Coin #1	Coin #2
T	H
T	T
H	T
H	H

The whole point here, as with rolling a die or two, is to get children to consider all the possible outcomes, which means all the possible combinations, and to understand that each outcome is just as likely to occur as any other. What would the chances be of tossing the coin ten times and having each flip come up heads? Some children (and adults) would say "impossible," or "a million to one," but you can show your children that each subsequent flip doubles the number of possible outcomes (1 flip = 2 possible outcomes, 2 flips = 4, 3 flips = 8, and so on). With 10 flips, there would be only 1,024 possible outcomes, so the chance of all ten flips being heads is 1 chance in 1,024.

One of the best home references for thinking about probability (and mathematics in general) is an inexpensive paperback titled *Innumeracy: Mathematical Illiteracy and Its Consequences*, by John Allen Paulos [510 PAU]. Here parents will find many examples of ways to bring numbers into their home and to make numbers an enjoyable and enduring part of their children's out-of-school activities.

USEFUL FAMILY RESOURCES

Innumeracy: Mathematical Illiteracy and Its Consequences, by John Allen Paulos (New York: Hill & Wang, 1988) [510 PAU].

Odds & Chances for Kids: A Look at Probability, by Manfred G. Riedel (Englewood Cliffs, N.J.: Prentice-Hall, Inc., 1979) [J 519.2 RIE].

Probability: The Science of Chance, by Arthur G. Razzell and K. G. O. Watts (Garden City, N.Y.: Doubleday & Co., Inc., 1967) [J 519 RAZ].

Rand McNally Mathematics Encyclopedia, by Leslie Foster (New York: Rand McNally, 1986) [J 510 FOS].

Reading the Numbers: A Survival Guide to the Measurements, Numbers, and Sizes Encountered in Everyday Life, by Mary Blocksma (New York: Penguin Books, 1989) [530.8 BLO].

Rules of Thumb, by Tom Parker (Boston: Houghton Mifflin Co., 1983) [031.02 PAR].

Math Stories and Math Tricks Can Be "Magic" in Your Home

Parents who want to bring numbers and arithmetic into their children's everyday lives can, as I have suggested, look for learning opportunities in the experiences their children have outside of school to see whether those experiences provide the basis for an activity that teaches or reinforces number concepts and skills. They can also take another path to this same end by initiating and creating learning situations instead of restructuring those that already exist.

For example, parents can make mathematics an interesting and enjoyable part of their family's conversations and activities by telling number stories at home and by doing "magic" tricks with numbers. All they need to do is look for stories and tricks that involve mathematics in some way, and the more ways the better. Children love stories and tricks, and they especially love stories that are told by their parents and tricks that they can learn to do themselves. So parents who acquire a stock of good math stories and math tricks will always have an eager and supportive audience, and they can choose from their stock as the situation demands—perhaps a calming tale or a diversion from boredom or crisis.

No parent has much success inspiring a child with the words "Let's do some math," but no parent I know has yet failed by changing the come-on to "Would you like to hear a story?" or "Let me show you a trick."

Here are a couple of my favorite math stories and tricks to show you what I mean and to get you started. Many, many more can be found in books from the 793.7 and 510 sections of the juvenile collection in your local library.

Doubling Does in the Miser

There was once a very rich, but very miserly old man who lived alone on a small farm. How he obtained his vast wealth no one knew, but he hoarded every penny and performed every chore around the farm himself rather than pay anyone to help him.

One day, however, he had an accident that would confine him to bed for an entire month. When he advertised for a hired hand to do the chores for that month, most applicants demanded $5 per hour, which was much more than the miser was willing to pay.

Then a young boy and his sister appeared at the door inquiring about the job. "We may be younger and smaller than most hired hands," the boy said, "but we'll work very hard, if you'll just give us the chance."

"And," his sister added, "we'll do all the work for just pennies a day."

Well now, this was music to the miser's ears, and he sat up straight in his bed. "Just how many pennies a day, dear child?" he asked with a sugary grin.

"Only a single penny on the first day, two on the second, four on the third, and so on, doubling the previous day's amount throughout the month," she replied.

What a deal! the miser gloated to himself, for he quickly calculated that an entire week would cost him considerably less than the others had asked for a single hour's labor. But he still felt compelled to make one last, penny-pinching demand. "Now that price is for the both of you. I'll not be paying a penny to each after the first day, will I?"

"No," the boy replied, "you just pay the amount we asked, and we'll divide the money between us. You see, we really want this job."

"Done!" the old man shouted, and he even made the children sign a contract requiring them to work the entire month and be paid according to the plan described by the little girl.

When the sun had set on their first day's work, the children drooped their way into the farmer's room for their pay. "Here's your wages," the farmer gloated as he placed a single copper coin into the boy's outstretched hand. "Now remember to divide that between you," he chuckled. "After all, you did sign a contract, and a bargain is a bargain."

The work was hard, but the children persevered, completing each chore and receiving their pay at the end of each day—2 pennies, then 4 pennies, then 8 pennies—so that after their tenth day of chores, the farmer was somewhat surprised to find that he owed them 512 pennies, or $5.12. On the seventeenth day, however, when he had to pay out $655.36 for their wages, he screamed, "This is an outrage! Why, tomorrow I'll have to pay you $1,310.72, and that's more than the other hired hands wanted for the entire month!"

"And there are still twelve days left for us to help you," said the little girl sweetly.

"After all," her brother added, "a bargain is a bargain."

How much were they due after the thirtieth day? Would you believe a whopping $5,368,709.12? But that's just the half of it. Added to the money they had already received, their total compensation for the month came to $10,737,418.23!

As you tell this story to your children, and just before you reveal the totals in the last paragraph, take a page from an old calendar and have them compute the amounts for each day's pay during the first week or so. Then have them use a calculator to see how much the children in the story would be paid on the thirtieth day, and what their total compensation for the month would be. How much more would they have received if the month they worked had thirty-one days instead of thirty?

There is one additional piece of learning that can come from this story and may be especially useful to parents and grandparents: Beware of any birthday present requests that begin "Just give me a single penny this year, then two next year, then four, and so on. . . ."

Fractions Save the Day

There was once a rancher who had lived a full life and who, though a widower for many years, had managed to raise three fine sons. And when the rancher passed away, he left strict instructions in his will that those boys should receive their inheritance according to the following formula: The oldest boy was to have $\frac{1}{2}$ of the rancher's estate, the second oldest was to receive $\frac{1}{3}$, and the youngest was to receive $\frac{1}{9}$.

Well, the money and the land that the rancher left were easily divided into the portions specified in the will, but the boys were stumped about how to divide the seventeen horses their father had left. Taking $\frac{1}{2}$ or $\frac{1}{3}$ or $\frac{1}{9}$ of the seventeen horses would leave each boy with part of a horse, and that would not be very beneficial to the boys, nor was it likely to be very popular among the horses. What were they to do?

Well, it happened that there was a lawyer in town named (here I like to use the name of the child who is hearing the story; let's use Melissa this time). Now Melissa had achieved great renown because not only was she very smart, but she also knew more about fractions than anyone in the territory. For example, she even knew that the word *fraction* came from the Latin word *fractus*, which meant "broken." That is why the whole is broken into parts called *fractions*; a broken bone is said to be *fractured*; breaking a law or a rule is an *infraction*; and a prism breaks a beam of light into its constituent colors by *refracting* it.

Well, Melissa looked over the will very carefully and then told the boys that she would solve the problem to everyone's satisfaction if they would pay her very sizable fee in advance. (I told you she was smart.) The boys agreed, and that very afternoon Melissa rode

120

her horse out to their ranch, removed the saddle, and turned her own horse loose into the corral containing the seventeen horses that were to be divided.

"Jamie," Melissa called to the oldest son, "you are entitled to $\frac{1}{2}$ the horses in the corral." Well, Jamie had little difficulty figuring his share because now there were eighteen horses to divide, and so he took nine for his own. Meanwhile Ken, the second son, easily figured out that his $\frac{1}{3}$ share of the eighteen horses would be six horses, and so he led them out of the corral. Finally Bill, who was the youngest son but by far the most handsome (yes, there are many advantages to being the one who tells the tale), took his $\frac{1}{9}$ share, and $\frac{1}{9}$ of 18 amounted to two horses.

Hmmm. Let's see. Of the eighteen horses, Jamie got nine, Ken got six, and Bill got two. That totals seventeen, and so one horse was still left in the corral. That horse was Melissa's very own, which she saddled up and rode back to town, having made everyone happy, and all because she knew so much about fractions.

You'll need to have a pencil and some paper handy when you tell this story, and let your child use them to figure the initial proportions—for example, what would $\frac{1}{2}$ of seventeen horses be? Now when the lawyer's horse is added to the others and the total is eighteen, have your child figure the proportions again, and one (whole) horse will remain.

There are also many math-related stories that aren't really "tales," as such, with a beginning, middle, and end, but are just as useful in teaching us and our children some lessons about mathematics and in developing our appreciation for the beauty of mathematics, as well. Keep an eye out for these little sketches and anecdotes in the course of your reading because they are very good memory aids that children can call upon to help them solve math problems both inside and outside of school.

For example, I was reading recently about a German mathematician named Johann Karl Friedrich Gauss [pronounced GOWSS] who was a mathematical genius even as a child. From the time he was three years old, he could solve complicated arithmetic problems without even the aid of pencil or paper.

When he was six, he was asked to add up all the numbers from 1 through 100. He paused for a few seconds and then announced the correct answer: 5,050. Amazing! I wondered how long would it take me to work out the same calculation?

Well, the fascinating part of this story, at least for me, lies not in **how long** it took Gauss to calculate the answer, but in **how** he went about doing so.

Gauss, you see, thought about the problem in a completely different way than most of us would. Instead of barging ahead with calculating a hundred different sums, he saw that the entire problem could be solved in just one step.

In those few seconds of deliberation, Gauss saw that if all the numbers 1 through 100 were arranged in a row, the first and last numbers would add up to 101 (1 + 100 = 101). So, too, would the second number and the second from the last number add up to 101 (2 + 99 = 101); and so would the pairs formed by the third, fourth, fifth, and so on, numbers from each end of the row. There would, then, be 50 such pairs of numbers (the last pair would be 50 + 51), each pair adding up to 101. So the sum of all the numbers 1 through 100 is really just 50 groups of 101, and 50 x 101 = 5,050. It's brilliant; a seemingly difficult problem reduced to just one simple calculation.

Adding the numbers from 1 to 100. Even though he was only a child, Gauss reasoned that this set of 100 numbers could be arranged into 50 pairs, each totaling 101.

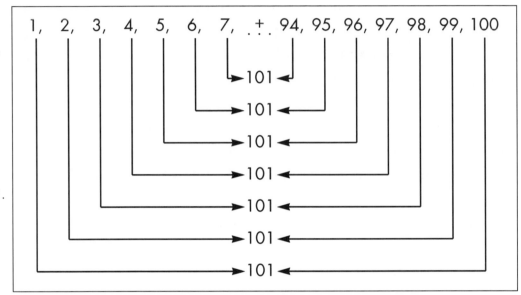

In explaining this problem to children, it is best to start out by considering the sum of all the numbers from 1 to 10. Write the numbers in a column or a row, then cross off the pairs formed by the two numbers on each end (e.g., 1 + 10 = 11, 2 + 9 = 11, and so on). Then total the five pairs of 11 for the correct answer of 55. Now let them try 1 through 100.

Think About the Problem

The lesson here is that not all problems are as difficult or as complicated as they may appear. The first thing to do is what Gauss did: Think about it. Maybe you won't come up with the astounding insights of a prodigy like Gauss, but maybe you'll see something that you didn't see before—some pattern that was concealed by the apparent and distracting complexity of the problem at hand.

My father gave me some very helpful advice about how to approach the countless story problems that were a never-ending part of my math homework and used to confuse me so much that I would come up with answers that made no sense whatsoever. "Substitute simple numbers first, and see if it makes more sense," he would say. And so the train that was traveling 54.92 miles per hour in the problem became a train that traveled 50 miles per hour, and the $13\frac{3}{8}$ gallons of syrup that dripped out of the holding tank every 3 hours and 45 minutes became 10 gallons dripping every 4 hours.

Now I could see what was really going on, and I could try different operations on my simple numbers until I understood how to go about solving the problem in a reasonable way. It was then just a matter of slugging in one set of numbers for another and carrying out the arithmetic. I still use this system today.

Stories About Mathematicians

Many years ago, I read a fascinating little story about the tomb of Archimedes [pronounced ark-uh-MEE-deez], a story that served to etch an important geometric concept permanently into my memory. It also revealed to me the power of stories as memory aids in math.

Archimedes, who lived in the Greek city of Syracuse on the island of Sicily in the third century B.C., was the greatest scientist and mathematician of the ancient world (see pages 175–76). His accomplishments and discoveries were many, but the one in which he took the most personal pride, the achievement he thought was the greatest of his life, was his solution to the problem of how to find the volume of a sphere. Archimedes proved that the volume of any sphere is exactly $\frac{2}{3}$ of the volume of the smallest cylinder that will enclose the sphere.

Think of a tennis ball that has been placed inside a soup can that is exactly as tall and as wide as the tennis ball. The width and the height of this cylinder, then, equal the diameter of the sphere inside it. Now, what Archimedes said was that if you want to know the volume of the sphere, just figure the volume of the cylinder first, and sphere's volume will be $\frac{2}{3}$ of that.

This was absolutely brilliant because it was (and still is) easy to compute the volume of a cylinder: just take the area of the circle that is the cylinder's base and multiply that times the cylinder's height. The area of the base is found by squaring the radius and multiplying by pi. Let's say our tennis ball is 3 inches in diameter (for easy figuring). The radius of the base of the soup can, then, is $1\frac{1}{2}$ inches (half the diameter), the area of the base is about 7 square inches ($1\frac{1}{2} \times 1\frac{1}{2} \times 3.14$). Multiply that by the height of the can, which is also the height, or diameter, of the tennis ball (3 inches), and the volume of the cylinder is 21 cubic inches. The volume of the sphere inside will be exactly $\frac{2}{3}$ of that, and so the volume of our 3-inch tennis ball is about 14 cubic inches.

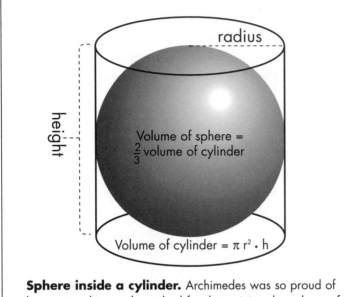

radius

height

Volume of sphere = $\frac{2}{3}$ volume of cylinder

Volume of cylinder = $\pi r^2 \cdot h$

Sphere inside a cylinder. Archimedes was so proud of discovering this simple method for determining the volume of a sphere that he made the symbol part of his gravestone.

Back to the story. Archimedes was so proud of this discovery that he asked to have this figure of a sphere inside a cylinder placed on top of his gravestone, and so it was. Years passed, and so did the memory of the great Archimedes for the people of Sicily. In fact, when Cicero, the Roman orator and philosopher, came looking for the grave a century and a half later to pay homage to the memory of Archimedes, the people of the town denied that such a grave even existed. But one old man suggested that Cicero search an overgrown plot on the outskirts of the city where he recalled seeing some gravestones when he was a boy.

So, Cicero and his men searched where the old man had indicated, and after cutting through thick weeds and vines, they discovered many ancient gravestones. Cicero recounted his search this way:

> I remembered some verses which I have been informed were engraved on his monument, and these set forth that on the top of the tomb there was placed a sphere with a cylinder. When I had carefully examined all the monuments . . . I observed a small column standing out a little above the briers, with the figure of a sphere and a cylinder upon it. . . . When we could get at it and were come near to the front of the pedestal, I found the inscription, though the latter parts of all the verses were effaced almost half away. Thus one of the noblest cities of Greece, and one which at one time likewise had been very celebrated for learning, had known nothing of the monument of its greatest genius.

Ever since hearing this little story, I have been unable to forget the relationship between spheres and cylinders, although I find many much simpler formulas difficult to recall.

Math Tricks

Math tricks are like stories, themselves, because they require a little "telling," that is, a little showmanship or presentation in order to achieve their greatest effect. So I suggest that you

Archimedes' tomb.
Cicero was able to identify the grave of Archimedes because the image of a sphere inside a cylinder had been carved into the tombstone.

practice a little before demonstrating any math tricks to your children, and I encourage you to select your tricks carefully and be mindful of your children's skill level as well as their interest level.

You will also find that it helps to have a pocket calculator on hand for doing some math tricks; in fact, it's a good idea to have an inexpensive calculator around the house and available for your children to use all the time. The beauty of the pocket calculator (beyond its being portable, inexpensive, and noiseless) is that it allows children to get past the tedium of computation and to see the underlying structure behind how arithmetic works and what numbers really mean. A simple problem like 15,873 × 7 = 111,111 can, with a calculator, be quickly followed by 15,873 × 14, then × 21, and so on until the child sees the pattern and can predict the next element in that pattern.

There are also many games that can be played on a calculator—even word games. Numbers such as 3, 4, and 5, for example, look like the letters *E, H,* and *S* when the calculator display is turned upside down. So parents can make up math problems for their children to work out on the calculator, the answers to which will form words when the display is turned upside down. For example: "What did the big spender have at the end of the month after he charged $32,896 and $17,554 and $7,268 on his credit cards?" (Answer: BILLS)

After a while, your children will be able to create word problems of their own for you to solve. They will start with the number that "spells" the desired answer, and then, using pencil and paper along with their calculator, they will work backward inventing computations that result in that answer.

Word problems of varying complexities, as well as many other calculator games and puzzles, can be found in such books as *Pocket Calculator Fun & Games*, by Ross and Pat Olney, and *Calculator Puzzles, Tricks & Games*, by Norvin Pallas, and similar books in the J 510 and J 793.74 sections of your library.

In choosing a pocket calculator for your child, let me recommend that you select one that automatically shuts off when not in use. Calculators with this feature, a memory function, and a percent key can be bought for as little as $5.

Now, with the aid of that calculator, you can show your children a couple of truly "magic" numbers. The first is the number 12345679 (the nine digits in order with the 8 removed). Now multiply this number by 9 and see what happens: $12345679 \times 9 = 111111111$. And when you use multiples of 9, the products jump up a notch: $12345679 \times 18 = 222222222$; $\times 27 = 333333333$ and so on.

Or take the number 142857 and see what happens when you multiply it by 1, then 2, then 3, 4, 5, and 6. The answers (142857; 285714; 428571; 571428; 714285; 857142) show that the order of the digits remains unchanged, but the 142857 sequence begins at a different position each time. You could write the number clockwise around a circle, then start at any point, and the answers would follow. Now multiply 142857 by 7 and be ready for a surprise. Magic, isn't it? (If 142857 is hard to remember, just divide 1 by 7—that's $\frac{1}{7}$ expressed as a decimal—and watch 142857 repeat to infinity!)

Here's a math trick in which you, without even using pencil and paper, can add up a column of figures faster than your children can add them using a calculator. Ask your children to write down any two numbers (small numbers are best) and, hiding the numbers from you, add them together so that their sum is now the third number in the column. For the fourth number, they should add the second and third, and continue in this pattern— each number is the sum of the two above it—until there are 10 numbers in the column.

For example:　3
6
9
15
24
39
63
102
165
267

When their task is finished, you take a quick glance at the column of numbers, draw a line beneath it, and—like magic—write down the total of all ten numbers combined! Even with the calculator it will take a minute or so for them to check your answer, but you'll be right every time. You must be a genius!

Well, not necessarily. You see, no matter what two numbers are chosen first, the total of the ten numbers will be exactly 11 times the seventh number in the series. So all you do is quickly count up four from the bottom to find that seventh number (63 in our example), multiply by 11 (63 X 11 = 693), and write that number as the sum of all the numbers in the column.

Multiplying by Eleven

Now the real trick is that multiplying by 11 is a snap. For a 2-digit number (let's call the digits A and B), 11 times that number is just the three digits A (A+B) B. For example, 63 X 11 is 6 (6+3) 3 or 693. It's easiest to work from right to left because you may have to carry a larger number over one place. To multiply 48 X 11, you write down 8 at the right, then 4 + 8 = 12, so write 2 in the middle and carry the 1. The 4 now becomes a 5, and the answer is 528. Check it out, 48 X 11 = 528.

Three-digit numbers require an additional step: ABC X 11 = A (A+B) (B+C) C, so that 426 X 11 = 4 (4+2) (2+6) 6 or 4686, but you, and even your children will, with a little bit of practice, be able to perform these calculations swiftly and accurately. (Come on, give it a try. 52 X 11 = ? 75 X 11 = ? 354 X 11 = ? 449 X 11 = ? Answers below.)

By practicing "magic tricks" like this one, children reinforce their knowledge of number combinations and operations; they also develop confidence in their own ability to play with numbers and, perhaps, to perform for their classmates as well. (Answers: 572, 825, 3894, 4939)

Here are a few other tricks that you can try, ones in which your children select their own numbers, but after they perform the operations you describe, you'll be able to "guess" the result accurately.

1. Have your children choose any number. Tell them to multiply that number by 100, and then to subtract the original number. Now have them add up the digits in their answer, and you guess the sum to be 18.

> EXAMPLE: 8 (number they select) X 100 = 800. Subtract original number (-8) = 792. When you add up the digits in the answer, 7 + 9 + 2 = 18. No matter what number they select, the resulting digits will always total 18.

2. Have your children choose any number. Have them add the next higher whole number. Then have them add 9, and divide the total by 2. Now have them subtract their original number. You guess their answer to be 5.

EXAMPLE: 15 (the number they select) + 16 (the next higher number) = 31. Add 9 = 40. Divide by 2 = 20. Subtract the original number (15) = 5. The result will always be 5.

3. Have your children choose a three-digit number in which all the digits are the same. Now have them add those three digits together, and divide their original number by this sum. You guess their answer to be 37.

EXAMPLE: 777 (the number they select) divided by 21 (the sum of 7 + 7 + 7) = 37. The result will always be 37.

4. Tell your child to get some loose change in any amount under $1. Now have your child write his or her age in years, double it, add 5, multiply the result times 50, subtract 365, add the cents value of the loose change, then add 115, and write down the total. You look at the result and see that the digit (or two) on the left is the child's age, while the two digits on the right reveal the value of the loose change.

EXAMPLE: Let's say the child is 11 years old and has 47 cents in loose change. The calculation begins with 11 x 2 = 22; + 5 = 27; x 50 = 1350; - 365 = 985; + 47 (loose change) = 1032; + 115 = 1147. The child's age is on the left (11), and the loose change is on the right (47).

Calculator Puzzles, Tricks & Games, by Norvin Pallas (New York: Sterling Publishing Co., 1976) [J 793.74 PAL].

Figuring: The Joy of Numbers, by Shakuntala Devi (New York: Harper & Row, 1977) [510 DEV or 513 DEV].

The I Hate Mathematics! Book, by Marilyn Burns (Boston: Little, Brown and Co., 1975) [J 510 BUR].

The Joy of Mathematics: Discovering Mathematics All Around You, by Theoni Pappas (San Carlos, Cal.: Wide World Publishing/Tetra, 1989) [510 PAP].

Magic House of Numbers, by Irving Adler (Vancouver, Wash.: John Day Co., 1974) [J 793.74 ADL].

Math for Smarty Pants, by Marilyn Burns (Boston: Little, Brown and Co., 1982) [J 513 BUR].

Mathematical Puzzles, by Martin Gardner (New York: Thomas Y. Crowell Co., 1961) [J 793.74 GAR or J 510 GAR].

The Pantheon Story of Mathematics for Young People, by James T. Rogers (New York: Pantheon Books, 1966) [J 510.9 ROG].

Pocket Calculator Fun & Games, by Ross and Pat Olney (New York: Franklin Watts, 1977) [J 793.74 OLN].

Learning About the Nature of Things:
SCIENCE

Introduction

There may be no area of study that is more in need of help from Family Learning than is the subject of science. New horror stories appear every week about the depths to which American students' scientific literacy has sunk and how poorly our children compare to those in other countries on international tests of science knowledge and skills. But the real problem is that our children, especially our adolescents, don't seem to care about the "why?" or the "how?" of things in the world around them. They aren't amazed or excited by the wonders of science even when these wonders are demonstated to them.

Still, some of our students do very well in science, but this only serves to perpetuate the myth that scientific skill is somehow a genetic attribute, and that, therefore, some children —perhaps most children—will never be able to achieve even a basic level of scientific understanding. Most discouraging is the fact that our schools of education do not require much in the way of scientific knowldege or fondness or even appreciation in those who will become our children's teachers, nor do our local schools demand these attributes in the teachers they choose to hire. Children need to see a curiosity about science and an everyday concern for "doing" science in **all** their teachers—in every grade and every subject—and, yes, in their parents, too. Only then will they come to understand that science is not some difficult, arcane, and avoidable school subject but is, instead, an expected part of everyone's learning and a necessary tool for thinking about and understanding every other field of study.

The situation is not as gloomy as it might seem, however, for there are many teachers who actually do enjoy science, and enjoy "doing" science with their students. It is also true that our schools have at their disposal many fine science books and other science materials and scientific equipment that can give our children all the learning opportunities and challenges they need to attain a world-class understanding of science.

However, before your children can take advantage of these teachers and these materials, they must come to understand that science is, above all, an attitude. It is this attitude—this way of thinking about the world—that Family Learning can provide for your children, and that they can then use to take advantage of every science-learning opportunity that is available to them in their schools. The essays that follow touch on only a few areas of science, and they describe only a few home experiments and activities, but the purpose of these essays is to focus on that scientific attitude and to get you started in doing things around the house that will encourage that attitude in your children. You may very well find yourself becoming interested in, and knowledgable about, some scientific principles that you see operating in the everyday world, and here you will find suggestions for methods and materials to expand and extend your own learning as well as that of your children. In increasing your own scientific literacy and understanding, you will be modeling that all-important attitude of inquiry for your children and, thereby, ensuring their success in science at school and their interest in science from then on.

FOR BETTER OR FOR WORSE © Lynn Johnson Prod., Inc. Reprinted with permission of UNIVERAL PRESS SYNDICATE. All rights reserved.

Ah, but where to begin?

Well, the best introductory resource I have found—a book that helps parents learn what science is and what science is not, and also helps them explain various scientific principles to their children—is titled *Teach Your Child Science: Making Science Fun for the Both of You,* by Michael Shermer [372.3 SHE], and is available in paperback.

Another good starting point for the Family Learning of science mirrors the practice I have recommended for making subjects like math, history, and character development part of normal, everyday family life: storytelling. Reading stories about science aloud to your children and telling stories about famous scientists, inventors, discoveries, and experiments will make your children familiar with many scientific names, terms, and ideas they will encounter later in school. You can find collections of stories about science in and around the 509 section of the adult and juvenile books in your local library. One that I particularly enjoy is titled *Marvels of Science: 50 Fascinating 5-Minute Reads,* by Kendall Haven [J 509 HAV].

Three Little Words Your Children Don't Often Hear

One of Albert Einstein's most lasting memories of his own childhood was the time when he was five years old and his father brought home for him a toy pocket compass. How fascinated he was with that swinging needle, which would always point in the same direction no matter which way the compass was turned!

Children are like this—not necessarily like Einstein, perhaps, but all children are curious about the workings of things. The eminent engineer, inventor, and philosopher of science R. Buckminster Fuller once put it this way:

> Children are born true scientists. They spontaneously experiment and experience and reexperience again. They select, combine, and test, seeking to find order in their experiences—"which is the mostest? which is the leastest?" They smell, taste, bite, and touch-test for hardness, softness, springiness, roughness, smoothness, coldness, warmness; they heft, shake, punch, squeeze, push, crush, rub, and try to pull things apart.

The whole idea of "experimenting" as a way of finding out about things comes naturally to children. But they don't "experiment" with the objects that fall into their reach in the methodical or orderly ways that we would prefer, and that is mainly because they haven't yet been taught that science is a "subject" and should be learned from a "science textbook." They'll get that message soon enough, and then most of them will come to dislike it and distance themselves from that same investigative instinct that both fascinated and nurtured them when they were young.

135

But while they're still curious about things like compasses and magnets and invisible forces, let's feed that curiosity and fascination, just as Einstein's father did.

In a variety store or toy store, you'll be able to purchase, quite inexpensively, a pocket compass and a bar magnet or two, which you and your children can use around the house to perform many scientific experiments, much as Sir William Gilbert—the man who first formulated the essential laws of magnetism—did long ago as a way of understanding how magnets behaved in the real world.

In the year 1600, Sir William Gilbert (who was at the time the personal physician to Queen Elizabeth I) published a scientific pamphlet in which he set forth his theory that the earth was a huge magnet, complete with north and south magnetic poles and connecting lines of force, just as though a giant bar magnet were running through its core. But is there actually a magnet in the earth? I mean, why exactly does a compass needle point to this "magnetic north pole" on our planet's surface?

Most adults, I've found, will offer one or both of the following explanations:

a) there is a huge deposit of magnetic material lying way up in northern Canada, which attracts the north-seeking end of a compass needle, or

b) the core of the earth is an ironlike material that somehow, perhaps by spinning through a gravitational field, has acquired the properties of a magnet.

In truth, the answer is c) none of the above, or even better still, "I don't know." Not only don't I know, but no one else does either. It's a wonderful mystery, which has produced many theories, but no hard answers.

Now many adults—parents and teachers, too—find these words, "I don't know," so difficult to say that they never use them in answer to a question from a child. Any answer, they think, even a wrong answer, is better than the baldfaced admission of ignorance: "I don't know." How sad this is, for many reasons, but especially because it helps destroy that fascination and wonder that children have about their world, and that we should have about our world, too.

(I am reminded here about a story that was often told in the school district where I used to teach. It seemed that there had been a high school coach who was assigned to teach a class in physical science—there being no openings for gym teachers at the time. It happened that this teacher was asked by some curious students one day about the reason for the high and low tides that occurred in the world's oceans. Now, an explanation of this fascinating phenomenon would involve a discussion of the gravitational tug exerted by the sun and the moon, and the rotation of the earth as well, but this teacher was apparently unable to say the words, "I don't know," and so began his response by pointing to the globe on his desk and saying, "Well, you can see that the earth is tilted, and so the ocean water on one side of the earth is falling faster than the water on the other side, and....")

Our children need to hear us say these three little words: "I don't know," when we are stumped by a question, whether that question involves science or history or geography or language. They will profit from this response by learning that no person can be the repository of all knowledge, even in a particular field. But they will profit even more if we will just include three additional little words at the end of our reply, so that instead of deflecting their questions or inventing some temporarily plausible answer, we say to them "I don't know; *let's find out*."

So, "let's find out" about magnets.

Learning With a Magnet

Earlier I said that no one, no scientist or teacher, knows precisely why the earth behaves like a giant magnet. But we have learned a lot about magnets in general, ever since our ancestors thousands of years ago unearthed some strange black rocks that seemed to hold an invisible and mysterious power over any particles or pieces of iron.

The Greek philosopher Thales [pronounced THAY-leez] was one of the first to study the properties of this mineral, and since he obtained his samples from an area called Magnesia, he called the mineral "magnes," from which we get our word *magnet* as well as the modern name for this iron oxide, *magnetite*. After several centuries, "magnes" became known as *lodestone*, which meant a "leading stone," because when it was allowed to move freely, it would point in a northerly direction, and so could "lead" ships on their proper course.

Having a compass and a bar magnet or two around the house is a great way to tap your children's innate curiosity about the physical world, and to encourage them to investigate and experiment with "hands on" science as well. It also provides parents a way to practice a set of behaviors that will encourage children to learn for themselves.

The first time that children see a magnet pick up a thumbtack off a table from an inch or two away, they will be amazed, but they will not have an uncontrollable need to know the scientific explanation for this phenomenon. Parents who launch right into a discussion of "lines of force" and "magnetic poles" will miss the opportunity to have their children experience for themselves the effect that this magnet has on a variety of materials. But if, instead, you try the magnet on all kinds of objects—a wooden match, a paper clip, various coins, some staples, toothpicks, safety pins, stamps, whatever is at hand—and preface each trial with a question like "What do you think will happen if we try...?" then your children will get a feeling for what magnetism is, and you will get a feeling for asking encouraging, open-ended questions.

We all have to make a conscious effort at developing this questioning skill, precisely because it is so easy to lean in the other direction and "tell" rather than "ask." Sometimes we phrase our questions so that we are really "telling" instead of "asking" at all: "Isn't it true that...?" "Don't you think that...?" or "Wouldn't it be better if...?" These questions don't lead the child to do any thinking at all, but questions that call for a prediction, and questions like "What do you think is happening here?" certainly do.

Let your children feel the tug between two bar magnets, then turn one magnet around and have them experience for themselves what the words *repel* and *repulsion* feel like and mean. (How about *repulsive?*)

Hang a chain of paper clips or tacks from the ends of your magnet. Can you make the same length chain closer to the middle? How many will hang from the exact middle? "What do you think will happen if...?"

Have them see whether the magnet's power to move tacks or clips will extend through various substances such as glass, plastic, water, and wood. "What materials do you think might block the magnet's power?"

Learning With a Compass

Now you can move on to the compass, which is just another magnet (a magnetized needle) housed in a case. By placing one end of the magnet close to the edge of the compass, your child can see that one end of the compass needle is attracted to the magnet, and the magnet can pull this end of the needle right around in a circle. But what happens when the other end of the magnet is placed at the edge of the compass? Why, it attracts the other end of the needle. Still, when the magnet is moved far enough away, the needle returns to its original position.

If this activity causes you to bring up the existence of "north and south poles" in a magnet and in a compass needle, be careful about your terminology, because your children may start to wonder how the "north" end of a compass needle can point to the "north" magnetic pole of the earth, if "like" poles are supposed to repel each other. Good question. That is why the poles of any magnet, including a compass needle, should be referred to as either a "north-seeking pole" or a "south-seeking pole."

Although you are not going to be able to answer the question of how or why the earth acts like a giant magnet—by the way, the temperatures at the earth's core are hot enough to demagnetize any known element, especially iron), you and your children will be able to learn a great deal about how magnets behave by looking through the books in the 538 section of the juvenile collection in your local library.

There is also a wonderful book called *Explorabook: A Kids' Science Museum in a Book*, by John Cassidy [J 507.8 CAS], which is a fairly inexpensive, miniature science laboratory and science museum all rolled into a single home-learning reference. It comes complete with its own bar magnet (along with a magnifying lens, a flexible mirror, and other science materials), and it explains the principles behind numerous experiments—in magnetism and several other areas of science—that are ideal for home learning with your children.

Parents will also find some home activities featuring magnets and compasses in Michael Shermer's wonderful home science resource titled *Teach Your Child Science: Making Science Fun for the Both of You* [372.3 SHE]. However, the main value of this book, like that of another good general resource titled *Awakening Your Child's Natural Genius: Enhancing Your Child's Curiosity, Creativity, and Learning Ability*, by Thomas Armstrong [648.68 ARM], is that here parents can find useful and helpful descriptions of ways to maintain their children's innate curiosity for experimentation and ways to involve their children in the process of science.

USEFUL FAMILY RESOURCES

Awakening Your Child's Natural Genius: Enhancing Your Child's Curiosity, Creativity, and Learning Ability, by Thomas Armstrong (Los Angeles: Jeremy P. Tarcher, Inc., 1991) [649.68 ARM].

Experimenting With Magnetism, by Alan Ward (New York: Chelsea House, 1991) [J 538.2 WAR or J 507.2 WAR].

Explorabook: A Kid's Science Museum in a Book, by John Cassidy (Palo Alto, Cal.: Klutz Press, 1991) [J 507.8 CAS].

My First Science Book: A Life-size Guide to Simple Experiments, by Angela Wilkes (New York: Alfred A. Knopf, 1990) [J 507.8 WIL].

Magnets: Mind-boggling Experiments You Can Turn into Science Fair Projects, by Janice VanCleave (New York: John Wiley & Sons, 1993) [J 538.4 VAN].

Physics for Every Kid: 101 Easy Experiments in Motion, Heat, Light, Machines, and Sound, by Janice Pratt VanCleave (New York: John Wiley & Sons, 1991) [J 530.078 VAN].

Simple Science Says: Take One Compass, by Melvin Berger (New York: Scholastic, Inc., 1990) [J 507.8 BER].

The Story of the Earth's Magnetic Field, by Germaine Beiser (New York: Dutton, 1964) [J 538.7 BEI].

Teach Your Child Science: Making Science Fun for the Both of You, by Michael Shermer (Los Angeles: Lowell House, 1989) [372.3 SHE].

Working with Magnets, by E. A. Catherall and P. N. Holt (Chicago: Whitman, 1969) [J 538 CAT].

SEPTEMBER 22 (APPROX.): *Autumn begins*

DECEMBER 21 (APPROX.): *Winter begins*

Family Science in Fall and Winter

Having inexpensive pieces of scientific equipment, such as magnets, compasses, mirrors, magnifying glasses, and the like available in the home is just one way to encourage the development of a scientific attitude in your children. This all-important attitude about science, however, depends less upon "things" and upon the equipment that is available, than it does upon the way a child looks at the world, wonders about the world, and investigates the world without any equipment other than an inquisitive mind, and, if the child is lucky, an eager parent for a guide.

Family Learning about science does not require that parents be scientists themselves, or that you be able to answer your children's questions about physics, or chemistry, or biology right off the top of your head. But when you acquire some knowledge about the scientific processes that go on in nature, you become much more likely to direct your children's attention toward some of the wonders of science that occur in the natural world. You model for them a sense of fascination about the processes that occur in nature, and even though you cannot answer all your children's questions about what is actually going on, you convey the idea to your children that science is at work here, and that understanding science will allow them to answer all those questions for themselves.

When parents learn to look closely at the world around them, they will see evidence and examples of *everything*—every law, every process, every experiment—that is in their children's science books at school. They will not only see the natural world as brimming with reinforcement for the science their children learn from a textbook, but they will start to use science, instead of folklore and pseudo-science, to explain and answer the questions that their children ask about the world they see changing before their eyes.

Why Leaves Change Color

Take, for example, the onset of fall, when children ask their parents "Why do the leaves change color?" and their parents sheepishly resurrect something they heard when they were children and reply "Jack Frost painted them," knowing full well that the first frost has yet to occur. Bang! Discussion over. All learning stops, and not because these parents didn't know *everything* about the scientific reason behind fall's changing colors, but because they didn't know *anything* about it, and really weren't interested in finding out about it, either.

So what can a parent say when asked about why leaves change color in the fall? Well, to begin with, you can tell your children how fortunate they are to be able to witness this annual spectacle, because it is only in North America that the bright yellows and reds of fall ever appear. The fall colors in England, Japan, eastern China, and west-central Europe are dull by comparison because the autumn months are usually mild and cloudy in these regions, and the brightest fall colors require a combination of clear, sunny days and crisp, but not frosty, nights. (An early frost can turn the leaves a drab brown almost overnight.)

Besides, nowhere in the world are the countrysides so scattered with *deciduous* [pronounced dih-SIJ-you-us] trees and shrubs. Deciduous plants shed their leaves in winter, whereas the leaves and needles of evergreens are insulated against the cold and, therefore, can be replaced a few at a time year-round.

Several months before fall arrives, these deciduous, broadleaf trees begin preparing for winter. They begin building a separation layer at the base of each leaf stem, a layer that is made up of cells that will shrink and weaken just before the onset of winter. These cells, then, form a little tear line between each leaf stem and the twig to which it is attached, rather like the perforations on postage stamps. Just below this layer of cells, they prepare another layer that is made up of tough, corklike material that will seal the wound where the leaf pulls away from the twig, thus protecting the twig from frost, insects, and bacteria that could enter and damage the tree if the wound were not sealed and protected.

Imagine that! All these trees have anticipated the coming of winter for several months, and have begun to build layers of cells that will permit their leaves to fall away without doing any damage to the tree in the process. And there's more. The trees have also begun shutting down their food factories until spring arrives again, and so they no longer manufacture the chlorophyll that gives leaves their green color. As the chlorophyll in the leaves fades, other colors—yellows, golds, browns—become apparent. These colors were in the leaves all along, but they were covered up by the chlorophyll's intense green. You might even say that a leaf's color in fall is its "true" color, which had been hidden by the green chlorophyll.

Trees and shrubs and animals all know when to begin preparing for winter by sensing the small but steady decrease in the length of daylight each day. After the third week of June, the daylight hours start to shrink, almost imperceptibly, and each night becomes a little bit longer. By the third week of September, the hours of daylight and darkness are equal, but each night thereafter continues to grow a little longer, and the daylight hours continue to shrink, so that by December and January our nights last more than two hours longer than our days.

You can help your children understand this process by following with them the table of sunrise and sunset that appears near the weather map in your daily newspaper (these times are also generally reported during the weather segment of a televised newscast). Mark these times on a calendar for a few consecutive days, then, perhaps, just once a week over the course of a few months, and have your children compare these times and the length of days and nights to get a feeling for the way that broadleaf trees anticipate the coming of the cold of winter, as well as the coming of the warmth of spring. Other home experiments and activities to acquaint your children with the wonders of fall can be found in an excellent resource titled *Fall Is Here!* by Dorothy Sterling (check the 525 section of your library's juvenile books).

Isn't it a wonder that every living thing in nature can sense these tiny variations in the length of daylight and darkness? And how inspiring it should be for us and for our children to know that it is precisely this ability that accounts for the leaves' turning color, and also for the annual migrations of swallows and caribou and butterflies.

The Wonder of Water and Ice

Now, just as the onset of fall presents parents with some scientific questions that are always asked by children, the onset of winter generates questions, too, most of which have to do with the scientific miracle we call *ice*.

I never thought of ice as a "miracle" when I was growing up, but I do remember wondering about the ice that formed each winter over the surface of our old swimming hole. The thing that puzzled me was that the ice just covered the very top of the pond and that there was liquid water underneath—a fact that any well-heaved boulder would confirm. What should be so puzzling about this, you ask?

Well, I remember being troubled by the fact that, in the summer, when we would splash about and try to dive as deep as we could, the temperature of the water got colder and colder the farther down we went in the water. But if the warmest water is at the top and the coldest water at the bottom, why would the water on the surface be the first to freeze? Shouldn't this swimming hole have frozen from the bottom up?

My bewilderment over this conflict between my experience and my observations turned out to be a topic that was deserving of bewilderment. In its solution lies the reason that life has been able to endure on this planet, which seems like a lot to learn from one midwestern swimming hole.

As common as water is, it is also one of the most unusual substances on Earth. Like most substances, water contracts as it gets colder—that is, it becomes more *dense*. Colder water weighs more than an equal volume of warmer water, and so that colder water sinks and heads toward the bottom of the pond. Sure enough, the deeper you dive, the colder the water feels on your skin.

But then a truly extraordinary event occurs. When the temperature of water drops to 39° Fahrenheit (4° Celsius), that is, just before it gets cold enough to freeze, water stops contracting and starts to expand! Suddenly the very coldest water becomes less dense than water of higher temperatures, and so this almost-frozen water rises to the surface. As water freezes into ice, it expands even further, so that ice weighs considerably less than an equal volume of water. Consequently, ice floats.

Just think what would happen if this remarkable reversal did not occur. Water would continue to become more dense as its temperature decreased. Ice would be heavier than the water surrounding it, and would sink to the bottom, where it would build up, protected from the warming rays of the sun. In time, or during an ice age, all the water on earth would turn to ice, and all living things that depend upon water would cease to exist throughout this lifeless, arctic wasteland.

And this is precisely the way almost every single substance in the world behaves—the colder it becomes, the more it contracts, the more dense it becomes—every substance in the world *except water*. (Ammonia and neon also behave in this way, but they do not freeze at temperatures that are common on the earth.) I find it just fascinating that the most common and ordinary substance in the world is so uncommon and extraordinary in the way it behaves.

Young children don't need to know the detailed characteristics of this most curious substance, but they can and should become familiar with some of the ways that water behaves, and especially with the concept of *density*. (For additional learnings on this topic, see the discussions of "Archimedes" and the "Plimsoll Line" on pages 174-78.)

Ice is larger—it takes up more room—than the water from which it was made. That is why the top surface of the ice cubes in your freezer tray is higher than the surface of the water was when you filled that tray. And that's why a sealed bottle of water (or juice or soda, which are mostly water) will shatter if you mistakenly put one in the freezer or leave it outside on a freezing winter night. That's also why ice cubes float in a glass of water, and why very large ice cubes—called icebergs—float in the ocean.

Would the ocean levels rise and swamp the coastal areas of our earth if some strange circumstance caused all the floating icebergs to melt? Well, you can set up a simple experiment in your kitchen to help you answer this question. Put several ice cubes in a drinking glass, and fill the glass with water right up to the very top of the brim. As the ice cubes melt, watch carefully to see how much water spills over the edge. Surprised? Well, the same scientific principles that operate on ice cubes in glasses of water also govern the behavior of icebergs in oceans of water.

Ice cubes and icebergs float because they are less dense than the water from which they were made. Let's put that another way: When any volume of water becomes cold enough to harden into ice, it will expand, it will become larger, it will take up more room than it did when it was in liquid form (about an additional $\frac{1}{9}$ of its original volume). It will still *weigh* the same as it did before it hardened (no water was added or lost in the transformation), but now that weight is distributed over a larger volume, and so the *density* of ice is less than the *density* of liquid water.

That is why about $\frac{1}{9}$ or $\frac{1}{10}$ of a floating ice cube or iceberg rides above the surface of the water. The portion that lies below the waterline represents the volume or space that the entire piece of ice would take up if it were liquid water instead of solid ice.

When that ice melts, therefore, it takes up only the space that its submerged portion did previously, and so the water level around it, whether that water is in a drinking glass or in an ocean, remains unchanged.

There are dozens of simple experiments that you can do at home with your children to acquaint them with the scientific wonders of water—whether it is in the form of a liquid, a solid, or a gas. Inexpensive paperback books such as *175 Science Experiments to Amuse and Amaze Your Friends*, by Brenda Walpole [J 507.8 WAL], and *Water: Experiments to Understand It*, by Boris Arnov [J 546.22 ARN], are available at or through any children's bookstore. There is also a free catalog of helpful and inexpensive science handbooks that I find ideal for home use, which you can obtain by sending a request to Dover Publications, Inc., Dept. 23, 31 E. 2nd. Street, Mineola, NY 11501. You will also find many useful collections of science experiments and explanations in the 500–507 sections of the children's books in your local library.

USEFUL FAMILY RESOURCES

Earthly Matters: A Study of Our Planet, by James J. O'Donnell (New York: Julian Messner, 1982) [J 550 ODO].

Fall Is Here! by Dorothy Sterling (Garden City, N.Y.: Natural History Press, 1966) [J 525 STE or J 574 STE or J 500.9 STE].

How Leaves Change, by Sylvia A. Johnson (Minneapolis, Minn.: Lerner Publishing Co., 1986) [J 581.1 JOH].

Measure, Pour & Mix: Kitchen Science Tricks, by James Lewis (New York: Meadowbrook Press, 1990) [J 507.8 LEW].

175 Science Experiments to Amuse and Amaze Your Friends: Experiments, Tricks, Things to Make, by Brenda Walpole (New York: Random House, 1988) [J 507.8 WAL].

The Reasons for Seasons, by Linda Allison (Boston: Little, Brown and Co., 1975) [J 500.9 ALL].

Science Experiments and Amusements for Children, by Charles Vivian (New York: Dover Publications, 1967) [J 507.2 VIV].

Science in Summer and Fall, by Georg and Lisbeth Zappler (New York: Doubleday & Co., 1974) [J 500.9 ZAP].

Water: Experiments to Understand It, by Boris Arnor (New York: Lothrop, Lee & Shepard Books, 1980) [J 546.22 ARN].

Chemistry in the Home Can Ignite the Flame of Learning

When I talk to parents about the absolute necessity of awakening their children to the science that goes on around them all day long, most parents begin to re-think their commitment toward Family Learning. They can be language models, they can be guides for their children in history or geography or even in simple mathematics, but expecting them to aid and direct their children's studies in subjects like chemistry and physics is simply asking too much. They readily admit that they never studied or never liked these subjects when they were in school, and they can't possibly learn enough now to make any real difference in the success their children will have in the classroom. So, how about leaving chemistry and physics to the schools, or at least let's wait until the kids are in high school and have textbooks that will help them know about these things?

Fine, except that by then the game will have already been lost. If children don't form a positive attitude about science early on, and if children don't see the most basic principles of science operating in all things, then they will not be able to take advantage of whatever scientific training and study are offered by the schools.

Parents must also realize that ability in the "hard sciences" is not particularly valued in most of today's colleges of education, and so many teachers come into the profession without having demonstrated any degree of mastery in chemistry or physics or biology; worse still, they don't have to display an interest in or love for science when they are certified, hired, or tenured. Consequently, the nonverbal message that comes across to children in far too many elementary and middle-school classrooms—especially to girls in the class—is this: Science is hard; science isn't any fun; if you're good in science, you won't be popular.

There is, however, a silver lining around this admittedly dark cloud, and in this case it is the fact that there are books and classes and teachers already in place, in every district and in every school, that **can** provide help and encouragement and world-class lessons in science for our children. But we must first put our children in a position whereby they can take advantage of these benefits without having their interest in science be destroyed by the negative forces and features that are also already in place and are a part of every district and every school.

This does not require that you be a scientist or an engineer, or even that you be knowledgeable in these fields. It does require, however, that you convey to your children a positive attitude toward science, that you eliminate all destructive spoken and silent messages such as those I mentioned earlier, and that you, yourself, begin to see scientific principles at work in the common and simple occurrences of home and family life.

Even in chemistry and physics, you say? Yes, especially chemistry and physics.

Chemistry in a Candle Flame

Take, for example, the magical glow of a fire in the fireplace or of candles flaming on a birthday cake. How many times have children looked wistfully at the burning logs or at the glowing candles and asked their parents, "What are flames made of?" or "What causes the fire?" How wonderful it would be if their parents could offer an explanation that incorporates the language of science! Even though that explanation may not be complete—even though that explanation may not be completely accurate—the mere use of scientific words to describe scientific principles that are at work in the home will, in itself, prepare the child for future learnings in school. If parents can just convey the idea that knowing the science behind such wondrous and fascinating things as candle flames does not diminish their wonder or fascination at all, and that observing and talking about basic scientific processes is a natural part of family life, then even young children can develop a vocabulary and an understanding about science that will allow them to continue learning about science and to grasp highly technical and complicated scientific concepts in the future.

Let's look at the chemistry that is responsible for that candle flame, and at the scientific vocabulary we can use in describing that chemistry to our children.

The wonders of a candle flame and the apparent disappearance of the wax base as the candle burns can be explained by telling children that the wax (or paraffin or tallow) is a mixture of substances called *hydrocarbons*—that is, molecules that contain atoms of hydrogen and carbon. Now, when these large molecules are heated, their hydrogen atoms and their carbon atoms get excited and begin to move about rapidly, crashing into each other and into other atoms nearby. When oxygen atoms happen to be nearby (oxygen makes up about a fifth of the air we breathe, most of the rest being nitrogen), the carbon atoms and the hydrogen atoms crash into, and link up with, these oxygen atoms to form completely new and different molecules. A single carbon atom can join with two oxygen atoms to form carbon dioxide (CO_2). Two hydrogen atoms can join with a single oxygen atom to form water (H_2O).

But in the process of breaking down the large hydrocarbon molecules into smaller molecules like carbon dioxide and water, energy is given off in the form of heat and light. The candle's yellow flame is actually just millions of hot carbon atoms that didn't link up with any oxygen atoms. These atoms glow (just like a piece of burning coal, which is also carbon) and then cool to form the black particles in soot and smoke.

You can't see the carbon dioxide or the water that the burning candle or paper or logs have changed into because they are sent into the air as gases and vapors. But if you invert a clean drinking glass and hold it above the burning candle, you can see the water vapor condense into droplets on the inside of the glass.

The candle wax itself won't burn very readily, so a cotton wick is used. Heat melts the wax into a liquid, which is then pulled up the wick by a process called *capillary action*. This process, which is the same way that trees pull ground water up through the very fine tubes that extend from their roots right up their trunks and branches, can be demonstrated by touching the corner of a paper towel to a puddle of water on the counter top. The water is pulled up into the towel just as liquid wax is pulled up through the wick. (This process works best in tiny, hairlike tubes and so its name is derived from the Latin word for hair: *capillus*.)

But even liquid wax will not readily burn, and so the heat from the flaming wick turns it into a gas. You can show your children that it is the gas, not the wick or the wax, that produces the flame by blowing out the candle and then quickly holding a lighted match an inch **above** the wick. Presto! The vaporized wax that has risen above the wick relights immediately, starting the entire chemical reaction all over again.

The Father of Modern Chemistry

Now, if your children don't grasp right away the idea that the heat from a match causes separate elements in the air and the wax (such as hydrogen and oxygen and carbon) to recombine in various ways and to give off energy in the form of heat and light (the candle flame), that is perfectly natural, normal, and understandable. Consider the fact that it is only very recently in the history of our species that the most scientifically literate and educated adults have understood this either. Until about two centuries ago, the wisdom of the scientific community said that a mysterious substance called *phlogiston* (pronounced flow-JISS-tun) was responsible for the phenomenon of burning. It was the phlogiston in a substance that was burned up by the fire, and that is why the burned ashes of a log, for example, weighed less than the original log itself. Anything that wouldn't burn simply didn't have any of this essential phlogiston to begin with.

But then along came a man named Antoine Laurent Lavoisier [pronounced lah-vwah-ZYAY or, sometimes, lah-vwah-zee-AA], who was born in Paris in 1743 and studied to be a lawyer, like his father. But he became interested in science instead, and today he is recognized as being "the father of modern chemistry." Still, most people don't recognize the name of Lavoisier at all, but that name should be part of any discussion you have with your children concerning candle flames, or burning logs, even the "burning" of food that takes place in our bodies (which Lavoisier also showed to be a type of combustion).

Lavoisier, you see, was the first person to suggest that nothing "burned up" in a fire at all—not the wood or the wax or any invisible and weightless and mysterious element like phlogiston. He said that if you measured *all* the substances that existed before and after any burning took place, you would find that the burning had merely caused these substances to change their form, not to disappear altogether. And that's just what he did. He very carefully and precisely weighed a small piece of combustible material, and he weighed the air that surrounded it in an enclosed chamber, then burned the substance inside the chamber and measured *everything* that remained. Voila! The weight remained unchanged; the fire had merely caused the original elements to combine in a different way. No matter what substances he burned, the products of that burning weighed exactly the same as the original substances did before burning. Here was the world's first chemical equation.

This was earth-shaking science at the time, and Lavoisier was hailed as a genius. But there was also the French Revolution at the time, and Lavoisier was jailed as an enemy of the people. He was tried, convicted, and beheaded all on the same afternoon, and, as a probably apocryphal legend says, when he appealed for a little time so that he might complete some important experiments, the presiding judge replied, "The Republic has no need of scientists." A more authentic tribute to Lavoisier's genius was framed by the great French mathematician Joseph Louis Lagrange, who, on the day after the execution remarked, "It took only an instant to cut off that head, and a hundred years may not produce another like it."

Chemistry and Family Life

Whether or not Lavoisier becomes a household name in your family is not as important as whether words like *atoms, molecules, capillary action, hydrocarbons,* and *oxygen* can be freely used and understood by both you and your children. This vocabulary, like any set of words, is learned over the course of time and through frequent use, so don't think that either you or your children have to be comfortable with scientific terms like these right away. You have plenty of time to weave the language of science into the language that you and your children use without pretense or embarrassment in your home.

Your children's learning in school will be enhanced not only by their understanding of scientific terms, but also by their understanding of very simple and basic scientific principles. For example, they will know more about the workings of the world around them, and will also be better able to take advantage of the science lessons in their school studies, if you will just encourage and reinforce their understanding of two vital concepts, both of which are enhanced by the glow of a candle flame: (1) whenever you apply heat to any substance, you cause its atoms to become excited, to move around faster, to crash into each other more vigorously; and (2) if there is no oxygen present—if you remove all surrounding air, for instance—there can be no burning, no flame, not even any smoke. By grasping these two concepts alone, your children will have a greater understanding of chemistry than did anyone in the world, up until the time of Antoine Lavoisier.

USEFUL FAMILY RESOURCES

Chemically Active! Experiments You Can Do At Home, by Vicki Cobb (New York: J.B. Lippincott, 1985) [J 540.78 COB].

Let's Experiment! Chemistry For Boys and Girls, by Jacqueline Harris Straus (New York: Harper & Row, 1962) [J 540.72 STR].

Marvels of Science: 50 Fascinating 5-Minute Reads, by Kendall Haven (Englewood, Colo.: Libraries Unlimited, 1994) [J 509 HAV].

Teach Your Child Science: Making Science Fun for the Both of You, by Michael Shermer (Los Angeles, Cal.: Lowell House 1989) [372.3 SHE], pp. 73-81.

Who? Famous Experiments for the Young Scientist, by Robert W. Wood (New York: TAB Books, 1995) [J 507.8 WOO].

JANUARY 4 (GREGORIAN CALENDAR)

OR DECEMBER 25 (JULIAN CALENDAR): *Birth of Isaac Newton*

Gravity and Other Weighty Matters

The whole science and subject of physics has gotten a bad rap, I think, primarily because few people can explain what "physics" really is. Children learn that it is a highly specialized and demanding subject that only the "nerds," the "gifted," and others on the "accelerated track" are allowed to take, and then only during their last year of high school. Most parents figure it has to do with things like atomic energy and the speed of light, and that goes well beyond their ability to provide much assistance for their children's school studies.

Yet physics is, perhaps, better suited to out-of-school study, tutoring by parents, and Family Learning than any other subject in the entire school curriculum. The reason for this lies in the fact that the study of physics is made easier and is enhanced by one's own experience, and adults simply have more experience than children do. What kind of experience, you ask? Well, the kind that comes from living in the real world, and from learning how things behave in the real world. That's what physics is about, primarily: the laws that govern motion, matter, and energy. You see these laws, you feel these laws, you are affected by these laws every day of your life. You understand the workings of motion, matter, and energy, but you've just never thought about them very much. Physics helps you to think about them.

What a shame it is that children have to wait until the end of high school to study the principles that govern the workings of their world, and that we only let certain children in on these secrets. Oh, I know that there are classes in "physical science" during junior high, but these usually lump a smattering of chemistry, astronomy, geology, meteorology, and a dozen other "ologies" into a single textbook and semester, thereby serving the general purpose of selecting and separating those who like science from those who hope never to partake of it again.

The real beauty of physics, I think, at least from a Family Learning standpoint, is that it is everywhere. It is ideally suited to out-of-school teaching, learning, and reinforcing because so much of it exists and occurs out-of-school. The Winter Olympics and other skiing, skating, and sledding competitions, for example, provide all of us with lavishly financed physics laboratories and opportunities to isolate and witness and learn about the laws of motion and friction and gravity. How wonderful it would be if *all* children could be studying the physics of motion in school at the same time they were viewing the application of these principles on television, watching the Olympics and other winter games. How sad it is, though, that so few actually are.

Out-of-school physics means more than just Olympic Games, however; in fact, these same principles of motion and matter and energy can be seen in the most mundane occurrences of everyday life. Even young children, therefore, can grow up learning about and witnessing the principles of physics in action, if we, as parents, will just learn to look for these natural demonstrations of physics, and learn the principles and laws they demonstrate.

The Mystery of Gravity

Family Learning stresses the idea that all of us—children and adults alike—can be taught to learn from everything around us, and there may be nothing that is more truly "around us" than gravity. The way that objects behave when they are affected by the force of gravity is a part of that subject we call physics. It probably was the first topic in physics that humans ever studied or experimented with in any way. Isn't it fascinating, then, to find out that nobody today has any idea what gravity is? That's right, not even the most highly trained rocket scientist can tell you what this force is or why it occurs. We call it *gravity* (from the Latin word *gravis*, meaning "heavy"), and that gives us a certain confidence that we understand it— or that at least somebody does—but we don't, and neither does anybody else.

Most of what we do know about this mysterious force, however, we owe to a man named Isaac Newton, a name I hope will become well known and honored in your home and among your family. Isaac Newton was indisputably a genius and was recognized as such in his own time and by every generation since. It can be fairly said that all of modern physics began with Newton, and so I think that some of his observations about gravity are a good place to begin your family's study of this most misunderstood subject.

Children usually hear about how Newton saw an apple fall to the ground (cartoons occasionally picture the apple hitting him on the head), and from that experience he devised his theory of universal gravitation. He may very well have made such an observation (the apple didn't hit him on the head, however), but there was really no single occurrence that caused this earth-shaking view of the world suddenly to come to him in a flash of genius. It was, instead, through a whole series of observations and measurements, and over a long period of ruminating, calculating, and creating experiments in his mind that Newton finally described for us the way that apples fall, and people fall, and planets, and satellites, too.

Newton said that the earth has gravity simply because everything has gravity; the bigger an object is (that is, the more matter or mass it has), the greater its force of gravity will be. The moon has gravity, but it is less than the earth's because the moon has less mass than the earth. Even people have gravity, although its force is very slight compared to the force of the earth's gravity. Newton was the very first human to realize that although the earth exerted a pull upon the apple, the apple pulled the earth, as well. Now, the effect of the apple's gravitational pull on the earth is very, very small, that's true, but it was this observation, this declaration by Newton, that shook the world and explained the workings of the universe at the same time.

You see, Newton was saying that the earth was really nothing special; it exerted a pull just as strong as any body would if that body were as massive as the earth. So, extremely massive objects, like our sun and huge planets like Jupiter and Saturn and Neptune, have a stronger gravitational force than Earth's, while less-massive bodies, like our moon and Mercury and Mars, exert a weaker force. The sun's gravity pulls at the earth, while the earth's gravity pulls at the sun; the earth's gravity pulls at the moon, while the moon's gravity pulls at the earth. These forces all contribute to the orbits of our planet and its moon, and to the orbits of other planets and moons, and they can all be measured and predicted, but Newton was the first to figure out how.

The second thing that all children need to know about gravity is that it accelerates all things equally; that is, gravity causes all falling things to increase their speed at the same rate, no matter what they weigh. The philosopher Aristotle, as wise as he was, didn't know this. He said that heavy objects fall faster than lighter ones, and while this would seem to make sense, it is dead wrong, and we can prove it in our own homes.

Take two objects that are similar in size but different in weight—such as a steel bearing and a glass marble, or a softball and a shotput, if you are outdoors—and drop them at exactly the same time from as great a height as possible. Have your children predict which one will hit the ground first, then have them observe and report on what actually happens. (Both objects should land at the same time.) If you can drop the objects from a second-story window, you can duplicate, in a way, Galileo's famous experiment at the Leaning Tower in Pisa, Italy. In this way, you can introduce these important names and images into your children's knowledge and vocabulary.

If we remove the effect of air resistance, we don't even have to use similar-shaped objects. This fact was demonstrated by the Apollo astronaut who dropped a hammer and a feather on the surface of the moon (there is no atmosphere on the moon and so no air to resist the fall of either object) and watched as they landed on the lunar surface at exactly the same time. You can perform a similar experiment in your own living room. Hold a large book flat in one outstretched hand and a small piece of paper in the other. Release both objects at the same time, and you will see that the book falls easily to the floor, while the piece of paper is affected more by the friction of the air, and so it floats down sometime later. Now hold the book out again, this time placing the paper flat on the top of the book. When you drop the book, it will displace the air beneath the paper, and so the paper will fall (for a while) without being impeded by air resistance, and, light as it is, it will fall at the same rate as the heavy book.

A Thought Experiment

These physical experiments you do in your home can help your children better understand difficult concepts, but also keep in mind that you and your children—especially your older children—can create "thought experiments" that may be even more instrumental in learning and reinforcing and remembering scientific principles. For example, together, try to imagine being in an elevator car that is stopped at the top of the tallest building in the world. On the floor of that car are various objects—several coins, a hammer, a feather, dust particles, and a bathroom scale. You step on the scale, and it shows your normal weight. Then, suddenly, the elevator cable snaps, and the car begins plummeting to Earth. What will happen inside the car?

The elevator is in free fall, and so is everyone and everything inside. Does the hammer fly up to the ceiling of the elevator car, or does it stay on the floor? What about the coins and the feather and the scale? Do they rise from the floor of the car? Does the feather rise higher than the coins and the scale? What about you? Do your feet remain on the floor throughout your descent? You see, if heavier things fell faster than lighter things, then the elevator car would fall faster than the hammer, or the coins, or the dust, or you, because it is heavier. And if you and the other objects didn't fall as fast as the car, you and they would end up on the ceiling because the ceiling would run into you on its way down. But, if all falling things increase their speed at the same rate no matter how much they weigh, then you and the hammer and the feather and the scale and the coins and the dust remain on the floor because you and they and the elevator car are all falling at the same speed at any given time.

Speaking of that scale, what do you think it would show your weight as being if you stood on it all through your descent? Well, since the scale and you are falling at exactly the same rate and speed, you would not be applying any pressure at all to the surface of the scale, and so it would show your weight as zero. (When you reached bottom, however, the reading would go up considerably!)

"Thought experiments" such as this one can allow you to grasp the mysteries behind gravity's effects upon astronauts and orbiting satellites. The bathroom scale in our falling elevator car shows your weight to be zero, and so during your entire descent you are "weightless." So is the hammer, and the paper, and even the scale itself; each still has weight, but in free fall each behaves as though gravity didn't exist at all.

Why Objects Stay in Orbit

So it is with the astronauts who seem to be "weightless" as they orbit the earth in their space shuttles. Most people think that the astronauts' freedom of movement is due to the fact that they have "slipped the surly bonds of earth" and have achieved an altitude that is beyond the force of Earth's gravity. But we know that can't be so because it is Earth's gravity that holds the moon in orbit, so the force of gravity must extend at least a quarter million miles into space, and the shuttles orbit only a hundred miles or so above the surface. So why are the astronauts "weightless" if there is gravity in space? For the same reason that everything inside the falling elevator car behaves as though it were "weightless": The astronauts, their equipment, their shuttle craft, and every satellite that orbits the earth—even our own moon—all are falling freely through space.

 A satellite's circular (or elliptical) orbit is actually the result of an ongoing struggle between the downward gravitational pull of the earth and the satellite's natural tendency to continue along the straight line on which it was launched. You can give your children a very memorable demonstration of these two competing motions by tying a weight (such as a couple of steel washers) to the end of a 3-foot length of string. Have your child observe from a few yards away as you swing the washers in a large circle with your arm extended in front of you. When the washers reach the very top of the circle, release your grip on the string and have your child observe the path that the washers take as they fly away. Do they continue in a circle? Do they fly straight up overhead?

No. When the tug of the string is gone, the washers go off in a straight line that is parallel to the ground, because that is the direction they were moving at the instant you released the string.

Now have your child swing the washers and predict what their path will be when they are freed from the tug of the string at other points around the circle. In every case, their path will be a straight line that is perpendicular to the line that the string made when it was released.

The string in this demonstration represents the tug of gravity, and it is this tug that keeps the washers moving in a circle, and that keeps our satellites and astronauts from flying off in a straight line, too. You see, there is plenty of gravitational pull, even as far away as the moon, and if a satellite (including the moon) were not moving along its orbit, it would fall straight down into the earth. It is the horizontal push we give these satellites (just like the initial thrust you had to give the washers) that balances the gravitational tug and keeps them aloft. If we sent our rockets straight up from Cape Canaveral, they'd come straight down (or nearly so). So we fire them out (or "down range"), as well as up, so that the distance that the earth curves away below them, during any period of time, will allow them to fall freely without getting any nearer to the earth's surface.

Another Thought Experiment

One of the best ways to think about this rather difficult concept is to imagine an extraordinarily high mountain—one whose peak rises 100 miles above the surface of the earth. Now imagine that you could stand on that peak, and imagine that you could throw a baseball very, very fast—180 times faster than Nolan Ryan—that is, a fastball with a velocity of 18,000 miles per hour.

If your imagination can carry you this far, let's go on and think about where that mighty heave would carry the baseball. Well, if you threw the ball out horizontally, parallel to the surface of the earth below, the ball would behave just like baseballs (and all other thrown objects) behave at more normal altitudes, that is, it would fall sixteen feet toward the earth during its first second of flight. But in that first second, the ball would have also traveled out five miles away from the mountain (18,000 miles per hour is about five miles per second).

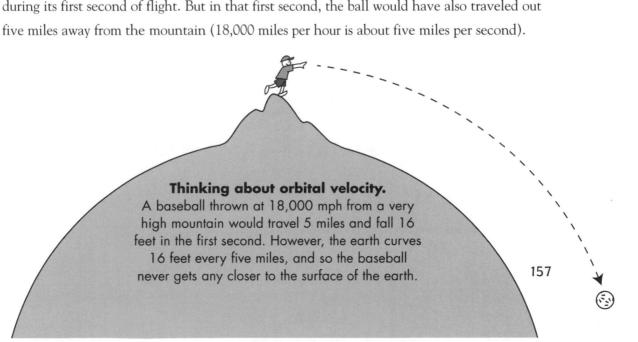

Thinking about orbital velocity.
A baseball thrown at 18,000 mph from a very high mountain would travel 5 miles and fall 16 feet in the first second. However, the earth curves 16 feet every five miles, and so the baseball never gets any closer to the surface of the earth.

157

Now here's the whole matter in a nutshell. The earth curves about sixteen feet over a distance of five miles, and so even though the ball has fallen sixteen feet in that first second, it is no closer to the earth's surface than it was before you threw it. As long as the ball (or a shuttle or a satellite) travels at 18,000 miles per hour, the earth will fall away (curve) at the same rate as the ball falls toward the earth, all around the earth, over and over again.

How does the ball keep going at that speed, without an engine of any kind? Well, if there's nothing to slow it down (friction with the atmosphere, for example), it doesn't need an engine. There actually is a little bit of atmosphere even 100 miles above the earth, and so satellites in such low orbits eventually lose their speed and fall back to Earth. But satellites in much higher orbits (like communication satellites that are 22,000 miles up, or our moon at 239,000 miles up) will stay in orbit for, well, who knows?

The other interesting thing about higher orbits is that they can be maintained with lower speeds. Remember that this orbital motion is a balance between two forces, and the force of Earth's gravity is weaker the farther away you get from the center of the earth. It takes a velocity of 18,000 miles per hour to balance the earth's pull at 100 miles, but only 6,800 miles per hour to balance the weaker pull at 22,000 miles. You can simulate this by again using the weighted string and having your children see how much more slowly they can swing a longer string, but how fast they have to swing the weight to keep it in "orbit" when the string is short.

The force of Earth's gravity is so comparatively weak at 239,000 miles, that our moon (or anything else at that altitude) needs a velocity of only 2,232 miles per hour to stay in orbit. Since the moon's diameter is 2,159 miles, you can look up at a full moon and imagine that it is loping along at just about one diameter each hour. It appears to be moving much faster across the sky, but that's because you (and the earth) are rotating in the opposite direction.

This whole idea that gravity is the key to the orbiting of satellites and moons and planets is one of the most fascinating concepts in all of science. But it is even more fascinating, I think, to know that Isaac Newton himself, as brilliant and learned as he was, used the learning technique of the "thought experiment" (just as I am suggesting for you and your children) to help him get a grasp of this whole idea, and he did it way back in 1666—centuries before space shuttles or communication satellites were ever dreamed of.

Newton wondered how fast a cannonball would have to be fired so that as it fell to Earth, the curvature of the earth would continue to drop away beneath the ball's path, and the ball would continue to fall without ever hitting the ground. It is precisely this same question that NASA scientists ask themselves in determining the "orbital velocity" of a spacecraft or a satellite.

This is not all there is to gravity, of course, nor is gravity all there is to physics. But gravity is a good topic to start your children thinking about some of the physical laws that govern the world they live in. Soon, and with your help, they will take notice of little things—like the coins that slide across the dashboard when your car makes a hard turn, or the way a train's horn changes pitch as the train rushes by. These are examples of the principles of physics at work in the real world, and when you understand the principles, your experience with the world will suggest to you dozens more examples that you can use in creating physical experiments and "thought experiments" for you and your children to better understand the world around you. Who knows, you may even begin to see ice skating and ski jumping and bobsleding in a wholly new way.

USEFUL FAMILY RESOURCES

Famous Experiments and How to Repeat Them, by Brent Filson (New York: Julian Messner, 1986) [J 507.8 FIL].

Famous Experiments You Can Do, by Robert Gardner (New York: Franklin Watts, 1990) [507.2 GAR].

Marvels of Science: 50 Fascinating 5-Minute Reads, by Kendall Haven (Englewood, Colo.: Libraries Unlimited, 1994) [J 509 HAV].

Observing Earth Satellites, by Desmond King-Hele (New York: Van Nostrand Reinhold Co., Inc., 1983) [629.437 KIN].

Science Around the House, by Robert Gardner (New York: Julian Messner, 1985) [J 507.8 GAR].

Teach Your Child Science: Making Science Fun for the Both of You, by Michael Shermer (Los Angeles: Lowell House, 1989) [372.3 SHE].

Thinking Physics: Practical Lessons in Critical Thinking, by Lewis Epstein (San Francisco: Insight Press, 1995) [530.0724 EPS].

Turning the World Inside Out (and 174 Other Simple Physics Demonstrations), by Robert Ehrlich (Princeton, N.J.: Princeton University Press, 1990) [530.078 EHR].

Sound Is a Good Teacher, Both Coming and Going

Another area of physics that is ideal for Family Learning is the study of sound, because we don't need a laboratory or scientific equipment to produce or investigate this invisible phenomenon. Sound is everywhere around us, and once your children begin to see that all sounds—no matter how loud or soft, high-pitched or low—are essentially the same, they will be able to use this understanding as a foundation for learning about other scientific mysteries in school.

There are dozens of experiments with sound that you can do in your own home and that can be found in books such as *The Magic of Sound,* by Larry Kettelkamp; *Science Experiments with Sound,* by Harry Sootin; and *Wonders of Sound,* by Rocco Feravolo (check the 534 section in the juvenile collection of your local library). But all these experiments and all their applications in the outside world depend upon your children's understanding of *vibration* and *wave motion.*

Wave Motion

Drop a stone into a pond and have your children focus on the ripples that it makes in the water. Here is a model for the way that sound travels through the air—outward in waves from its source. Notice that the ripples become less and less distinct the farther away they travel from the stone's point of entry, just as sounds get weaker and weaker the farther they travel from their source. Perhaps there is a leaf or a twig that is floating motionless on the water's surface, but it begins to move when the first ripple arrives, just as the membrane we call our eardrum begins to moves when sound waves arrive through the air.

This modeling of sound waves in a pond tells your children two important things about the creation, the transmission, and the reception of any sound. First, in order for there to be any sound at all, something has to move: no movement, no sound. Second, that movement causes movements in the molecules of whatever is around it—air, water, steel, whatever—until it finally moves our eardrums and we hear a sound.

From these two concepts alone, your children will be able to grasp all sorts of fascinating learnings and teachings about the science of sound. I have selected as examples just two areas pertaining to this topic: the speed of sound and the pitch of moving sounds.

The Speed of Sound

Your children may have already heard about supersonic airplanes such as the Concorde that can fly faster than Mach 1, and perhaps you, yourself, have wondered about this designation and exactly what speed it represents. Well, the name comes from an Austrian physicist and philosopher of science named Ernst Mach [pronounced MOCK], who died in 1916 and is famous in the scientific community for his teachings about space and time (his work had considerable influence on Albert Einstein, for example). He is most widely known, however, for his pioneering studies of shock waves, high-speed aerodynamics, and for developing the "Mach number." A plane flying at Mach 1 is traveling at the same speed as the sound made by its engines. Mach 2 refers to a speed that is double the speed with which sound would move *through the same medium*.

And therein lies the lesson with which all children should be acquainted: Sound travels at different speeds through different substances.

Sound needs something to travel *through*—that is, sound must have a carrier of some kind to conduct its waves to our ears. The substance or material that carries the sound waves is called a *medium* (from the Latin word *medius*, meaning "middle"). Most often this medium is the air around us, which serves as the "middle" or go-between that carries sound vibrations from their source to our ears. The molecules of air nearest the source are forced to bump together—back and forth—by the vibrating object that is causing the sound. These molecules, in turn, bump into the molecules next to them—back and forth at the same frequency—and so on all the way to the air molecules right inside our ears. These air molecules bump into the eardrum, which sets the eardrum vibrating and sends these vibrations to the inner ear, where they are picked up by tiny hairs that send nerve impulses to the brain telling us that we are hearing a sound.

Whew! And to think that this chain of molecule bumping—back and forth, one way and then the other—goes on anywhere from thirty to 20,000 times each second for every sound we hear!

But air is not the only medium that can carry the vibrations of a sound to our ears. In fact, the molecules of many substances bump together much more efficiently than do the molecules in air, and so these molecules can carry a sound to our eardrums more quickly, more clearly, and from greater distances than air molecules can.

If you place a wristwatch with a sweep-second hand on one end of a bare wooden table, and press your ear flat against the other end of the table, you will be able to hear the ticking even though the sound is too faint to hear through the air alone. Wood is a better medium for conducting sound than air is.

Water conducts sound waves four times faster than air does. That is why you hear the sound of the running water that is filling your bathtub much more intensely if you lie back and submerge your ears in the bath water.

Sound is usually said to travel through the air at approximately 1,100 feet per second (750 miles per hour). But that's in the dense air near the earth's surface; the thinner atmosphere at higher altitudes does not conduct sound as efficiently, and so sound travels more slowly the higher up you go. The speed of sound at 40,000 feet, for example, is about 660 miles per hour. So Mach 1 is by no means a fixed number. The speed of sound depends upon the medium through which it travels.

But one thing that does remain fixed is the need for a medium of *some* kind to carry the sound. In the emptiness of outer space, for example, there is no air at all, and so there are no molecules that can bump together and conduct sound to a person's ears. Contrary to what movies like *Star Wars* would have us believe, then, a battle in outer space would be conducted in absolute silence. Did the astronauts and their vehicles make any sounds at all on the surface of the moon? No, because there was no atmosphere on the moon to act as a medium. We could hear the astronauts speak, but only because they transmitted their voices through microphones, which converted the sounds to radio waves, which were then beamed to Earth and converted back into sound waves.

The speed that sound travels through any medium does not depend upon how loud that sound is. A whisper travels just as fast as a shout through the air; it just won't travel as far. Remember the stone that you threw into the pond? The ripples would travel at the same speed through the water no matter whether you threw a large stone or a small one; no matter whether you threw it hard into the pond or just let it drop.

All sound waves, therefore, reach our ears at the same speed, and so the differences we hear in the pitch of various sounds has nothing to do with their speed, but with their *frequency*, instead. Waves that arrive close together produce high-pitched sounds, while waves that are farther apart produce lower-pitched ones. This connection between pitch and the frequency that sound waves collide with our eardrums is the solution to a real-world mystery that you and your children may have already encountered and puzzled over and wondered about.

The Doppler Effect

When you stand beside a railroad track and listen to the whistle or the horn of a passing train, the pitch changes from higher to lower as the train rushes by. (Try imitating the steady blare of a train horn with your voice, and then quickly lower the pitch to see if this doesn't resemble the sound of a passing train.) But if the train's horn has only one pitch, why do we hear two distinctly different ones as the train goes by? Well, a nineteenth-century Austrian physicist and mathematician named Christian Doppler wondered that, too, and he became the first person to figure out the answer.

We have already learned that sound, all sound, travels in waves or pulses that are sent out in ever-expanding circles from the source of the sound, in this case the horn on the locomotive. The vibrations of the horn are duplicated in vibrations of the air molecules that cause our eardrums to vibrate in the same pattern. The more frequently these waves arrive, the higher the pitch of the sound we hear, while less frequent waves produce a lower pitch. (When explaining this principle to your children, it is a good idea to draw semicircles representing sound waves, along with a horn and an ear, on a piece of paper. Even better illustrations can be found in a children's encyclopedia under "sound" or "Doppler effect," or in the books from the 534 section of the children's collection in the library.)

As the train moves toward the listener, these waves are pushed together by the forward motion of the train. The waves are still being produced at the same rate, but they are now arriving at your ear more frequently, and so they have a higher pitch. After the train passes, the waves are stretched out—pulled away from you by the train. The waves arrive at your eardrum less frequently now, and you hear a lower-pitched sound.

It may be easier for you to picture a rifle on top of the train instead of a horn—a rifle that fires one bullet every second. As the train races away from the target, the bullets have to travel farther, and so each subsequent bullet takes more time to reach that target. But as the train approaches the target, each bullet is fired from a place that is closer to the target than was the previous bullet, and so the bullets hit the target at a frequency that is greater than one per second.

So it is with sound, which takes longer and longer to reach our ears as the train speeds away simply because it is being generated at points that are farther and farther away. But as the train approaches, each wave of sound is generated from a point closer to our ears, and so the

163

waves arrive more frequently than if they had been generated by a stationary horn and train.

This "Doppler effect" applies to more than just speeding trains, of course. The sounds of race cars and gas-powered model airplanes seem to change pitch after they begin moving away from you. You can even create a "Doppler effect" by listening for the sound of an airplane flying overhead, then quickly bringing your head down to the level of your knees and up once again. The pitch of the airplane's sound will seem to lower as you bring your head down, and then rise as you stand up again, all because you have temporarily "stretched out" the pattern of the sound waves being generated by the plane. (The "Doppler effect" also applies to light waves and is essential to a field known as radio astronomy.)

Another convenient and reliable demonstration of this effect can be performed by having your child stand along a remote stretch of road while you drive by blowing the car horn. In fact, this is precisely what a scientist in Holland did in 1844, two years after Doppler had proposed his explanation for the phenomenon that had begun puzzling listeners since the advent of trains. He hired a group of professional trumpet players, experts who could blow a sustained note through a horn without having the pitch waver at all, and he placed these trumpet players on a flatbed railroad car, which was pulled by a locomotive down an isolated length of track. Near the middle of the course, he positioned another group of professional musicians, all having perfect pitch and all able to detect the slightest change in the tones coming from any instrument. He ordered the trumpet players to sustain a predetermined note all along the route, and he directed the listeners to write down the exact notes they heard as the trumpeters approached and as they receded into the distance. Doppler's mathematical predictions proved correct and were shown to describe exactly what occurred. No matter what note the trumpeters played or what speed their car was pulled, the tone sounded higher to the observers at trackside when the train approached and lower after it passed.

It is important to remember that this effect is all relative, which means that what you hear depends upon where you are. Anyone riding on the train itself will hear a train horn of constant pitch, just as though the train had been standing still. But they will experience the "Doppler effect" in any sound that originates from the ground. So the clang of the crossing bell, which we hear as a single pitch while waiting in our cars for the train to pass, sounds higher to the passengers who are on that train as they approach the crossing, and then lower after they begin moving away from the sound of the bell. Can you or your children imitate the bell sound those passengers would hear?

Famous Experiments and How to Repeat Them, by Brent Filson (New York: Julian Messner, 1986) [J 507.8 FIL].

Famous Experiments You Can Do, by Robert Gardner (New York: Franklin Watts, 1990) [507.2 GAR].

Let's Experiment, by Martin L. Keen (New York: Grosset & Dunlap, 1968) [J 507.2 KEE].

Sound and Ultrasonics, by Ira M. Freeman (New York: Random House, 1968) [J 534 FRE].

What Makes the Wheels Go Round? by Edward G. Huey (New York: Harcourt Brace and Co., 1952) [J 530 HUE].

JANUARY 20: *Birth of Daniel Bernoulli* JUNE 16: *First helicopter flight*
MAY 20-21: *Lindbergh's flight* NOVEMBER 21: *First untethered balloon flight*
JUNE 9: *Birth of John Gillespie Magee, Jr.* DECEMBER 17: *Wright brothers' flight*

Balloons, Airplanes, Helicopters, and Flights of Fancy

One of the fundamental principles of Family Learning is that we can learn from the world around us, and just as gravity and sound are ideal vehicles for learning because they are around us all the time, so is that wonderful and mysterious and invisible substance we call *air*.

We live at the bottom of an ocean of gas that is composed of 78% nitrogen, 20% oxygen, and small amounts of a few other gases as well. (Are you surprised to learn that only about one-fifth of our air is oxygen?) We know of nowhere else in the entire universe that this same mixture of gases exists. And our atmosphere, that ocean of air that is held against the earth by gravity, is surprisingly shallow, too. Three-quarters of all our atmosphere (a region called the *troposphere*, in which all our world's storms and clouds and weather changes occur) lies within seven miles of the earth's surface. To put that in perspective, if the whole Earth were the size of your family's globe (about 12 inches in diameter), the atmosphere we breathe would be just about the thickness of the protective wax coating on the surface of that globe!

Now, if you and your children begin with the general topic of "air," and you look for lessons and experiments that can be done in your own home to further their understanding of this miraculous combination of gases, you will find that your study can branch off along many different paths. The composition of air, for example, and the process by which our bodies extract oxygen from it and exhale carbon dioxide (while plants take in carbon dioxide and give off oxygen) is vital to your children's understanding of biology. Similarly, the concept of "air pressure," is vital to their understanding of why and how changes in weather occur (see "Children Should Know Which Way the Wind Blows" p. 183).

Another learning path that your study of air might lead you along is the concept of flight, for it is our atmosphere that makes it possible for balloons and airplanes and helicopters to lift themselves off the ground. We can't perform or devise any home experiments that will simulate the experience of flying, but we can create some activities that will help our children to understand the scientific principles of flight, and we can encourage them to think about these principles whenever they see aircraft of any kind in person or on television.

Principles of Balloon Flight

We can also join them in taking "flights of fancy"—wholly imaginary trips in which we simulate the experience of flying, and which become learning experiences as well when we focus our mind's eye on the physical processes that cause our imaginary craft to lift us away and bring us home again. An imaginary flight in a hot air balloon, for example, will be much more vivid and much more meaningful if we understand what actually happens, and why it happens, when the basket we are riding in leaves the surface of the earth and sails over the countryside.

One of the basic principles of science that children of all ages should understand is that hot air rises and cold air falls. Now the reason that hot air is lighter than cold air is that heat excites the molecules in the air and drives them apart. Consequently, a gallon jug filled with warm air would contain fewer molecules than a gallon of colder air, and therefore would weigh less than the gallon of colder air.

Try this experiment with your children: Blow up a round balloon and measure its widest circumference with a length of string or with a measuring tape. Now put that balloon in the  refrigerator for a while, then measure its widest circumference again. It still has the same amount of gas that you blew into it, but now that gas takes up less space because it has cooled, and so its molecules are not bounding about as excitedly as they were before. Place the balloon in a warmer environment—over a hot radiator or in the warming rays of the sun, for example—and that same amount of gas will push the walls of the balloon out even farther than they were at room temperature. So even though the warm air balloon and the cold air balloon weigh the same, the warm one is much larger; you would have to add more air to the cold balloon to make it equal the other's size, and so the cold air balloon would weigh more than a warm air balloon of equal size. Warm air, then, is lighter than cold air, and so warm air rises while cold air falls.

The beginning of our imaginary flight occurs near dawn, when the air outside the balloon is cool and the winds are light. The propane burner in our wicker gondola roars and heats the air trapped in the balloon until that air expands and expands even more. Soon the combined weight of the hot air, the balloon, the gondola, and everything in it, including us, is less than the weight of the same volume of outside air.

We lift gently off the ground as friends below wave, wish us well, and become smaller and smaller, almost invisible now, though we can still hear their conversations (between blasts from the burner) because the earth bounces their voices up to us as we stand in absolute silence and peacefulness in our basket above.

A gust of wind carries us away from our launch site, and we sail over houses and trees and farmlands. Is our hair blowing in the stiff breeze? No, we feel no wind at all because we *are* the wind! We are being carried by the wind; we are going just as fast as the wind, and so to us the air always feels calm.

Can we turn back toward our launch site? No, we are prisoners of the wind, which carries us where it will. We can climb and descend with our burner, but we have no control over our direction. Our friends will have to follow us with a truck in order to get the balloon and gondola back home.

Now the day heats up, and as we fly at treetop level above a hot, blacktop parking lot, does our balloon rise or drop? Surprisingly enough, it is sucked downward because the hot air from the parking lot is not much different in temperature from the air inside our balloon. But then the wind carries us away from the parking lot, and we pass above a cool, wet marsh. Do we rise or drop? We rise, because the air inside the balloon is now much warmer, and therefore much lighter, than the cool air above the marsh.

It's getting late now, and we'll need time for our crew to find us and get everything loaded into the truck before dark. There's a meadow straight ahead, if we can just clear those telephone wires. A few blasts from the burner slow our descent, and soon we bounce and skid across the meadow to a stop.

Some good books to look for in a bookstore or a library (the 507.8 and 629.133 sections of the juvenile collection) to help you and your children better understand the principles of hot air balloons include *Balloons: Building and Experimenting With Inflatable Toys*, by Bernie Zubrowski, and *Balloons and Ballooning*, by William Bixby.

Principles of Airplane Flight

But if giant balloons can rise above the ground because hot air is lighter than cold air, how do airplanes accomplish this feat with wings and propellers instead of a gas bag and a burner?

There is a fundamental piece of science that all children must grasp before they can understand how a heavy metal object like a jumbo jet can fly through the air, and you can help them learn this principle through some simple demonstrations right in your own home. This principle was discovered by a Swiss mathematician and physicist named Daniel Bernoulli [pronounced ber-NEW-lee] back in the mid-eighteenth century, but it took more than 150 years before the Wright brothers could incorporate the principle into the first machine that would carry a human being through the air on December 17, 1903.

Bernoulli's Law, as it is called today, says that the pressure of air decreases when the speed of its flow increases. Air that is moving, therefore, exerts lower pressure than air that is stationary, and faster-moving air has lower pressure than air that is moving more slowly.

The Wright brothers knew that if they designed their wings with a flat bottom side and a slightly curved upper side (a shape that is call an *airfoil*), the air that flowed over the curved top would have to travel farther, and therefore faster, than the air that took the more direct route along the flat bottom side of the wing. According to Bernoulli's Law, that would mean less air pressure on the top of the wing than there would be on the bottom, and the greater pressure underneath would push the wing—and everything attached to it—up.

You can demonstrate Bernoulli's Law quite easily by cutting off a strip of paper about three inches wide and twelve inches long. Hold one end of the strip by the corners against your lower lip, and let the other end hang down. Now blow across the top of the strip and watch the paper rise. Why does the paper strip rise, even though you aren't blowing up against its bottom side? Well, the air that is moving across its top has less pressure than the stable air across its bottom side, and so the higher pressure from below forces the strip upward.

You can also demonstrate this same principle by inflating two identical balloons and suspending them from pieces of string so that the balloons are just a couple of inches apart. Now blow a stream of air through a soda straw aimed between the balloons. The balloons come together because the moving air between them has less pressure than the stable air on the opposite sides.

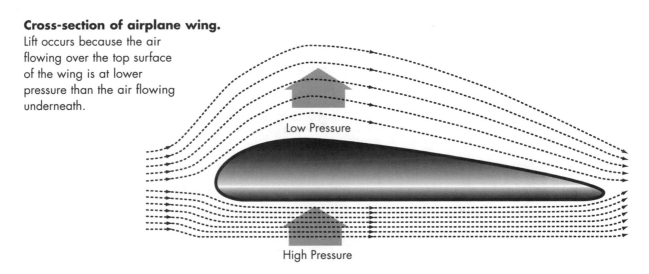

Cross-section of airplane wing.
Lift occurs because the air flowing over the top surface of the wing is at lower pressure than the air flowing underneath.

Low Pressure

High Pressure

Or when you are riding in a car, open one window slightly and watch as smoke or soap bubbles or a balloon heads toward the area of lower pressure, the moving air outside the car.

I remember as a child being fascinated by what I assumed was the remarkable intelligence of mosquitoes, butterflies, and other insects I would see heading right toward the windshield of our speeding car, then suddenly shoot up into the air just high enough to avoid being smashed against the windshield. How could they change direction so fast, and why did they wait until the last possible instant to make their move?

Later, when I learned about Bernoulli's Law and airplane wings, I realized that the shape of an automobile—relatively flat on the bottom and curved from the hood to the trunk—was the shape of an airfoil. So air rushing at the car from the front and going over the top of the car would travel farther, and therefore faster, than would the air that took the lower route between the roadway and the bottom of the car. This faster-moving air created lower pressure along the upper surface of the car, and so the insects were merely being pushed, or sucked, upward without any thought or effort of their own.

Bernoulli's Law also explained for me why the convertible top of our car would lift up an inch or more off its metal supports when the car was going at highways speeds. The top was being lifted into the region of lower air pressure on its upper side. In fact, the entire car was being lifted because its shape made it act like an airplane wing, and so the car "weighed" less when it was moving than when it was standing still.

It doesn't matter whether the car or airplane is moving through the air or whether air is being blown over and under the stationary airfoil, as is the case in a wind tunnel. A propeller or a jet engine on an airplane, therefore, is just a means for creating that flow of air over the wings so that Bernoulli's Law can take effect. The propeller or jet engine won't produce flight all by itself; it is the plane's wings—specifically, the shape of the plane's wings—and the scientific principle we call Bernoulli's Law that permit us and our machines to fly through the air.

I can hear the questions now: "If it's the wings, rather than the engine, that produces flight, how can a helicopter, which has no wings, fly just like an airplane?" Well, the blades that rotate above a helicopter are just like airplane wings—curved on the top and flat on the bottom. So while an airplane uses its engine to pull its wings through the air, a helicopter uses its engine to rotate its "wings" around in a continuous circle. As these rotor blades are pulled through the air, Bernoulli's Law tells us that the air moving across the curved top surface of each blade must travel farther, and therefore faster, than the air that passes under the flat bottom side of the blade. Just as with a fixed-wing aircraft, then, there is lower pressure on the top side of each blade, and so the higher pressure on the bottom side forces each blade upward. But unlike a fixed-wing plane, the helicopter can hover because it doesn't need forward motion in order to make air pass above and below its "wings."

Bernoulli's Law applies not only to air, but to fluids like water as well. There is less pressure in a region of faster-moving water than in a region where water moves more slowly. Put a cork or a floating toy in the water as you fill the sink or the bathtub and watch as it moves toward the region where the water is coming from the faucet. Here the water is in motion, and so it is at lesser pressure than the rest of the water in the tub or bowl. The cork, therefore, moves with the water around it toward that area of lower pressure (just as the insects move with the air around them over the top of a car).

Or try this demonstration in your kitchen. Have your children hold two tablespoons loosely in either hand between the thumb and index finger. Let the spoons hang down with their backs facing in, and hold them on either side of a stream of tap water. As your children bring the spoons slowly closer and closer to the sides of the moving stream of water, have them predict what they think will happen when the spoons touch the stream.

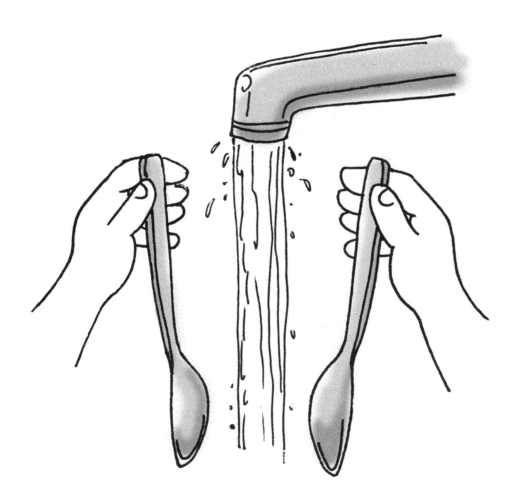

Bernoulli's Law.
When the spoons touch the water, the stationary air around them will exert more pressure than will the moving stream.

Surprise! As the spoons just touch the sides of the running water, they are not pushed away, but are pulled together instead! Gently pull the handles apart, and the spoons continue to cling together in the stream. Because the water is moving, it exerts lower pressure than the stationary air on the other side of the spoon, and so the spoon is pushed by the higher pressure on one side toward the lower pressure on the other—just like an airplane wing or a helicopter blade.

While we can devise many activities and experiments around the house to demonstrate the principles of flight, nothing we do can ever replace the experience of flying itself. And that is why the wonder of flying has captivated the imagination of children and adults for as long as there have been children and adults. Humans have always dreamed about how it would feel to soar above the ground, looking down upon it as the birds do. There is the ancient myth of Icarus and Daedalus, who fashioned wings for themselves from seagull feathers, which allowed them to fly away from the island of Crete, where they had been imprisoned. Stories about the wonder of flight can be found in every land and every culture, and they tell of such fantasies as riding flying carpets, or flying horses, or being carried aloft by the wings of eagles or other birds.

Your children need to know the science of flying, to be sure, but they can also learn much from the wonder of flying as well, and so these myths and tales can make excellent family read alouds and can make literature and art part of your family's learning about science. The exhilaration of flying wherever we choose to go is an experience that only pilots and astronauts know firsthand, and they find it a very difficult one to describe. The very best description, I think, is in a poem called "High Flight," written in 1941 by John Gillespie Magee, Jr., who was a fighter pilot for the Royal Canadian Air Force during the early years of World War II.

When you read this poem aloud to your children, remember not to pause at the end of a line unless there is a punctuation mark of some kind.

 "High Flight"

Oh, I have slipped the surly bonds of earth,
And danced the skies on laughter-silvered wings;
Sunward I've climbed and joined the tumbling mirth
Of sun-split clouds—and done a hundred things
You have not dreamed of—wheeled and soared and swung
High in the sunlit silence. Hov'ring there
I've chased the shouting wind along and flung

My eager craft through footless halls of air.
Up, up the long, delirious, burning blue
I've topped the wind-swept heights with easy grace,
Where never lark, or even eagle, flew;
And, while with silent, lifting mind I've trod
The high untrespassed sanctity of space,
Put out my hand, and touched the face of God.

John Gillespie Magee, Jr., is buried in northern England, where he was killed during a training accident three months after he penned the words of this poem. On his tombstone are the words from "High Flight" that President Reagan used in eulogizing the seven Challenger astronauts: "Oh, I have slipped the surly bonds of earth, put out my hand, and touched the face of God."

John Gillespie Magee, Jr., was 19 years old when he died.

USEFUL FAMILY RESOURCES

Air and Flight, by Neil Ardley (London: Franklin Watts, 1984) [J 533 ARD].

Air in Fact and Fancy, by Alfred Slote (Cleveland: World Publishing Co., 1968) [J 551.5 SLO].

Explorabook: A Kids' Science Museum in a Book, by John Cassidy (Palo Alto, Cal.: Klutz Press, 1991) [J 507.8 CAS].

Flight! Free As a Bird, by Siegfried Aust (Minneapolis: Lerner Publications Co., 1990) [J 629.12 AUS].

Marvels of Science: 50 Fascinating 5-Minute Reads, by Kendall Haven (Englewood, Colo.: Libraries Unlimited, 1994) [J 509 HAV].

Physics for Every Kid: 101 Easy Experiments in Motion, Heat, Light, Machines, and Sound, by Janice Pratt VanCleave (New York: John Wiley & Sons, 1991) [J 530.078 VAN].

Science Experiments with Air, by Sam Rosenfeld (Irvington-on-Hudson, N.Y.: Harvey House, 1969) [J 551.51 ROS or 507.2 ROS].

Thinking Physics: Practical Lessons in Critical Thinking, by Lewis Epstein (San Francisco: Insight Press, 1995) [530.0724 EPS].

What Makes a Plane Fly? by Scott Corbett (Boston: Little, Brown and Company, 1967) [J 629.132 COR].

"Eureka!": Finding Science All Around the House

For parents who still aren't quite convinced that they can make a difference in their children's understanding of science, it is helpful to remember that parents—all parents—are already much better scientists than they think they are. Parents are also learners, too, and so they can learn along with their children some scientific principles that will make their home life and their work life more understandable and rewarding, and they have in their homes already all the scientific equipment they need to help themselves and their children acquire this new understanding.

Take this miraculous substance we call water, for example, which can provide a world of opportunities for parents and children to observe together and learn together some scientific principles that are essential to understanding the world in which we live. Indeed, the use of water as an aid in home learning is an important part of one of the most famous science stories of all time.

Archimedes' Principle

In the third century B.C., there lived, in a Greek city called Syracuse on the island of Sicily, a king who had decided that he needed a new crown. He wanted it to be a magnificent treasure, one of purest gold, and so he handed over a precise amount of gold from the royal treasury to the royal goldsmiths who were to fashion it into the new royal headpiece.

Several days later, the work was finished, and, oh, what a crown it was! The gold had been hammered into wondrous leaves and points all around, and its gleam attested to its purity. But the king was just a little suspicious; he wondered whether his royal artisans might have kept a bit of the gold for themselves. So he put his new crown on a very precise scale, but it turned out to weigh exactly the same as the gold he had personally withdrawn from the royal treasury.

Still the king had his doubts. What if the workers had substituted a cheaper metal— silver, for instance—for the gold they had pocketed for themselves. The crown would not be pure gold, but by adding enough of the cheaper and lighter metal, they could make it weigh the same as pure gold. How could he ever tell if he had been cheated?

Now it just so happened that there lived in Syracuse at that time a man named Archimedes [pronounced ark-ih-MEE-deez], who was the greatest scientist, the greatest mathematician, and the greatest inventor in all the ancient world. The king called upon Archimedes to find a way to tell whether his new gold crown was, indeed, made of gold and nothing but gold.

The great Archimedes was stumped by the problem presented him. Everyone knew that silver was lighter than gold, and so if this crown contained any silver at all, it would be larger than a crown of the same weight that was pure gold. But how could you ever measure the volume of such an irregular object as a crown?

Archimedes spent several days pondering the problem without success. Then one morning, deeply absorbed in contemplation, he stepped into his bath, which he had thoughtlessly filled to the brim, and he noticed that the volume of water spilling over the side equaled the volume of his own body under the water's surface. That was it; that was the answer! If the crown had nothing but gold in it, it would displace the same amount of water as would a piece of gold of equal weight. A crown that contained a lighter metal would be bulkier for the same weight, and so it would displace more water.

"Eureka!" [pronounced you-REE-ka], he cried, (which is Greek for "I have found it!") as he jumped out of the tub and, mindless of the fact that he was still stark naked, ran through the streets of the city toward the royal palace.

The king ordered the test performed immediately, (and also ordered some clothes for Archimedes to put on). Sure enough, the crown displaced more water than did a bar of pure gold that weighed exactly the same amount. So the king now had proof that his new crown was not made of pure gold after all, because the water test had proved that the crown was less dense (and therefore larger) than it should have been. The workers were arrested and hauled off to prison, and the king lavished praise and many fine gifts upon Archimedes.

What Archimedes had learned from the water in his bathtub is the principle of *buoyancy*, which is also known today as "Archimedes' principle." We can help our children learn this principle and see it operating in bath water and sink water and ocean water, too, and we can prepare them for later lessons in school by making them familiar with such terms as *buoyancy* and *density* as we stimulate their curiosity about why some things float on the water's surface and others sink to the bottom.

 The idea behind the principle of buoyancy is that when any object is released into a pool of water, that object will receive support, or will be pushed up, by the water that is beneath the object's bottom surface. Consequently, things seem to weigh less when they are submerged in water than they do outside of that water because water exerts more upward pressure on the object than air does. You know this from your own bathtub experiences, for in a well-filled tub, you can raise your whole body with just a little pressure from your hand on the bottom of the tub. This would be impossible to do if you were outside the water.

What Archimedes discovered was that the reduced weight of any object in water is exactly the same as the weight of the water that the object displaces. In other words, even an object that sinks to the bottom of a perfectly full bathtub is buoyed up by a force that is equal to the weight of the water that flows over the rim of the tub. So, if an object weighs more than the water it displaces, that object will sink. If an object weighs less than the water it displaces, it will float on the surface. Any object will sink into the water until it reaches a point where the portion below the surface has displaced enough water to equal the weight of the object itself.

Density

What matters, then, is the *density* of an object, that is, how heavy it is for its size. One liter of water weighs 2.2 pounds, and so any object that has a volume of exactly one liter, but a weight of more than 2.2 pounds, will sink in water. This knowledge offers us and our children a way to predict whether any object will sink or float. Try to imagine how much that object would weigh if it were made entirely of water. (Yes, this does require a vivid imagination.) If the actual object weighs less than this amount, it will float; more than this amount, it will sink.

Now, the reason that a huge battleship can float on water even though it is made of a heavy and dense substance like steel is that the ship is not made *entirely* of steel. A solid lump of steel would, of course, sink quickly in water, but the frame of a steel ship encloses a great deal of hollow space (mostly in the hull), which weighs virtually nothing. The density of the ship, then, is much less than the density of steel because the *total* volume of the ship includes the volume of all that empty space as well as the volume of the steel. If all that empty space contained water instead of air, the ship would sink, which is precisely what happens in a shipwreck.

A battleship or a sailboat or a canoe will displace a volume of water that weighs as much as the boat itself. If we load an extra 100 pounds, say, into that boat, it will sink into the water a little farther and will displace another 100 pounds of water. The more weight we load into the boat, the farther it must sink in order to displace that exact weight of water.

Once you understand this principle of buoyancy, there are many activities and experiments that you can do in your home to help your children grasp it, too. In the 546 section of your library's juvenile collection, you will find helpful books such as *Rub-a Dub-Dub: Science in the Tub*, by James Lewis, and *Water: Experiments to Understand It*, by Boris Arnov.

Plimsoll Line

You can also be on the lookout for photographs of large freighters and tankers and cruise ships, and especially for a mark called the "Plimsoll line," which will appear on the hull of  these vessels. This line, or series of lines, can help us in teaching our children about the concepts of buoyancy and density and displacement, and it can remind us also about a brave individual who fought so hard to improve the working conditions on merchant ships that he became known as "the sailors' friend."

Samuel Plimsoll [pronounced PLIM-saul] was born in England on February 10, 1824 (and February 10 is today celebrated in many places as Plimsoll Day). He was elected to Parliament in 1868, a time when British merchant vessels were capsizing and sinking with such frequency that they were dubbed "coffin ships" by the hapless sailors who risked their lives on them.

The reason that so many ships and so many men were being lost at sea was that greedy and unscrupulous ship owners were packing their vessels so full of cargo that the ships would lie dangerously low in the water and would be virtually unseaworthy in the slightest storm. And because these cargoes were invariably overinsured, merchants made a handsome profit even if the ship went down—with all hands aboard.

Samuel Plimsoll fought hard for legislation that would end such practices, but when all the bills he proposed were defeated, he resorted to writing a book about the tragic conditions that British merchant sailors faced on the seas. That book, *Our Seamen*, so aroused the general public that Parliament was forced to pass the Merchant Shipping Act in 1876, which required strict inspections of all vessels before they were allowed to put out to sea.

Another of the reforms that came about as a result of Plimsoll's efforts was the mandate that every merchant vessel have a symbol painted on both sides of its hull, which would always be visible above the waterline and would mark the limit to which that ship could be safely loaded. Originally, this "Plimsoll line" (or "Plimsoll mark") appeared as a circle with a long horizontal line extending through its center, and it gradually became adopted as a maritime reform for merchant ships throughout the world.

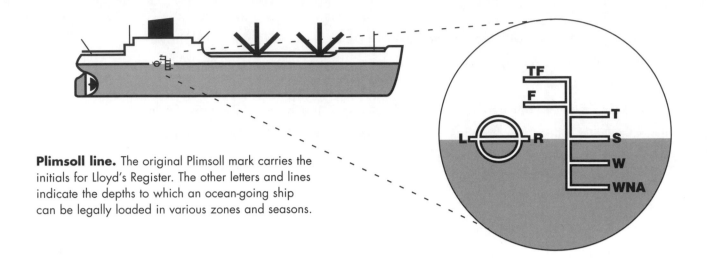

Plimsoll line. The original Plimsoll mark carries the initials for Lloyd's Register. The other letters and lines indicate the depths to which an ocean-going ship can be legally loaded in various zones and seasons.

Today's ocean ships and tankers bear, usually in addition to the original Plimsoll line, a series of horizontal marks arranged like the rungs of a ladder. These marks are labeled (from top to bottom) *TF, F, T, S, W,* and *WNA* and indicate the safe load limits for voyages in freshwater (Tropical Fresh, Fresh) and in saltwater (Tropical, Summer, Winter, Winter North Atlantic).

Cold water, you see, is more dense than warm water, and so it can support a heavier load. Remember that each ship will displace a volume of water that weighs as much as the ship. Well, if the water that is displaced is more dense—that is, heavier for the same amount—then the ship will need to displace less of this denser water than it would if the water were less dense. So a ship will displace less cold water than warm water, and it will ride higher in the water in cold water than it will in warmer water. It can, therefore, be loaded with more cargo when traveling through cold water and still be as seaworthy and safe.

Similarly, saltwater is more dense than freshwater, and so a cargo ship (or even a human body) will sink deeper into freshwater than it will into saltwater. (That's why it is much easier to swim in saltwater than in freshwater.) The Plimsoll line designating the safe load limit for ships traveling through tropical freshwater (*TF*), therefore, is at the very top of the scale because warm (tropical) freshwater is the least dense of all and will cause the ship to sink farther into the water than would be the case in colder waters or ocean saltwater.

Children will be able to see that saltwater provides more buoyancy than freshwater if you fill a large glass or tumbler with tap water and try to float an egg on the surface. The egg will sink to the bottom. Now remove the egg and stir about three tablespoons of salt into the water in the glass. When you put the egg back in this salt solution, it will bob up and float on the surface. The overall density of the egg is greater than the density of tap water, but it is less than the density of saltwater.

The principle of buoyancy applies to floating liquids as well as solids. One liquid will float on another only if its density is less than the other's. Gasoline floats on water because gasoline weighs about six pounds per gallon while water weighs about eight pounds per gallon; gasoline, therefore, is less dense than water. It is this difference in density that causes the salad oil to float on the surface of the vinegar when you prepare a salad dressing, and it is also the reason that cream rises in milk and floats on the top.

Kitchen Science

And now we have moved our science experiments, and demonstrations, and applications from the bathroom to the kitchen. Here we can find abundant resources and opportunities to help our children acquire the scientific attitude and understanding they will need to take advantage of the science lessons they are taught in school. We can, for example, help  them grasp the workings of the entire food chain by just playing "Plant or Animal?" and having them guess the original source of each food on the table (How about spaghetti? cheese? margarine?). After all, with the exception of water and salt, every single thing we eat comes either from a plant or an animal. One of the most helpful resources I have found for guiding children through the science of food production is a 1987 paperback book produced by the Ontario Science Centre titled *Foodworks* (see the 641.3 section of the juvenile books in your library).

Then there is the science that is involved in cooking and baking, including the physics of heating and freezing, and the chemical reactions that explain such mysteries as why a sliced apple turns brown and what causes a cake to rise. Parents can find many demonstrations of kitchen science and can familiarize themselves with the scientific principles and terms involved in these processes by consulting the library's J 502.8 section. My favorite is a recently updated version of the 1972 classic by Vicki Cobb titled *Science Experiments You Can Eat*, which is not a children's recipe book at all but is rather a guide to using foods in ways that will demonstrate science to young people.

And that is how I think cooking and food preparation can be best used as a Family Learning technique—not with our aim being to help children become better able to prepare various meals and follow various recipes (although there is merit in these goals, also), but with an eye toward helping children realize that cooking **is** science, and real science, too. Just because cooks use the name "salt" instead of "sodium chloride," or just because they don't refer to mayonnaise as "an emulsion of two immiscible liquids" does not mean that the science they are doing is any less respectable than the experiments carried out in a laboratory.

In fact, as Vicki Cobb points out, we and our children can profit from realizing that our kitchens actually **are** scientific laboratories—and well-equipped ones at that. Consider some of the similarities: both have measuring instruments, a source of heat to stimulate reactions, a source of water for preparing solutions and cleansing equipment, a refrigerator for slowing reactions and storing chemicals. The only real difference is that the people who work in a kitchen don't even think of themselves as really "doing science," but this is one educational misconception that is in our own power to change.

Balance

Other rooms in the house can be used for science experiments and demonstrations, too, and these rooms are every bit as good as any classroom or physics laboratory for learning certain basic principles of science. Take, for example, the whole idea of balance and the scientific concept called the "center of gravity," which refers to a single, imaginary point around which an object balances.

Have your children try to balance some common objects on the tip of their index finger—a ruler, a thin book, the lid of a jar. The center of gravity is at the center of each of these objects, and the objects will balance only when that point is directly above the point on which they rest (your child's fingertip).

Human bodies have a center of gravity, too, only our "balancing point" moves every time we do. Stand straight with your legs together and your arms at your side. Your center of gravity is now near the middle of your stomach, but directly above your feet. What happens when you put your right leg out as far as you can to the right? Did you lean to the left or throw your left arm out to avoid falling over? When you moved your leg, your body formed a new shape, and its center of gravity was a little bit to the right of where it had been before. It was no longer directly above its point of support, and so you either reconfigured your shape or you fell over. In either case, your center of gravity found a new position directly above its base.

Have your children try standing with their back to the wall, keeping their heels against the wall, and bending at the waist to pick up a coin off the floor in front of them. As they bend, their center of gravity moves out over their supporting feet, and they can no longer balance on those feet. They will be able to get a better grasp of this concept if you sketch the situation for them with "stick figures." Have them put an X where the center of gravity is on the standing figure, then another X at the center of gravity of the figure that is bending at the waist. They will see that the first X is directly above the figure's feet, but the second X is not.

You might also have them perform the simple act of rising from a sitting position in a chair, but now have them think about the act and about how they were able to change positions without losing their balance. In order to stand up, they first had to put their center of gravity directly over their feet, either by bending the trunk of their body forward, or by holding their arms out in front of them. Again, sketch the action and have them mark the center of gravity for each position. Next, let them see if they can rise from the chair without moving their torso or arms forward. Have them sit with their arms folded on their chest, and have them try to rise from the chair, keeping their back straight.

Now have them stand on one foot on a narrow object, like the edge of a brick, for instance. Is it more difficult with their arms at their side or with their arms extended sideways? Their outstretched arms don't actually lower their center of gravity, but they do make it easier for them to keep their center of gravity directly above the edge of the brick. The long, flexible pole carried by a tightrope walker in the circus really does lower the acrobat's center of gravity and keeps it closer to the base of support—that is, the tightrope. The lower that center of gravity is toward its base, the easier it is for the entire object to balance. (That is why it is difficult to walk on stilts: Your center of gravity is higher above its base.)

Perhaps now your children will start to realize how wondrous it is that their bodies can remain in balance and can change their center of gravity so quickly and so precisely, without any conscious thought on their part. Perhaps they will acquire a new appreciation for the struggle that babies must go through in developing and refining their sense of balance, and for all the struggles that attend the simplest movements of those whose misfortunes in birth or in life have caused a crippling of any kind in their bodies and in their balance.

USEFUL FAMILY RESOURCES

Balance It! by Howard E. Smith, Jr. (New York: Four Winds Press, 1982) [J 530.8 SMI].

Foodworks: Over 100 Science Activities and Fascinating Facts That Explore the Magic of Food, by Ontario Science Centre (Reading, Mass.: Addison-Wesley Publishing Co., Inc., 1987) [J 641.3 FOO].

Fun with Physics, by Susan McGrath (Washington, D.C.: National Geographic Society, 1986) [J 530 MCG].

Kitchen Science: A Compendium of Essential Information for Every Cook, by Howard Hillman (Boston: Houghton Mifflin, 1981) [641 HIL].

Learning Science Through Cooking, by Barbara Davis (New York: Sterling Publishing Co., 1964) [J 641.5 DAV].

More Science Experiments You Can Eat, by Vicki Cobb (New York: J. B. Lippincott Co., 1979) [J 502.8 COB or J 507.8 COB].

Physics for Every Kid: 101 Easy Experiments in Motion, Heat, Light, Machines, and Sound, by Janice Pratt VanCleave (New York: John Wiley and Sons, 1991) [J 530.078 VAN].

Science Around the House, by Robert Gardner (New York: Julian Messner, 1985) [J 507.8 GAR].

The Science Chef: 100 Fun Food Experiments and Recipes for Kids, by Joan D'Amico and Karen Eich Drummond (New York: John Wiley and Sons, 1995) [J 507.8 DAM or J 641.3 DAM].

Science Experiments You Can Eat, by Vicki Cobb (Philadelphia: J. B. Lippincott Co., 1994) [J 502.8 COB or J 507.8 COB].

What Makes the Wheels Go Round? by Edward G. Huey (New York: Harcourt Brace and Co., 1952) [J 530 HUE].

Children Should Know Which Way the Wind Blows

There is an abundance of low-cost educational materials to be found in any home, although we often don't recognize their learning potential, or we don't have enough knowledge ourselves to be able to use these materials to help our children learn. Let me show you what I mean by looking at just one of the features that is included in every daily newspaper: a weather map.

The styles of weather maps and the arrangement of the information they contain vary from paper to paper; some are highly detailed, while others show only the most basic weather information. But let's think a moment about what is "basic information" on a weather map. That is, what understanding should an educated adult or child be able to take away from a simple newspaper weather map?

Well, as with almost every other area of learning, the things you can learn from a weather map will depend in large part upon the knowledge you are able to bring to that learning opportunity in the first place. If children aren't aware of the basic scientific concepts that govern the movements of air, they can't be expected to learn anything from the letters and symbols that the map uses to describe those movements. Fortunately, these basic scientific concepts can be learned at home, and the use of a newspaper weather map, as well as the maps and explanations offered during the weather segments of television news programs, will enable us to reinforce those concepts and apply them to everyday life as well.

No matter how limited the detail of a weather map may be, it will always show the centers of high and low pressure around the country, usually labeling them *H* and *L*. Yet, an understanding of these two symbols alone requires a level of scientific literacy that very few children have today, even those in high school and college.

Air Pressure

Children need to realize that they are living at the bottom of an ocean of air, which extends several miles above their heads and is held against the earth by gravity. That column of air directly above them weighs a great deal, for although air doesn't seem very heavy, when it is piled up for miles and miles, it exerts a pressure that is tremendous—roughly fifteen pounds per square inch or about a ton per square foot! That's about 200 pounds of pressure on the surface of your open hand, but you don't feel the weight because there is air pushing up beneath your hand as well.

Take a sheet of paper and lay it on top of your open hand. Now cover the paper with a piece of cardboard held in your other hand. Lift the cardboard quickly and watch what happens to the paper. For just a moment, the cardboard has carried some of the air away from the top side of the paper, and so the greater air pressure on the bottom pushed the paper toward the cardboard.

Here is another activity that can help you show your children just how powerful this force called *atmospheric pressure* really is. Run water into a sink or a large bowl and submerge a drinking glass in that water. Turn the glass upside down and slowly lift it up, above the water's surface but not all the way to the brim. Water stays in the glass because the atmosphere is pressing down on the surface of the water in the bowl with a pressure of about fifteen pounds per square inch of surface area, and that pressure is forcing the column of water up into the glass. (You can find many other similar home activities and experiments in books like *Science Experiments With Air*, by Sam Rosenfeld, in the 551 section of your library's juvenile books.)

Newspaper weather map.
The symbols on this map confirm that winds flow clockwise around an area of high pressure and counter-clockwise around an area of low pressure.

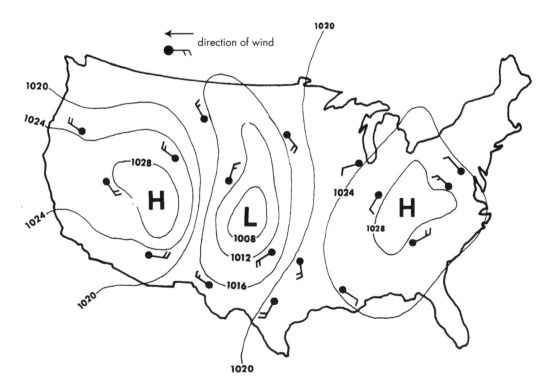

184

Now this ocean of air, just like an ocean of water, does not have a smooth upper surface. Our atmosphere is constantly moving and forming high peaks of air that spill into low valleys of air. (It is easiest to explain and visualize this idea if you have a globe of the earth at hand.) As one of these high peaks passes over your head, the column of air above you is taller, weighs more, and therefore exerts greater pressure on you than the shorter column would if you were standing beneath a valley of air.

And that, for the most part, explains those H and L symbols on your weather map. The H shows the center of a tall mountain in our ocean of air (high pressure), while the L shows the center of a shallow valley in that atmospheric ocean (low pressure).

Air in Motion

Nature tries to even out those crests and troughs of air, and so air spills or flows down from a mound of high pressure into a valley of lower pressure. Now the flow of that air would be straight downhill if it weren't for the fact that the earth rotates toward the east, causing the outflowing air (in the Northern Hemisphere) to twist to the right as it rushes down and away from the center. This deflection is known as the *Coriolis* [pronounced kore-ee-OH-liss] *force* and causes winds around a high-pressure center to follow a clockwise path; winds around a low-pressure center flow counterclockwise. (In the Southern Hemisphere, the opposite is true.)

With just this knowledge alone—that the winds around a high-pressure area flow clockwise, and the winds around a low-pressure area flow counterclockwise—you and your children can look at a newspaper or television weather map, predict which direction the winds should be blowing in your area, and then confirm your prediction by going outside and looking at a waving flag or a column of smoke or some blades of grass tossed into the air. (Just think what's going on here, in an educational sense. Your children are not only involved in learning about the science of wind and weather, but they are learning about geography, too, from that weather map, and they are reinforcing their knowledge of compass directions as well.)

The steeper that mound of air is, the greater the wind speed will be around it. Detailed weather maps show this with a series of concentric lines around each high and low. These lines connect regions of equal pressure, and so they are called *isobars* [pronounced EYE-so-barz], from the Greek words *isos*, meaning "equal" and *baros*, meaning "weight." Isobars that are spaced close together show great pressure differences within a short distance and warn of high winds and rough weather.

A change in the wind direction or speed often brings a change in the weather, but an even better way to predict weather change is to measure changes in air pressure directly. Having a barometer (again from the Greek *baros,* meaning "weight" and *metron* meaning "measure") in your home or classroom will allow you to see when and how the weight of the air overhead changes.

Your weather map will also show the position of weather "fronts," which form at the borders between masses of warm air and cold air. When two air masses of differing temperatures meet, they don't mix very well, and they struggle for control. Colder air is more dense and, therefore, heavier than warmer air, and so it is able to push the warmer, less-dense air up and out of the way. (You might demonstrate to your children how this looks on a small scale by putting tap water in a glass and then slowly pouring in some chocolate syrup.) The lighter, warmer air is forced to rise. It cools as it expands in the lower pressure of the upper altitudes, and, because now it can't hold as much water vapor as it did when it was warmer, some of that vapor is released in the form of clouds or precipitation.

You can use your weather map, a barometer (or the pressure readings given in the newspaper or on television), and some scientific observation of your own to confirm that air pressure usually falls as a front approaches, rises after the front passes, while winds usually shift in a clockwise direction.

More information about weather and weather maps can be found in the 551 section of both the juvenile and adult collections in your local library. There is also a very handy and inexpensive paperback book titled *Weather,* from Golden Press, that is available in most bookstores and on drugstore book racks. Another excellent home learning resource is *The Weather Classroom,* by Karen Wenning Moore. This 76-page paperback is published by The Weather Channel and covers a wide range of interesting topics dealing with climate and weather. You can obtain a copy of *The Weather Classroom* by sending a check for $6.95 to Weather Channel Enterprises, P.O. Box 510243, Livonia, Michigan 48151, or call 1-800-294-8219. You can also order a week's worth of very detailed and instructive "Daily Weather Maps" from the U.S. government by sending a check for $1.50 (payable to Department of Commerce, NOAA) to Daily Weather Maps, Climate Prediction Center, Room 811, World Weather Building, Washington, D.C. 20233, or you can download these maps from the Internet by visiting the National Weather Service's home page at http://www.nws.noaa.gov.

Once you and your children start to learn more about weather, you will find that there is more to learn. You can branch off in so many different learning paths, and you can use your new-found knowledge to explain natural occurences, which will cause you to wonder about others that you cannot explain. This is a feature of Family Learning that is not generally available or even possible in school learning, because schools are tied to a class or grade or textbook curriculum that does not permit each child to go off on an individual learning path that he or she finds interesting. Again, I am not saying that school curricula *should* be geared this way, just that the approach is available to families and that it allows children to take better advantage of whatever learning opportunities exist in their schools.

Your children might, for example, wonder about the science behind various weather conditions that occur from time to time. Take fog, for instance. What exactly is fog? Why does it form when and where it does? What makes it disappear? Or hail, or a tornado, or a ring around the moon. The weather resources mentioned earlier and at the end of this chapter can explain the science that explains these events, and your children can use this knowledge not only to better understand the world around them, but to provide the necessary associations and applications for the science lessons they learn in school as well.

Let's look at just one weather-related topic that can provide a science learning path for your children to follow, namely, lightning.

Science and Lightning

Ever since Benjamin Franklin proposed his famous, and extremely dangerous, kite experiment to demonstrate that lightning was actually electricity (it is unclear whether Franklin actually carried out this experiment himself), people have tried to understand the science behind this atmospheric wonder and have used that science to dispel many ancient notions about the causes of both lightning and thunder. But even today, most adults don't really understand what is occurring during these natural sound and light shows, and much of what they think they know is not scientifically accurate.

For example, did you know that many of the lightning flashes we see streaking down to the earth from a cloud are actually streaking *up* to a cloud *from* the earth? That's a fact; our eyes trick us into thinking we see a downward motion when it's actually the other way around. But then, if we believed only what we think we see, we'd still insist that the sun actually rises in the morning, moves across the sky, and sets at night.

Most lightning flashes take place inside a cloud, and only a relative few of these giant electric sparks can be seen jumping between two clouds or between the earth and a cloud. But with about 2,000 thunderstorms taking place above the earth every minute of the day and night, there's enough activity to produce about 100 lightning strikes on Earth every second—that's more than 8 million each day!

Here is a very brief description of what actually happens during a typical discharge of lightning. The negatively charged particles at the base of a thundercloud streak downward in invisible, halting jumps or steps—each about fifty yards long and lasting about a millionth of a second—until they are met by positive charges rushing upward from the earth through the tallest object in the area (a tree or tall building, for example). A route between the cloud and the earth is now complete, and this ionized path conducts a very bright and very powerful "return stroke," which we see as the flash or bolt of lightning.

A typical lightning flash discharges about 100 million volts of electricity and heats the air in its path to a temperature of 50,000 degrees Fahrenheit—that's five times hotter than the surface of the sun! This heat creates tremendous air pressure in the channel; the molecules of heated air fly out in all directions, colliding with other air molecules and creating a sound wave that we call thunder. This sound wave may bounce off clouds or hills before it reaches our ears—thus producing a series of deep, rumbling sounds—or it may arrive unimpeded as a single loud clap or crack.

Parents can use thunder and lightning to help their children learn about other areas of science besides meteorology. For example, when children understand that the light of the lightning flash reaches their eyes almost instantaneously (it travels at the speed of light, which is about 186,000 miles per second), but the sound of the thunderclap, which was created at the same time, takes about five seconds to travel just one mile (sound travels about 1,100 feet per second in air at low altitudes), they can begin to time the interval between the flash and the crash to learn how close they were to the actual spark. If they hear the thunderclap arrive ten seconds after they see the lightning flash, for example, then they will know they missed what would have been a truly memorable experience by only two miles.

Look at the learning that is involved in just this activity alone. Here we have not just the weather-related science that explains lightning and thunder, but also an understanding of the speed of light, the speed of sound, the length of a mile, and the arithmetic that relates all three together into a meaningful measurement of an earthly event.

Oh, and one thing more—Clement Moore, in this case. When this author of the famous poem titled "A Visit from St. Nicholas" (which is usually called "The Night Before Christmas") chose the names for Santa's reindeer, he included *Donder* and *Blitzen*, which are the German words for *thunder* and *lightning*.

All About Lightning, by Martin A. Uman (New York: Dover Publications, Inc., 1986) [J 551.63 UMA].

Marvels of Science: 50 Fascinating 5-Minute Reads, by Kendall Haven (Englewood, Colo.: Libraries Unlimited, 1994) [J 509 HAV], pp. 41-44.

Simple Weather Experiments with Everyday Materials, by Muriel Mandell (New York: Sterling Publishing Co., 1990) [J 551.5 MAN].

Weather (Earth Science Library Series), by Martyn Bramwell, (New York: Franklin Watts, 1994) [J 551.5 BRA].

Weather (Just Look at...Series), by John and Mary Gribbin (Vero Beach, Fla.: Rourke Enterprises, Inc., 1985) [J 551.5 GRI].

The Weather Classroom: A Complete Workbook for Understanding Meteorology, Climatology, and the Environment, by Karen Wenning Moore (Atlanta: The Weather Channel, 1994).

Weather Forecasting: A Young Meteorologist's Guide, by Dan Ramsey (Blue Ridge Summit, Penn.: Tab Books, 1990) [551.63 RAM].

Learning About the Earth and the Heavens:
Geography & Astronomy

Introduction

I have coupled these two learning areas—geography and astronomy—together because they both deal with the common question "Where am I?" Geography helps us know where we are on Earth, and astronomy tells us where that Earth is in the universe. Both areas, of course, deal with other questions as well, which often require us to combine our knowledge of both geography *and* astronomy (as, for example, questions about climates and seasons and their effect upon various populations).

Geography and astronomy might seem a strange pair at first, for one appears to be in constant flux while the other is fixed and everlasting. New countries are formed, national borders change, cities and nations are renamed so frequently now that globes and atlases simply cannot keep up with the pace and are often considered out of date as soon as they reach the market. Even the land itself is changing. The shifting crust of the earth is moving North America westward about two inches every year, for example, and so Columbus would have had to sail an additional 120 feet or so if he tried to cross the Atlantic today.

But the heavens seem so permanent and dependable. We can predict with absolute surety precisely when and where certain stars and planets will appear overhead, and we can know the exact times that the sun will rise and set for many years to come. Still, it is the variation within all this permanence that makes astronomy so wondrous, and the time we spend learning about astronomy so rewarding. The changing path of the sun across the sky, the changing faces of the moon, the changing positions of the stars from season to season— each takes on new meaning and importance once we feel comfortable in knowing what changes to expect and why those changes occur.

Too many school districts think that astronomy can be taught only at night, and so they never offer children even a rudimentary understanding of Earth's place in the universe, and they disregard all the lessons that children can acquire from observing one very prominent star: our sun. The slighting of geography in the school curriculum over the past thirty years has been so pronounced that it has given rise to a widely told joke about a research study that reportedly found that all high school geography teachers had the same first name: "Coach."

Yet, there are some districts in which individual teachers have had such a passion for studying the heavens and the earth that they have created, on their own, lessons in astronomy and in geography, which their students learn in school and then practice at home. I am sure that these teachers are convinced, as I am, that children who learn to marvel at the majesty of a starry sky, or who yearn to know more about "far away places with strange sounding names" are much less likely than their peers to mug the cashier at the local 7-Eleven store.

But no matter what status geography and astronomy have in your own school district, they remain ideally suited to Family Learning, for adults and children alike. Through learning activities designed for the home and family, geography and astronomy will no longer appear to be "subjects" at all, but pathways to help us answer the question "Where am I?" and help us see that our lives are made richer and fuller by this knowledge.

MARCH 5: *Birth of Gerardus Mercator*
TUESDAY AND WEDNESDAY AFTER MEMORIAL DAY: *National Geography Bee finals*
SECOND WEEK OF NOVEMBER: *National Geography Awareness Week*

Mercator Made Me Do It

Developing and encouraging geographical knowledge in the home is no different from any other area of Family Learning, for it begins with, and is dependent upon, the parents' **attitude** toward learning, not the parents' own knowledge or skill. Geography must be seen by your children as being important to you; knowledge of geography must be respected and worthy of praise in your home. Even more important, your children must see you as someone who is eager to learn about geography—one who is curious enough to ask questions, and concerned enough to search for their answers.

Using Maps and Globes

Most people think that learning about geography and demonstrating an inquiring attitude about geography require you to have maps all over the house, but this view, I think, has the practice reversed. What really happens is that when people become interested in geography and when they have an inquiring mind about various places on the earth, then they will begin to acquire all sorts of maps because they will have an appreciation for the learning that can come from those maps and is found in no other learning resource. Too often, people think that having maps or globes around the house is all that is necessary for children to excel in their geography studies at school, but they find that those wonderful resources go unused because neither the children nor the parents know how to avail themselves of all the learning these maps have to offer.

A world atlas and a globe of the earth ought to be part of the learning resources in every home and family, yet globes are not cheap and atlases can be downright expensive. Until we get our communities and our school districts to recognize the advantages of using their buying power to make these learning tools available to every family at a reasonable price, we will just have to budget for these items down the road or tie them into a special occasion such as a birthday or a holiday gift. Until then, we can focus our attention upon the many maps that are available in our homes already, and those that we can obtain for a nominal price.

A map of the United States appears in the first several pages of almost every phone book nowadays to show the boundaries of area codes and time zones. Another is printed each day in the newspaper to show weather patterns across the nation (see page 184), and, of course, we see a regional and national map on the weather segment of televised news programs every evening. There is no law that says we must use these maps **only** for the purposes they were intended, nor is there any reason that we can't come away from looking at these maps with more information than we sought from them in the first place.

Using a Road Atlas

Let's say that your family is watching the weather report on television together, and that as you look at the weather map, both you and your children are using it to help suggest questions about the United States that might be asked to one another as part of a contest. For example: What four states come together at a single point? What states border the Gulf of Mexico? Now the newspaper weather map or the map in the phone book can be used to provide answers and to suggest additional questions as well.

In addition to these and other maps that are available at almost no cost whatsoever, there is one extremely valuable geography resource that should become part of every home and is surprisingly inexpensive. The resource I am referring to is a road atlas or highway atlas—a collection of maps covering the United States, Canada, and Mexico. (Collections published by Rand McNally, Mobil, and Hammond are the most common of these paperbound atlases, and each sells for approximately six to eight dollars.) This handy reference is more likely to be used in your home if you make sure to find a place for it **near the television set**. If it is handy, it can be called upon immediately, but if it is tucked away in a desk or a bookcase in another room, the chances are that it will seldom be consulted.

In many families, it is the television set that provides most of the inspiration for geography questions and most of the need for geography knowledge, because it is on television that families see together news broadcasts concerning other states, sporting events from various places in the country, and movies that are set in faraway cities. When your children hear you wonder aloud about the location of a certain city or lake or mountain, and when they see you reach for the road atlas to satisfy your curiosity, they will, in time, become eager to help you use the maps to find what you want to know.

As with a dictionary or an encyclopedia, each trip to the road atlas can, and should, produce much more information than just the answer you were originally seeking. What states border the one you are looking at? Which direction is that state from your home? What is the name of its capital city? You can encourage your children to invent questions like these and to ask them of you as they look through the maps. Then reverse the roles, and have them use the maps to answer questions that you create. (For example: Which two states are bordered by eight others? — Missouri and Tennessee. Which of the five Great Lakes is located entirely within the United States? — Lake Michigan.)

The maps in the road atlas are also ideal for plotting family trips and for fixing in your children's mind the cities and states where their relatives live, the domains of storybook characters, and the location of historic landmarks. One parent wrote me to say how she has used old road maps as wall decorations in her child's room by gluing the maps around rectangular pieces of Styrofoam. Another parent taped a national map over a dart board, and so the family's dart games required each player to aim at a certain state, or players to team up and combine their skill and geographic knowledge into various games of fun and chance and learning, as well.

Preschoolers can get a good start on understanding the positions of our country's states with a wooden jigsaw puzzle of the United States, while older children with access to a computer will find geography programs such as *Where In the World Is Carmen San Diego?* absolutely fascinating. The Internet offers countless aids to those who are interested in studying geography, and there are several books available to guide you down this superhighway to geographical learning. For example, *NetAmerica*, by Gary M. Garfield and Suzanne McDonough, gives Internet addresses for learning about every state in the nation, and several learning activities related to each state as well.

Distortion in Maps

As your family's interest in geography increases, and as geography becomes an increasingly common part of your family's discussions and activities, you may start to acquire all sorts of maps for use at home, even wall maps like the ones found in most classrooms. If so, be sure you understand that all maps contain distortion—that is, all maps portray some areas as being larger or smaller than they actually are. This is not an error or a mistake on the part of the mapmaker, but it can cause you to make mistakes if your don't understand why and where the distortion occurs.

I still remember how this problem of distortion caused me to make an embarrassing mistake way back in the seventh grade. During the first week of geography class, our teacher asked the class to name all the countries that were larger in area than the United States. Well, after the initial flock of hands flew up to get credit for Canada and what was then called the Soviet Union, I confidently volunteered the answer "Greenland," because I had remembered how massive Greenland appeared on the map. A stunned silence fell over the class and was broken only by the teacher's incredulous response, "Greenland? Why, Greenland is only one-fourth as large as the United States."

What had I done? How could I be **that** wrong? Greenland just **couldn't** be that small.

Well, it is that small, but on the map I remember, and on the map your children probably see hanging on their classroom wall, Greenland is a huge country, quite a bit larger than the continental United States. The size of Greenland on these maps, you see, is greatly distorted, and this distortion is all due to a sixteenth-century Flemish mapmaker named Gerardus Mercator [pronounced mer-KAY-tur] who produced one of the most famous and most useful maps that has ever been created. Indeed, the most common map of the world in homes and classrooms today is called the "Mercator projection," which is characterized by its vertical lines of longitude (instead of the curved lines that all meet at the poles, as on a globe).

In creating his map, Mercator faced the identical problem that has faced every mapmaker for thousands of years and is still a problem for them today. The surface of the earth is curved, but a map of that surface must be flat, so something's got to give. You can't just peel off the printed covering of a globe, for example, and lay it out flat; it just won't squash down without tearing or buckling.

Try peeling an orange or a grapefruit so that the peel comes off in two identical halves. (Penetrate the peel with a sharp knife all the way around the circumference and then carefully inch your thumbnail between the fruit and the peel.) The two hemispheres will represent the eastern and western hemispheres of the earth's surface.

These curved surfaces cannot be flattened out without tearing. But if you make several cuts with your knife along the edges, each an inch or so long and extending out from the "north and south poles," the formerly curved surface now flattens out with ease.

Try this same procedure on the other hemisphere, only this time use a marking pen to draw identical circles all over the surface of the peel before making any cuts in it. These circles now represent equal areas of the earth's surface—continents, countries, oceans, lakes—as a globe would show them. Make the several cuts at the poles, flatten out the peel, and look at what has happened to the shape of the circles. The ones near the middle (the "equator") are intact, but the circles near the poles are broken. If we reconnect the lines of the broken circles by filling in the areas where the breaks occurred, their areas are much larger than their original areas were when we drew them.

A Mercator projection does much the same thing with an entire sphere (the surface of the earth) that we did with a hemisphere of orange or grapefruit peel. The distortion in a Mercator-style map of the earth is greatest near the north and south poles. All the lands and waters near the poles on this style map appear much larger than they actually are—much larger than they appear on a globe of the earth.

The closer to the equator you get on a Mercator-style map, the less distortion there is, and for navigators and travelers who didn't need to concern themselves with the far north and south latitudes, this map was an accurate and practical marvel of cartography.

But if you were in the seventh grade, and you had never tried to lay an orange peel out flat, you'd swear that Greenland was one of the largest countries on the earth.

USEFUL FAMILY RESOURCES

All About Maps and Mapmaking, by Susan Marsh, (New York: Random House, 1963) [J 526.8 MAR or J 912 MAR].

Earthsearch: A Kid's Geography Museum in a Book, by John Cassidy (Palo Alto, Cal.: Klutz Press, 1994) [J 372.35 CAS].

The Map Catalog: Every Kind of Map and Chart on Earth and Even Some Above It, edited by Joel Makower (New York: Vintage Books, 1992) [912.0294 MAP].

NetAmerica: Travel the 50 States on the Information Highway, by Gary M. Garfield and Suzanne McDonough (Parsippany, N.J.: Good Apple, 1996).

Understanding Maps: Charting the Land, Sea, and Sky, by Beulah Tannenbaum and Myra Stillman, (New York: McGraw-Hill, 1969) [526.8 TAN].

Where, on Earth, Are You?

At some point in your work with maps and globes, you and your children will encounter the words *longitude* and *latitude*, and at this point, your geographic understanding of the world will begin. This system of imaginary lines that people throughout the world use to identify locations on the earth is essential to your knowledge of geography—and astronomy, too—but I know that many people think of it as "school knowledge" and think they can neither teach it nor learn it at home. This is absolutely false, and, in fact, the home may very well be the best of all settings for teaching and learning this system.

In order for you and your children to feel comfortable with these imaginary lines called longitude and latitude, you must first realize that this is not the type of lesson that can, or should, be learned in a single session. So, don't be upset if you or your children don't "get it" right away, or if you get confused by the rather strange designations and terminology. This is a subject that you have to come back to from time to time, and from many different directions, so just keep an eye out for any opportunities that might allow you to think about and to talk about longitude and latitude with your children.

If you don't have a globe of the earth in your home, use one at your public library to acquaint your children with the imaginary lines that make the surface of the earth into a giant grid. Notice that any point on Earth can be described as being at the intersection of two lines: one running north and south, and the other running east and west. And because everyone on Earth uses this same system, all we have to do is identify which two lines we are talking about, and everyone else will know the exact position we are referring to.

Latitude and Longitude

The lines that are called *latitude* run east and west, or on a map from side to side, and their name comes from the Latin word *latus*, meaning "side." Notice that all the lines of latitude are parallel, and that is why they are also known as *parallels*.

The lines that are called *longitude* run north and south, from pole to pole. They are also called *meridians*, which comes from the Latin word for *midday*. When the sun is directly overhead, it is midday to all the people who live along that particular line of longitude, that meridian.

Notice that the lines of longitude are not parallel; they get closer together as they approach the poles, where they meet. So, the distance between any two lines of longitude varies depending upon how close you are to the equator, but the distance between any two lines of latitude remains exactly the same all around the earth.

The very best visualizing technique I have ever heard for this system came from one of my readers who wrote me that she saw the lines of longitude (the meridians) as being like the cuts in an apple after have you have pushed down one of those apple slicers over it. And the lines of latitude (the parallels) were like the cuts in a hard-boiled egg after you have sliced it with an egg slicer. Try slicing an apple and an egg for your children (after explaining longitude and latitude first with a globe), and see if this technique doesn't help them, too.

Your house, your child's school, and every other point on the entire earth lies along a specific parallel and along a specific meridian. Make sure your children understand that the several lines they see drawn on the globe are just reference lines, and they represent only a few of the thousands of imaginary parallels and meridians that crisscross the earth. If **all** the lines were drawn in, you wouldn't be able to see anything else on the globe.

Your "Global Address"

One of the best ways I have found to get children interested in understanding this system of longitude and latitude is to have them try to figure out their own "global address"; that is, the *exact* lines that intersect at *your own house*. The numbers that identify these specific lines, then, will—all by themselves—show anyone in the entire world *exactly* where you live.

The hardest thing for children (and adults) to get used to in this system is that it is not based on the usual zero to 100 range, as is the system of percent, for example. Instead, it is based on the idea that there are 360 degrees in a complete circle, 180 degrees in a half circle, 90 degrees in a quarter circle, and so on, which applies to other things as well (such as compass directions, for example) and is a valuable concept for children to know.

Although most mapmakers agreed long ago that there should be 360 lines of longitude extending from pole to pole in one complete trip around the earth, there was no agreement at all about where the numbering of these lines should begin; that is, which line should be labeled as the first or "prime" meridian. Almost every country thought that this designation rightfully belonged to the meridian that passed through its own capital, and so there was much confusion in the map world until 1884, when it was agreed that the "prime meridian" would be the one that passed through the Greenwich [pronounced GREN-itch] Astronomical Observatory in London, England.

All points along that line are labeled 0 degrees longitude. Meridians east of that line are labeled from 1 to 180 degrees "east longitude," and meridians to the west are labeled from 1 to 180 degrees "west longitude." Consequently, the 180-degree line is exactly halfway around the world from the prime meridian and is called the "international date line."

There was never any dispute, however, about the zero point for the lines of latitude because the equator provided a natural and accepted middle line between the North Pole and the South Pole. The lines north of the equator, then, were labeled from 1 to 90 degrees "north latitude," and the lines south of the equator were labeled from 1 to 90 degrees "south latitude."

Try picking out some coordinates for your children to locate on the globe (10 degrees south latitude, 75 degrees west longitude is in the country of Peru, for example). Then have them give you some coordinates to find.

In order to pinpoint areas more precisely, however, we have to divide these degree lines into smaller units (each degree of latitude covers about sixty-nine miles). The system chosen was to divide each degree into sixty *minutes*, and to divide each minute into sixty *seconds*. When conveyed in writing, minutes are usually followed by a single apostrophe (') and seconds by a double apostrophe ("), although they sometimes are given after decimal points. So 37°27'12"N and 37.27.12N both mean 37 degrees, 27 minutes, 12 seconds north latitude.

Even with a small globe, you can get your children to see approximately what the "global address" of their hometown is, and they should make a note of its approximate longitude and latitude. They can refine this estimate a little more by using the state and local maps in the road atlas (the Rand McNally version includes longitude and latitude marks along the edges of each map).

But to get an accurate fix on exactly where you are on the earth, try visiting the engineering branch of your city or county department of public works. They have highly detailed maps of your specific area along with precise descriptions of various points in longitude and latitude. (I have also found that most of the engineers and other employees who work with maps and precise coordinates every day, are so thrilled to find young people who are interested in learning about longitude and latitude that they often go out of their way to provide whatever information and materials they can.)

Another excellent resource that you can obtain quite inexpensively for your home is a very detailed map covering $7\frac{1}{2}$ minutes of longitude and latitude around your town. These "$7\frac{1}{2}$ minute," or "quadrangle" maps are available for $4 each (plus $3.50 postage), and you can find out exactly which map depicts your area by writing for the free *Catalog of Topographical Maps* from the U.S. Geological Survey, Earth Science Information Center, 507 National Center, Reston, VA 22092.

Once armed with a "quadrangle map" of your area, and a working knowledge of how degrees, minutes, and seconds of longitude and latitude can pinpoint the position of any spot on Earth, you and your children can embark upon an outdoor learning adventure together in which you will be doing some actual hands-on geographic study.

Bench Marks

By using a magnifying glass, you'll be able to comb the map for symbols that indicate the exact placement of survey markers, or "bench marks," that have been set into the earth, in very precisely measured positions, throughout the United States by various government agencies. (Some positions will be marked on the map with a black X, while others will be indicated by the letters *BM*.) No matter where you live, you can usually find several of these bench marks within a short distance from your home.

Bench marks.
Bronze discs like this one have been set in concrete all across the country (often in the sides of bridges and buildings) by government surveyors, and their positions measured precisely and recorded.

202

Another way to find out where these bench marks are located in your area is to contact the National Geodetic Survey Data Center on the Internet (http://ngs.noaa.gov). Just click on to the "NGS products" category, page down past the data sheets, and you'll find a feature that will list for you descriptions of, and directions to, all the bench marks that exist within a two-mile radius of any point (in longitude and latitude) you enter on your computer.

Now you and your children can have a fun-filled and rewarding time going out on a hunting expedition together to find each of these bench marks. Your map will put you in the right general area, but from then on what you'll be looking for will be a bronze disc, about four inches in diameter, that has been set in concrete and that bears the inscription of the surveying agency that placed it there.

This disc will also be inscribed with the *exact* elevation of that particular place on Earth—some report the elevation to $\frac{1}{1,000}$ of a foot above sea level, and the most recent ones to $\frac{1}{10,000}$ of a foot. Other markings will tell you the year that the bench mark was placed at that site, and an identifying number that you can use to learn the *exact* longitude and latitude of the site.

All you need do is telephone the government agency that surveyed the area and placed that particular bench mark in the earth (the U.S. Geological Survey can be reached at 314-341-0851, and the U.S. Coast and Geodetic Survey at 301-443-8631), and give them the identifying number that you found on the disc. They will then tell you the position of that marker with a precision of at least two, and sometimes three or four decimal places!

Just think for a minute about how precise a measurement that really is. Each degree of latitude (and longitude at the equator) covers about sixty-nine miles of the earth's surface, and so if you describe your "global address" in degrees only, you identify a spot that could be anywhere within a space of about 5,000 square miles. But a second is $\frac{1}{3,600}$ of a degree (a second covers about 100 feet of latitude), and so if you state your global address in degrees, minutes, and seconds, you will describe a plot of Earth that is about 100 feet on a side. Now, if you can report your position in hundredths (two decimal places) of a second, as even the oldest of these bench marks do, then you are identifying an individual and specific *square foot* on the entire surface of our planet!

Maps Can Mislead

When you and your children become familiar and comfortable with this general system of longitude and latitude, you will begin to see how it can reveal where the distortion exists in any flat map, and how difficult it is to portray the curved surface of the earth on the flat surface of a map. A "Mercator projection" of the earth, for example, shows all the lines of longitude as running straight up and down—that is, running north and south, *parallel to one another*. But we know that these lines are **not** parallel on a globe, and that they converge at the North Pole and at the South Pole. So, on a Mercator map, our view of the earth becomes more and more distorted as we get farther away from the equator.

But *every* type of flat map misrepresents the surface of the earth in some way, and it is by knowing how the system of longitude and latitude creates an imaginary grid on a globe that we can determine just where the distortion in any flat map occurs, and how much better a globe really is in giving us an accurate picture of the earth's surface. (You can obtain a free poster describing eighteen different map projections, highlighting their uses and their areas of distortion, by calling the U.S. Geological Survey's Earth Science Information Center at 1-800-USA-MAPS.)

Some maps of the United States, for example, mislead children into thinking that the northern border of our country is greatly curved. It certainly appears on these maps that the our border with Canada slopes southward from Washington state across Idaho, Montana, North Dakota, and Minnesota (and, that the state of Maine must contain the most northern lands in all the continental United States). But when we see our country outlined on a globe, we can tell right away that this stretch of our northern border is actually a line of latitude—the 49th parallel, specifically—and so it runs due east and due west all round the earth and is not "curved" at all. As we follow this 49th parallel to the east, we can see that it passes a hundred miles or so north of the most northern tip of Maine, and so we know that Maine is actually well south of the northern border of these other states.

Many state borders and national borders follow lines of longitude and latitude because those lines can be described and identified even though they are imaginary. In fact, almost every time you see a straight line on a map (or a gently curving line on some map projections), it will really be a parallel or a meridian. There are a few that are angled (the state borders of South Carolina, Georgia, Nevada, for example), but the vast majority of all these long, straight lines point exactly east and west or exactly north and south.

Using Parallels and Meridians

By understanding this fact, children can use state maps and national maps and even a globe of the earth to make geographic comparisons of various points in the United States and around the world. Look at the western United States, for example. The northern border of California is the 42nd parallel, which is also the northern border of Nevada and Utah. But if you follow this line due east, you will discover that the 42nd parallel is also the northern border of Pennsylvania. Along the way, it has passed right through O'Hare Airport in Chicago (there is a restaurant in the airport called the 42nd Parallel), and it will cross the eastern border of the

United State, in Cape Cod, Massachusetts. Continuing to the east, the 42nd parallel passes through Barcelona, Spain, and Rome, Italy. Did you ever think that Chicago could be just as far south as Rome? Well, continue tracing the parallel to the east and you'll see that both Chicago and Rome are also hundreds of miles *north* of Tokyo, Japan!

Once you and your children start following individual parallels and meridians on your globe, you'll come up with all sorts of astounding observations. For example, did you know that Reno, Nevada, is actually *west* of Los Angeles, California? Or that if you travel due south from Indianapolis, and leave the United States along the panhandle of Florida, the next continent you meet is *Antarctica?* (That's right. The entire continent of South America lies east of Indianapolis.)

Have your children ever heard about or thought about "digging a hole to China"? Well, the idea of digging a hole straight through the center of the earth and out the other side has been a popular fantasy for generations, in spite of the impossibility of the venture. But what if you could do the impossible? Would you surface in China?

Having a globe of the earth at your disposal and knowing your longitude and latitude, is really the only way to demonstrate to your children that if they started digging anywhere in the continental United States, they would come out in the waters of the Indian Ocean— thousands of miles south of China. Only if they started their journey in Hawaii would they emerge on land (the Kalahari Desert in southern Africa). And just where should they begin digging in order to wind up in China? (Try Chile or Argentina.)

Where, on Earth, are you, anyway? If that question came to you from a pen pal on another continent, or if it arrived in a radio signal from some being on another planet, would you be able to respond with your own "global address"?

USEFUL FAMILY RESOURCES

Family Geography Challenge.
For information about how to establish these workshops in your community, write or call the National Geographic Society, Geography Education Program, 1145 17th Street NW, Washington, DC 20036-4688; (202) 828-6661.

Helping Your Children Learn Geography, by Carol Sue Fromboluti (Washington, D.C.: U. S. Department of Education, 1996) [372.891 FRO]. To obtain a copy of this resource for your home, send $.50 to Geography, Dept. 372 D, Consumer Information Center, Pueblo, CO 81009.

National Geodetic Survey Data Center, 1315 E. West Highway, Silver Spring, MD 20910, telephone: 301-713-3242.

Understanding Maps: Charting the Land, Sea, and Sky, by Beulah Tannenbaum and Myra Stillman, (New York: McGraw-Hill, 1969) [526.8 TAN].

Where in the World Are You?, by Kay Cooper (New York: Avon Books, 1990) [J 910 COO].

The World Almanac and Book of Facts (contains longitude and latitude for the United States and world cities, $7.95) [032.02 WOR].

JANUARY 26: *Australia Day*

FEBRUARY 22: *Birth of George Washington*

MARCH 9: *Birth of Amerigo Vespucci*

APRIL 27: *Death of Ferdinand Magellan*

JULY 1: *Canada Day*

Many Roads Lead To Geography

I often complain that geography isn't given much attention in many schools today, but I do not mean by this that I think it should be treated as a separate and distinct course of study. Just as math shouldn't be taught only in math classes, and "proper English" shouldn't be reserved only for the speaking and writing that occurs in English classes, the study of geography ought to be a natural and common part of every class a child takes in school.

If you look for it, you'll find geography in everything, and this is just the advantage that the Family Learning of geography has over the rigid, subject-oriented curriculum that is found in most schools. Indeed, the ultimate purpose of this Family Learning approach is to get your children to see lessons about geography and opportunities for learning and applying geographic knowledge in all their classes and studies.

Linking Geography and Language

Think for a moment about the many obvious links and ties there are between the study of geography and the study of language: places and words. Just as we can trace the origin of many English words to the names of individual human beings from the past (for example, *guillotine, czar, sideburns*), so, too, can we find dozens of common, everyday words that owe their existence to the name of a particular city, country, river, or other identifiable place or feature on the surface of the earth. This provides us an interesting way to gain not only a better understanding of certain words, but also a way to connect those words to the names of places that we and our children can locate on a globe or map.

Look, for example, at the number of common foods that have taken their names from the cities where they were popularized. Today's *hamburger* started out as "Hamburg steak"

and was brought to America by immigrants from Hamburg, Germany. When you have found Hamburg on a map of Germany, have your children also locate the German city of Frankfurt, and they will find the home of the *frankfurter*. Brussels, Belgium, is the source for our *Brussels sprouts*, and on a map of Italy they'll find the cities of Bologna (*bologna* sausage), and Parma (*Parmesan* cheese), and the island of Sardinia (*sardines*). They can also look for the source of *lima* beans (Lima, Peru), *tangerines* (Tangier, Morocco), and the ever-popular *Swiss* cheese.

Many types of drinks have eponymous (see page 60) names, too, such as the wines called *Burgundy*, *Bordeaux*, and *champagne*, which are the names of the French regions in which they are produced. You'll find other regions and districts on the map that have equally familiar names, such as *Chianti* (Italy), *Daiquiri* (Cuba), and *Tequila* (Mexico).

You and your children will also find that the names for many things you wear appear on world maps, although often in somewhat different forms. A popular cotton fabric was originally called *serge de Nimes*, after the manufacturing town of Nimes [pronounced NEEM] in southern France, and *de Nimes* gradually collapsed into our common word *denim*. What we call *jeans* today can be traced to Genoa, Italy, just as *cashmere* derives its name from a state (Jammu and Kashmir) in northern India, which was formerly called Cashmere. And what do you think originated in Cologne, Germany?

 By linking language to geography, you'll help your children build their map skills and also their dictionary skills, because most of these word origins can be found within the appropriate entry in a good desk-size dictionary. (See whether your family dictionary will lead you to the geographic origins of the following words: *bikini, madras, fez, limerick, donnybrook, shanghai*.) For a more complete explanation of how various places became words, you'll need to browse the 422–423 section of your library for collections of word histories (such as *The Dictionary of Eponyms*, by Robert Hendrickson, and several by Charles Earle Funk). Here you'll find that the word *meander*, which means "to wander aimlessly," has a geographic origin in the name of a Turkish river that twists and turns many times on its way to the Aegean Sea.

Linking Geography and Science

The scientific world, too, can provide some interesting paths for you and your children to follow in your study of geography. I know of several families, for instance, who make it a practice, whenever they travel to a new state, to pay a visit to the highest point in that state. At home, they keep a map record of all the state summits they have attained, along with the elevation above sea level for each.

How does this link science to geography? Well, in order to understand how "the highest point" can be determined and measured, your children will need to learn about the scientific concepts of *sea level* and *air pressure*.

The elevation that is listed on a road map or in an almanac will tell you the height in feet above sea level. But just what is sea level anyway, and how can anybody know what that is, since none of the seas is ever level?

Good question. Tides and waves are constantly changing the heights of all the ocean waters, and so "sea level" actually refers to an average of all the hourly readings taken over a 19-year period (which spans all the tidal variations). The important point for your children to understand, though, is that sea level is the reference point or baseline for all measurements of the elevation of natural features such as mountains or lakes. Buildings, on the other hand, are measured from the ground up, and so while the country's tallest building, the Sears Tower in Chicago, rises 1,454 feet above the ground, its top is actually higher in the air than the highest natural point in 16 different states because the ground that the Sears Tower is built upon is already 595 feet above sea level. (However, the top of this building is still more than a thousand feet below the *lowest* natural point in Colorado!)

But just how can anyone know or measure the distance above or below sea level at any point on the earth? Well, here again, a little scientific knowledge—in this case the concept of air pressure or atmospheric pressure—can lead us to a fuller understanding of geography.

Atmospheric Pressure

Children need to understand that there is considerable weight to the several miles of air that is stacked up in a column directly overhead. Have them hold the palm of their hand out horizontally, and then have them imagine and visualize the column of atmosphere— nineteen miles high—that is pressing down on the surface of their hand with a force of almost 300 pounds! It's true. The air molecules directly above your hand, all the way to the edge of the atmosphere, exert a downward pressure of approximately 14.7 pounds per square inch on your hand, and if there were no air underneath your hand to exert an equal pressure upward, you wouldn't be able to lift your hand off the floor.

Having your children visualize air pressure or atmospheric pressure as the weight of the air directly above them encourages them to see that the higher up into the air they go, the less air there will be to press down on them, and the lower will be the weight of that column of air. So, you should be able to tell your elevation just by weighing the air above you.

And that's exactly what a barometer does. The name *barometer* is derived from the Greek words *baros*, meaning "weight," and *metron*, meaning "measure." If you affix a barometer to a scale that shows elevation instead of air pressure, you will have an instrument known as an *altimeter* [pronounced al-TIMM-it-er], which pilots use to tell them how high they are flying above the ground, and which some motorists attach to their dashboards to show them the elevation of the terrain they are crossing.

If you and your children are interested in learning more about the highest points in the various states, you might want to write to a group called the Highpointers Club, whose members try to visit each state's summit, from the highest (20,320 feet) in Alaska to the lowest (345 feet) in Florida. Yearly dues are $5. Address your letters to Highpointers Club, P.O. Box 327, Mountain Home, Arkansas 72653-0327.

Linking Geography and History

Another subject in which you can find many tie-ins to geography is in the study of history. These two areas—history and geography—are really inseparable because the course of history depends so much upon location and climate and resources, and with a little imagination, you can come up with many other connections that will launch you and your children from history right into geography. For example, many schools use the occasion of George Washington's birthday to focus children's attention and study on Washington's contributions to our country and on the historical events in which Washington was involved. But think of the learnings in geography that can branch off from a focus on Washington's name alone. The Father of Our Country holds the all-time record for having the most places named after him, and this is an international record, too, for no other country has so honored any one human being. Washington is memorialized not only in the name of our nation's capital, but in the names of 1 state; 33 counties; 121 cities, towns, and villages; 257 townships; 10 lakes; 8 streams; 7 mountains; and thousands of streets, parks, schools, and other human creations. (There is even a mountain in Colorado that is named for his wife, Martha: Mount Lady Washington.)

Do your children know of any streets or buildings in your town that are named after our first president? Is there a city or a county in your state that is named Washington? How about in the states that border your own, or in states that your children have visited?

Have your children look in the "Index" section in the back of a road atlas. The location of each listed city is usually given as a set of coordinates on a particular map, for example: "Washington, Georgia, p. 23, G-10." The map on page 23 of my atlas shows the state of Georgia. Sections labeled with the alphabet extend down one side of the map, and sections labeled with numbers run across the top. The intersection of the areas labeled "G" and "10" is the area in which I should look to find the city of Washington on this map.

All right, now let's branch off into the names of other presidents and see where their names are memorialized. There are no states named for presidents other than Washington, but there are four state capitals that bear the names of presidents (Madison, Wisconsin; Lincoln, Nebraska; Jefferson City, Missouri; Jackson, Mississippi). Use the index of the road atlas again and have a contest with your children to see whether a state that you pick has more towns that are named after U.S. presidents than the state your child picks. In a search like this, you'll come across many curious facts; for instance, you'll find towns named Lincoln in fifteen of our states, but not one of those states lies below the Mason-Dixon line. Here, then, is a great opportunity to branch off even further into discussions and investigations about the Civil War, names of Confederate heroes, or the meaning of "Mason-Dixon line."

Naming the Americas

The names of other historic figures are even more closely tied to the study of geography—famous explorers, for example. The entire continent on which we live, and the continent to our south, as well, bear the name of an explorer about whom our children may know nothing at all. But it would be truly unfortunate if they also knew nothing about the continents. Let's take a brief look at the history of the name *America*, and use it to launch us toward a better understanding about the seven land masses that form the surface of the earth.

North America and South America were named for Amerigo Vespucci [pronounced ves-PEW-chee]—a fifteenth-century merchant and adventurer from Florence. He was not the first explorer to reach these continents, nor did he ever suggest that they should be named for him. In fact, he died without ever knowing that they were. But the name America became applied to the lands of the New World anyway, in part because a young German mapmaker had simply not heard about the voyages of Christopher Columbus.

Amerigo Vespucci did, indeed, explore the coast of what is now South America on four separate voyages. His several letters describing his exploits (and some forgeries of those letters that contained even more sensational descriptions) came to the attention of Martin Waldseemuller, who was preparing a book of maps showing all the lands that were known to exist at the beginning of the sixteenth century. Waldseemuller drew in the land masses described in Vespucci's letters, and in the introduction to his book, he suggested that these new lands "be called Amerigo...or America" in honor of their discoverer. Later, when he learned of Columbus's voyages, he removed the designation "America" from his maps (calling the area "the Land Unknown"), but by then his earlier work had gone through several editions, and people had become accustomed to calling the New World "America".

Unlike Columbus, Vespucci did recognize that these new lands were not part of Asia but were an entirely separate continent instead. Now, just what is a continent, anyway?

Continents

A continent is usually defined as "a large continuous landmass located on the surface of the earth." I said earlier that there were seven continents, and when we help our children to locate and identify these continents on the globe, some questions are sure to arise.

Listed in order of their size, the seven continents are Asia, Africa, North America, South America, Antarctica, Europe, and Australia. But your children will probably notice that only two of these landmasses are "superislands," that is, unconnected to any other continents: Australia and Antarctica. North America and South America are connected at the Isthmus of Panama (*isthmus* comes from an ancient Greek word that meant "narrow passage"). Knowing this, can they tell which continent contains Mexico and the countries of Central America? (Answer: North America)

Africa is connected to Asia at the Isthmus of Suez, and Europe is really just a large peninsula on the giant landmass called Asia. So, you could say that there are just four "large continuous landmasses located on the surface of the earth," and, indeed, the boundary between Europe and Asia is so artificial that many people today refer to the entire landmass as "Eurasia." But in studying the globe with your children, what you want to concentrate on is not the definition, but the recognition of the positions and the shapes of the seven continents listed above.

If they ask why Antarctica is a continent but the northern polar cap is not, make sure they know that beneath all the ice of Antarctica is actual land, which, like all land, is part of the earth's crust, but the ice at the North Pole floats in the Arctic Ocean.

Voyage of Magellan

Some of the voyages of famous explorers are so well documented that we can make this necessary tie between history and geography simply by tracing their exact routes on a globe or a map. I remember how this simple exercise helped me provide the correct answer to a "trick" question that appeared on a test I took some time ago—a test written by someone who didn't even know this was a "trick" question. The question was "Who was the first person to sail completely around the earth?" and the suggested answers included "Christopher Columbus," "Ferdinand Magellan," "Vasco da Gama," "Marco Polo," and "none of the above." I answered "none of the above" because, although most people associate the name Ferdinand Magellan with the first circumnavigation of the globe,

Magellan was killed by natives in what is now the Philippine Islands on April 27, 1521, and so he never completed the last leg of the trip back to Spain.

Actually, Magellan never intended to sail around the world in the first place. He thought that the "Spice Islands" (which are called the Moluccas [pronounced muh-LUCK-uz] today and lie just west of New Guinea) and their treasures of pepper, cloves, and nutmeg, could be reached more quickly by sailing west from Spain instead of east. Like many others of his day, Magellan believed that the ocean surrounding the Spice Islands was quite small, and so these islands must be very near the lands of the New World.

You really have to look at a globe of the earth to see how wrong Magellan was about this, and tracing his route on that globe with your children can be a great geography lesson because it is "peppered" with familiar names that we owe to Magellan himself.

From southern Spain, Magellan's five ships and 240 sailors headed south and west, skirting the African coast until they neared the equator, and then headed across the Atlantic toward the east coast of today's Brazil. Magellan was sure that a passageway existed that would connect the Atlantic to the ocean on the other side of the New World, but no one had found it yet. Balboa had seen that ocean from Panama and had named it *El Mar del Sur* ("the South Sea") because, as you can see by looking at Panama on the globe, the Atlantic Ocean is to the north and this other ocean lay to the south. (We still use this name when we speak of the islands of the Pacific as the "South Sea Islands.")

As Magellan continued down the coast of South America looking for this passage, he sighted a tall mountain and exclaimed "Monte video!" (meaning, "I see a mountain!"), which is how the modern capital of Uruguay got its name.

Finally, Magellan's party ventured into a narrow passage that eventually opened onto that South Sea, which Magellan renamed "Pacific" because it appeared so calm and peaceful. This narrow waterway—which is still called the Strait of Magellan—can be seen on the globe near the southern tip of South America. And notice the spelling of the word *strait*, which means "narrow" or "restricted" and comes from the Latin word meaning "to draw together." This meaning and spelling (not *straight*) are also part of *straitjacket*, *strait-laced*, and *in dire straits*.

Now look at the 10,000 miles of "peaceful" ocean that lies between the Strait of Magellan and the Philippines. Sailing this enormous distance required much more food and water than Magellan's ships had on board, and the crew eventually resorted to eating rats and rawhide and even sawdust to stay alive. Still, many died of hunger and dehydration before the ships finally reached the island known today as Guam.

The westward route was not the shorter way after all, as Juan Sebastian del Cano—who assumed command after Magellan's death (and whose name is probably the best answer to the question about who first circumnavigated the globe)—confirmed when he continued on around Africa's Cape of Good Hope and north to Spain once again, arriving with just one of the original five ships and only seventeen of the 240 original crew.

Now just think of all the geography knowledge that your children would have missed if their study of Magellan had been confined to the subject of history only. And just how could they have gotten any worthwhile understanding of Magellan's voyage if their study had not included a globe of the earth as a featured learning device?

We can find worthwhile and useful geographic ties to history in more places than in just the lives of historical characters. Countries, themselves, have both a history and a place on the earth, and because that history is tied to that place, any understanding of the country must include knowledge about both.

Learning About Canada

What do your children know about our northern neighbor—Canada—for example? Is the extent of their knowledge confined to just a few wistful images of Eskimos, ice hockey, and red-coated mounties? Do they know the names and locations of any of the ten provinces and two territories that make up this second-largest country in the world? (Russia is the largest.)

Our general ignorance about Canada is especially vexing in that our two peoples are so closely tied, sharing as we do the longest undefended border on the planet. Two-thirds of all the people in Canada live within 100 miles of the United States, and 90 percent live within 200 miles.

But our ties with Canada are historical as well as geographic. After we won our independence from the British in 1781, for instance, more than 40,000 colonists who remained loyal to the king fled to Canada. When these Loyalists demanded a colony of their own, the British government carved out a section of Nova Scotia for them and called it New Brunswick.

Canada celebrates its birthday on July 1 every year, a date that commemorates the passage of the British North America Act in 1867, which united four provinces into the Dominion of Canada. Even this holiday, which is called Canada Day, shows how closely and how long our two nations have been tied, for the unification of the Canadian provinces into a single country came about, in part, because the end of our own Civil War created a fear among many that the United States would seek to control all of North America and would soon mount an invasion against the disunited colonies to its north.

We can help introduce Canadian history to our children through library books (look in the 971 section of the juvenile collection), but our first duty is to help them understand where Canada is in the world and where it is in relation to the United States. With a globe of the earth at your disposal, you can show your children not only how immense Canada's area is, but also how much of its territory is made up of islands. Canada contains three of the world's ten largest islands; Baffin Island itself is as large as the country of Spain. Canada has over a million lakes and contains about one-tenth of all the freshwater on Earth.

The maps of Canada in an inexpensive road atlas will be even more useful in helping you and your children become familiar with the names and positions of Canada's provinces and major cities. Family questions and games can then be generated by any mention of a Canadian baseball or hockey team (In what province do the Expos play their home games? Answer: Quebec), or by such common images as the Labrador retriever (part of Newfoundland lies on the Labrador Peninsula) and Niagara Falls (it separates the province of Ontario from the state of New York).

Learning About Australia

Or perhaps you might celebrate Australia Day in your home, and make this island-nation a focus of your family's discussions and activities on that day. Once again, the combination of geography and history will give your children a better understanding about Australia than will either subject studied separately.

Australia Day is celebrated on January 26 and commemorates the arrival (in 1788) of the first European settlers on the continent of Australia. The eleven ships that anchored in what is now Sydney Harbor carried about 1,000 passengers, three-fourths of them convicts who were being shipped from London to ease the overcrowding in the prisons there and to work off their sentences as laborers in this uncharted wilderness.

Australia was not only uncharted, but also entirely unknown to explorers from the rest of the world well after all the other continents had been located and mapped with some precision. In fact, Australia got its name from the mysterious land that mapmakers back around 1500 had drawn in the South Pacific without any evidence that such a land actually existed. They labeled this imagined land *Terra Australis Incognita*, which were the Latin words meaning "the Unknown Southern Land."

Australis, in Latin, means "southern," and that is why the dazzling visual display we call the *aurora borealis*, or "northern lights," is called *aurora australis* ("southern lights") in the southern polar regions. (*Aurora* is the Latin word meaning "dawn.")

Australia is very similar in size to the forty-eight contiguous United States. Indeed, Australia even looks a little like the shape of the United States, if we flip our country over so that the southern tip of Florida and Texas are pointing north.

This idea might suggest a way to help your children recognize the shapes of various countries and continents. Trace the outlines of all the continents and of easily identifiable nations (such as the United States, Canada, India, Italy, Australia, France, Brazil, Chile, Argentina, Mexico, China, and any others you wish to focus on) on tracing paper from the large globe at your library or from the maps in a world atlas. Then use these shapes to make cutouts from heavy construction paper, which you can then use in a guessing game (rather like flashcards) with your children—and don't forget to let them quiz you as well.

"Concentration"

Another game idea that you might try as a way to combine geography with other areas of your children's studies is a television game that used to be called "Concentration." This format can be adapted to almost any subject or topic or combination that you want to focus on with your children, and so I will show you just one adaptation, and you can apply it to other areas as you wish.

Let's say that we are trying to help our children associate various cities and countries in the world with certain symbols and images that are commonly linked to them. The image of the Eiffel Tower, for example, is often used to represent the city of Paris in pictures and drawings, just as the Golden Gate Bridge is identified with the city of San Francisco. The Washington Monument symbolizes Washington, D.C., the Acropolis symbolizes Athens, and London is represented by the Clock Tower of Parliament ("Big Ben" is really the bell, not the clock, in that tower).

Cut out pictures of these buildings and monuments from travel magazines (particularly the advertisements) and from the free brochures that are given out by airlines, cruise lines, and local travel agents. Then take about twenty blank file cards and paste a cutout on half of them; you might include the name of the structure as well. On the other ten cards, write the name of the city and country that is associated with the structure.

Lay all the cards out in columns and rows on a table, with only their blank side showing. Each player turns two cards over, looking for a matching pair (New York City, for example, would be a match for the Statue of Liberty). If the cards match, the player collects them into a pile of his or her own and gets another turn. If the cards don't match, they are returned to their blank side, and the next player gets to take a turn.

You may choose to include some buildings that stand for countries instead of specific cities. The Pyramids, for instance, could symbolize all of Egypt; the Taj Mahal is identified with India, while the Leaning Tower could stand for Italy or the city of Pisa.

216

Australia—A Lucky Land, by Al Stark (New York: Macmillan Child Group, 1987) [J 994 STA].

The Book of Where: Or How to Be Naturally Geographic, by Neill Bell (Boston: Little, Brown and Company, 1982) [J 910 BEL].

Don't Know Much About Geography: Everything You Need to Know About the World but Never Learned, by Kenneth C. Davis (New York: Morrow, 1992) [910.76].

The Naming of America: How Continents, Countries, States, Counties, Cities, Towns, Villages, Hamlets, & Post Offices Came by Their Names, by Allan Wolk (Nashville, Tenn.: Thomas Nelson, Inc., 1977) [929.4 WOL or 973 WOL].

The Science Chef Travels Around the World: Fun Food Experiments and Recipes for Kids, by Joan D'Amico and Karen Eich Drummond (New York: John Wiley & Sons, 1996) [J 507.8 DAM or J 641.5 DAM].

Stories of the States: A Reference Guide to the Fifty States and U. S. Territories, by Frank Ross, Jr. (New York: Thomas Y. Crowell, 1969) [J 973 ROS].

Why Do They Call It Topeka? How Places Got Their Names, by John W. Pursell (New York: Citadel Press, 1995) [J 912 PUR].

Why in the World: Adventures in Geography, by George J. Demko (New York: Anchor Books, 1992) [910 DEM].

Astronomy Begins at Home, and Our Home Is Earth

For many parents, as for many adults in general, the mere mention of *astronomy* conjures up images of telescopes and other expensive pieces of equipment, along with notions about how difficult it is to understand the workings of the universe and how it is best left to professional scientists and astronomers anyway. I don't know where this reluctance about studying astronomy originates, or why people believe that basic astronomy is beyond the mental powers of the general population, but I suspect that it has something to do with our failure to understand the difference between *learning* and *schooling*.

Schooling has always been conducted during the daylight hours, and so the study of astronomy has never been thought of as an appropriate element in the science curriculum for grade schools or high schools or for schools that train teachers, as well. Consequently, the general population—adults and children alike—hear about astronomy only from experts on those special occasions when an occurrence in the heavens happens to be a newsworthy event: an eclipse of the sun, the appearance of a comet, the photos of planets and galaxies sent back from satellites and space probes.

Other than that, we hear about the stars and planets only from science fiction writers, astrologers, and astrophysicists, and this suggests to most people that astronomy is fanciful, or fraudulent, or philosophical. But astronomy has as little to do with *Star Wars* as it does with knowing your birth sign, and because we are led to believe that astronomers are only concerned with the physics of black holes and "the big bang," we overlook the fact that astronomy involves things that are important to us—things like weather, and climate, and tides, and the feeling of wonder that wells up inside us when we look up at a starry sky.

218

The Family Learning of astronomy is concerned with the practical, everyday lessons that can be learned and reinforced through common experience. Its purpose is not to explain the origin of the universe or distract our attention from problems and responsibilities we have here on Earth, but neither is it so rooted in the practical that it diminishes our sense of wonder about celestial bodies and about our place in the universe.

Just as the Family Learning of geography makes our children aware of where they live on the surface of their planet, so the Family Learning of astronomy helps them to see that planet as their "home," and to find out where their home is in relation to other objects in the universe. Our goal, as learners ourselves and as guides for our children's learning, is to be able to walk out under an open sky, daytime or nighttime, and feel a sense of familiarity—a sense of understanding and belonging—with the sun and the moon and the stars and the planets that share with us the vastness of space.

The Family Learning of astronomy, however, will probably not find any direct application in our children's schoolwork, and so in this one subject area we must provide all the inspiration and motivation and materials and reinforcements if we want our children to understand the movements of the earth and to know their way around the night sky. We must, therefore, use a variety of paths in our approach to astronomy. Rather than treating it as a subject itself, we must be constantly vigilant for opportunities to relate facts and events of daily life to their celestial causes and origins.

Time Zones

For example, when your family hears a television announcer say that a certain football game will be televised at "eight o'clock in the East, seven in the Midwest, and five Pacific time," do your children understand how and why the same game can be occurring at different times in different parts of the country? Or perhaps you might want to use the twice yearly resetting of the nation's clocks (daylight saving—not savings—time begins on the first Sunday in April and ends on the last Sunday in October) as appropriate occasions for getting your children to see how an understanding of time changes, time zones, and even the time of day itself requires an understanding of astronomy and the movements of the earth. This family focus on what time it is in different parts of the country and different parts of the world offers an ideal bridge from the study of geography to the study of astronomy because it allows children to progress from seeing their world as a stable and fixed surface on a map or globe to seeing it as a planet that is in constant motion through space.

As the earth rotates toward the east, the morning sun becomes visible to the people in, let's say, New York while it is still dark in Chicago, Denver, and Los Angeles. Morning occurs along the East Coast of the United States about an hour before it occurs in the Midwest, two hours before it occurs in the Rocky Mountains, and three hours before it occurs along the West Coast. The same can be said for noontime (the sun is directly overhead in the eastern United States three hours before it will be directly overhead to people living in the West), and for nightfall as well. I am constantly amazed at how few schoolchildren understand that it is the rotation of the earth that causes this to be so.

The best way to introduce your children to the way that the earth's rotation causes daytime and nighttime around the planet is to place a globe in a darkened room and hold a flashlight (representing the sun) just above the equator. Let the edge of the flashlight beam fall on the east coast of the United States and have your child turn the globe slowly to the east so that the edge of the beam approaches the Midwest, then the West Coast, then Hawaii, and so on around the earth. Your children should understand that when the edge of the beam approaches any area, it corresponds to the first rays of morning light for the people who live there. The trailing edge of the beam corresponds to the dusk of evening wherever it falls.

As your children turn the globe slowly to the east (hold the flashlight still so that you reinforce the concept of a fixed sun and a moving Earth), have them estimate what time it would be (morning, noon, evening, or night) in various cities across the United States and around the world. They should begin to see that when morning breaks in New York, let's say 7 A.M., it is quite dark in San Francisco, and that if we all used the same clock setting, sunrise wouldn't occur until 10 A.M. there, and not until after noon in Honolulu! Obviously, there have to be "time zones" in order to make sunrise, noon, and sunset occur at approximately the same clock hours all around the world.

When this idea is firmly fixed in their minds, look in the first few pages of your local telephone directory for a map titled Time Zones and Area Codes. Now use the flashlight again to create an artificial dawn over the East Coast on this map as your child moves the map to the east and watches the "sun" come up in the Central Time Zone, the Mountain Time Zone, and the Pacific Time Zone.

Here's where our knowledge of geography can be put to good use. The entire earth rotates through 360 degrees (a full circle) in twenty-four hours, which figures out to fifteen degrees every hour. So the sun's light appears to move across the face of the earth at a rate of 15 degrees of longitude (the lines that extend from pole to pole) each hour. Did you ever wonder why the only longitude lines that are shown on most globes are 15 degrees apart? That's how far the edge of daylight and the edge of darkness move every hour. These 15-degree segments correspond roughly to the twenty-four time zones that begin in Greenwich [pronounced GREN-itch], England, and circle the entire earth.

Look at the telephone book map again and you'll notice that the actual boundaries of our time zones are not the straight, north-south lines of longitude. Instead, they conform with some state boundaries and some local boundaries, so it is often difficult to know whether a town that lies near the border of two zones sides with its neighbors to the east or to the west. But if you think that our boundaries are irregular, you should look in a multivolume encyclopedia (under "time zones") for a map of world time zones. There you'll learn that clocks on the island of Newfoundland (off the east coast of Canada) are set **a half hour** ahead of those in the rest of eastern Canada! That's right: When it's noon in New Brunswick and in Nova Scotia, it's *12:30* P.M. on the island of Newfoundland. Clocks in India and in the central territories of Australia are also **a half hour** different from time zones to their east and west. China spans four time zones, but all the clocks in that country are set to the time in its capital, Beijing.

Movements of the Earth

By having your children begin their study of astronomy close to home—that is, by focusing on the rotation of Planet Earth instead of faraway stars and galaxies—you have put them in an ideal position for carrying on their investigation of the heavens. It is absolutely necessary for them to use their imagination and their knowledge to "look back at Earth" from a position somewhere in space. This is just what they are doing when they see the flashlight beam fall on the rotating globe, and it is what they must do in order to understand the other movements of the earth as well.

What other movements, you ask? Well, sit down in a comfortable chair, and try to remain very, very still. There, now how fast would you say you are going?

Since we all are on the surface of the earth, and since that earth is constantly rotating, we all are in motion even when we think we're sitting still. In fact, because the earth makes one complete rotation every twenty-four hours, and because the circumference of the earth at the equator is approximately 25,000 miles, anyone living at the equator would be traveling at a constant speed of 25,000 miles in twenty-four hours, or a little more than 1,000 miles per hour.

Now, you don't live at the equator, and so you aren't going that fast. The distance around the earth (along any latitude) gets smaller as you move away from the equator, and so the nearer to the poles you live, the less distance you'll travel during each rotation, and the slower your speed will be. People living in the southernmost part of the United States, for example, are whirring around at about 900 miles per hour, while those in Anchorage, Alaska, are going only about 500 miles per hour. And at the North Pole? Well, there your speed would be zero.

But wait a minute. This planet we are riding on is not only spinning on its axis, it is flying through space as it orbits the sun, too. Each year our planet travels 584 million miles in its orbit around the sun, and so all of us, no matter where we live, are cruising around this loop at an average speed of 18.5 miles every second, or 66,600 miles per hour. But there's more.

Not only is our planet in motion, but so is our solar system. All nine planets, and all their moons, and our sun are moving together in space. Astronomers have noticed that the stars near Vega (the third brightest star in the sky) and those in the constellation Hercules seem to be moving away from one another, and they reason that this is because we are moving closer toward them. Our solar system, therefore, is moving in the general direction of Hercules, and scientists have measured the speed of this movement to be about twelve miles every second—that's another 43,000 mph. Brace yourself, there's still more.

Our sun is just one of billions of stars that make up the galaxy known as the Milky Way. This galaxy seems to be in the shape of an incredibly huge disc or saucer, and we live about two-thirds of the way out from its center. The entire galaxy is turning or spinning like a wheel, and it makes one complete revolution every 200 million years. The farther away from the center of the galaxy you happen to be, the greater distance you will travel during those 200 million years, and so the faster your speed will be. The best estimate we can make about our own speed of rotation is that it is more than 500,000 miles per hour.

But our Milky Way appears to be doing more than rotating. In fact, all the galaxies (and there are millions that we know of) appear to be moving away from one another at speeds that approach the speed of light.

So, how fast are you going, even when you are sitting very still? Who knows? A tremendous speed, to be sure, but because everything and everybody else is moving at that speed, too, we think and feel that we are motionless, and for all practical purposes we are. But this exercise is a good way to get children to think about the wonders of their universe, and to see their own planet as being nested in larger and larger systems, rather like a set of huge Russian eggs that all fit inside one another. And in order for them to imagine each successively wider view of their universe, they must push their imaginary viewing platform farther and farther out into space.

Viewing Earth From Space

Now let's bring that platform back closer to Earth once again, so that we can get a picture of how our planet looks from satellites that orbit above it, and how it looked to the astronauts who viewed it from the moon.

Until 1959, when the very first photo of Earth was transmitted from space by the *Explorer VI* satellite, every model and likeness we had ever made of our planet had been based upon conjectures. But that first satellite photo, which was taken from 19,500 miles above Mexico, showed us a world that was in many ways very similar to the one represented by our classroom globes. Yet it was much different, too, for the countries of the world and the states of the United States weren't separated by differing colors or by artificial boundary lines, nor was there any sign of the equator or the Arctic Circle or the international date line, which are all prominent features and reference points on our globes. Though a globe of the earth is a wonderful and necessary home learning aid, it can create some confusion for us as well, if we think of it as a perfect representation of how Earth would appear to an observer in space.

Place a globe of the earth on a table, and have your children imagine that they are astronauts looking back on their home planet from the surface of the moon. This requires some vivid imagination, for the only surface distinctions they would see would be the different colors of land, water, and ice.

They could locate the United States, but could they see the entire outline of any individual state? (Yes: Hawaii.) Which countries could they trace completely? (Island-nations like Australia, Greenland, Iceland, Sri Lanka, and Madagascar, and others that have rivers and lakes for boundaries, but none whose borders follow a straight line. Nature herself does not make long, straight lines.)

Globes can confuse us even more if we aren't careful to view them with an accurate sense of proportion. Some models, for instance, have a raised surface to indicate the various mountain ranges of the world. These "relief" globes are usually quite expensive, and they can also lead us to a distorted view of the earth. If a twelve-inch diameter globe represents an Earth whose diameter is approximately 8,000 miles, then each $\frac{1}{4}$-inch bump on a relief globe would represent a mountain 167 miles high! (That's more than thirty times the height of Mt. Everest.) Our earth has, in fact, a surprisingly smooth surface when you consider how vast that surface really is. If the earth were reduced, in perfect proportion, to the size of a billiard ball, it would have a smoother surface than any billiard ball ever manufactured.

Children need to develop this sense of proportion about the earth, and you can help them do so. Put your globe in the corner of the living room and then explain to your child that each globe diameter you move away represents one Earth diameter, or 8,000 miles. Our moon is about thirty Earth diameters away (approximately 240,000 miles), so to see how our planet would look to someone on the moon, have your child move back thirty feet and see what features can be recognized on the globe. How would the earth look to someone standing on Mars? You'd have to move back more than three-quarters of a mile to get this perspective.

Now let's come back a little closer to Earth. Most of us think that our shuttle astronauts orbit the Earth from the distant reaches of space, while actually, the shuttles operate in a very low Earth orbit—about 175 miles above the surface. Where would this be in proportion to the size of your globe? Well, if you hold the globe about a quarter of an inch from your eyes, you'll have the same view of Earth that the shuttle astronauts have during a space walk.

There is one more way that we can use a globe to give our children a sense of proportion about their planet and its place in the universe. The layer of air that sustains all life on Earth and in which all the world's weather occurs (the portion of the atmosphere known as the troposphere) is only eight or ten miles deep, and only about half that deep over the poles. So, all the plant and animal life on Earth depends for its existence upon a layer of gases that is so thin it corresponds to the thickness of the wax coating that covers your globe! What better image can there be for helping our children understand how important and how fragile this layer of irreplaceable, life-sustaining atmosphere really is?

USEFUL FAMILY RESOURCES

Comparisons: Of Distance, Size, Area, Volume, Mass, Weight, Density, Energy, Temperature, Time, Speed, and Number Throughout the Universe, by The Diagram Group (New York: St. Martin's Press, 1982) [530.8 DIA].

Earth—Our Planet in Space, by Seymour Simon (New York: Four Winds Press, 1984) [J 525 SIM].

The Earth: Planet Number Three, by Franklyn M. Branley (New York: Thomas Y. Crowell Co., 1966) [J 525 BRA].

Earthwatch: Space-time Investigations with a Globe, by Julius Schwartz (New York: McGraw-Hill Book Co., 1977) [J 525 SCH].

MARCH 20 (APPROX.): *Spring equinox* SEPTEMBER 22 (APPROX.): *Autumn equinox*
JUNE 21 (APPROX.): *Summer solstice* DECEMBER 21 (APPROX.): *Winter solstice*

Shadows Help You Celebrate Solar Holidays in Your Home

One of the benefits of Family Learning is that it doesn't have to conform to an artificial calendar of certain weekdays in which school happens to be in session, and so it can take advantage of those learning opportunities that don't happen to fall conveniently into the school year. There are, in fact, four very special days each year that are opportune times for your children to obtain a better understanding of Earth's orbit around the sun, yet only two of these days occur during the school year, and then only occasionally. So, unless we are alert to these opportunities and avail ourselves of them in our homes, our children will probably have less knowledge of the sun's changing arc in the sky than the most unschooled peasants had thousands of years ago.

Special Points in Earth's Orbit

The four special days that I am referring to are the spring equinox [pronounced EE-kwih-nocks], the summer solstice [pronounced SOUL-stiss], the autumn equinox, and the winter solstice. I like to think of these four days as being "solar holidays" because each marks a special point in the earth's orbit around the sun, and because each of these days was known to our ancient ancestors and celebrated by them as a special day long before calendars were ever invented.

Parents who want their children to understand why these four days are so special, and who want to use the solstices and equinoxes as "refresher points" during the year to reinforce their children's knowledge about the workings of the solar system, may want to make these solar holidays special by creating family traditions and celebrations to accompany them. For example, some families I know prepare their children's favorite family dinner on each solstice and equinox. Others exchange little gifts or create their own greeting cards to share within their family on these four days.

What do these little celebrations have to do with learning? Well, having these four family celebrations that children can look forward to each year provides an opportunity for those children to wonder what it is that they are celebrating. Bingo! The door is open, and now the explanations and demonstrations and reinforcements that you do with them all have purpose and are much more likely to lead to real learning.

The best way for parents to reinforce their own knowledge of the earth's path around the sun, so that they can explain and demonstrate to their children why these four solar holidays are such special occasions, is to head for the children's section of the local library. It is in the books designed for children that adults will find the clearest descriptions and the most useful and understandable drawings of the relationship between our planet and its sun. The adult books that deal with this topic assume that the reader already has a basic understanding of Earth's orbit and astronomy in general, but the children's books make no such assumptions, and so they can give adults the basic understanding that will allow them to make use of more advanced sources later on.

As you roam through the 523–529 section of the juvenile books in your library, look especially for *Exploring the Sky*, by Richard Moeschl, and *Earthwatch: Space-time Investigations with a Globe*, by Julius Schwartz. These books offer many useful activities and projects (such as making a family sundial out of an old flowerpot) that your and your children can do at home to better understand the earth, sun, moon, and stars.

But, for now, I will give you a brief introduction to these four special days so that you can see why they have been so special throughout human history and how they can serve as "refresher points" throughout the year to help reinforce your children's knowledge of the solar system.

The earth's axis (the imaginary line that extends through the poles) is not perpendicular to the plane of earth's orbit; that is, the poles don't point straight up and down as our planet runs its annual course around the sun. If you were standing on the sun, you would see the Earth follow a flat, almost circular path, but you would also see that the spin of the earth was not on the same level as this path. The earth's axis is tilted $23\frac{1}{2}$ degrees away from being straight up and down (perpendicular to its orbital plane), just as it appears on your globe.

The $23\frac{1}{2}$-degree tilt of the earth's axis means that the northern hemisphere is pointed away from the sun for six months of the earth's orbit and pointed toward the sun for the other six months. When it is tipped away from the sun, there is winter above the equator;

the days are shorter; the nights are longer; the sun traces a path low in the southern sky. But beginning with the day of the winter solstice>, this pattern starts to reverse. The days begin to grow longer; the sun begins to pass higher overhead; winter gradually looses its grip on the northern latitudes; spring begins and summer will soon follow. So, it is this tilt in the earth's axis that causes all the differences between summer and winter, and the changing seasons have nothing whatsoever to do with the annual variations in the earth's distance from the sun. (In fact, Earth is actually about three million miles *closer* to the sun at the beginning of January than it is at the beginning of July!)

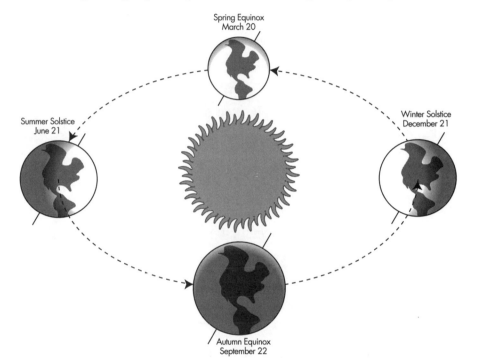

Earth's orbit.
On each equinox, the suns rays light the earth's surface from pole to pole. The entire Arctic Circle is without sunlight on the winter solstice, but will have sunlight all day and all night long on the summer solstice.

Equinox

The spring equinox, marks the midpoint between the long nights of winter and the long days of summer. On this special day, which occurs each year around March 20 (the variation has several causes, including the addition of a day each leap year), the night and the day will be of exactly equal length (exactly twelve hours), and that is why this day is called the equinox. *Equinox* comes from two Latin words and means "equal night" (Nox was the Roman goddess of night).

There will be no other day just like the equinox for another six months, because the spring equinox and the autumn equinox are the only two points in the earth's orbit during which the sun is directly above the equator. If the sun remained directly above the equator all year around, then the climates on Earth would be constant all year around—there would be no difference between summer and winter; there would be no spring and no fall.

Because the sun is directly above the equator on the day of the equinox, you might expect that anyone living on the equator would see the sun appear to rise exactly in the east, pass directly overhead at noon, and set exactly in the west. And that is precisely what they would see. But this day is exceptional for everyone else in the world, too, for on the day of the equinox—and only on the day of the equinox—the sun rises exactly in the east and sets exactly in the west *everywhere in the world*. And not only are there equal periods of daylight and darkness *everywhere in the world* on the equinox, but if you could look back at the earth from a position out in space on this special day, you would see that the circle of sunlight bathing the earth's surface extends from the North Pole to the South Pole, and that the edges of daylight and darkness conform precisely to the lines of longitude that run from pole to pole on your globe.

I say "everywhere in the world," but I really mean everywhere except at the poles. If you were standing at the North Pole or at the South Pole on the day of the equinox, you would see the top of the sun just peek up above the horizon and remain in that same position all day long, and all night long, for the entire twenty-four hours.

Humans have known about the equinox and have celebrated its arrival for thousands of years. Even though the ancients thought the sun moved and the earth remained fixed, they knew that when the days and nights were of equal length, it was time to plant their crops. And they knew that when this situation occurred again, it would signal the time for them to harvest their crops before the onset of winter.

So this is truly a day to celebrate—a celestial holiday that parents and children can plan for and study about and confirm by themselves when it arrives. This is a day to begin a year-long plotting of two vitally important objects in the universe: the sun and your house. Pick out a window or two that face southeast or southwest and allow a view of the horizon. Now pick a viewing position from which your child can see the sun make its first appearance (sunrise) or last appearance (sunset) on the equinox. Note and write down the feature on the horizon that corresponds to the position of the sun. (For example, "Right over the fire hydrant on the corner," or "Just on the left edge of Mrs. Carter's house across the street.")

Repeat these observations every two weeks, and each time write down the reference points that mark the position of the sun. You will notice that the sun moves farther and farther away from the point you observed on the equinox, and it will continue to do so for three full months. Then, one morning, your child will find that the position of the rising or setting sun will be heading back again in the other direction. And, when the next equinox occurs six months from the first, you'll find the sun to be precisely in the position you described it in your first observation.

The sun, of course, doesn't move at all, but it is only by understanding the tilt and orbit of the earth, and by thinking about them long and hard and often, that you and your children will be able to grasp both the reality and the majesty of what is really going on. Together you can predict where the sunrise and sunset will appear from your observation point during the days and months to come. Together you will have created a calendar.

You can also use this day to start becoming aware of shadows, for they can tell you so much if you are only curious enough to think about why they are where they are. Look for something near your home that is tall and sits straight up in the ground—a flagpole or a telephone pole, for example. On the equinox, no matter where you live, the shadow from that pole at sunrise will point due west, and the shadow at sunset will point due east. Be sure to have your children mark these directions, and from them determine where true north and south lie, as well.

If there is any shadow at all when the clock strikes noon (1 P.M. for the autumn equinox because of daylight saving time), then you are not living at the equator, for the sun will be directly overhead at noon along the equator. Therefore, the longer the noontime shadow, the farther away you are from the equator. In fact, this is precisely the method by which an ancient astronomer proved that the earth was round, not flat, and this discovery was made centuries before Columbus was born.

Eratosthenes and the Solstice

It was on June 21, in about 240 B.C., that a man named Eratosthenes [pronounced air-uh- TAHS-thin-eez] allowed his own curiosity to lead him to one of the great discoveries in all of human history. Eratosthenes happened to be the director of the great library at Alexandria, in northern Egypt, and one day he came across a scroll on the shelves of the library, in which the author stated that at midday in the city of Syene [pronounced sie-EEN], on the longest day of the year (June 21), vertical sticks and vertical columns cast no shadows whatsoever.

Eratosthenes thought he would check out this observation for himself, and so when June 21 came around, he pounded a long stake straight up and down into the ground and waited for noon to arrive. As midday approached, the shadow from the stake grew shorter and shorter, but it never disappeared. At noon, his vertical stake still cast a shadow, but the scroll said that in Syene vertical stakes didn't cast shadows. How could this be?

June 21 is the day of the summer solstice, the day on which the sun's most direct rays fall on the latitude we call the Tropic of Cancer, $23\frac{1}{2}$ degrees north of the equator. This is the farthest latitude north on the planet that these direct rays will fall, and because the Tropic of Cancer is south of the continental United States (it passes very near Havana,

Rays from sun are parallel

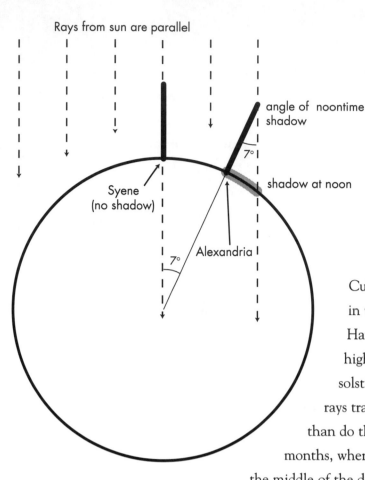

angle of noontime shadow

7°

shadow at noon

Syene
(no shadow)

7° Alexandria

Eratosthenes' proof.
By using geometry (when parallel lines are cut by a transversal, alternate interior angles are equal), Eratosthenes reasoned that the angle between the tip of the stake and the tip of the shadow was identical to the arc between Alexandria and Syene.

Cuba), the sun is never directly overhead at any time in the year anywhere in the United States (except Hawaii). Still, these rays are more direct, and the sun is higher in our sky around the time of the summer solstice than at any other time, and these more-direct rays transmit much more of the sun's warmth and energy than do the glancing rays that fall on us during the winter months, when the sun never appears very high in the sky even in the middle of the day.

The town of Syene (which was located near the modern city of Aswan) lay right on the Tropic of Cancer, and that is why the noonday sun cast no shadows there, for the sun was directly overhead on June 21. But it was not quite overhead in Alexandria, which lay about 500 miles to the north, and so Eratosthenes reasoned that the earth's surface must be curved; it could not be flat.

It is helpful for us and for our children to follow Eratosthenes' reasoning by picturing the earth as he did.

Eratosthenes reasoned that the angle that the sun's rays struck his stake in Alexandria would be the same angle formed by the lines extending the two stakes into the center of the earth (see diagram). So he marked the tip of his stake's noontime shadow, extended a straight pole from the tip of the shadow to the top of the stake, and measured the angle at the top of the stake. This gave him the angle (in degrees) that separated Alexandria from Syene on a round Earth.

The circumference of the whole earth, he knew, would equal 360 degrees (as with all circles), and the angle he measured (which was approximately 7 degrees) would represent a fraction of that complete circle ($\frac{7}{360}$ or about $\frac{1}{50}$). So the distance between Alexandria and Syene was actually $\frac{1}{50}$th of the distance around the entire world.

Now, if only he knew the exact distance between the two cities, it would be a simple matter to estimate the circumference of the planet. In order to learn this vital measure, Eratosthenes hired a company of soldiers (because soldiers were trained to march with a fixed and precise stride) to step off the exact distance between the two cities. When they returned and reported the distance to be 500 miles, Eratosthenes knew that 500 miles was $\frac{1}{50}$th of the earth's circumference, and so the total distance around the earth must be 500 x 50, or 25,000 miles.

His estimate was accurate to within *one percent* of what we know the circumference of the earth to be today, and remember, Eratosthenes figured all this out around 240 B.C.!

Eratosthenes made his famous measurement on the day we call the summer solstice. *Solstice* is a combination of the Latin words *sol,* meaning "sun" and *sistere,* meaning "to stand still." Early humans saw that the arc of the sun's path changed slightly each day as the sun traveled across the sky. In the winter, that path was very low, but each day the sun would climb higher and higher, and in six months it would be directly overhead. But it would not continue heading in the same direction, for, at this point, it would "stand still" and then head back the other way. For the next six months it would carve out lower and lower arcs in the sky. Then it would "stand still" once again, and the whole pattern would begin anew.

These two extremes in the sun's path across the sky—the summer solstice on June 21 and the winter solstice on December 21—are excellent times to begin your family celebrations of "solar holidays." If you have a globe of the earth in your home or at your local library, you can show your children the pattern of light that exists during the day of the solstice. Position the globe so that its axis is tipped toward you. Now have your children hold a flashlight near enough to the globe so that the entire Arctic Circle is bathed in light but so that no light at all falls on the Antarctic Circle. When they have achieved this pattern, they will find that the flashlight, just like the sun itself on the summer solstice, is directly above the Tropic of Cancer, $23\frac{1}{2}$ degrees north of the equator.

So, if you lived anywhere along the Tropic of Cancer, the sun would be directly above your head at noon on the day of the summer solstice. Turn the globe and see how many countries you can name that lie along the Tropic of Cancer. The people who live in these countries, if they ventured out into the sunshine exactly at noon, would cast no shadow at all. Hold a short pencil straight up (that is, pointing to the center of the earth) from any of these countries as your child shines the flashlight from above. No shadow. Now hold the pencil straight up from the area where you live while your child holds the flashlight still. Is there a shadow?

Now position the flashlight so that its beam covers the entire Antarctic Circle, but none of its light extends above the line that marks the Arctic Circle. This shows the position of the sun on the day of the winter solstice. The sun is directly above the line of latitude called the Tropic of Capricorn, which your child can confirm by having you hold the pencil straight up from the parallel that is $23\frac{1}{2}$ degrees south of the equator; the pencil should cast no shadow because the flashlight is directly above it.

With the flashlight in this position, move the pencil to several points in the United States and notice how long a shadow it casts. Also notice how narrow the pattern of light is on regions in the northern hemisphere, and how much of any particular latitude is in darkness. This should confirm for you that daylight hours decrease in the winter, and that we have fewer hours of daylight on the winter solstice than on any other day in the year. (Conversely, the summer solstice gives us our longest day and shortest night of the year.)

Determining When Midday Occurs

You can also make use of the summer solstice (and your child's summer vacation from school) to determine exactly when "midday" occurs at your house. The middle of the day—that is, the time at which the sun is at its highest point in the sky—will not very likely be on the hour, and it will almost certainly not be at 12 o'clock noon.

Think of it this way. Although the clocks all across your time zone show 12 o'clock noon occurring at the same instant, the sun can't possibly be at its highest point everywhere in the zone at the same time. Just as sunrise and sunset occur along the eastern edge of a time zone approximately one hour before they occur along the western edge of that zone, so, too, does midday occur first in the east, then successively later and later throughout the hour as the time zone turns beneath the sun.

But we can't make midday coincide with the clock hour of noon all across each time zone because then clocks in one town would be a few seconds ahead of clocks in the neighboring town to the west, and both would be several minutes behind clocks in the neighboring state to the east. In fact, this is precisely the condition that prevailed until 1883, when the railroad companies in the United States and Canada adopted a system of standard time that we still use today.

Each time zone spans approximately 15 degrees of longitude (although political and geographical considerations make the boundaries extremely irregular). There is a central meridian, then, for each time zone, and approximately $7\frac{1}{2}$ degrees of the zone lies east of that meridian, and $7\frac{1}{2}$ degrees lies to the west. The middle of the Central Time Zone in the United States, for example, is the 90th meridian, which runs from the eastern tip of

Minnesota down through the Mississippi delta in Louisiana. When the sun reaches its highest point in the sky (midday) over this imaginary line, it is exactly noon all across the Central Time Zone. Twenty minutes later, the earth will have turned a couple hundred miles, and now people living in central Minnesota and eastern Texas are directly beneath the sun. It is midday to them, and to everyone living along the 95th meridian, but the clocks show the exact time to be 12:20 P.M.; midday, yes, but not 12 o'clock noon.

If you live east of the central meridian in your time zone, midday will occur anywhere from one to thirty minutes before twelve o'clock noon; if you live west of that central meridian, midday will occur after noon. The 75th meridian is the middle of the Eastern Time Zone; the 105th meridian is the middle of the Mountain Time Zone; and the 120th meridian is the middle of the Pacific Time Zone. Use a globe or a map of the United States to show your children where these lines of longitude run, and look for cities that are situated close to these meridians. For instance, both Memphis, Tennessee, and New Orleans, Louisiana, lie almost directly on the 90th meridian, and so noon in those cities marks almost exactly the time when the sun is at its highest point in the sky.

The summer solstice is an ideal day for you and your children to replicate Eratosthenes' experiment and to discover when midday, or "solar noon," occurs where you live. If you don't have a telephone pole or light pole nearby, you'll need a long stake (about four feet) to pound into the ground (make sure it is vertical). You'll also need a tape measure, a notepad, a pencil, several Popsicle sticks or other marking sticks, and a watch set to the correct time.

Because we move our clocks ahead one hour each spring, midday will occur sometime between 12:30 P.M. and 1:30 P.M. (unless your region does not observe daylight saving time). So, starting around noon, begin measuring and recording the length of the shadow cast by the stake about every five minutes. Several children can participate in this experiment (and you'll find neighborhood children eager to do so). One can hold the tape measure against the stake, while another holds the watch and calls out the exact time; one can mark the shadow's tip with a marking stick, while another measures the length of the shadow. Either you or another child can record each measurement and the time of each measurement on the notepad.

These five-minute intervals will clearly show a measurable decrease in the length of the shadow. When 12:30 P.M. arrives though, begin taking measurements ever minute, and although the differences between successive measurements will be quite small, a point will come when the shadow stops getting shorter and starts getting longer. The time at which you measured the shortest shadow of all will be the time at which the sun was most directly overhead. This is midday or "solar noon" at your house.

Determining True North

Remove all the other marking sticks, but leave the midday stick right where it is. This point and the position of the stake that cast the shadow are very important places on the earth, and you might want to mark them in a more permanent way. If you draw a line between these points, that line will point due north and south. No matter what a magnetic compass reads, (they can be deflected by as much as twenty degrees in some parts of the country), this line points to true north and true south. If you take your children out later on to look at the stars, sight right down this line looking north and you'll find it points almost exactly to Polaris—the "north star."

Now that you know exactly when midday occurs at your house, you can set up your shadow stake on the other three solar holidays, too. In December, on the day of the winter solstice, mark the position of the shadow's tip at precisely the time you determined to be midday (but use standard time). Your children will be amazed to find that this point lies exactly on the north/south line you drew back on the summer solstice in June.

Determining Your Latitude

On the days of the spring and autumn equinoxes, precisely at midday (again, using standard time), place a marker at the tip of the shadow that is cast by the stake. Stretch a string or place a yardstick from that marker to the top of the stake and use a protractor to measure the angle between the ground and the line that extends back from the tip of the shadow to the top of the stake. No matter where you live, the reading of this angle will be exactly the same as your latitude on the earth.

You and your family can prepare for these solar holidays by referring to an almanac (such as *The Old Farmer's Almanac* [031.02 OLD]) for the exact time of their occurrence. News reports and some calendars will also refer to "the first day of spring" (or summer, or fall, or winter), but people who aren't interested in looking at shadows on those days, or thinking about their place in the universe on those days, probably won't see much importance in them, and they'll miss out on the chance for some great family celebrations, too.

Cosmos, by Carl Sagan (New York: Random House, 1980) [520 SAG].

Earthly Matters: A Study of Our Planet, by James J. O'Donnell (New York: Julian Messner, 1982) [J 550 ODO].

Experiments in Astronomy for Amateurs, by Richard Knox (New York: St. Martin's Press, 1977) [523 KNO].

How Did We Find Out the Earth Is Round? by Isaac Asimov (New York: Walker and Co., 1972) [J 525 ASI].

The Old Farmer's Almanac, by Robert B. Thomas (Dublin, N.H.: Yankee Publishing, Inc., 1996) [031.02 OLD].

Once Around the Galaxy, by Roy A. Gallant (New York: Franklin Watts, 1983) [J 523 GAL].

The Practical Astronomer, by Colin A. Ronan (New York: Bonanza Books, 1984) [520 RON].

The Reasons for Seasons: The Great Cosmic Megagalactic Trip Without Moving from Your Chair, by Linda Allison (Boston: Little, Brown and Company, 1975) [J 500.9 ALL].

Science for Kids: 39 Easy Astronomy Experiments, by Robert W. Wood (Blue Ridge Summit, Penn.: Tab Books, 1991) [J 522.078 WOO].

Shadow Science, by Robert Gardner (Garden City, N.Y.: Doubleday & Co., 1976) [J 535.2 GAR].

Sundials: How to Know, Use, and Make Them, by Robert Newton Mayall and Margaret L. Mayall (Boston: Charles T. Branford Company, 1958) [529 MAY].

The Wonderful World of Mathematics, by Lancelot Hogben (Garden City, N.Y.: Doubleday & Co., 1968) [J 510 HOG].

Family Learning by the Light of the Silvery Moon

The most prominent feature in our night sky is the moon, and here is where astronomy begins for most people. The moon is not only the subject of their first astronomical investigations, it is also the inspiration for their study, as well.

Humans have always looked up at the moon with a sense of wonder, and it is precisely this sense of wonder—this fascination about something so beautiful, yet so unattainable and so much larger than life—that we can use to stimulate our children's interest and encourage their understanding about the universe.

The Family Learning of Astronomy

There are three features about the Family Learning of astronomy that make this subject one of the best of all the areas that can be learned or reinforced through out-of-school activities. The first is, of course, that astronomy is not taught in many schools. Most elementary-school children learn nothing about the phases of the moon, and even most high school students have no knowledge of the constellations, save what they hear from their classmates who are "into astrology." So, if you think it is important for your children to know their way around the night sky, then that knowledge will have to be encouraged and attained at home.

The second reason astronomy is such an ideal topic for Family Learning is that it is ideal for adult learning, too. Very few parents have ever received any schooling about the planets and the stars, and so their own education in astronomy must begin at home. Haven't you ever wanted to look up at the starry sky and feel familiar with the objects and patterns and splendors that are offered to you free of charge almost every night? Well, here is an opportunity for parents and children to enjoy the learning of an entire subject together—from the ground up, as it were—and for children to see their parents as learners, too. Studying astronomy is not a lonely activity when a parent and child can plan for, and then experience together, an evening under the stars, with binoculars in hand, observing and pointing out to each other and wondering together about the majesty of their private learning laboratory.

Then, too, the heavens provide a moving panorama to stimulate and guide our learning. So many other subjects and topics are static by nature, that is, our study must be focused on learning all we can about things that don't move or change much from one day to the next: mathematics, geography, language, etc. But every single trip out under the stars offers us a different picture—we can see the moon moving across the sky right before our eyes, and each night we see a little more or a little less of its surface.

Still, the Family Learning of astronomy adheres to the same general principles we used in the other areas of learning, especially the idea that it cannot be learned or taught as a "subject." Nobody—no child, no adult—can grasp or even think about a subject that is as vast as astronomy, and so we have to approach it in a series of limited and topical investigations. A knowledge of astronomy will be the result of all those topics and investigations—the accumulation of all the little pieces of learning we acquire along the way.

Locating Tranquillity Base

For example, our study of the moon might begin with an event that commanded the attention of the entire world back in 1969, when astronaut Neil Armstrong became the first human being ever to walk on the surface of a world other than the earth.

Did you ever look up at the moon and wonder just where it was on the lunar surface that Armstrong walked? You don't need a powerful telescope; your naked eye is sufficient to locate this general area of the moon. But having a good pair of binoculars is the best way to become acquainted with many of the features of the moon, and is also the best way to ignite a child's interest in the wonders of the night sky.

Take a look, for example, at what we and our children can learn from just this one search for Tranquillity Base, the spot where Armstrong told the world, "The *Eagle* has landed."

First, let's remember that whenever we see the moon, we're always looking at that landing spot. Only one side of the moon is, or has ever been, visible to people on the earth. The reason for this is that the moon rotates on its axis, just as the earth rotates on its axis, but the moon takes exactly as long to make one complete rotation as it takes to make one complete orbit of the earth: 27.33 days.

It may seem, therefore, that the moon doesn't rotate at all, but you can demonstrate to your children that it does by using a globe or a basketball to represent the earth, and a grapefruit to represent the moon. Place the globe on the floor in the middle of the room. Now draw a face on one side of the grapefruit (to represent the "man in the moon"), and have your child move the grapefruit along the floor in a large circle around the globe. In order to keep the face on the grapefruit always aimed at the globe, your child will have to turn the grapefruit one complete turn with each complete orbit.

Or think about how the moon would appear if you were viewing it from the sun. You would see it make a complete orbit of the earth in the course of a month, and from your viewing position you would see the entire surface of the moon as it turned completely around during its orbit.

So now we're in the correct half of the moon, but in order to find Tranquillity Base we have to also remember that NASA wanted to select a smooth landing site, and so it chose one of the large dark spots that are so easily seen on the moon's surface. These spots are the result of huge meteor collisions with the moon, which formed great crater basins. Molten lava from beneath the moon's crust oozed into these basins, cooled, hardened, and created large patches that early astronomers thought were filled with water. They called these areas *maria*, which in Latin meant "seas," and still today these dark spots are known by such names as the Sea of Serenity, (the left eye of the face in the moon) and the Sea of Rains (the face's right eye).

The Sea of Tranquillity is the dark area that we see as the face's left cheekbone, just outside and below the face's left eye (which appears on our right-hand side). On the lower left edge of that dark area, Armstrong and Buzz Aldrin left their footprints back in 1969, and because there is no air or water or wind or weather of any kind on the moon, those footprints remain there today, exactly as they were left, and they'll stay just that way for perhaps millions of years to come.

Phases of the Moon

The best time to look for Tranquillity Base is, of course, during a full moon, because you can use the features of the "face" to guide your exploration. But to study the details of the basins and craters and mountains that can be seen with the aid of binoculars, the best time for viewing is when only half the moon is bathed in sunlight—phases that are called the "first quarter" and "third quarter." Instead of having the ridges and valleys washed out of our view by the glare of sunlight shining directly down upon the moon's surface, during these phases the sun strikes the surface at an angle, and there is a distinct dividing line between sunlight and darkness. This line is known as the terminator, and along it we can see the very vivid shadows made by the moon's deep craters and rugged mountain ranges. Look, for example, at the shadows that extend down the nose of the "face in the moon." These are caused by a mountain range known as the Apennines [pronounced APP-ih-nines] and named for a similar mountain range that runs through the middle of Italy.

It is also interesting, I think, to realize that whenever we look at a "first quarter" moon, we are looking at the exact point in space where the earth was just $3\frac{1}{2}$ hours earlier.

You can find many excellent books to guide you on your initial investigations of the moon's surface in the 523.3 section of both the adult and children's collections in your local library. There are also two very handy and inexpensive pocket-size books that you can get in most bookstores and drugstores: *Stars* and *Planets* are both part of the Golden Guide series, and both contain much useful information about the phases and features of the moon. Rand McNally also publishes a wonderfully detailed wall map of the moon, which can be ordered with a credit card by calling Omni Resources at 1-800-742-2677; the price is $7.95 (plus shipping), and the product number is 71-8100.

The date on which the moon will be in each of its phases, along with the time for the rising and setting of the moon each day, is given in the weather section of most daily newspapers, and so parents can plan their lunar observations several days in advance. There are other astronomical events, however, that require longer-range planning, and for these you will need an almanac of some kind—such as *The Old Farmer's Almanac*, which can be found in the 031 section of your library's reference collection as well as in bookstores and in the magazine racks of most supermarkets (for about $3.95). With this reference aid, you'll be able to learn when, for example, there will be an eclipse of the sun or an eclipse of the moon that will be visible in your area. These events, too, can be excellent springboards to inspire you and your children toward the Family Learning of astronomy.

Eclipse of the Moon

In order to acquaint your children with the mechanics of a lunar eclipse, have a flashlight on hand, along with several common spheres, such as a marble, a Ping-Pong ball, a tennis ball, or a grapefruit, that you can use to represent the earth and moon. By placing a marble or Ping-Pong ball on a table, and holding a lighted flashlight near the table's surface, you can create a long shadow that extends from the object and narrows like a cone down to a point. (This shadow is called the umbra, from the Latin word for *shadow*, which is the root for our word *umbrella*.)

The earth casts this same type of shadow in space—twenty-four hours a day—because the earth is always standing in the path of some of the light from the sun. This circular shadow is widest at the earth's surface, and when people on the earth rotate into the shadow, they call the shadow "night."

From there this same shadow stretches some 850,000 miles out into space, but the circle gets smaller and smaller before it narrows down to nothing. In all that immense distance, however, there is only one object that the shadow can fall upon. Every once in a while, our moon, which is whizzing around the earth at about 2,280 miles per hour, will cross the path of this shadow, and some or all of the sunlight falling on the moon's surface will be blocked out until the moon emerges from the shadow once again.

By using the flashlight and two of the spherical objects, you can demonstrate why an eclipse can only occur during the time of a full moon. The moon has to be in line with the earth and the sun in order to enter the earth's shadow, and so anyone on the night side of the earth would see the moon fully lighted until it touches that shadow.

Why don't we have an eclipse during every full moon? Well, first of all, that alignment is incredibly precise. Think of trying to align a grapefruit (the earth), and a Ping-Pong ball twelve feet away (the moon), and a large house about a mile down the road (the sun). Even more critical than this, however, is the fact that the moon doesn't orbit the earth on the same plane that the earth orbits the sun. The moon's orbit is tilted about five degrees, and so the moon usually passes above or below the earth's shadow.

When some ancient Greek thinkers, such as Pythagoras and Aristotle, saw this phenomenon we call a "partial eclipse," they noticed that no matter where in the sky the eclipse occurred, the shape of the shadow on the moon was always curved in the arc of a circle. They reasoned that if the earth were flat, this shadow would at some time cast the image of the "edge" of the earth on the moon, but it never did; the shadow was *always* curved in the arc of a circle. The only shape that could cause such a shadow from all perspectives was a sphere, and so they concluded—hundreds of years before Columbus sailed the Atlantic—that the earth could not be flat after all; it must be a giant sphere.

Moon Illusion

Another pathway you might follow to begin your Family Learning about the moon involves an illusion—a trick that the moon's image plays on our senses. The moon looks considerably larger to us when it is near the horizon than when it is overhead. It has appeared this way to people for as long as there have been people, but no one knows why. The ancient astronomer Ptolemy [pronounced TOL-uh-mee] came up with the explanation that when the moon is near the horizon, we compare it with the images of trees and houses we see in the distance, and increase its size in our minds. Well, that sounds good, but the illusion also happens out on the sea, where there are no houses or trees for comparison.

And it is an illusion—the moon doesn't actually decrease in size, nor is it any farther away when it is overhead. In fact, you can show your children that their eyes are deceiving them by having them hold a dime out at arm's length when the moon is near the horizon. Even though this horizon moon looks large, the dime should just cover its image. After a few hours, when the moon has risen high overhead and appears to be much smaller, have your children hold that dime out again, and again it will just cover the image of the moon.

Or you could take some photos of the moon when it is near the horizon and again  after it is overhead. When your pictures come back, you'll see that the camera's eye wasn't fooled at all.

Another experiment you can try is to look at the large moon through the end of a  mailing tube or a rolled-up length of paper. Does the moon look as large now? Or try looking at the moon backward through your legs, like a football center snapping for a punt. Some people find that this, too, makes the horizon moon appear much smaller.

What we have here is not really an "optical" illusion at all, but a "psychological" one instead. This illusion is different from the truly optical variety of tricks that we see in our sky every day and that we can explain with some basic science. The sun, for example, appears to change color from yellow to red as it nears the horizon, but even though our eyes detect this change in color, we know that the sun has not undergone any change, so this must be an optical illusion. It is.

Color of the Sun and Sky

The apparent change in the color of the sun is caused by the fact that when the sun is near the horizon, its light takes a longer path through the atmosphere before it reaches our eyes; the light travels through less atmosphere when the sun is directly overhead. Molecules of air, water, and dust in the atmosphere scatter some of the sun's light before it can reach our eyes. These molecules and particles scatter about ten times more light from the blue end of the spectrum than from the red end of the spectrum, and so the setting (and rising) sun appears red.

You can diagram this for your children by drawing a circle about two inches in diameter to represent the earth, and another, slightly larger one, around the first to represent the layer of Earth's atmosphere. Place a small X at the very top of the earth (representing a person); draw one line straight up from that X to the outside circle and another horizontally to the left until it, too, reaches the outside circle. Notice that the vertical line

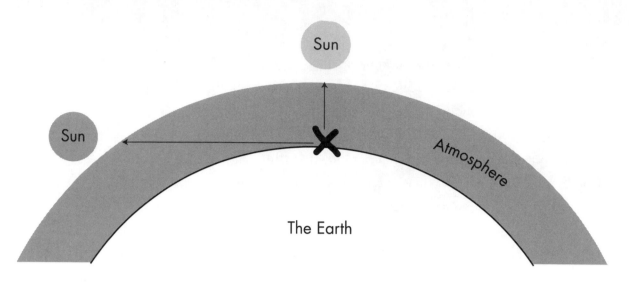

Sunlight's path through the atmosphere. The rays at sunrise and sunset are more scattered because they must pass through more atmosphere before reaching observers on Earth.

is quite a bit shorter than the horizontal one, which shows that sunlight coming to the earth from the horizon must pass through more atmosphere, and so there is more chance that some of its light—and color—will be scattered.

What is the sun's "real" color? Not yellow—because that color is a result of scattered light, too—but white, which is how it appears to astronauts in space. The blue light that is scattered by the atmosphere is the reason for another optical illusion: our apparently blue sky. The sky itself has no color at all, and so it should appear black, just as it does to the astronauts, and even to us during the one time we are allowed to see its "true" color—at night.

Earth's atmosphere is the cause for other natural illusions, too, such as the "twinkling" of stars and the mirages that we commonly see on highways during hot summer days. And while all of these illusions can be explained (with the single exception of the "moon illusion"), their explanations should in no way diminish their wonder and fascination to us or to our children. In fact, these illusions can serve us as daily and nightly reminders of the science that goes on around us all the time and is just sitting out there waiting for us to take advantage of the lessons it can teach. But too often we choose to build new science laboratories in our classrooms before we even consider availing ourselves of this most wondrous laboratory that has already been provided for our use.

Astronomy for All Ages: Discovering the Universe Through Activities for Children and Adults, by Phillip Harrington and Edward Pascuzzi (Old Saybrook, Conn.: The Globe Pequot Press, 1994) [J 529 HAR].

Astronomy Projects for Young Scientists, by Necia H. Apfel (New York: Arco Publishing Co., 1984) [J 520.78 APF].

Experimenting With Illusions, by Robert Gardner (New York: Franklin Watts, 1990) [J 152.148 GAR].

Exploring the Night Sky, by Terence Dickinson (Ontario, Canada: Camden House Publishing, 1987) [J 523 DIC].

Exploring the Sky: 100 Projects for Beginning Astronomers, by Richard Moeschl (Chicago: Chicago Review Press, 1989) [J 523.007 MOE].

The Moon (Space Science Series), by Heather Couper and Nigel Henbest (London: Franklin Watts, 1986) [J 523.3 COU].

The Moon, by Michael Jay (New York: Franklin Watts, 1982) [J 523.3 JAY].

The Moon and Its Exploration, by Necia H. Apfel (New York: Franklin Watts, 1982) [J 523.3 APF].

The Moon: Steppingstone to Outer Space, by Dorothy E. Shuttlesworth and Lee Ann Williams (Garden City, N.Y.: Doubleday & Co., 1977) [J 523.3 SHU].

New Guide to the Moon, by Patrick Moore (New York: Norton, 1976) [523.3 MOO].

To Learn About the Stars, We Must "Become As Little Children"

The Family Learning of astronomy does not have to begin with a focus on the earth and then proceed to the moon and, eventually, to the stars. There is no reason at all why you and your children can't start right off with an investigation of various stars and planets, although you may find, as I did, that a basic understanding of the movements of the earth can help in explaining the changing positions of these other heavenly bodies throughout the year.

There is a certain advantage, though, in beginning your astronomy study together by focusing on the most distant objects—the stars—first. By doing so you are pulled along by the undeniable wonder that both you and your children feel every time you look up at a sky full of stars. Chet Raymo, in his book titled *365 Starry Nights,* which I urge you to find in a bookstore or in the 523 section of your library's juvenile collection, makes the point this way: "The night sky possesses an unparalleled power to excite the human imagination. Intimate, yet infinite. Dark, yet full of light. Near, yet unreachably far. No part of our world displays such immediately accessible patterns of order, and no part of our world remains so deeply mysterious."

I often wonder, though, how many of us almost avoid marveling at this majesty because we don't understand what we're looking at, and we don't want to admit to anyone—including ourselves—how much we don't know.

A Strategy for Learning

But even if we decide that we want to learn our way around the night sky, and that we want our children to acquire this knowledge as well, the question that puts a halt to most adult learning about astronomy before it can ever get off the ground is, simply, "What do I do now?" Where can and should adults go to learn about a subject like astronomy—a field in which they don't know any answers, and don't even know what questions to ask?

Perhaps you are like some parents I have known who wanted to learn about astronomy, and who began their study by seeking out whatever relevant books they could find in their local library and bookstores. This thoroughly commendable learning strategy, which may have been a successful one for these parents in many other fields, produced nothing but disappointment and discouragement for them in astronomy because the books they found generally presumed they already had a basic knowledge of the subject, and it was precisely that basic knowledge that most of them were seeking. If this has been your experience, let me suggest that you are in the right church, but the wrong pew.

One of the learning strategies that adults often overlook is to swallow their pride and head for the children's section of a library or a bookstore. Here you will find resources that don't presume any initial command of the subject, and somewhat surprisingly perhaps, resources that aren't embarrassingly simplistic either.

Astronomy books for children will tell you not only where to find the most prominent stars and constellations, but how to pronounce their names as well, so that you can comfortably and confidently talk about, and learn about, the subject with others.

H. A. Rey, whose many "Curious George" books have been children's classics for decades, has also written some of the best beginning astronomy books I have ever seen, including *Find the Constellations* [J 520 REY] and *The Stars: A New Way To See Them* [J 523.8 REY]. Another excellent paperback primer is Terence Dickinson's *Exploring the Night Sky* [J 523 DIC], which won the 1987 Children's Science Book Award.

What books like these allow you to do is to become a participant in the extravaganza of light that is given for our benefit and enjoyment almost every night of the year. They allow you and your children to locate quickly patterns of stars—such as the Big Dipper, for example—and use them as a home base, from which you can launch out in various directions to locate the positions of other stars and constellations.

Each of these beginning steps can be accompanied by wondrous stories about how the constellations came by their names, and so stargazing with your children becomes a natural time for storytelling as well, and we all know how much children look forward to story times with their parents. Here, then, is a natural inspiration and stimulation for learning not only about the stars and constellations, but for extending that learning into mythology, as well, by sharing with your children other classic tales from myths of all cultures.

Notice that this method for beginning your study of the stars does not require the purchase or use of a telescope or any other expensive paraphernalia. Astronomy was studied for thousands of years before telescopes were ever invented, and so a telescope is by no means essential to your understanding. What is essential is that you and your children become comfortable about finding your way around a starry sky without being tied to any fixed position or any piece of optical equipment. You may very well grow so interested in knowing what is out beyond the view of your naked eye that you and your family will decide to purchase a good pair of binoculars, and then, perhaps, a family telescope. But these will be purchases with a purpose, and that purpose will be a greater understanding of the world around you, which is just what Family Learning is all about.

You may find that, just as in other areas of Family Learning, a basic understanding about the brightest stars and major constellations can be stimulated by subjects that don't appear to have much to do with astronomy at all. And, that by having a working knowledge of basic astronomy, your children will be able to take advantage of, and benefit from, lessons and topics that are covered in a variety of courses and subjects in school. Science and mythology, of course, come quickly to mind, but let me give you an example of how a knowledge of basic astronomy can illuminate one's understanding of a topic that would appear to have no connection at all to the stars.

Finding the north Pole

During their history studies in school, your children may hear about or read about an event that occurred on April 6, 1909. It was on that day that two U.S. explorers became the first humans to reach the North Pole. Most history textbooks will report that Robert E. Peary and Matthew Henson (along with four Eskimos they had hired) traveled by dogsled over hundreds of miles of snow and ice, and braved temperatures of 50 degrees below zero and winds of hurricane force for seven grueling months, until they finally arrived at the "top of the world."

Did you ever wonder how they knew they had reached their destination and could stop looking? I mean, there is no physical "pole" or marking of any kind; in fact, the North Pole isn't even on land, just a floating pack of ice. So how did they know exactly where it was? Well, first they had to know *what* it was, and so should we.

The "pole" that Peary and Henson were looking for was the *north geographic pole*, which is the northern end of the earth's axis and is the point at which all the earth's lines of longitude meet. This "pole" is invisible, but it is not imaginary, for there is a point in the Arctic (and one in the Antarctic) on which you could stand and have the entire planet Earth turn below your feet.

So why didn't Peary and Henson just follow a compass needle right to the pole? Because magnetic compasses point to the *north magnetic pole*, which has nothing to do with the *north geographic pole* or the earth's axis. In fact, the north magnetic pole is about a thousand miles away from the geographic pole, and its position is constantly changing, moving many miles in just a few years.

So they must have determined their position by the stars, right? In a way, yes. But remember that the North Pole experiences six months of daylight and then six months of darkness each year. You wouldn't want to try to find your way across the snow and ice in constant darkness, and so you—like Peary and Henson—would time your expedition for a period following the spring equinox (around March 20). There would be no nighttime, but neither would there be any stars to use as guides. Except one—the one we call the sun.

During the daylight months at the North Pole, the sun will appear to rise and sink in the sky, but it will never drop below the horizon (and so it is visible twenty-four hours a day). By measuring the angle of the sun over the horizon, and then measuring it again twelve hours later, and by knowing how many days had passed since the equinox, Peary and Henson were able to figure out exactly where they were and to know with reasonable certainty that they had arrived at the North Pole.

Finding the North Star

Try to locate the North Star, Polaris [pronounced poe-LAIR-iss], with your children one night, and help them to understand that this star lines up very closely with the axis of the earth. Therefore, it will point north to everyone on the planet who can see it (people below the equator can't see it at all), but it will appear at different heights in the northern sky depending upon the latitude from which it is seen. Can your children imagine how Polaris would appear to someone standing at the North Pole during the six months when stars can be seen from the top of the world? Because Polaris lines up with the earth's axis, it sits almost directly over the North Pole and so would appear straight overhead—and stay there every day of the year. All the other stars would pivot around Polaris and swing around the sky in circles that are parallel to the horizon. No stars would rise or set as they do in the sky we see; instead, they would stay at a fixed height above the horizon all year around.

The stars, of course, don't actually pivot around Polaris or move at all. It is we who are rotating, turning around the axis of the earth once each day, and so we see the stars from different angles throughout the night (and the day, too). If you locate a star pattern—such as the Big Dipper, for example—early one evening, and then search for it again several hours later, you won't find it in the same sector of the sky where you saw it earlier. It will have moved around in a giant circle, with Polaris at the center of that circle, one quarter of the way in six hours, halfway in twelve hours, three-quarters in eighteen hours, and back again to (almost) its original position twenty-four hours after you first noted its position in the sky.

It's not just the Big Dipper that appears to rotate around Polaris but every star and every constellation that you can see seems to rotate in the same way, though in greater or lesser arcs in the sky. The Little Dipper, for example, which appears to hang from Polaris (the last star in its handle), will swing its bowl around like the hour hand on a celestial clock, but Polaris itself remains fixed and motionless among all the stars in the sky.

The best way to help your children find where Polaris is in the night sky is first to locate the Big Dipper. Polaris, you see, is really not a very bright star at all—it ranks only forty-ninth among the stars in brightness. But because it stays in the same position throughout the night and throughout the year, it is easy to relocate once you know where to look.

The Big Dipper is useful as a guide because it is one of the few groups of stars that actually look like the things for which they were named. This particular "dipper" has four stars making up its bowl and three stretching out to form its handle. Like all the stars and constellations, the Big Dipper appears to make one complete orbit around Polaris every twenty-four hours, but we must remember that every "celestial clock" runs about four minutes fast; that is, all stars make just a bit more than one complete revolution each twenty-four hours. Consequently, they appear in different positions in the sky at different seasons of the year.

But no matter where or when you see the Big Dipper, you will find that the two stars on the outside of its bowl will always point directly to Polaris. These two stars are, therefore, commonly called "the pointers"; if you draw a line between them and extend that line about five times its length (up from the bowl), you'll find Polaris, and you'll know that Polaris will be right there all night, all year—and all day, too.

Locating the North Star.
The Big Dipper appears to rotate $\frac{1}{4}$ of the way around Polaris every six hours. "The pointers" in the bowl of the Dipper will always be in line (approximately) with Polaris.

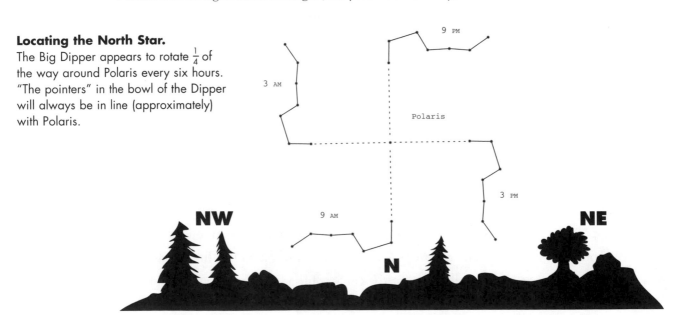

I say "all day" as a reminder to parents that we and our children are easily duped by another great illusion—that the stars "come out" at night. It is such a good illusion that we have to remind ourselves, and make our children aware, that the stars are always "out"—daytime as well as nighttime—but their faint light blends into the overpowering light from our own star—the sun.

Here is a simple activity that can help your children understand how starlight can be "washed out" by sunlight.

Use a paper punch to make several holes in a three-by-five-inch index card, and place that card in a white letter envelope. In a well-lighted room, have your children hold the envelope out in front of them while you shine a flashlight on the front of the envelope (that is, from the same direction your child is looking) from about two inches away. Can they see the holes in the index card? Probably not. Now move the flashlight so that it shines on the back of the envelope, and the holes in the card become quite distinct. When the flashlight is shining from behind the envelope, the area surrounding the holes is darker than the area in the holes themselves, and so the holes become visible. Similarly, the stars don't become visible until their light is greater than the background light we see in the sky, and that doesn't happen until our earth begins to block the sun's light from our view.

USEFUL FAMILY RESOURCES

Astronomy for Every Kid: 101 Easy Experiments That Really Work, by Janice VanCleave (New York: John Wiley & Sons, 1991) [J 520 VAN].

Astronomy for All Ages: Discovering the Universe Through Activities for Children and Adults, by Phillip Harrington and Edward Pascuzzi (Old Saybrook, Conn.: The Globe Pequot Press, 1994) [J 529 HAR].

The Big Dipper and You, by E. C. Krupp (New York: Morrow Junior Books, 1989) [J 523.8 KRU].

Exploring the Night Sky, by Terence Dickinson (Ontario, Canada: Camden House Publishing, 1987) [J 523 DIC].

Find the Constellations, by H. A. Rey (Boston: Houghton Mifflin Co., 1976) [J 520 REY].

The Friendly Stars, by Martha Evans Martin (New York: Van Nostrand Reinhold Co., 1982) [523.8 MAR].

Glow in the Dark Constellations: A Field Guide for Young Stargazers, by C. E. Thompson (New York: Grosset & Dunlap, 1989) [J 523.8 THO].

Guideposts to the Stars: Exploring the Skies Throughout the Year, by Leslie C. Peltier (New York: Macmillan, 1972) [J 523 PEL].

Look to the Night Sky: An Introduction to Star Watching, by Seymour Simon (New York: Viking Press, 1977) [J 523 SIM].

The Night Sky Book: An Everyday Guide to Every Night, by Jamie Jobb (Boston: Little, Brown & Co., 1977) [J 523.8903 JOB].

Stars: A Guide to the Constellations, Sun, Moon, Planets, and Other Features of the Heavens, by Herbert S. Zim and Robert H. Baker (New York: Golden Press, 1985) [J 523 ZIM].

The Stars: A New Way to See Them, by H. A. Rey (Boston: Houghton Mifflin Co., 1967) [J 523.8 REY].

Stories from the Stars: Greek Myths of the Zodiac, by Juliet Sharman Burke (New York: Abbeville Kids, 1996) [J 133.5 BUR].

Sundogs and Shooting Stars: A Skywatcher's Calendar, by Franklyn M. Branley (Boston: Houghton Mifflin Co., 1980) [J 523 BRA].

365 Starry Nights, by Chet Raymo (Englewood Cliffs, N.J.: Prentice-Hall, Inc., 1982) [J 523 RAY].

Learning From the Past:
History

Introduction

What is there about the study of history that makes it so unattractive and wearisome when it is taught badly, yet so fascinating and memorable when it is taught well? Why can we always remember the history teacher we had in junior high, high school, or college who made the subject come alive for us and who made us feel that the study of history was important to our own lives and to our futures as well? Why did we all have to suffer through so many other history classes in which the dominance of dates and facts drove out all the enjoyment, and all the intrigue, and all the stimulation, and in the process drove us away from any further pursuit of history?

The answer to all these questions, I think, is that some very good teachers actually enjoy history themselves, and they realize that what makes the subject so intriguing is that *history is about people*, not about dates or facts. This should be the guiding principle behind everything we do in encouraging our children's learning about the wonders of the past.

Children don't often think of the people from the past as being *real* people—the knights of the Round Table, George Washington, even their own great-grandparents. Historical figures, to them, have a two-dimensional, cardboard appearance, and so we must help them understand that these people really lived, and that they had the same everyday concerns and problems that modern adults and children have. We must, in a very real sense, bring history to life for them.

Because our efforts at home will all be aimed at the human side of history, we can broach the subject from many different areas. We can look at the language people used; how they heated and lighted their homes; how they obtained their food; even how they managed without television. What we are trying to instill in our children, after all, is a feeling for the people who lived in the past, no matter how far back that past may be, and an understanding that the people of the past had the same concerns that people have today. It is those human concerns that are the single unifying thread in all of the history that your children will ever study, inside or outside of school, and they are also the focus of the learning activities that are included in the following sections.

APRIL 14: *Lincoln's assassination*

JUNE 25: *Custer's last stand*

Laying Down Life Spans Makes History Come Alive

Learning historical dates is not the same as learning history. But dates and eras and centuries do provide us with a worthwhile backdrop for any historical study. What we must do, then, is provide for our children a view of history that includes important dates and fixes the time of important events but that treats these dates and times as a means to an end, and not as the end itself.

Our whole concept of "centuries" works against us in this regard, for we have created a system of 100-year segments that is a convenient way of working with numbers but has almost nothing to do with the lives of real people. If we want to personalize history for our children, if we want them to understand that what we call "history" is a collection of human happenings, and if we want them to get a feeling for the human beings that created the history they are studying, then we must find ways to tie historical events to human lives instead of to these artificial spans we call centuries.

One way to help your children place historic events in time, and to help them connect their own lives to the lives of historic people as well, is to think about and talk about history as being a succession of human life spans instead of a succession of centuries. Let me illustrate what I mean by looking at one significant historical event: the assassination of Abraham Lincoln.

Lincoln's Assassination

On April 14, 1865, President Abraham Lincoln and his wife attended a benefit performance of a play titled *Our American Cousin* at Ford's Theatre in Washington, D.C. Only five days earlier, Confederate General Robert E. Lee had surrendered at Appomattox, ending our nation's longest and bloodiest war, and the president (who looked much older than his fifty-six years), could at long last enjoy an evening away from the White House and away from the stresses of the Civil War.

Although the story of Lincoln's assassination that evening, and the manhunt that resulted in the death of John Wilkes Booth, is well known to most adults and children, there is one very small item in this story that I find both fascinating and instructive. It is this: I could have talked with someone who was actually there at Ford's Theatre on the night of the assassination. And possibly you could have talked with him, too.

The last survivor of the 1,675 people who were in the audience that fateful night, one Samuel J. Seymour, passed away in 1956—that's right, *1956*. Five-year-old Sammy Seymour had come to Ford's Theatre with his father and a family friend who lifted the boy up so he could see Mr. Lincoln sitting in the presidential box. Seymour was ninety-five years old when he died, but throughout his long life he remembered clearly, and often spoke about, seeing Booth leap from that balcony box and fall onto the stage as he made his escape.

Now, what I find so instructive about this historical footnote is that it brings a piece of history out of the musty pages of a textbook and makes it a part of my life. No, I didn't talk to Mr. Seymour, but our lives overlapped, and so the Lincoln assassination and I are joined by that single life span. Events just don't seem like ancient history anymore when you realize you could have talked to someone who was actually there at the time.

Abraham Lincoln, Gettysburg, Robert E. Lee, slavery—all the people and facts and events surrounding our Civil War—seemed so far away to me when I was in school, almost as though they weren't about "real people" at all. This view was due partly to the fact that these people and events were taught as belonging to a different century, a century so unlike the one I was living in that it had no connection whatsoever to me or to anyone I knew. Yet, here was a man—an old man to be sure, but a living human being just the same—who was alive during the Civil War and also during my childhood. I have never looked at the Civil War, or felt about the Lincoln years, in the same way since.

Measuring History in Life Spans

Let's say that a life span is seventy-five years. Now think about the year that your own father or mother was born. Their lives overlapped the life span of someone who was born seventy-five years earlier. Zoom! You're already back into the days of wagon trains, the California gold rush, and the pony express. That is, your parents could have talked to someone who lived during those happenings in history. Or start with your grandparents; go back seventy-five years from their birth and you might find the Monroe Doctrine or Noah

Webster's first dictionary—and people like Thomas Jefferson and John Adams and James Madison, who were still alive then. Just think of the stories they could have told!

No, your grandparents probably didn't speak with anybody who spoke with Monroe or Webster or Jefferson or Adams, but don't you wish you knew all the people with whom they did speak? Not only does this idea of "laying down life spans" help us see how really close we are to people and events we used to think of as belonging to "ancient" history, but it also encourages us to mine all the sources of oral history that are still in our own families and in our neighborhoods and in our towns. For example, when my English grandmother was a little girl, she attended the funeral of Queen Victoria, in 1901. I didn't discover that fact until after I had studied the Victorian Age in school and had taught my students about Victorian literature, but nothing "Victorian" has ever seemed the same to me since.

Once you start laying down life spans (your grandfather could have talked to someone who could have talked to...), you find yourself traveling back through history with tremendous speed and ease, eating up seventy-five-year chunks at a time. It takes only three links in this chain of human history to connect your children with the American Revolution; only five to join them with Shakespeare; only seven and they are sailing with Columbus.

This method or technique for looking at history and thinking about history is best suited, I have found, for showing children how recent the history of their own country actually is. This is why the Civil War still fascinates and captivates so many people today, because it didn't happen that long ago. The ruts made by Conestoga wagons carrying pioneers out west can still be seen etched into the mountain trails they crossed in Utah, Nevada, and California. Even the founding of our country is a relatively recent event in human history, and so the study of it is, therefore, quite unlike the study of the history of England or France or China. We need to take advantage of this difference and use it in linking our children's lives to the lives of the men and women and boys and girls who lived but a few life spans ago.

Focusing on Human History

 When we focus, then, upon an event in history—especially in American history—we should look for ways to show our children how close this event really is to the present, instead of how different things were "way back when." Linking the event by life spans to the present is but one way to create this vision and this feeling about history in our children. Instead of looking only at the event itself, try focusing on the humans who participated in the event or who lived during that time, and then think about how long these people may have lived and about all the people to whom they could have told their stories. (For example, the last Civil War veteran of the Union army died in 1956; the last Confederate soldier died in 1959.)

I have been told that there were four Sioux Indians who participated in the Battle of the Little Bighorn and who also lived past the year of my birth. (The oldest of these survivors, Chief Iron Hail of the Oglala Sioux, died on a reservation in South Dakota in 1955 at the age of ninety-eight.) In other words, I could have talked to or known or touched four people who were actually present at Custer's Last Stand, and that event occurred in 1876. The entire story of that battle, including its causes and its aftermath, became much more important to me after I learned this little fact. When I thought about how it was entirely possible for me to be connected to people who actually lived in 1876, the events of that time took on a feeling of closeness that they never had before. If I could have touched someone who was alive in 1876, then I could have also "touched" or been "touched" by events such as the invention of the telephone, the publication of *Tom Sawyer*, and the 100th birthday of our country, too—all of which occurred in 1876.

Knowing the dates and eras and centuries of significant events in history *is* important, and we should not be quick to follow the "modern" trend in teaching history, which advocates ignoring these facts altogether. We must, however, use the time line of history as a backdrop for better understanding the human beings and the human events that make up history. When we know the date of a historic event, for example, we can help our children imagine what children their own age were doing at that time, and how long those children might have lived, and to whom they might have told their stories. History starts coming to life, both for children and adults as well, when history starts being about life itself.

USEFUL FAMILY RESOURCES

The Last Time When, by George Gipe
(New York: World Almanac
Publications, 1982) [031 GIP].

If Those Walls Could Talk, What Tales They Would Tell

Another strategy or technique that parents may find useful in developing their children's sense of history is one that was suggested to me by an exhibit I saw during a visit to the Muir Woods, north of San Francisco. The forest service had sliced off a thin cross section from the trunk of a giant redwood tree that had died after many years and had fallen in the woods. How many years had this tree lived?

Well, the rings in the cross section of tree trunks are really layers of sapwood that trees form once each year, just underneath their bark, and the space between any two rings represents one year's growth in the thickness of the trunk. By counting the number of rings in a trunk, we not only can tell the age of the tree, but we can also pinpoint the exact ring that was formed during any particular year.

This particular redwood tree had more than 2,000 of these concentric rings visible in its trunk, and so the rangers decided to label some of the rings with markers to indicate just what was going on in the world during various stages of the tree's growth.

It makes quite a display, and practically every visitor to these woods stops by the exhibit and reflects a little while about the events that this one tree had "seen" during its life on Earth. For example, one of the outer markers, far away from the center, pointed to a ring that was within a few inches of the bark, and the marker read "Signing of the Declaration of Independence." That particular ring had been formed in 1776, and this particular tree was a very old tree even then.

Other markers identified rings that were formed at the time of Columbus's arrival in the New World, the Norman Conquest of England, the fall of Rome, the birth of Jesus, and the death of Julius Caesar.

It occurred to me that the reason this display and this listing of historic events was so impressive and so different from the usual printed "time lines" of human history was that you had the feeling of being in the presence of something special—something that had lived through it all and had been an actual witness to human history in progress. Of course, the tree hadn't "seen" or even been near any of these historic events, but it had been around just the same, and it had shared their time in history.

Thinking About Old Buildings

Some buildings are like that—oh, not many remain standing as long as a giant redwood tree—but there are buildings in every city that are older than any human in that city. There are buildings in your own area and town that have been "witnesses" to events that you and your children know only from books and history lessons.

There is an urge to say "If those walls could talk, what tales they would tell!" and that is precisely what you and your children can imagine when you come upon a building or a monument whose cornerstone or inscription tells you when it began its vigil over that particular spot on Earth. Did that building watch over the street outside as the first motor car came to town? When was that, anyway? And those soldiers marching by, they never seem to age, yet their uniforms keep changing from blue or gray to olive, then khaki, then a mottled green, then a dusty sand.

This feeling and longing for the tales that walls could tell is what creates the awe and the hushed reverence we experience in a visit to an identifiably historic setting such as Independence Hall, or the Alamo, or the decks of "Old Ironsides." We even imagine, when walking through the lands around Gettysburg, for example, or Dodge City, or the Little Bighorn, that the ground itself might somehow be implored to reveal its secrets and to recount the stories that were played out on its surface years ago.

What if the walls and the lands could talk? Would we know what to ask? Do our children have a sufficient knowledge of history to take advantage of such imaginative speculations? What I am suggesting here is that we can use this fanciful idea as a basis for discussions with our children and as encouragement for their writing about history as well. Not only can they devise their own historical tales from a building's point of view, but you can trade parts with them in "interviewing" various walls about what they have seen and what was going on in the world at that time.

Sound Techniques Focus on the Past

This technique of "personalizing" history for your children is well-suited to the whole idea of Family Learning because it relies upon opportunities for learning that exist all around you—opportunities that you can experience with your children even on weekends and during summer vacations—and it will prepare your children to better understand and to apply whatever history lessons they are taught in school.

Now, don't be alarmed that this approach may appear, on the surface at least, similar to the "new age" or cultish techniques that some education professors claim will help children "discover their inner selves." Imagining what tales various buildings or monuments could tell focuses on *the past*—not the present or the future.

Let me explain it this way. There is a big difference between imagining a conversation with Eleanor Roosevelt as a way of making decisions or planning actions that you, yourself, will take, and imagining what Mrs. Roosevelt would say about her own life and her own decisions and actions. The first has virtually nothing to do with history (or learning in general), while the second puts a premium on it. The more history you know, the greater the understanding you'll be able to achieve because your imagination will have history for its guide, and your musings will have a context and a background that will provide a test for their validity.

Indeed, "if those walls could talk" is very similar to the kind of history lessons that come from stage performances featuring actors who portray historical characters by embellishing as well as quoting their speeches and writings. (Productions focusing on Mark Twain, Harry Truman, and Will Rogers come quickly to mind.) It is also in keeping with a television show from the 1950's and 1960's titled "You Are There," in which Walter Cronkite would pretend to be on the scene of historic events, such as the signing of Magna Carta or the trial of Joan of Arc, and would "interview" the principal characters about what was taking place.

 This technique can also be useful in sharpening and reawakening your own interest in history. If, for example, you could "talk" to any building in the world, which would it be— the White House, perhaps? the Texas Schoolbook Depository? the Colosseum in Rome? that stable in Bethlehem?

USEFUL FAMILY RESOURCES

My Backyard History Book, by David Weitzman (Boston: Little, Brown and Co., 1975) [J 973.07 WEI].

Underfoot: An Everyday Guide to Exploring the American Past, by David Weitzman (New York: Charles Scribner's Sons, 1976) [973.072 WEI].

History Is More About "Why?" Than "When?"

In Richard Lederer's hilarious collection of mistakes and bloopers culled from the writings of high school and college students across the country, I find one recurring theme, and that is the sense among many students today that history somehow just "happens." Perhaps it's the way we teach the subject—too often as a series of unconnected occurrences—but for some reason our children think that historic events just spring into existence all of a sudden and without any apparent cause. Look, for example, at these student observations concerning the Elizabethan Age: "It was an age of great inventions and discoveries. Gutenberg invented the Bible. Another important invention was the circulation of blood. Sir Walter Raleigh is a historical figure because he invented cigarettes and started smoking. And Sir Francis Drake circumcised the world with a 100-foot clipper" (from *Anguished English*, by Richard Lederer [420.207 LED]).

I don't mean to suggest that our children should see history as a "linear" series of occurrences, that is, one in which each specific event can be traced to a specific cause. Indeed, there is probably no event in all of human history that could be said to have had only one cause. There are many forces and factors that converge at a moment in time and result in a single historic event, and each of those events causes many changes to occur in various fields of human endeavor.

So any useful study of history will have to expand upon the usual time line model and, instead, encourage children to think about the causes and the effects of a historical event rather than just the facts of the event itself. I'm not saying that the question of "when?" is unimportant in our children's study of history; I am saying that the question of "why?" is even more important.

Asking "Why?" About Historical Events

When your children were very young, they used to ask you "why?" about everything, and no matter what your answer would be, they would ask "why?" again, and again, and again. Well, when you talk about history with your children—whether as part of a school assignment or when using some of the Family Learning techniques I have suggested in this book—you can take advantage of the opportunity to switch roles with them, for now you can be the one to ask "why?" They may learn in school that the Pilgrims came to America from England in 1620. Yes, that date (or at least an approximation of it) *is* important for them to know (especially since a recent study showed that more than one-fourth of our high school seniors could not place this event in its proper century). But what I am suggesting is that if our focus is on "why?" the Pilgrims left England, then the "when?" will take care of itself.

The whole purpose of asking your children "why?" about every historic event—and asking "why?" about the causes, and "why?" about the effects, too—is to encourage them to adopt the practice for themselves and to start asking themselves "why?" about the history they read. Many history textbooks put review questions at the end of each chapter or each unit, but the real students of history don't wait for the textbook to catch up with their curiosity. They ask themselves "why?" throughout their reading. Sometimes the answers are revealed as their reading continues, but if not, then the "why?" remains and identifies for them the gaps in their understanding. These children will have a useful and working knowledge of history no matter how well or how poorly the subject is taught to them in school. They will continue to acquire a knowledge of history and a feeling for history throughout their lives, and our goal should be to give them the tools by which they can point their lives in this direction.

In order to focus our children's attention on the "why?" of historic events, we must look for examples that will show them how the history of any period will "come to life" for them if they will just look at what life was like, and how lives were lived, during that time. This is what the most compelling history books do, and what our children's history textbooks rarely do.

It was the focus on real people—the men, women, adults, and children—and their real-life situations and struggles that made Alex Haley's "Roots" the most-watched television series of all time, and made "The Civil War" the highest-rated series ever broadcast on public television. People are drawn to historical tales, but only when those tales concern the lives and the hardships and the hopes of real human beings, because those human concerns don't change over the centuries. They tie us to the people of the past no matter how deep into the past we go.

262

Asking "Why?" About Columbus's Voyage

Let me give you an example of how this focus on "why?" can change the way you help your child look at the study of history. I'll use Columbus's voyage to the New World as an example, but what I want you to see is that you can use this same technique to guide your own study of history and to give your children a tool that will further their understanding of any historic event.

In 1492, Columbus sailed the ocean blue.

Why?

It surely wasn't to prove that the earth was round, for the roundness of the earth was pretty well taken for granted at the time. (Columbus, however, thought the earth was much smaller than the size estimated by most scholars of his day, and on this point he was dead wrong.) But an expedition like this would have cost a great deal of money, and so the people who financed it surely expected some return on their investment. Just what was it that Columbus convinced them he would find?

In the 973 section of your local library, you will come across books about American history that are quite unlike the textbooks your children read in school. These books are different because they don't have to conform to the political views and demands of the many special-interest groups that decide what will be presented in your children's textbooks and how that material will be taught. And so here is a good place to look for answers (sometimes you'll find several different answers) to your "why?" questions about American history.

It was here that I came across Alistair Cooke's *America*, which is the book version of the wonderfully thought-provoking, thirteen-part television series that PBS broadcast back in 1972. Alistair Cooke's explanation of the reason for Columbus's voyage makes us think about what living conditions were like in the fifteenth century, and through it we can help our children see how their own human needs and desires are just like those of human beings who lived 500 years ago.

Salt was the only known food preservative in Columbus's time, but it was nothing like refrigeration or freezing for keeping foods fresh. So most foods—especially meats—arrived at the table already spoiled and tasting of decay. (Knowing this, perhaps your children will think more highly of refrigerated leftovers and will not take frozen dinners so much for granted.) To mask the taste and odor of their putrid food, people all across Europe depended upon spices: cloves, nutmeg, cinnamon, pepper—especially pepper. During this time, pepper was, quite literally, worth its weight in gold.

But these all-important spices were found only in the Spice Islands and the Orient, and so Europeans had to pay dearly for them to be transported across Asia along a trade route that passed through the city of Constantinople [pronounced con-stan-tin-OH-pull], which we call Istanbul [pronounced ISS-tan-bool] today. That route became blocked however, when the Turks conquered Constantinople in 1453, and the flow of spices to Europe was cut off almost completely.

Can you imagine what meals were like without any way to keep foods fresh, and without any spices to mask their taste and smell? (Use a globe of the earth to point out to your children where the Spice Islands were located and how the spices passed through Constantinople on their way to Spain, Italy, Portugal, and France. Today the Spice Islands are known as the Moluccas [pronounced muh-LUCK-uz], and can be found in Indonesia, east of Borneo, south of the Philippines.)

So the search for spices—and pepper in particular—supplies the "why?" for Columbus's four voyages to the New World. Columbus, you see, had convinced the king and queen of Spain that he could reach these spice-bearing islands from the other direction, by sailing west across the Atlantic Ocean, and throughout his life he maintained that he had done just that, refusing to believe that he had discovered any "new" lands at all.

Developing a "Sense" of History

To help your children get better acquainted with their own senses of smell and taste, make sure they know that these two senses are related: It is very difficult to taste anything that you cannot smell. Have your child pinch shut his nose and then put a few grains of fresh ground coffee or a little ground cinnamon in his mouth. Can he taste what he is chewing? Now have him breathe through his nose and feel the instantaneous rush of flavor that accompanies the return of his sense of smell.

Does your child think she can tell the difference between the taste of an apple and the taste of a potato? Have her put on a blindfold and pinch her nose closed; then let her taste a piece of each food separately and try to guess which is which.

Your eyes work in conjunction with these other senses, too. Try to identify the smells of various spices in your kitchen (the little bottles of flavoring extracts are ideal for this) without seeing their labels first. You'll probably recognize several familiar scents, yet be totally unable to name them. (You can find many other home experiments to help your children better understand and appreciate their sense of smell in the 612.8 section of the juvenile books in your local library.)

So, here is an instance of history "coming to life" because you and your children will better understand the condition of life in Columbus's time, you will have a feeling for the human desires and needs that caused his historic voyages, and you will know more about the human senses of taste and smell that tie you directly to the people of the fifteenth century and to Columbus himself. All this is better learned—more easily learned—in the home than in the school, and it all begins by asking "why?"

USEFUL FAMILY RESOURCES

America, by Alistair Cooke (New York: Alfred A. Knopf, 1973) [973 COO].

How to Really Fool Yourself, by Vicki Cobb (New York: J. B. Lippincott Publishers, 1981) [J 612.8 COB].

Touch, Taste and Smell (part of the Human Body series), by Brian R. Ward (New York: Franklin Watts, Inc., 1982) [J 612.8 WAR].

OCTOBER 12: *Columbus arrives in America*

NOVEMBER, FOURTH THURSDAY: *Thanksgiving Day*

DECEMBER 21: *Pilgrims land at Plymouth*

Bringing History Into Your Home

Many parents who begin using Family Learning activities in their own homes find it is easier to identify and create learning opportunities in the kitchen, or in the bathroom, or out in the back yard, when the learning has to do with science, or math, or even language. But the Family Learning of history often poses a problem because it is difficult to see how one's home life offers much opportunity for teaching or learning the lessons of the past, and not many families can take their children on frequent vacations to historic places around the country or around the world.

Well, the Family Learning of history *is* different, and that difference is due to the fact that we as parents must *create* home learning opportunities in the study of history, while we can often just uncover them in the other subjects. We have to be creative and resourceful and opportunistic in finding as many ways as possible to bring history into our homes and into our home life with our families. Just as our primary goal in helping our children to understand their lessons in science was to create in them a scientific attitude, we must instill in our children an attitude that values the lessons of history, too, if we want them to benefit from those lessons and from their history classes in school.

Valuing History in Your Home

How, then, do parents go about making history important to their children and encouraging the study of history in their homes? Well, just as it is with the Family Learning of any subject or topic, the first step is to show your children that history is important to you. It is your attitude about history that they will carry with them to school, and no matter what that attitude may be, they will find plenty of reinforcement for it from their classmates and

266

teachers. If you think that "history is more or less bunk," as Henry Ford once said, or if your children hear you discourse about how boring and worthless your own history classes were in school, then I guarantee that they will struggle with the subject themselves and will very likely have little interest in it for the rest of their lives.

If, on the other hand, you show them an interest in the events of the past, if you let them know your feeling of kinship with the people who lived and died in other times, and if the atmosphere in your home is one of eagerness and encouragement for knowing and learning about the people and places of long ago, then your children will very likely exhibit an interest in history that will grow with them and will become a passion in their later years.

There are materials available that can help you bring history into your home and can help you create this atmosphere of appreciation for things of the past. One of the best resources I have found (and one that will interest adults and children alike) is a 12-page, tabloid "newspaper" called *Old News*, which is published by a Pennsylvania family (including the children and grandparents) and features stories about historical events and the people who participated in them as though they were fast-breaking news events. "Henry VIII Seeks Divorce" screams one banner headline, beneath which is a thorough retelling of the events in 1527 that led the king of England to discard his queen, Catherine of Aragon, in favor of the twenty-year-old Anne Boleyn. "Confederate Spy Ring Exposed in Washington, D.C." shouts another, while feature stories include an "interview" with Al Capone and Heinrich Schliemann's description of his expeditions to find the ancient city of Troy. You can obtain a one-year subscription to this excellent family resource (nine issues per year) by sending $15 to *Old News*, 400 Stackstown Road, Marietta, PA 17547 (telephone: 717-426-2212).

There is also *American Heritage* magazine, which is aimed at adult readers and is ideal for improving your own knowledge and appreciation of American history. The features are well written and include many photographs and paintings as well as helpful information about planning family visits to various historical places. A yearly subscription (eight issues) costs $32 (telephone: 1-800-777-1222).

Whether your resource materials are inside your home or inside your local library, you and your children must learn to look for lessons from the past. You must be curious about historic events and about what you can learn from those events that you can apply to your life today and tomorrow. National holidays, for example, create natural opportunities for families to think about just what it is that they are celebrating on each particular day. But knowing the history of the event or the history of the person being celebrated is only a beginning, for the history alone will be static and stale if we don't take that next and necessary step of asking ourselves how that history affects our lives today and what there is in that history that can be a benefit to us in helping us lead better lives.

Learning the History of Thanksgiving

Let's look at our celebration of Thanksgiving, for example, to see how making history part of our homes can help us and our children get a better feeling for the people of the past, and for the lessons they have to teach.

Is the traditional Thanksgiving dinner designed to replicate the food that the Pilgrims ate during the celebration of their first harvest? No, not really. But if we can talk with our children about what Thanksgiving Day really commemorates before we sit down to our Thanksgiving feast, we all will be able to enjoy that meal a little more and appreciate the many comforts and pleasures we take for granted in our lives, because history will be present in our minds and hearts around that table and throughout that day.

The Pilgrims who landed at Plymouth Rock in 1620 didn't call themselves "Pilgrims," and the name wasn't used to refer to them until almost two centuries after their arrival. They were "Separatists," who believed that the Church of England was an ungodly institution and could not be reformed, and they were hounded out of England for this belief.

They left in *two* ships—the *Mayflower* and the *Speedwell*—but after getting about 300 miles out into the ocean, the *Speedwell* began to leak, and so both ships returned to port and all 102 travelers huddled into the *Mayflower* for their overly crowded, sixty-four-day voyage to the New World. Only forty-one of these passengers were Separatists; the rest were coming to America to find their fortune, not to practice their religion.

We know very little about the Pilgrims' first Thanksgiving; in fact, there is only one firsthand account of what occurred that day (a letter back to England describing athletic contests and an outdoor feast for the company and about ninety Indians). It certainly doesn't describe the scene most of us picture as having taken place. Did they eat turkey? cranberries? pumpkin pie? popcorn? No one knows for sure.

What we do know is that this hearty little band of somewhat kindred souls had endured a wearying sea voyage only to reach land in the cold of winter—the barren, rocky, almost-desolate shores of Cape Cod. But here they stayed, in spite of disease, and exposure to cold, and inadequate food—which combined to kill almost half their number during that very first winter. Forty-seven men, women, and children were buried in unmarked graves, this to prevent hostile Indians from learning the extent of the group's losses.

Still, they endured, and when the spring came, they planted crops, and in the autumn, when they harvested those crops, they saw that there would be enough to nourish them through the coming winter. They would not starve. Thank God!

We cannot imagine how they must have felt, but we can wonder with our children just how we would have reacted to these terrible hardships, and how thankful we would have been to know that our hope and our lives would not be snuffed out by forces we were powerless to control. We can share with our children the story of the Pilgrims' perseverance, we can admire their strength and their tenacity, and we can learn not only that hardships can be overcome, but also that we should be thankful for our many blessings every day of the year.

Learning the History of Holidays

A multi-volume encyclopedia is a good place to find the history behind various holidays and celebrations, but the 394 section of the reference books in your local library also has other resources that focus on American history and American holidays. My personal favorite is *The American Book of Days* (third edition), edited by Jane M. Hatch [R 394.26973 HAT].

You will find that a Family Learning focus on holidays will allow your children to get a perspective on history and to find lessons in history that they are no longer able to get in school. The histories behind most of our religious holidays—for example, Christmas, Easter, Hanukkah, Passover—are left untouched by our public schools, but even our secular celebrations have become occasions for our children to learn how unheroic their national heroes really were. Columbus Day has become a time to ridicule Christopher Columbus rather than praise him or to better understand the importance of his achievements. He is scorned by "revisionist" writers and teachers who believe that children and adults are better served by learning about every fault and blemish of the people they have come to admire.

I am certainly not suggesting that we shield our children from these facts of history or that we tell them only the myths and not the truths about historical heroes like Columbus or George Washington or Martin Luther King. What I am suggesting is that there are reasons behind the elevation of men and women to hero status, reasons that both transcend the myths and give rise to them. All human beings are going to have human faults and failings, but not all human beings have the ennobling qualities, the uncommon characteristics, that allow heroes to perform heroic acts.

Family Learning, unlike classroom learning or textbook learning, allows us to focus on these heroic characteristics because the goal of Family Learning is self-improvement. We want to use the lessons that exist everywhere in the world around us as ways to help ourselves become better, more knowledgeable, wiser people, and to encourage our children to adopt this inexhaustible, self-perpetuating lifestyle of learning as well.

Admirable Qualities in Columbus

So, what can we learn from Columbus that will help us and our children become better people? Well, we can see that among his admirable qualities was the ability to dream great things for himself and then to back up his dreams with hard work and diligent preparation. (This particular quality brings to mind one of my favorite quotations, from Henry David Thoreau: "If you have built castles in the air, your work need not be lost; that is where they should be. Now put the foundations under them.") Columbus was also a man of extraordinary persistence, who would occasionally get discouraged but would never give up. And he was a lifelong learner as well, a man who had taught himself four languages, navigation, and meteorology, and who read everything he could find that would be of benefit when his opportunity finally came.

We can use the occasion of Columbus Day to focus on these attributes in our homes and with our families, and we can take similar advantage of other holidays as well, but first we must see the study of history as being useful to our own personal growth and development and to that of our children.

USEFUL FAMILY RESOURCES

The American Book of Days, Third Edition, edited by Jane M. Hatch (New York: The H. W. Wilson Company, 1978) [R 394.26973 HAT].

Celebrations: The Complete Book of American Holidays, by Robert J. Meyers (Garden City, N.Y.: Doubleday and Co., Inc., 1972) [394.26973 MYE or R 394.26973 MYE].

The Folklore of American Holidays, edited by Hennig Cohen and Tristram Potter Coffin (Detroit: Gale Research, 1987) [R 394.26973 FOL].

My Backyard History Book, by David Weitzman (Boston: Little, Brown and Company, 1975) [J 973.07 WEI or J 921.1 WEI].

Old News, 400 Stackstown Road, Marietta, PA 17547, telephone: 717-426-2212; $15 per year (nine issues).

APRIL, THIRD MONDAY: *Boston Marathon*

JUNE 14: *Flag Day*

SEPTEMBER 9: *Battle of Marathon*

Don't Wait for Holidays to Celebrate Historic Events

National holidays, school holidays, religious holidays—all these dates are ideal for focusing our children's attention on specific events and people in history, and on the lessons we all can learn from history, because the rest of society is helping to reinforce our message. There are special newspaper features and television programs and celebrations in the community that encourage the learning and understanding of history on these special days.

But what about all the days that aren't so special? Must the subject matter for the Family Learning of history be restricted to only the people and events that are important enough to merit a holiday?

Surprisingly enough, the answer is "yes," but *every day* can be a historical holiday in your home. One of the most useful techniques in the Family Learning of history is to have parents and children select their own occasions in history to celebrate in their homes and to use these occasions as a focus for learning about the history behind famous people, places, and events.

Often these family celebrations will be suggested by something that is taking place in the world and is of special interest to you or to your children. The tie-in to history, then, may not be a specific calendar date, or that date may be just a minor historical fact that you will discover during your study.

History of the Marathon

Let's take, for example, the running of the marathon during the Olympic Games, or the annual Boston Marathon, or perhaps a marathon race that is being held in or near your community. Can you see how these events might be more interesting and more rewarding and more memorable if your children knew the history behind why the race is called a *marathon* and why it is the length it is? Do you also see how your children's attention to the marathon—the television coverage of the race, for instance, or their knowing someone who is running in the event—is an ideal motivator for this particular historical study, and is an advantage that the Family Learning of history has that the classroom learning or textbook learning of history simply cannot share?

Let's see what a brief look into both ancient history and modern history can tell us about the origin of this event and about why all marathon races are exactly 26 miles, 385 yards long.

 The name *marathon* comes from a plain in eastern Greece where one of the most famous battles in history was fought in 490 B.C. The Athenian soldiers were outnumbered six to one by the invading Persian army, yet they routed the Persians at Marathon that day, killing several thousands and sending the rest fleeing to their ships.

Legend has it that a runner named Phidippides [pronounced fie-DIP-ih-deez] dashed full-tilt from the battle scene back to the city gates of Athens, some twenty-five miles away. Thoroughly exhausted from his run, he managed to utter only one dying word: "*Nike!*"— the Greek word for "Victory!"

You might use your children's familiarity with the name of a certain shoe manufacturer to lead them into this story and lead them to the 292 or 938 sections of the juvenile collection in your library, where they can learn more about the famous Battle of Marathon.

Although the marathon run acquired its name from this story, the connection stops there. Phidippides' heroic dash, you see, is almost certainly pure fiction. The story appears to have originated about six centuries after the Battle of Marathon took place. Nor was the run commemorated during the ancient Olympics, for the longest race in the original games was about three miles.

 In fact, it was not until the 1908 Olympic Games in London that the marathon acquired its distance and its stature. A race of twenty-four or twenty-five miles had been added when the modern Olympics resumed in 1896 (after having been discontinued for over 1,500 years). But during the Games of 1908, the starting line was moved hundreds of yards back to the royal lawn of Windsor Castle so that the grandchildren of King Edward VII and Queen Alexandra could watch the race begin.

Well, this 1908 Olympic marathon turned out to be one of the most thrilling and most famous distance races ever run. Dorando Pietri [pronounced pee-AA-tree], a twenty-two-year-old Italian candymaker, staggered into the Olympic Stadium at the end of the race needing only to circle the cinder track once and cross the finish line in first place. But he was so fatigued from his grueling run that he began running *in the wrong direction* around the track! With 70,000 spectators screaming for him to turn around, Pietri stumbled and fell to his knees. British officials and doctors ran to him, pulled him up to his feet, and shoved him off in the right direction. Three more times he fell, but three more times he somehow summoned enough strength to stagger onward. Finally he collapsed in a heap just a few yards from the finish, but some officials picked up his arms and literally dragged him across the tape just seconds ahead of his nearest pursuer.

Pietri was disqualified for not finishing the race under his own power, but his courage and the similarity between his struggle and that of the legendary Phidippides caused Olympic officials to remeasure the course that he ran. Several years later, the precise distance of the 1908 marathon was established as the standard for all future marathons—26 miles, 385 yards.

So by tracing the history of this sporting event, we and our children acquire not only a closer personal bond with the human beings who made it the event it is today, but we also find ourselves following various learning paths through which we hear about and talk about places like Athens and Persia and London and Windsor Castle. There is no chapter or unit in any history textbook that would include mention of all these places together, and that is because most history texts deal with centuries or ages, while the Family Learning of history focuses on topics.

History of Our National Anthem

Let's look at another learning topic that can spring from a sporting event, at the history lessons it can teach, and at the geography and language skills that can be acquired along the way. Suppose you are going to see a professional game—it could be baseball, basketball, football, or hockey—or even a college game or high school game, for that matter. There is  one activity that precedes all these contests: the playing and singing of our national anthem. Why not take advantage of the situation by using your children's interest and excitement in attending the game to focus their attention on the national anthem as well as on the game itself? Spend a few minutes with them finding out what they know and don't know about "The Star-Spangled Banner," and you'll see how a better understanding of history and geography and language can all spring from this one learning opportunity.

Just what are *spangles*, anyway? Do your children have any idea what the words to our national anthem really mean—words like *perilous*, and *o'er*, and *ramparts*? Find a copy of the lyrics (look in the 973 section of your local library for books like *The American Reader: Words That Moved a Nation*, by Diane Ravitch), and have your children look up the meaning of any words that are unfamiliar to them in a dictionary. The song may still not make much sense, and that is because your children do not understand why it was written or what the lyrics were attempting to describe. And here is where the history lesson comes in.

 The words were composed during the War of 1812 by a lawyer from Washington, D.C., named Francis Scott Key, whose involvement in the whole matter was quite accidental. Key had been persuaded by several friends of a physician named William Beanes, who had become a prisoner of war, to negotiate with the British Navy for the release of the doctor. Dr. Beanes had—for some reason—been picked up by soldiers off the streets of Washington during a British assault on the city that had resulted in the burning of the White House, the Capitol, and several other public buildings. He was taken back to the British naval ships that had blockaded Chesapeake Bay, where Francis Scott Key went to obtain his release.

The talks were courteous and an agreement was reached, but other talks were under way at the same time, on that same ship, and these talks concerned the battle plans for that night's attack on Baltimore and on Fort McHenry, which guarded the city. The British didn't know how much of their plans Key and Dr. Beanes had overheard, and so they detained the Americans until after the battle had commenced.

From here on the story is, or should be, rather well known by all American schoolchildren. Key was so taken by the bombardment he witnessed from the deck of the ship that night (the British lobbed more than 1,800 bombs and rockets into and around the fort), and he was so stirred upon seeing the American flag still flying over the fort at daybreak, that he hastily composed several verses of a poem on the back of a letter or an envelope he found in his pocket. That poem, which appeared shortly thereafter in a Baltimore newspaper under the title "The Defense of Fort McHenry," became the words for what we know as "The Star-Spangled Banner."

 Now recite the anthem for your children like a poem and have them paraphrase or "translate" it into more modern or more common vocabulary. When they sing it with you at the game (and every time they sing or hear the anthem thereafter), they will be reinforcing their knowledge of history and their vocabulary as well, and they will be reminded of this Family Learning experience for the rest of their lives.

Learning From the Flag

You can take this lesson a step further by recognizing that not only will they be hearing "The Star-Spangled Banner," they will be looking at the American flag, too. Just what do they know about this national symbol?

We think of our flag as having fifty white stars on a blue background, and thirteen red and white stripes. (Are there more red stripes or white stripes? Answer: seven red, six white.) These thirteen stripes represent the thirteen original colonies, which became the thirteen original states. (Can you name all thirteen? Answer: Delaware, Pennsylvania, New Jersey, Georgia, Connecticut, Massachusetts, Maryland, South Carolina, New Hampshire, Virginia, New York, North Carolina, and Rhode Island.) But the flag that Francis Scott Key saw flying above Fort McHenry in 1814 had *fifteen stars* and *fifteen stripes!* You see, we used to add both a star and a stripe each time a new state was added to the union, and that is what Congress did in honor of the fourteenth state (Vermont) and the fifteenth state (Kentucky). This fifteen-stripe flag was also the one that Lewis and Clark carried across the continent in 1805, and the one under which General Andrew Jackson defeated the British at the Battle of New Orleans.

But by 1818, six more states had been admitted, and Congress felt that the addition of so many stripes would clutter the look of the flag. So from 1818 until now, each new state has added a star to the flag, but the stripes remain fixed in honor of the thirteen original states. (When was your state admitted to the union, and how many stars were on the flag at that time?)

USEFUL FAMILY RESOURCES

The American Reader: Words That Moved a Nation, edited by Diane Ravitch (New York: Harper/Collins Publishers, 1990) [973 AME or 081 AME].

Don't Know Much About History: Everything You Need to Know About American History but Never Learned, by Kenneth C. Davis (New York: Crown Publishers, 1990) [973 DAV].

Flags of the USA, by David Eggenberger (New York: Thomas Y. Crowell, Co., 1964) [J 929.9 EGG].

Panati's Extraordinary Origins of Everyday Things, by Charles Panati (New York: Harper & Row Publishers, 1989) [031 PAN].

The Story of Our Flag, by Carl Glick and Ollie Rogers (New York: G. P. Putnam's Sons, 1964) [J 929.9 GLI].

What So Proudly We Hail: All About Our American Flag, Monuments, and Symbols, by Maymie Richardson Krythe (New York: Harper and Row Publishers, 1968) [929 KRY or 917.3 KRY].

SEPTEMBER 17: *Signing of the Constitution*   DECEMBER 15: *Ratification of the Bill of Rights*

SEPTEMBER 27: *Matchbook patented*   DECEMBER 31: *Edison's electric light demonstrated*

Creating Holidays to Celebrate in Your Home

Although many events and activities outside the home can suggest tie-ins for the Family Learning of history, parents who want to increase the frequency of their children's "brushes with history" will look for ways to learn about the past inside the home as well. One of the easiest and best methods for doing this is to create celebrations in your home to honor specific historic events—events that are important for your children to understand, but ones that do not merit a holiday of their own and are not likely to be studied in school.

Celebrating the Constitution and Bill of Rights

For example, the United States Constitution, the Bill of Rights, and the Declaration of Independence may be the three most important documents in the history of our country, yet only the last is honored with a holiday (and that happens to fall during a school vacation). One way to focus your children's attention upon the other two is to make them the focus of your family's attention on a date that is significant to each document. The Constitution, for instance, was signed by the delegates to the Constitutional Convention in Philadelphia on September 17, 1787, and so September 17 might be an excellent time to celebrate the Constitution in your home and to discuss this document and its history and its importance with your family.

Children should understand that although the Declaration of Independence was signed in 1776, we didn't begin the process of creating a constitution for our new nation for almost eleven years, and the document wasn't ratified and didn't go into effect until 1789. In fact, our Constitution would never have been ratified at all if those who had

276

framed it and were promoting its adoption (Franklin, Jefferson, Madison, and Hamilton, for example) hadn't agreed to add a list of guaranteed freedoms and fundamental rights to the document. These guarantees became the Bill of Rights, and on December 15, 1791, they became the first ten amendments added to the Constitution. So, December 15 is another excellent date for a family celebration that focuses on the history of our country's founding and on the ideals that the people of the time thought should be embodied in the spirit and laws of our country.

It is difficult for children today to understand the importance that our ancestors attached to this statement of fundamental, individual rights and freedoms. We can only vaguely imagine what it must have been like to have soldiers quartered in our homes or to be prevented from meeting with others to discuss whatever we might wish. Indeed, it is somewhat harder now to find examples of nations that deny their people the right to pray or speak or assemble in any way they choose. But December 15 may be an ideal time to have your family consider not only what life *was* like before the Bill of Rights, but what life *would be* like today if the freedoms we take for granted were not guaranteed to us by this most remarkable document.

Parents and children can become familiar with our Constitution and its Bill of Rights without having to think of themselves as Constitutional scholars. Nor should they think of these wonderfully well-written and surprisingly brief documents as just some ancient parchments preserved in a distant shrine. You can make the Constitution, the Bill of Rights, and the Declaration of Independence part of your home learning resources so that they, just like a dictionary, a globe, or an atlas, can be readily available for occasional family readings and discussions.

To receive a pocket-size book containing all three documents, send a request for "The Constitution" (stock number 052-003-01411-4) along with a check for $1.75 made out to Superintendent of Documents, and mail it to Superintendent of Documents, P.O. Box 371954, Pittsburgh, PA 15250-7954. Or order by phone (202-512-1800) and have your Visa or Mastercard number handy.

There are all sorts of historic dates that you can make into family celebrations to encourage learning in your home, and just how you go about celebrating each event can be designed to fit your particular family and the interests of your children. In fact, you will want to open up and expand your ideas of what constitutes a "historic" event in the first place, for this will allow you to see the many opportunities for teaching and learning history that lie all around you but that appear to deal with subjects other than history.

Celebrating the Electric Light

Take, for example, the light bulbs in your home. They are called *incandescent* bulbs because the filament inside them glows with an intense heat, and the Latin word *candescere* meant "to glow white." (A similar Latin word, *candidatus*, meant "a person dressed in white," and was applied to those politicians who wore clean, white togas when they campaigned among the people. From this root we get our modern words *candidate* and *candid*.)

One way to introduce the "science" of the incandescent light to your children is to have them look at its history instead, and a good time to do that might be on December 31, for it was on New Year's Eve back in 1879 that Thomas Edison gave the first public demonstration of his new electric light. Have your children think about all the ways that the world began to change because of what happened on that New Year's Eve just a little more than a century ago. Businesses, for example, could now be open after sunset; factories could run night shifts; hospitals could provide round-the-clock medical service.

But why did the electric light spring into existence at this time in history, and just what did Edison do that no one had been able to do before?

Although human curiosity over electricity dates back many years, the simple fact is that we had no way of generating a sustained electric current until several decades into the nineteenth century. So Edison was living at a time when people were just learning about ways to apply this new and exciting source of power. It was not he who came up with the idea of making a wire glow by passing electricity through it; he was, however, the one who solved the problem of how to keep that wire glowing.

Edison knew that because oxygen was needed for anything to burn, he must remove all the air from inside the glass bulb and seal the bulb so that no oxygen could reach the glowing filament inside. The filament would have to be able to withstand tremendous heat without breaking, and so Edison experimented with more than 1,600 different materials (even a whisker from a friend's beard), but each lasted only a few minutes, some only a few seconds, before breaking (and thereby cutting the flow of electricity). Finally he carbonized a piece of cotton thread—carbon having the highest known melting point at that time— and the lamp glowed with the light of about sixteen candles for more than forty hours. The first practical incandescent light was born.

Edison's patent on the invention became a principal part of the Edison Electric Light Company, but he also founded the Edison Lamp Company to manufacture the bulbs, the Edison Machine Works to manufacture the dynamos that produced electricity for the bulbs, and the Edison Tube Company to make junction boxes and underground tubing. All these companies later merged to form the Edison General Electric Company, which became the conglomerate we know today as General Electric.

Your children will understand better how an incandescent bulb works if you carefully break the glass in one to expose its filament, or if you obtain a model in which the glass is clear instead of frosted. Today's light bulbs glow so brightly because the filament inside them is so hot—perhaps 4,500 degrees Fahrenheit! Consequently, modern filaments are made of a metal called tungsten, which has a melting point of 6,100 degrees. A thin strand of tungsten half the thickness of a human hair is coiled, then coiled again, so that its original twenty-one inches form a filament only $\frac{5}{8}$ inch from end to end. When this delicate filament breaks after hundreds of hours of heating and cooling, your children can hear it rattle around inside the globe as they shake the burned-out bulb.

Your children should understand, too, that the amount of light given off by an incandescent bulb depends upon how much electricity it uses. The wattage listed on a light bulb tells how much electrical power the bulb uses in making its filament glow. Some bulbs have two filaments of different wattages—a 50-watt filament and a 100-watt filament, for example. If current is channeled through these filaments separately, the lamp could glow like a 50-watt bulb or a 100-watt bulb, but when both filaments are glowing together, the lamp produces the light of a 150-watt bulb. Have your children look at the rating of any three-way bulbs in your house to see for themselves how the sum of the lower wattages always equals the highest wattage.

The invention of the electric light, then, had an identifiable cause and can be placed in its proper time period because it could not have existed prior to its cause. And that's what we should want our children to understand about historic events in general, that they are caused by earlier events and that they have effects upon later events. Children who look at history in this way will be asking and learning "why?" instead of just focusing on "when?" and they will realize that knowing the causes and effects of any occurrence will place that happening for them in its proper period of time.

Celebrating Famous Inventions

Studying and celebrating the history of important inventions with our children lets them see history in a new way, one that is quite different from the focus on wars and rulers and centuries that is common in most of their history textbooks. When we understand why an invention sprang into being at a certain point in history, why it couldn't have come about any earlier, and how that invention changed people's lives at the time and contributed to future change as well, then we will see wars and rulers and centuries as somewhat useful backdrops to the real story of human history, and not as the entire story themselves.

This was the idea behind James Burke's 1979 BBC television series called "Connections," which is still being rerun on Public Broadcasting stations in this country today. In this series, Burke shows that inventions and events occur as a direct result of inventions and events that preceded them, and that both are inextricably intertwined. If we can get our children to see such things as how the use of stirrups led to the Norman Conquest of England, and why Gutenberg's printing press contributed to both the Renaissance and the Reformation, then they will be on their way to having a useful command of history, instead of the comparatively useless knowledge of historic dates alone.

You can find the book version of "Connections" [609 BUR], as well as the guide to Burke's subsequent television series "The Day the Universe Changed" [509 BUR] at bookstores and in your local library.

Celebrating Everyday Inventions

Another way that we use inventions to help our children learn about and think about history is to focus their attention on those simple, everyday conveniences that we don't think of at "inventions" as all. The zipper, for instance, or the umbrella, or the flush toilet, or shampoo, or . . . , you get the idea.

We rarely think about the way life was really lived by our ancestors—life without all the modern conveniences we enjoy today—and most children find it difficult to imagine that life could have existed at all before there were such things as mirrors and sunglasses and Velcro. But just imagine the learnings that can grow out of giving some family thought to questions like "What did people use before they had _____?"

Take, for example, the relatively modern convenience called the matchbook. It may not seem like an invention at all, and yet somehow it came into existence, and somehow people managed to get on with their lives before it came into existence. The matchbook entered our history on September 27, 1892, when an attorney from Lima, Pennsylvania, named Joshua Pusey received a U.S. patent for his idea of putting fifty paper matchsticks, along with a chemically treated striking surface, together in a small, paper booklet. Unfortunately, Pusey designed his booklet with the striking surface on the *inside* of the cover, and so accidental sparks frequently ignited all the matches in the pack. However, when the Diamond Match Company bought Pusey's patent three years later, they moved the striking surface to the outside of the cover, creating a design that is still used today.

It is hard to envision a world without matches, and yet our own age needs them less than any other in all of history. We have electric lights, furnaces instead of fireplaces for warmth, and stoves and ovens that start with a push of a finger. And so we find it almost primitive when we read Charles Dickens's report of how it took most people in the mid-1800s almost a half hour to start a fire using flint and steel.

Could you have shown the people of that time how to make matches? This is just the type of question that can help us, and especially our children, learn science and history at the same time. What I am suggesting here is that instead of focusing all our scientific and technological interest on complicated and intricate, modern inventions—the workings of a computer, a television, or an electric motor, for example—we can profit from investigating and understanding the basic science behind the simple, everyday, yet extraordinary devices that we take for granted, but would be considered wonders and marvels to people in ages past.

The history lessons come from our wondering and imagining and investigating how people ever got along without these everyday wonders and common conveniences. How did the people who settled our frontier start the fires they used for cooking their meals? How did our colonial ancestors light their fireplaces?

Then, too, we can test our understanding of these "simple" devices by imagining ourselves living in an earlier age, attempting to create these wonders out of the materials available. (This method for understanding basic science and technology is highlighted repeatedly in a wonderful novel to read aloud with your children—Mark Twain's *A Connecticut Yankee in King Arthur's Court*—and is also similar to a theme that was woven into every episode of the television series "MacGyver.")

The whole process starts by reviving your own curiosity and by allowing yourself to wonder and to investigate how things work. We allow children to wonder how matches work, or how a zipper works, or how soap cleans, or how an eraser makes pencil marks disappear. But most adults are embarrassed to wonder about such things themselves, and so we find that we have surprisingly little help to offer our children when they ask us to explain these marvels to them.

We have to redouble our efforts within our homes and among our family members to investigate these simple, everyday wonders of science and technology. It is just such little investigations as these, more so than lengthy school reports, that provide an ideal use for a multi-volume encyclopedia. Another good resource is the 031 section of the juvenile books in your library, where you'll find books like *The Big Book of Tell Me Why*, by Arkady Leokum.

USEFUL FAMILY RESOURCES

The Big Book of Tell Me Why, by Arkady Leokum (New York: Purlieu Press, 1989 [J 031 LEO].

Connections, by James Burke (Boston: Little, Brown and Company, 1978) [609 BUR].

The Constitution (includes the Bill of Rights and the Declaration of Independence), send $1.75 to Superintendent of Documents, P.O. Box 371954, Pittsburgh, PA 15250-7954, telephone: 202-512-1800.

The Day the Universe Changed, by James Burke (Boston: Little, Brown and Company, 1985) [509 BUR].

"Documents of Liberty" posters. Parchment-like reproductions of the *Constitution, Bill of Rights, Declaration of Independence,* and *Gettysburg Address* from LibertyTree Network 1-800-927-8733; item #2044, $9.95 (four documents).

Fire of Genius: Inventors of the Past Century, by Ernest V. Heyn (Garden City, N.Y.: Anchor Press/Doubleday, 1976) [608.7 HEY].

The History of Invention: From Stone Axes to Silicon Chips, by Trevor I. Williams (New York: Facts on File Publications, 1987) [609 WIL].

Inventing, Inventions, and Inventors: A Teaching Resource Book, by Jerry D. Flack (Englewood, Colo.: Teacher Ideas Press, 1989) [607.1 FLA].

Panati's Extraordinary Origins of Everyday Things, by Charles Panati (New York: Perennial Library, 1989) [031 PAN].

The Smithsonian Book of Invention (Washington, D.C.: The Smithsonian Institution, 1978) [609 SMI].

APRIL 18: *San Francisco earthquake/Paul Revere's ride*
SEPTEMBER 2: *Calendar Adjustment Day*
OCTOBER 28: *Statue of Liberty dedicated*

History Can Lead You Down Many Paths to Learning

Throughout this book, I have suggested calendar dates that you could use to focus your children's attention upon specific events in history, and that you might celebrate in your home. I have done this primarily because I know that the most difficult part of any Family Learning activity is the broaching of it—beginning it with your children, suggesting it, and getting them involved. After that, the learning takes on a life of its own and is much easier to continue and expand than it was to begin. So these calendar dates can be a help by providing parents with a convenient "excuse" for beginning an activity on a certain date and for focusing the family's attention on a specific event in history.

In spite of the prevalence of dates throughout this book, however, it is important for us all to understand that knowing the day of the month on which an event took place is just about the least important thing that a child can learn about any historic happening. The year in which an event occurred places it in time and helps us see why an event occurred when it did and how it affected events that followed. But the calendar itself has changed over the years, and so an event that appears to have taken place exactly 300 years ago today, actually occurred 299 years and 354 days ago, instead. Why? Well, back in the year 1752, everyone in the British Empire—including everyone in the colonies that would soon become the United States—went to bed on September 2 and awoke on September 14! No, they didn't oversleep; they were just paying the price for a small miscalculation that had been made many centuries before.

History of the Calendar

It was on September 2, 1752, you see, that the British government finally accepted the fact that their calendar was wrong and had been wrong since the time of Julius Caesar.

All of us, and especially our children, think of the calendar as one of those fixtures of the world that has existed forever. There are twelve months in a year, and "thirty days hath September," and every fourth year is a leap year. That's how it's always been, right? Well, no.

For most of human history there were no calendars at all, nor was there any need for them. But agriculture, warfare, and money lending, among other things, brought about a need to know—first of all—just how many days there were in a year. The number of months and their irregular lengths are artificial divisions, but the year itself is a very precise period of time.

It is important for children to understand the idea that a year is the time it takes for the earth to make one complete orbit of the sun, and you can demonstrate this idea to them by using a basketball and a golf ball, for example, to represent the two bodies, and have your children call out the months as they move the smaller object (representing the earth) around the larger one (which remains fixed, representing the sun).

In 46 B.C., Julius Caesar's chief astronomer determined that there were exactly $365\frac{1}{4}$ days in each year. Caesar then devised a calendar of twelve months (it used to have only ten) totaling 365 days, and, to take care of that $\frac{1}{4}$ day, he invented the leap year, which would add an extra day every four years. This was a brilliant scheme, except for one thing: The earth doesn't take exactly 365.25 days to make a complete orbit of the sun; it takes exactly 365.2422 days.

Now this may not seem like much of a discrepancy, but every year following 46 B.C., that little .0078 of a day deviation put Julius's calendar (which is called the Julian calendar) more and more out of whack with the actual solar year. In other words, each year according to Julius's calendar took about eleven and a half minutes longer than the earth did to make a complete orbit of the sun, and this amounted to about three days every four centuries. The Julian calendar would say that the sun should be in a certain place in the sky at noon on a certain day, but the sun wouldn't actually be in that position until several days later.

After more than 1,600 years of this slippage, the Julian calendar had deviated ten full days from the solar cycle it was designed to represent, and Pope Gregory XIII decided to correct the calendar by lopping ten days off the current year, decreeing that Thursday, October 4, 1582, would be followed by Friday, October 15, 1582.

Although some countries adopted the Gregorian reform (named for Pope Gregory) right away, England and its colonies didn't accept the change for another 170 years, and by that time almost eighteen centuries had passed since Caesar had issued his calendar, and the deviation over those centuries amounted to a full eleven days.

Calendar Adjustment Day

Those eleven days simply vanished when the British Calendar Act decreed that Wednesday, September 2, 1752, would be followed by Thursday, September 14, 1752. History records that there was rioting in the streets throughout the far-flung Empire by those who felt they had been cheated out of eleven days. Renters, for example, had to pay for a full month even though that month had been reduced by eleven days, and people who had borrowed money now had eleven fewer days in which to pay it back. Many people of the time believed that their lives had somehow been shortened by eleven days, but landlords, moneylenders, and salaried workers, as you might expect, applauded the change.

For most people, however, the change was nothing more than a minor inconvenience. George Washington, for example, continued to celebrate his birthday on February 11, even though the new calendar pushed the date up to February 22, the date we now recognize as his birthday.

But it took many years for all the countries of the world to recognize and adopt the Gregorian calendar, and in the meantime, travelers and people doing international business had to keep track of what the local date was in various regions, just as we, today, need to know what the local time is when we contact someone far away by telephone or computer.

As an example of the mix-ups that resulted from this calendar confusion, consider the plight of our Olympic athletes back in 1896 when they traveled to Athens, Greece, to compete in the first modern Olympic Games. The "team," which was really just a collection of several Harvard and Princeton trackmen at that time, knew that the games would begin on April 6, and so they set sail for Europe on March 2 and expected to have two weeks time for training after their voyage. However, they had based their calculations on a calendar that hung in one of their dormitory rooms, and so they were unaware that the Julian Calendar was still being used throughout Greece.

You can imagine how shocked they were when their ship docked in Athens on March 24 (according to their calendar), and they were informed that it was, in fact, April 5 in Greece! The first events were scheduled to take place on the very next day.

Besides eliminating the days between September 2 and September 14, 1752, the British Calendar Act also changed New Year's Day from March 25 (approximately the day of the spring equinox) to January 1, and it decreed an adjustment in future leap years so that the calendar would continue to correct itself. Centenary years—those ending in two zeros (such as 1800 and 1900)—which would normally be leap years, would not have that extra day in February unless they could be evenly divided by 400 (such as 1600 and 2000). So, although we usually think of leap years as coinciding with the years in which we elect our presidents, the months of February in both 1800 (election of Thomas Jefferson) and 1900 (election of William McKinley) had only twenty-eight days.

Yet the changes and adjustments that calendars have undergone throughout history, although very suitable for a historical study themselves, are not the only reasons we should avoid focusing our children's attention on the specific date of a historic event. There are, quite simply, a great many more significant historic events than there are days in any one calendar year, and so every day of every month is the anniversary of several important happenings in history.

Historic Events Share Celebration Days

This idea was brought home to me on a recent trip from San Francisco to Boston, and it was all because I happened to be traveling on April 18. When I left San Francisco in the morning, much of the city was commemorating the anniversary of the great earthquake and fire back in 1906 that killed hundreds of people and left a hundred thousand homeless. When the plane touched down in Boston later that day, I found many of the residents there celebrating a historic event, too, but it had nothing to do with earthquakes or fires. April 18 also happens to be the date back in 1775 when Paul Revere and William Dawes rode out across the Massachusetts countryside to spread the news that the British were coming. Some of you may recognize this date as being featured in the most famous lines from Longfellow's "Tales of a Wayside Inn":

> Listen my children, and you shall hear
> Of the midnight ride of Paul Revere,
> On the eighteenth of April, in Seventy-five;
> Hardly a man is now alive
> Who remembers that famous day and year.

So these two historic events were both being celebrated on the same day but on opposite coasts of our country, and each event was relatively unknown to the celebrants in the other's region. Who, other than the people who happened to be traveling between San Francisco and Boston on that date, would even know that these events both occurred on April 18?

I'll bet Clarence Darrow knew. I looked it up and found that this great American attorney, who had helped shape the meaning of American freedom and justice by defending lost causes and underdogs (such as John Scopes in the famous "monkey trial") was born on April 18, 1857. So, April 18 was an important date to Clarence Darrow, and I am sure that he recognized his birthdate in Longfellow's poem about Paul Revere's ride, and I'm also sure that he remembered hearing about the disaster in San Francisco as he was celebrating his forty-ninth birthday.

All Children Have "Historic" Birth Dates

Just like Clarence Darrow, children like to think of their birth date as special, and so they are eager to identify the events and the people in history who share this special day with them. Of course, they will need to learn about why these events and people are famous, but this common date will serve not only to encourage their learning, but will cause them to remember what they have learned, as well.

A junior high teacher I know makes use of this technique with her classes each year by having each student "become" a character from history who was born on that student's birth date. The student studies the character's life and times and then adopts that character's identity (and costume) during a class session that features interviews with student "reporters" and discussions with other figures from world and American history.

There are several ways that you can use your children's birth date in helping them acquire a better understanding of history. For example, you can order a back issue of a weekly news magazine (such as *Time* or *Newsweek,* or even *Life* magazine) that came out on the week your child was born, or you can visit your local library and photocopy the front page from the *New York Times* or another major newspaper that was published on your child's birthday. These resources will help your child understand what was going on in the rest of the country, and what the people in the rest of the world were thinking about while you were concentrating on the birth of your child.

You can also use the library to help acquaint your children with the historic events that happened on their birth date but in other years than the year they were born. In the 031 and 394.2 sections of the reference collection, you will find several books that group historic happenings and the birthdays of famous people according to the day of the month, rather than the year, they occurred. My personal favorites include *Chase's Annual Events; From Day to Day: A Calendar of Notable Birthdays and Events,* by David E. Johnson; and *Famous First Facts,* by Joseph Nathan Kane.

But no matter whether you use your children's birth dates as aids in encouraging them to focus on the history behind various people or events, or whether you use family celebrations of historic happenings and famous inventions for this purpose, you will soon discover a fundamental difference between the Family Learning of history and the way in which history is presented in many classrooms and textbooks.

Family Learning does not see history as a grand subject that can stand alone and be bundled up neatly in the pages of a book. History is, instead, a combination of all the other subjects, and so there are many paths that a person can take to come to a better understanding of history. You and your children might decide to begin your learning by heading down one interesting path, and then discover that you want to branch off and follow another that was suggested by something you learned while treading the first. Family Learning allows you—in fact, encourages you—to let your curiosity be your guide. In this way, children come to know that it is perfectly all right to wonder about and to investigate all sorts of things, even things that won't ever be asked them on a test. Let me show you what I mean by taking just one history lesson and looking at some of the possible learning paths that can branch out from it.

Family Learning About the Statue of Liberty

Which of our national monuments can your children recognize, and what do they know about these famous structures? Surely the Statue of Liberty would be on your list, but what about this statue would you like your children to know? They can probably identify its image already, and so they will get it right on a "matching" test in school, but they may not know anything else about it.

If we ask the question "when?" about this statue, we can learn that it was officially dedicated on October 28, 1886, by then-president Grover Cleveland (and so we might use October 28 as a day of celebrating the Statue of Liberty in our homes). But even a cursory knowledge of this topic must certainly include the "where?" and "why?" of the statue as well. An encyclopedia will tell you that the statue stands on Liberty Island in New York Harbor, but do your children know where that is and why that site made the statue so symbolic to the millions of immigrants who came to this country seeking a new life? If you show them on a globe where New York is and where the European immigrants came from during the decades just before and just after the turn of the century, your children may be curious about why these people left their own lands, how they arrived, and what happened to them once they were here. If they follow their curiosity, they will come to learn about Ellis Island and how many family names were summarily changed by immigration officials, and how those changes can still be seen in family names today.

The encyclopedia will also tell you that the statue is 305 feet tall, but many children have never visited this monument, and so they don't understand what a gigantic structure it is. Have your children look at the tallest building in your area and imagine how tall a thirty-story building (the height of the statue) would be standing next to it. Here they will be estimating and extrapolating and multiplying and comparing.

Half that height is made up of the base and the pedestal, which were built and paid for by the United States. But the statue itself was a gift from the people of France to commemorate our centennial (1876), although it took ten years longer than expected to build and deliver. The statue was built in Paris using large copper plates welded to an iron framework that was designed by Gustave Eiffel (who would later build the Eiffel Tower). The entire structure was then taken apart, piece by piece, packed into hundreds of huge wooden crates, shipped across the ocean, and reassembled on its new pedestal. (Just think of the science and engineering lessons involved in this feat alone.)

As for the language lessons that come from the study of this statue, try reciting and explaining to your children the last five lines from Emma Lazarus's sonnet to the statue, which were inscribed on a bronze plaque in the pedestal in 1903:

> *Give me your tired, your poor,*
> *Your huddled masses yearning to breathe free,*
> *The wretched refuse of your teeming shore,*
> *Send these, the homeless, tempest-tossed, to me:*
> *I lift my lamp beside the golden door.*

What do the "huddled masses" refer to, and how did they come to be "tempest-tossed"?

And one last language note: Our word *gadget* also came into being in 1886, and may well have come about from a Monsieur Gaget [pronounced ga-ZHAY], who was a partner in the French construction firm of Gaget, Gauhier & Cie., which built the Statue of Liberty. He devised the money-making scheme of selling miniature models of the statue to Americans living in Paris, and they began referring to these souvenirs as "gadgets," mispronouncing his French name.

These are just a few of the learning paths you might choose to follow. Once you and your children start to see learning opportunities all around you, even in little things, you will realize that learning does not have to be confined to "subjects" or "classes" or "periods" but can follow your own particular interests instead, and the learning that results will be just as good, just as useful, and even more memorable than if you had gotten it in the conventional way.

USEFUL FAMILY RESOURCES

The American Book of Days, Third Edition,
   edited by Jane M. Hatch (New York:
   The H. W. Wilson Company, 1978)
   [R 394.26973 HAT].

Chase's Annual Events (Chicago:
   Contemporary Books, 1997)
   [R 394.26 CHA].

Famous First Facts, by Joseph Nathan Kane
   (New York: The H. W. Wilson
   Company, 1981) [R 031.02 KAN].

The Folklore of American Holidays, edited
   by Hennig Cohen and Tristram Potter
   Coffin (Detroit: Gale Research, 1987)
   [R 394.2 FOL].

*From Day to Day: A Calendar of Notable
   Birthdays and Events,* by David E.
   Johnson (Metuchen, N.J.: The
   Scarecrow Press, 1990)
   [R 394.2 JOH].

Learning From the Present:
The World Around You

Introduction

Although I have grouped the previous suggestions about out-of-school learning activities into categories that seem very much like school subjects (language, science, math, etc.), I have also tried to make it clear that Family Learning is not subject-centered at all. Each of the topics in the previous chapters could lead you or your children down learning paths that are well outside the particular subject that began your journey, and each of these topics can be reached from a variety of directions, too. In fact, one of the clearest distinctions between Family Learning and "school learning" is that parents and children can let their learning follow their interests when that learning is not confined to class hours or textbooks that must be read in consecutive chapters.

There are, however, a great many learning opportunities that occur throughout everyday life that don't fit neatly into any "school subject" classifications yet are every bit as valuable as those more conventional learning topics in helping us help our children better understand the world around them. These areas, too, can be the inspiration for investigations into other subjects and topics, or they might just happen to lie along a learning path that was, itself, inspired by a piece of learning acquired in a completely different area.

The areas I will focus on in this section are merely suggestions, and you should understand that there are thousands of similar learning topics and activities that lie all around you every day, no matter who you are or where you live. The whole point of these suggestions is to awaken you to the fact that out-of-school learning opportunities exist in abundance and that they hold powerful learning benefits for adults and children alike, even though they don't fit neatly into any textbook or course curriculum.

Individual Characteristics Teach Us About Ourselves and Others

Throughout the previous chapters I have talked about the need for parents to encourage a "language attitude" or a "science attitude" or a "history attitude" among their children, by which I mean that parents play a pivotal role in getting their children to be curious about, and to find some benefit from, various things that they observe in the real world, which also happen to be subjects commonly taught in school. In the following pages, however, I want you to see that your goal must be to encourage a "learning attitude" among your children—a general curiosity about everything, not just about school subjects, and a deep-seated belief that knowing is better than not knowing.

This general "learning attitude" among children is created by a "learning atmosphere" in the home, and by parents who encourage their children to wonder about and to investigate even the smallest, the most commonplace and seemingly insignificant objects and occurrences from daily life. Parents do this by modeling a "learning attitude" themselves—by being curious about the world around them, by taking pride in their learning, and by exhibiting a sense of satisfaction and growth from every new understanding they acquire. In such a "learning atmosphere," children come to see how a little piece of learning in one area can be applied to another area, and how the lessons they may learn from some seemingly unimportant experience can be generalized and applied to much larger facets of life, so that learning is not an end in itself but a means to understanding the world, and to living a richer and fuller life.

Learning About Fingerprints

Parents and children should pay special attention to the learning opportunities that they carry around with them every day—that is, the many facets and features of their own bodies. Take, for example, the curious and complex patterns that appear on the tips of your fingers, which we know as fingerprints. Here is clear evidence of our individual identity, and so here is a constant reminder that each of us, and each of our children, is unlike anyone else on Earth. Our children's individual strengths and talents may not appear until later in life, and so they need to be reminded throughout childhood that they are unique and special and one of a kind. A family study of fingerprints can confirm this to be true.

You might choose to launch this study on February 15, for that was the birthday, back in 1822, of an Englishman named Sir Francis Galton, whose studies of heredity led him to make two important conclusions about the nature of fingerprints: (1) that no two people could possibly share the same set of fingerprints, and (2) that a person's fingerprints remained unchanged through the entire lifespan.

Fingerprint identification card and the eight basic fingerprint patterns.

These observations so impressed the British government that a committee was formed—headed by Sir Edward Richard Henry, who later became commissioner of the London police force known as Scotland Yard—to see whether fingerprints could be used as a means of identifying criminals.

Henry completed his study in 1901 and introduced a system of classifying all fingerprints into a few basic types and variations. Though this system has been modified and refined over the years, it remains the basis for the system of classification that is used by the FBI and most police departments today.

In order to show your children the ridge patterns that are a permanent part of their fingertips, and how these patterns differ from yours and everyone else's (even identical twins have different fingerprints), you will need a magnifying glass, a stamp pad, and some paper. First, use the glass to examine your own ridge patterns and those on your child's fingers. These patterns will fall into the general classifications of "loops" (the ridges begin on one side of the finger, curve back, and end at the same side), "arches" (the ridges begin on one side of the finger, rise, then end on the other side of the finger), and "whorls" (the ridges form a circle or spiral pattern).

Make an impression of your child's fingerprints by rolling each fingertip on the stamp pad, then rolling it again on a piece of card stock or paper. Now label each print according to the finger from which it came (e.g., left hand: thumb, index, middle, ring, little). Then make a record of your own fingerprints, and those of the other members of your family. You will be amazed to find how easy it is to see the differences between your fingerprints and those of your children. You may also be surprised to discover that your prints don't all fall into the same general classification; it is quite common that a person will have a "tented arch" on one finger and a "double loop" on another. (That is why it is impossible for the FBI or anyone else to make a positive identification from a single fingerprint, despite what some television shows and movies would have us believe.)

You can look at all types of fingerprint patterns by taking your magnifying glass down to a local post office or police station to see the prints of posted criminals. You can also learn about the ways to differentiate among various patterns of loops, arches, and whorls in books from the 364.1 section of your library and from an excellent and inexpensive booklet on fingerprinting that is published by the Boy Scouts as part of their Merit Badge Series.

Perhaps your children's interest in fingerprints will encourage them to read detective stories and adventures about how an investigator's understanding of human nature and knowledge of human characteristics led to the solution of a crime, as in the stories about Sherlock Holmes, for example. Holmes, of course, was a fictional character, having been created by a British doctor named Arthur Conan Doyle. Doyle, in fact, modeled his hero after one of his former medical school teachers, Dr. Joseph Bell at Edinburgh University. Dr. Bell had a genius for taking note of every detail about his patients and then using those observations to aid him in making his diagnoses.

So, too, is Sherlock Holmes a master of observation and deduction. Nothing escapes his notice, for even the smallest piece of information can be useful to him in understanding a person's behavior and eventually solving a crime. He often upbraids his companion, Dr. Watson, for not being sufficiently attuned to all the clues that can be found in the dress or the speech or the bearing of the client or suspect with whom they have just been conversing. "You see well enough," he says, "but you do not observe."

Learning From Observations

There is a great lesson here, I think, and a great opportunity as well for all of us, but especially for our teenage children. It lies in the use of observation—not to aid in the investigation of others—but to help us see ourselves through the eyes of others.

We can play at being Sherlock Holmes and Dr. Watson with our children by focusing our attention on an object—an automobile, let's say—and observing what its license plate, age, model, and even its dents can tell us about its owner. When we watch a movie or a television show together, we can focus on one character and try to determine what that person's dialect or dress or mannerisms are designed to convey to the audience. I especially like to use television commercials in this way because their creators have only a minute or less to transmit their desired impressions, and so there are an abundance of clues to be found.

Now why, you may ask, did I say that this was a particularly good learning opportunity for teenagers? Because the purpose of all this observation is to help our children come to realize for themselves that they, too, are being observed and that they, too, are sending messages and creating impressions. When teenagers begin to identify the "Valley talk" or the jargon of the surf or rock or rap culture as being a badge of ignorance for characters who use it in movie or television scripts, they may not wish to convey a similar impression of themselves, at least outside their peer group.

More important, though, is the benefit that teenagers can receive from knowing that their own actions are being observed and are being interpreted and are having an effect on other people. An "inconsiderate" teenager is often just thoughtless, not malicious. By becoming more sensitive to the thoughts and feelings of others, our teenagers can, for perhaps the first time, live outside themselves and look back on themselves from another's perspective.

Sherlock Holmes's technique of detailed observation, then, can lead us to see the wisdom both in the adage about "walking a mile in another person's shoes," and in the words of the poet Robert Burns (with a slight transposition):

To see ourselves as others see us,
It would from many a blunder free us.

There are many human characteristics, however, over which people have limited control, or no control at all, and that they must simply make accommodations for throughout their lives. Again, we and our children will never be able to understand the burdens that others bear until we are able to get outside our own lives and see the world from another person's point of view. A very simple but highly instructive method for accomplishing this involves the plight of those who favor their left hand but who must contend with a right-handed world.

Learning About Left-handers

Maybe you have a child who is left-handed; certainly your child will have classmates who write with their left hand, or who eat with their left hand, or who throw, or catch, or bat that way. Well, an organization called Lefthanders has created a special day each year, August 13, to alert the rest of us to the special needs and frustrations of left-handers. Here, then, is a day we might use to help our children see how difficult some very simple acts can be for those who just happen—through no wish of their own—to be members of this left-handed minority.

It's a large minority, to be sure. Estimates of left-handedness in the U.S. population range between 10 and 15 percent, but it might be as high as 35 percent if parents and social customs didn't force or encourage left-handed children to favor their right hand. Still, the majority of the population in every country is right-handed, and that has been true for almost all of human history.

No one knows why humans came to favor their right hand over their left, but it is certain that left-handers—and all things associated with the left side—have been seen in an unfavorable light for thousands of years.

Our word *sinister* is the same word that the Romans used for "left," while *dexter,* the Roman word for "right," gives us such favorable words as *dexterous* and *dexterity.* Adding the Latin prefix *ambi-,* meaning "both," creates the word *ambidextrous,* which literally means "having both right hands." Other negative connotations for words that refer to the left can be found in dozens of languages including French, German, Italian, and Spanish.

But lefties learn to tolerate or ignore such linguistic vestiges as these and such invidious phrases as a "left-handed compliment" or someone's "right-hand man." It is the physical features of a right-handed world that pose real problems and cause real frustrations for left-handed people, especially for children, who all-too-frequently blame themselves for struggling with these simple, everyday items and who see themselves as being clumsy or inept.

For this one day, let the right-handers in your family pretend that they actually favor their left hand over their right. They won't, of course, be able to write very well, but have them try the task anyway just to see for themselves how our custom of writing from left to right means that left-handers cannot see what they have just written and will frequently smudge their work as they drag their writing hand behind the pen or pencil. Then have them try to sharpen that pencil by reaching their left hand all the way over to turn the crank that is always on the right side of the sharpener.

Now have them try taking a picture with a camera (the shutter button is on the right); wind or set a wristwatch (the stem is on the right); cut a piece of paper with a scissors (the action of the left hand causes the blades to pull away from each other); use an ice cream scoop (the thumb lever is designed for right-handers). In the car, show them how the gear shift lever, the ignition switch, and the radio are all designed for right-handers.

All these little inconveniences can help your children see how different the world can look from another's point of view, and how they cannot, therefore, just blindly assume that their own view of the world is the "correct" one. The left-handers in your family can also find encouragement in knowing that there have been countless lefties (not just sports heroes) who excelled in this right-handed world, including Julius Caesar, Napoleon, Leonardo da Vinci, Michelangelo, Benjamin Franklin, Albert Einstein, and three historic figures who all, strangely enough, had exactly the same middle name: Alexander the Great, Billy the Kid, and Jack the Ripper.

Estimating Distances

Other learning opportunities that can emanate from the characteristics of a child's own body include lessons in mathematics, physics, and biology as well. With the aid of a common tape measure (such as a ten-foot or twenty-foot steel rule), for example, you can help your children learn how to use their bodies to estimate and calculate various distances.

This activity has some lessons for us in history and in language, too, for it holds the answer to why the English word *mile* should look so much like the metric and Latin prefix *mil-*, meaning "a thousand" or "a thousandth part."

The story goes back to the days of the Roman Empire and to the Roman legions, who were taught to march with a very precise and uniform stride: Each pace (which was two steps) took them exactly five feet. So a thousand paces, which the Romans called *mille passus*, measured exactly 5,000 feet. With this measure, the legions could map all the territories they conquered, which is just what they did to the British Isles in the time of Julius Caesar.

The English used this 5,000-foot mile for centuries, until Queen Elizabeth I stretched its length to exactly eight furlongs (a furlong was and still is 220 yards). So, the mile was no longer a thousand paces but 1,760 yards, or 5,280 feet, instead.

How does the length of your stride compare with that of the Roman soldiers? How far would your children travel in a *mille passus*?

Select a flat stretch of sidewalk and use a tape measure to mark off a distance of exactly 52 feet, 10 inches (52.8 feet, which is $\frac{1}{100}$ of a mile). Now walk that course with your normal stride as your children count out each complete pace. (If you start with your left foot, each pace will be marked with your right toe.) If you took exactly 11 paces over the $\frac{1}{100}$ of a mile, then you would walk a mile in 1,100 paces, and half a mile in 550.

Then count your children's paces over that measured course and have them multiply the result by 100, 50, and 25 to see how many steps they take in each mile, half mile, and quarter mile.

Now they can do some rather precise measuring of their own, and they can calculate such distances as the length of each city block, for example, or the trip to their school by various routes, or the distance to a friend's house. In each case, have them first make their best estimate of the distance in fractions of a mile. Then have them walk the trip in their measured stride and calculate the result. Do you get a similar measure when you walk the same course and count your paces?

Another way to use the tape measure in helping your children calculate various  distances is to wrap it around the front tire of a bicycle and thereby know the distance covered with each complete revolution of that wheel. Paint a white mark on the side of the tire so that your children can count the number of complete revolutions the tire makes as they walk the bike along the path they wish to measure.

The Wonders of the Human Body

The lessons that can be learned by focusing on the characteristics of the human body are almost infinite, and they range from the microscopic to the astronomic. Not all are explainable by parents or are suitable to home activities and demonstrations, yet it is important that children acquire an early understanding of the basic systems that go on in their own bodies, if only to get them to see how fantastic and miraculous and worthy of admiration and care the human body really is.

Children can, for example, learn early in life about the role that their own bodies play in keeping them well and in defending them from illnesses of almost every kind. In the 612 section of the children's collection at your local library, you will find a number of books that will help you explain the wonders of the human immune system to your children, and once they begin to see the human body in this light, they will then be able to see many common and ordinary body actions as being part of the body's attempt to maintain its own health. Coughs and sneezes, for instance, will now have meaning to them, for they will be understood as methods that the body uses to expel microscopic invaders it believes to be harmful.

How "awesome" the body is! And by that I mean that the human body should constantly be looked upon with a sense of awe. Too often we misplace that awe and think that it is the knowledge and skill of medical professionals that causes our return to good health. Their talents are important, to be sure, but most doctors and nurses (with very few exceptions) will admit that they don't actually *cure* anybody of anything. Their skill, instead, can be accurately described as knowing how to put the body in a condition whereby it can cure itself.

Do your children marvel at the wonders that their own bodies work in their behalf? Do they understand, for example, that the redness of a sunburn is the redness of their own blood, which the body has sent to soothe and heal the damaged area? Do they know that the fever that accompanies many of their minor illnesses is just their body's way of raising its own temperature to a level at which harmful microbes cannot live? Do they realize that when their body detects a drop in temperature, it signals its muscles to tighten and loosen over and over again until this shiver generates enough heat to get the body back to normal?

The human body's defenses are truly miraculous, at least against those diseases and ailments that are within their power to attack and heal. I think that children who can understand and marvel at these miracles will also be more likely to see that their bodies are not very good at defending against or fighting against a host of new invaders, enemies that the human body just wasn't designed to repel, such as bullets, tobacco, and cocaine.

The Ambidextrous Universe, by Martin Gardner (New York: Basic Books, 1964) [501 GAR].

Fingerprinting: Magic Weapon Against Crime, by Eugene Block (New York: David McKay Company, 1969) [364.125 BLO].

How & Why: A Kids' Book About the Body, by Catherine O'Neill (Mr. Vernon, N.Y.: Consumers Union, 1988) [J 612 ONE].

Junior Body Machine, by Dr. Christiaan Barnard (New York: Crown Publishers, 1983) [J 612 JUN].

The Left-Handed Book, by Rae Lindsay (New York: Franklin Watts, 1980) [J 152.335 LIN].

Lefthander Magazine, P. O. Box 8249, Topeka, KS 66608; phone 913-234-2177; subscription is $15 per year (6 issues).

The Left-handers Handbook, by James Bliss and Joseph Morella (New York: A & W Visual Library, 1980) [152.335 BLI].

The Left-hander's World, by Alvin Silverstein and Virginia B. Silverstein (Chicago: Follett Publishing Co., 1977) [J 612 SIL].

Learning Opportunities Lie All Around the House

Creating a "learning atmosphere" in your home does not mean turning your living room into a classroom. Living rooms, after all, are for living. But learning can occur in living rooms—and in kitchens, and bathrooms, and backyards, too—because learning is a part of living, and it can become a more prominent part of the living that goes on in your house if you and your children will look for and recognize the myriad learning opportunities that exist all around you, every day.

I don't want to discourage parents from acquiring various learning aids and reference books as resources for their home, but neither do I want them to think that their family's learning is dependent upon such acquisitions. What I am suggesting is that parents focus their attention first on using the objects and activities that are already part of their home and family life in ways that will promote learning. Any learning aids and references they then acquire will be appreciated and used instead of just sitting on a shelf.

Let's look at a few of the things that you already have in your home but that you probably don't see as stimulants to your learning. The whole point here is to get you into the habit of wondering about everything—not just about stars and the Big Bang and the purpose of life on Earth, but about the smallest, the most common objects and experiences, as well. Once you start to see that everything around you can be used to test your understanding, and to launch you down learning paths that can lead you wherever your interest directs, then you will realize that you and your children already live in a stimulating learning environment, a place just brimming with learning suggestions and opportunities for the taking, no matter where you live and no matter what your learning interests might be.

Learning From a Dollar Bill

Take, for example, something as common as a dollar bill. We see it every day, but we don't see it as an object that could stimulate our learning. We think all its designs and numbers are part of some specialized code that is useful to someone, perhaps, but certainly not to us. Well, let's see how we can use this dollar bill in stimulating and reinforcing our children's knowledge.

Washington's picture on the front of the bill invites us to think about the portraits on the other denominations. Are they all of U.S. presidents? (No. Alexander Hamilton—$10 bill—was our first Secretary of the Treasury, and Benjamin Franklin—$100 bill—was famous as a statesman, scientist, philosopher, and author.)

Children should know something about all the people portrayed on our currency, and about the designs on the back of each bill. You can open up a miniature world for them by having an inexpensive magnifying glass around the house. With this learning tool you can show them the detail in each drawing and have them search for tiny features (such as the names of the states carved into the Lincoln Memorial on the back of the $5 bill) as you talk with them about each building and person.

Seal of Federal Reserve Bank. Letter inside identifies Federal Reserve district and corresponds to first letter in serial number.

Letter and number show bill's position on printing plate.

Number corresponds to Federal Reserve district's position in the alphabet.

Not all portraits are of presidents, but no living person may be pictured on our currency.

Scales of justice are part of the seal of the United States Treasury.

"Annuit Coeptis" is Latin for "God has favored our undertakings."

Roman numerals representing the year of the signing of the Declaration of Independence, 1776.

"E Pluribus Unum" means "One out of many."

Two sides of the Great Seal of the United States.

On the left side of the front of each bill, printed in black, is the seal of the Federal Reserve Bank that issued that note. This seal has a large capital letter in its center, which is always the same letter that appears at the beginning of the bill's serial number. This letter's position in the alphabet also corresponds to the four black numbers on the face of the bill. So, every time you see a letter G in the middle of the black Federal Reserve seal, you will also see four black 7's on the face of the bill because G is the seventh letter in the alphabet. (Check some other bills and see if the letter in the seal matches the letter at the beginning of the serial number and the alphabetical position of the four black numbers on the inside corners of the face.)

There are twelve Federal Reserve Districts, each with a Federal Reserve Bank that issues currency to state and local banks throughout its district. The Federal Reserve Banks are numbered as follows: 1 = A = Boston, 2 = B = New York, 3 = C = Philadelphia, 4 = D = Cleveland, 5 = E = Richmond, 6 = F = Atlanta, 7 = G = Chicago, 8 = H = St. Louis, 9 = I = Minneapolis, 10 = J = Kansas City, 11 = K = Dallas, 12 = L = San Francisco. It is likely that most of the bills in your pocket will bear the letter and number of the Federal Reserve Bank closest to your home.

There is also a tiny letter and number printed in black at the upper left of each bill, which shows the position of this particular bill on its printing plate. Each plate contains thirty-two bills that are arranged in eight columns (letters A through H) of four rows each (numbers 1 through 4). If your bill shows a tiny "F 4" at the upper left, for example, then this bill was at the bottom of the sixth column on its printing plate. The same capital letter also appears in black at the lower right of the bill, but the tiny number that follows it is the serial number of that particular printing plate.

The back of each bill has no black printing at all, and most denominations feature the image of an important building or memorial. The $1 bill, however, bears the image of the two sides of the Great Seal of the United States. On the left is an unfinished pyramid, which symbolizes the continuing quest for a more perfect government and the addition of new states. The eye in the sparkling triangle at the top of the pyramid signifies an all-seeing deity, while the Latin phrase above, *Annuit Coeptis*, means "God has favored our undertakings."

At the base of the pyramid is the Roman numeral form of 1776, the year of the Declaration of Independence. (How would the present year be written in Roman numerals?) Beneath this is the Latin phrase *Novus Ordo Seclorum*, which translates as "A new order of the ages."

The more familiar side of the Great Seal, at the right, features the American eagle holding a ribbon that is inscribed with the Latin phrase *E Pluribus Unum*, which refers to the joining of the original thirteen colonies into one nation and means "One out of many." Notice how many other symbols of the thirteen colonies there are in this seal—thirteen leaves and thirteen berries on the olive branch, thirteen arrows clutched in the eagle's talons, thirteen stripes on the shield, thirteen stars in the wreath of clouds, there are even thirteen steps or layers in the pyramid. (Can you name these thirteen original states? Answer: Delaware, Pennsylvania, New Jersey, Georgia, Connecticut, Massachusetts, Maryland, South Carolina, New Hampshire, Virginia, New York, North Carolina, Rhode Island.)

Learning From a Penny

Or you might use your magnifying glass to introduce your children to the history and geography and architecture that they can discover on the coins in their pocket. Take the

common penny (which is known in the coin world as a "cent"), for example, and look at the image of the Lincoln Memorial on the back (which is called the "reverse"). Your naked eye sees only the building (can your children recognize this memorial and do they know where it is?), but with a magnifying glass you can detect another image— the statue of Lincoln himself between the central pillars of that building. (You have to look very closely, and make sure that the surface of your coin is not worn.)

Did you know that Lincoln's portrait was the first to appear on an American coin? Before the Lincoln Head cent was introduced in 1909, the one hundredth anniversary of Lincoln's birth, our coins carried images of eagles, symbolic Native Americans, and various designs of Lady Liberty, but no portraits of presidents or other famous Americans. (In fact, the only things that, by law, must appear on every U.S. coin are the phrases *E Pluribus Unum*, *United States of America*, *In God We Trust*, and the word *Liberty*. Look at several other coins to see where these words and phrases appear.)

The magnifying glass will also lead you into some U.S. geography because the tiny "mint mark" on a coin will tell you the city in which that coin was struck (for example, *D* for Denver, *S* for San Francisco, and no mark for Philadelphia), a custom originated in Roman mints thousand of years ago.

But the most instructive feature of any coin may be the date stamped into its surface, which identifies the year that coin was minted. These dates point out quite clearly how enduring coins really are. They survive long after the monuments pictured on them, and they even outlive the civilizations that produced them.

The date on a coin can also help bring history to life for a child, because it identifies a piece of history itself. When children hold in their hands an old Indian Head cent that an uncle or grandmother, perhaps, had secreted away in a jewelry box up in the attic, and when they read the numbers "1860" on its face, they can imagine—and who can deny?—that this particular coin was held and spent by a Civil War soldier or even by President Lincoln himself. A local coin dealer may allow your child to hold (by the edges please) coins that Washington or Napoleon may have spent—and spent to buy what, do you suppose?

A child's journey into the world of coins begins with that magnifying glass, the books in the J 737 section of the library, and a parent's interest in supplying each day's loose change and encouraging its examination. A particularly good book about the historical significance of common coins is Frances Williams Browin's *Coins Have Tales To Tell* [J 737.4 BRO].

The American Numismatic Association will also send you pamphlets about how to introduce your children to coin collecting. They offer a "student membership" in the association (age 22 and younger) for $11 per year. Just send an addressed and stamped enveloped to them at ANA, Membership Department, 818 N. Cascade Avenue, Colorado Springs, CO 80903-3279, or visit their web site at http://www.money.org.

Simple Toys as Learning Tools

Bills and coins are just examples of the many common objects that could be used to stimulate our learning, but are frequently overlooked primarily because they are so common. For some reason we think that learning aids have to be complex, intricate, and, most of all, expensive in order for them to have real educational potential.

In doing so, we completely overlook the work and the genius of a German educator named Friedrich Froebel, who back in 1837 created an educational revolution that he named by using the German word for "children's garden": kindergarten. Froebel believed that all children were like unfolding flowers, and that the knowledge they accumulated about the world would be enhanced through guidance, not coercion. He was convinced that early childhood learning was fostered best through "directed play." So he created a series of simple toys (wooden blocks, cylinders, spheres, hoops) that his kindergarten children would use, with the guidance of their teacher, to create whatever their imaginations could conceive as a way to better understand the relationships that exist among things in the natural world.

As a child, Frank Lloyd Wright was given a set of these maple-wood blocks by his mother, and he spoke often throughout his life about the value of these simple toys and the role they played in shaping his ability and his desire to restructure the world around him. It is interesting to note that it was Frank Lloyd Wright's son, John L. Wright, who invented a construction toy back in 1916 that has entertained millions of children and is still popular today: Lincoln Logs.

Now, obviously, these smooth maple blocks did not create or cause the architectural genius of either Frank Lloyd Wright or his son, and they won't ensure that your children will have any architectural genius, either. But the simplicity of these blocks, coupled with the guidance of a concerned parent, allows young children to discover, just as Frank Lloyd Wright did, that the most basic geometric forms lay hidden in the appearance of all things, including the most magnificent buildings and in the works of nature as well.

Can your children see these basic shapes imbedded in the larger images of houses and other buildings? As you look at a house across the street or at a picture of a famous building, try to isolate and trace the rectangles (an outside wall or window frame, for example), the triangles (a porch roof), the partial sphere of a dome or cupola, the partial circle in the arch over a doorway. Whenever possible, try to draw their attention to the way nature's shapes are repeated in human constructions, such as the four-leaf clover in a freeway interchange or the petals of a daisy in a stained-glass window.

Architecture involves more than just shapes, however. It is the art and craft of building, an idea that can be seen in the origin of the word itself. The ancient Greek prefix *arkhi-* meant "the highest rank, the principal, the master" and can be seen in the meaning of *archbishop* and *arch* enemy. The Greek word for carpenter or builder was *tekton,* and so an architect is, literally, a "master builder."

Children all-too-often think of buildings as being pre-packaged and having no human creator. They never see how buildings are designed and that each element of that design—inside and out—has a reason behind it. This happens because most of the buildings we see most often in our lives—houses—are, in fact, pre-packaged. They take on their owner's individual identity through their landscaping, furnishing, and decorating instead of their design. Yet even here children can relate the lessons of their wooden blocks to the ways that columns and arches and roofs are constructed. When a child attempts to build an arch of her own out of wedge-shaped blocks, she will come to see firsthand that the arch is held together by the force each block exerts on its neighbor, and that the whole structure is locked in place by the indispensable one in the middle: the keystone.

There are two books published by Preservation Press that are wonderful for getting children involved with both the art and the craft of architecture. *What It Feels Like to Be a Building,* by Forrest Wilson [J 690.21 WIL], is aimed at younger children. Through very simple drawings, it conveys the idea of the various forces that are involved in construction by imagining how a person would feel if that person were a column, or a beam, or a block in an arch. *I Know That Building!* by Jane D'Alelio [J 720 DAL], is composed of many cutouts that can be folded and glued to make all sorts of buildings, and it also includes a card game in which players match eleven famous architects with pictures of buildings that they designed.

Students in junior high and above can learn much from a fascinating book by David Macaulay titled *City* [J 711.4 MAC]. Through his wonderfully detailed illustrations and a historically accurate text, the author shows how the first-century Romans would have designed and constructed an entire city. Here architecture is used to serve the public, and readers of all ages will have a new appreciation for a time when "long-term" city planning meant looking beyond the next election.

Wooden blocks, of course, are not essential to any child's learning, nor is architecture all that can be learned from them. These blocks, though, are an example of how we can, very inexpensively, provide stimulating objects and activities in our homes that will help children develop their natural impulses to know and to invent. Too often we fall victim to the glitz and the flash of television and video games, thinking that these colorful, moving images will inspire our children and expand their interest in the world. But we fail to understand that these technologies do all the inventing themselves and leave little room for children to create things of their own imagination that will be equally amazing and fantastic. But playing with simple construction toys, just like hearing a swashbuckling tale read aloud or living out fantastic adventures in a sandbox, encourages invention and imagination and creativity, and costs much less than a single video game cartridge.

We all occasionally fall into the trap of unfolding our children's flowers for them. We provide them with the "best" toys on the market—that is, the most explicit, the most detailed re-creations of real-world planes or guns or vehicles. What can a child's mind make these things become? They are what they are, and the better they are at being what they are, the more difficult it is for the imagination to transform them into anything else.

The year-in, year-out success of Lincoln Logs, Tinkertoys, the Erector set, Legos (a contraction of two Danish words meaning "play well"), and even those simple wooden blocks, all of which allow children to imagine the details for themselves, and especially the length of time these toys remain in the play area, should tell us that children have both a desire and a need to dream their own dreams and to create worlds of their own design.

American Numismatic Association, 818 N. Cascade Avenue, Colorado Springs, CO 80903-3279; phone: 719-632-2646; http://www.money.org.

City: A Story of Roman Planning and Construction, by David Macaulay (Boston: Houghton Mifflin, 1974) [J 711.4 MAC].

Coin Collecting As a Hobby, by Burton Hobson (New York: Sterling Publishing Co., 1986) [J 737.4 HOB].

Coins Have Tales to Tell: The Story of American Coins, by Frances Williams Browin (Philadelphia: Lippincott, 1966) [J 737.4 BRO].

I Know That Building!: Discovering Architecture with Activities and Games, by Jane D'Alelio (Washington, D.C.: Preservation Press, 1989) [J 720 DAL].

Reading the Numbers, by Mary Blocksma (New York: Penguin Books, 1989) [530.8 BLO].

A Treasury of American Coins, by Fred Reinfeld (Garden City, N.Y.: Hanover House, 1961) [737.4 REI].

What It Feels Like to Be a Building, by Forrest Wilson (Washington, D.C.: Preservation Press, National Trust for Historic Preservation, 1988) [J 690.21 WIL].

JANUARY 15: *Birth of Martin Luther King*   OCTOBER 25: *"Charge of the Light Brigade"*
MARCH 23: *Patrick Henry's speech delivered*   NOVEMBER 19: *"Gettysburg Address" delivered*
APRIL (FIRST WEEK): *Opening of baseball season*

Every Day Can Be a Holiday for Learning in Your Home

What traditions does your family observe? Most, I would guess, are relegated to holiday times, and that is to be expected. But the advantages that we as families receive and enjoy through these holiday traditions can be applied at other times of the year as well, and so we can benefit year-round by creating traditions and customs and themes that help bind the family together and encourage individual growth through focusing the power of the family unit.

Family Meals

Traditions are, after all, just activities that have a momentum of their own; their force pulls everyone along in spite of anyone's feigned or fervent will to resist. Parents today need that extra force behind them because it is so easy to be swayed by those small voices of reluctance or resistance. The simple ritual of dining together as a family at Christmas or Hanukkah or Easter—which may not seem like a tradition to you but surely qualifies as one—has year-round advantages for adults and children alike. How often, other than on holiday occasions, do you sit down to dinner in your own home, with your own family, without the television or stereo or newspaper there to distract your attention and stifle your conversation? I know there are severe pressures of school activities, multiple careers, and the like, but the daily family dinner is certainly a tradition worth all your efforts to create and preserve. The language benefits to your children are so great, and the benefits to you of being able to use this time to better understand and to soothe the day-to-day concerns of your family are so hard to realize in other ways.

Leo Buscaglia, in a book titled *Papa, My Father,* tells about the way his immigrant father used the tradition of the family dinner to promote learning among his children. Each child was required, at the end of the meal, to present one fact that he or she had learned during that day. Sometimes the children would scurry to the encyclopedia or dictionary just before dinner to arm themselves with the required fact for the day, but each piece of knowledge, no matter how trivial, was accepted and discussed and elaborated upon, and the tradition endured.

"In retrospect," Buscaglia writes, "after years of studying how people learn, I realize what a dynamic educational technique Papa was offering us, reinforcing the value of continual learning. Without being aware of it, our family was growing together, sharing experiences, and participating in one another's education. And by looking at us, listening to us, hearing us, respecting our opinions, affirming our value, giving us a sense of dignity, Papa was unquestionably our most influential teacher."

Family Read-alouds

There are other holiday traditions and rituals, too, that hold great benefit for everyone in the family and could become useful traditions to adopt in your home throughout the year. Consider the simple act of reading aloud, which is so common at Christmastime and is an accepted and anticipated part of that holiday season. Christmas read-alouds have been enjoyed in countless homes for hundreds of years, partly because winter demands more indoor activities, and partly because this season of wonderment and fantasy is ideally suited to the visions and images that each person's imagination creates differently after hearing the same well-told tale.

There is also a wealth of great Christmas literature for us to choose from, and these stories and poems seem so inappropriate for presenting at other times of the year that we feel a special urgency to share them with our families while we have the chance. Children may have heard "A Visit from St. Nicholas" dozens of times, and perhaps they know every detail of O. Henry's classic Christmas tale called "The Gift of the Magi" [pronounced MAY-jye], yet they can look forward to hearing these works again each Christmas without having to admit, as they grow older, how much this annual ritual means to them. It is, after all, a tradition, and so it has a momentum all its own.

I remember a struggle I had in choosing and editing the selections for *Classics to Read Aloud to Your Children* [J 808.8 RUS], for I was faced with the dilemma of omitting entirely Charles Dickens's *A Christmas Carol,* because it was a very long and difficult work to read aloud, or cutting it back severely and running the risk of losing its original flavor. I chose to cut it back, primarily because I wanted parents to be able to create a family tradition of reading that story aloud together on Christmas Eve or Christmas Day. If that reading required more than an hour, I believed, this particular bonding and learning tradition would never achieve the momentum that it would need to overcome all the seemingly good reasons for omitting it this year, and then the next. But if it took no more than an hour, then the little ones would listen intently for, perhaps, ten minutes this year, then twenty, and so on. And teens would grumble about having to read a particular part each year, but they, too, would find their presentation more persuasive every time, and the tradition would hold the work itself as a constant, while every reader and listener grew and changed from year to year.

Why can't reading aloud become a more common tradition in our families? I'm not talking about just bedtime stories, but about expanding that Christmas tradition of presenting certain works orally to and with our children at certain times of the year. Here is where parents and teachers can use their combined knowledge and imagination to come up with appropriate poems and stories and excerpts that families can tie into various events and activities that occur both during the school year and during school vacations.

Oh, there are works that are natural complements to other holidays and can become traditional family read-alouds on Thanksgiving, Halloween, or St. Patrick's Day. And certainly Martin Luther King's "I Have a Dream" speech or his "Letter from Birmingham City Jail" could become traditional read-aloud selections to share in your family on the anniversary of his birth every January 15. But what I am encouraging parents to do in creating these family read-aloud traditions is to expand their ideas about what constitutes an appropriate occasion for a family tradition.

Creating Read-aloud Traditions

If reading aloud is important to you, and if you want to encourage your children to become presenters as well as listeners in these family read-aloud sessions, then you have to look for annual events that you can turn into family traditions, whether those events rate a holiday among the general populace or not. I know a number of families, for instance, that have adopted an annual custom of reading Ernest Lawrence Thayer's "Casey at the Bat" aloud together to celebrate the opening day of each baseball season. This particular poem makes a wonderful read-aloud because it is filled with actions and facial expressions that are ideally suited to performing, and so it is as much fun to present as it is to hear. In these families, the children act out the parts of Casey and the pitcher and the umpire as their parents recite the poem, and then the next year the roles are reversed. Sometimes props are added, sometimes background music is played, but every year this poem provides something for each family to look forward to, and something that binds and identifies each family as well.

"Casey at the Bat" is not ideal for every family to adopt as a read-aloud tradition, but it is an example of the wonderful opportunities that await all of us if we will just be open-minded in selecting our family celebrations, and will allow those celebrations to make use of the special characteristics that identify us within our family and identify our family, as well.

Family read-alouds also permit us to acquaint our children with literature that they no longer encounter at school, and to link that literature with some knowledge and information about history or geography or science when there are natural tie-ins available.

Consider, for instance, the famous "Charge of the Light Brigade," by Alfred Lord Tennyson, which begins,

Half a league, half a league,
Half a league onward,
All in the valley of Death
Rode the six hundred.

Tennyson wrote this six-stanza poem after reading a newspaper account of the Battle of Balaklava [pronounced bah-luh-KLAH-vuh], which took place on October 25, 1854, during the Crimean War. Owing to the confusion and stupidity and rivalry of certain British officers, a brigade of sword-wielding cavalry was ordered to attack some entrenched batteries of Russian artillery, and, of course, the brigade was cut to pieces, with only a quarter of the original 600 troops returning from the senseless and fruitless attack.

This poem used to be standard reading in public school classrooms not so long ago, but it has fallen out of favor in these "politically correct" times. So the mention of "The Charge of the Light Brigade" connotes nothing whatsoever to many of our young people today, and the poem becomes another piece of our cultural heritage that will be lost altogether unless it is shared within our homes and families.

I look at this as a wonderful opportunity, both for children and their parents, because the home provides a learning environment in which many subjects and topics can be brought together to provide background and to enrich both the reader's and the listener's understanding of this poem. An encyclopedia and a world atlas or globe can tell you where in the world the Crimea is, which countries were fighting in the Crimean War, and how it was in this war that Florence Nightingale became a legend.

"Good Mrs. Murphy"

But if you read this poem aloud to your children, as I hope you will, I would also like you to consider another often-overlooked area of learning that must precede the reading itself. I am referring to the need for children to know the meanings of the words they hear read to them. Now, this is a little different from the kind of vocabulary work that might precede a selection that children read for themselves, and it is different because reading aloud does not usually allow listeners to get any visual clues about the meaning of an unfamiliar word or phrase. They know only the sound of the word or phrase, and so they often confuse it with another word or phrase that is already part of their vocabulary.

Take the phrase *light brigade*, for example. If a child does not know what a *brigade* is, and that *light* refers to their weapons (as opposed to *heavy* infantry or *heavy* artillery), then the phrase *light brigade* sounds more like something out of *Star Wars* than the Crimean War. If children don't know that a *league* is a measure of distance (about three miles), what will they make of the poem's opening lines: "Half a league, half a league,/Half a league onward"? Some, I am sure, will hear the lines as "Happily, happily, happily onward...," and both the purpose and the power of the poem will be completely lost.

Children (and adults, too) use what they already know as their first resource in any search for meaning, and so it is easy to see how a youngster could recite "I pledge a pigeon to the flag...," or could think that the *Twenty-third Psalm* says "Surely Good Mrs. Murphy will follow me all the days of my life...."

"Good Mrs. Murphy" happens a lot more frequently than we think, and so a wise parent (or teacher) will give special attention to providing children a preview of any unfamiliar words and phrases they are about to hear, so that they can acquire a fuller understanding when they hear those words used in context.

Famous Speeches as Read-alouds

When you choose selections to read aloud with your family—not just for creating annual family traditions, but for general family read-alouds as well—remember to include the great speeches of history along with the stories and poems you select. We and our children can all learn so much from reading and hearing these oratorical masterpieces, yet they are seldom taught in the classroom, and so must be shared in the living room. Too often we hear or remember only the "trumpet phrase" that identifies a historic speech, such as Patrick Henry's closing line: "I know not what course others may take, but as for me, give me liberty or give me death!" And, to be sure, the very best speeches have in common a memorable, eloquent, and concise passage that was designed to ring in the ears and minds of those who happened to hear it. But the real craftsmanship of a great speech is not visible in that trumpet phrase alone, nor can the true meaning or intent of that phrase be seen if it is removed from the foundation on which it rests.

By letting your children hear how words and phrases have been crafted for the express purpose of persuading others and moving them to action, you help them tune their ears to the power and beauty of spoken language—the vocabulary, the timing, the emphasis that are all so different from writing, which was meant only to be read in silence. Children also need to hear and read and understand the great speeches of the world because they are so unlikely to hear polished speaking of any kind today. Unbridled and vulgar fanaticism has replaced reasoned eloquence in campus and political rallies, and our leaders now create "sound bites" for the television cameras instead of polished and persuasive arguments for human audiences.

Indeed, parents who not only let their children hear great speeches at home, but also encourage their children to read those speeches aloud themselves, give their children an educational advantage that will serve them well in school and in later life. This practice helps children of all ages develop self-confidence in their ability to speak in public, and that is a skill that very few graduates carry with them from either high school or college. Today, having to make a speech in public is at the very top of the list of things that Americans dread most.

The classic addresses by Churchill, Frederick Douglass, Gandhi, FDR, and others can be found in the 808.85 section of your library. There is also a wonderful book titled *The American Reader: Words That Moved a Nation*, by Diane Ravitch [081 AME or 973 AME], which contains speeches, songs, and essays that have proved important in our country's history, many of which are ideal for family read-alouds.

USEFUL FAMILY RESOURCES

An American Primer, edited by Daniel J. Boorstin (Chicago: University of Chicago Press, 1966) [973 BOO].

The American Reader: Words That Moved a Nation, by Diane Ravitch (New York: HarperCollins Publishers, 1990) [081 AME or 973 AME].

Lend Me You Ears: Great Speeches In History, edited by William Safire (W.W. Norton & Co., 1992) [808.85 LEN].

A Treasury of the World's Great Speeches, by Houston Peterson (New York: Simon & Schuster, 1965) [808.85 TRE].

Learning About Living a Good Life:
Character Development

RIGHT

WRONG

Introduction

You may wonder what a unit on character development is doing in a book that focuses on ways in which parents can help their children succeed in school. Well, in my view, there is no area of learning that is more instrumental in determining whether or not children succeed in school than character development. The difference in our views about the place and importance of character development may lie in what we mean by "succeed in school."

We all want our children to get good grades, but surely that can't be the only measure of success or else we would consider competent cheaters to have "succeeded" in school.

We want them to learn a lot—at least enough to attend a good college or choose a good career. But we all know of learned people who lived wretched lives and famous professionals who were not respected or admired by anyone with whom they dealt. Success in school can't be defined by what our children will do, but rather by who they will be.

In a way, this unit turns the rest of the book inside out, for while the Family Learning of subjects like geography and science focuses on the outside world and the lessons we can find to improve our knowledge and understanding, character development looks inside first and focuses on the noble human qualities that we want to display in our dealing with the outside world.

There are, of course, out-of-school activities and adventures through which parents can share their own learnings about character and virtue, and this unit will offer many suggestions for ways in which character development can become part of everyday home and family life. But first we have to slog through some difficult territory in order to feel comfortable and confident about our own understanding of what "good character" is in the first place, and what qualities and behaviors we want to encourage in our children—and in ourselves.

Catch Them Being Good

Today, campaigns in almost every election—local, state, and national—are filled with pronouncements about "values," especially "family values," but very rarely do we ever hear anyone explain just what these values actually are. For most people, I think, "family values" are defined much the way people define pornography or art: "I know it when I see it." And that, to me at least, is part of the problem: We don't know it, so we don't often see it. And even when we do see it, we're at a loss because we can't define what it is, and so we can't discuss it or encourage it in our children.

Parents, just like teachers and coaches, need to know very clearly just what learnings and behaviors they want children to adopt and display before they can devise appropriate techniques, lessons, and activities that will help them achieve their goals. So, let's see if we can take some of the fuzziness and uncertainty out of the subject of character development so that we can begin to feel comfortable and confident in sharing these types of Family Learning activities and adventures with our children, too.

Pursuing "the Good Life"

First, let's agree that our goal in this area of study is the same as our goal in the more traditional "school subjects"; namely, self-improvement. The only difference is that the learnings and activities that focused on language or science or geography in previous chapters were designed to improve our knowledge and understanding of these fields, while the self-improvement we hope to achieve through character development is truly that: improvement of the self, which leads to living a better life.

Isn't this, after all, what we want more than anything else for our children and for ourselves as well? We want our children to be happy, certainly, but we want that happiness to be real and enduring, not just a succession of temporary, worldly pleasures. We want them to be, as the U.S. Army ads say, "all that they can be"—to realize their fullest potential as human beings no matter what career they choose to follow. In short, we want them to be good people, to feel the glow of their own self-worth and to know that it has nothing to do with their net worth. All their schooling and training and learning will be for naught if it doesn't help them fulfill the rich promise that is their birthright as human beings. As the nineteenth-century writer and social critic, John Ruskin, once said:

> Education does not mean...teaching the youth the shapes of letters and the tricks of numbers, and then leaving them to turn their arithmetic to robbery and their literature to lust. It means, on the contrary, training them into the perfect exercise and kingly continence of their bodies and souls. It is a painful, continual, and difficult work to be done by kindness, by watching, by warning, by precept, and by praise, but above all—by example.

Without our help, our children's idea of "the good life" will be fashioned in large part by the entertainment industry—including movies, television, and rock videos—and by the advertising industry, neither of which cares one whit about self-improvement or character development of any kind. Hundreds of times every day, our children are bombarded by highly polished, alluring messages that tell them and show them that "the good life" is a life of unlimited physical pleasure, and the goal of life, therefore, is to experience as much pleasure and as many pleasures as possible.

Dr. David Walsh, in his book titled *Selling Out America's Children* [305.23 WAL], lists the messages that business and entertainment and professional sports send to our young people this way:

1. Happiness is found in having things.
2. Get all you can for yourself.
3. Get it all as quickly as you can.
4. Win at all costs.
5. Violence is entertaining.
6. Always seek pleasure and avoid boredom.

Is it any wonder at all that after having these "goals" and "ideals" held up as defining "success" in life, our teenagers are more reluctant than any other teenagers in history to endure the rigors of demanding homework, less willing to resist the temptations of alcohol, drugs, and sex, and less likely to see marriage and parenthood as lifetime responsibilities? Yet, even though the "heroes" who deliver these messages become, in time, perfect advertisements for the tragedy and emptiness that are the inevitable consequences of the life they espouse, our teens refuse even to consider that such an end might be in store for them.

You can find numerous instances where this same story has played itself out in newspapers and movies of today, as well as in classic tales throughout history: Whoever sets out on an untempered pursuit of money (King Midas, Gordon Gekko in *Wall Street*) or power (Michael Corleone in *The Godfather, Part II*, Charles Foster Kane in *Citizen Kane*), or fame (Jessica Savitch, Rosie Ruiz) or physical pleasure (Jim Morrison, John Belushi) inevitably finds that the striving and the attainment of those goals do not produce a happy or satisfying life.

Indeed, the very best example to share with your children is the story of a man who pursued **all** these illusory goals, and attained every one of them, so that he might discover which would bring him true happiness.

Three thousand years ago, King Solomon was the richest, wisest, most powerful man on Earth. He had more money than John D. Rockefeller, J. Paul Getty, and Bill Gates combined. But, as Solomon himself tells us in the *Bible*'s book of Ecclesiastes [220 BIB], all the pleasures he could purchase with that wealth—worldly possessions, the finest foods and wines, sexual experiences—proved not to bring happiness at all, only a feeling of emptiness and despair. "I denied myself nothing my eyes desired; I refused my heart no pleasure" (Ecclesiastes 2:10). In the end, everything that came from his vast wealth was meaningless and unsatisfying. "All is vanity and a chasing after wind" (Ecclesiastes 1:14). Today, Solomon might express it this way: "Been there; done that; b-o-r-i-n-g."

How many examples from the worlds of politics, athletics, and entertainment will it take before our children realize that power or wealth or fame or physical sensations do not produce happiness in the end? How many miserable and wasted lives (and deaths) must we point to before they understand that there are certain fundamental, core values and virtues that are indispensable to good living? Without these essential, guiding principles, power and money and fame lead inevitably to tragedy and despair. With them as a base, a person can endure poverty or wealth, adversity or success, and live both nobly and happily throughout childhood and adulthood.

Virtues, Not Values

Now, just as we have the benefit of being able to draw upon thousands of years of human history to find examples of goals and attributes and acquisitions that do **not** bring happiness and satisfaction, we also can look to the thoughts and the writings of the wisest men and women throughout the ages to help us know what "the good life" really is. The beauty of such a search is the discovery that people in every age and every culture have asked these same questions about fulfillment and happiness in life, and every age and every culture has come to a common set of conclusions. That is, we humans have, over time, agreed that goodness in life can be realized by adhering to certain beliefs and behaviors that are good *for all people, at all times, and everywhere.* Talk about true "multi-culturalism," this is it!

We call these qualities "virtues," a term that always has a positive connotation—that is, there couldn't be any "bad" virtues. Notice that the term "values" is somewhat different in that it implies a more personal choice, and it admits the possibility of there being values that we don't all consider necessarily "good." (For example, I'm sure that Hitler was proud of his values and that lynch mobs think they are acting to protect theirs.) Values, then, fall more into the category of "preferences," while virtues are universal and timeless verities. Indeed, the things you value in life are outgrowths of the principles by which you live—the virtues you have or strive to attain.

So, let's focus on virtues instead of values, and let's use the term "virtues" with our children so that they come to know that there actually **are** understandable, definable, recognizable, principles and attributes that are good for all people, at all times, and everywhere. Just this knowledge alone will provide your children an indispensable base on which to build the moral framework for their lives, and it will distinguish your teenagers from their cohorts when they go off to college or embark upon a career. The very first line of Dr. Allan Bloom's 1987 book, *The Closing of the American Mind* [378 BLO or 973.92 BLO], states: "There is one thing a professor can be absolutely certain of: almost every student entering the university believes, or says he believes, that truth is relative."

We begin our list of universal truths and goods with the four "cardinal virtues," which were promulgated by the ancient Greek philosophers and celebrated in the classic tales of Greece and Rome: *wisdom, justice, temperance,* and *courage.* (*Wisdom* is sometimes referred to as "prudence," *temperance* as "self-control," and *courage* as "fortitude.") The name *cardinal,* here, comes from the Latin word for "hinge" or "axis" because a good and moral life hinges or is centered on these principles.

Now, while each of these virtues is unquestionably "good" and worth focusing upon by itself, one of the necessary understandings we must have about the cardinal virtues is that good character demands that all four be working together. In fact, each of these virtues is defined by its relationship to one or more of the others.

Take *courage,* for example. It would not be an act of courage merely to run out onto a battlefield in the midst of withering rifle fire because such an act would show no wisdom or discernment. The virtue of wisdom, then, helps us understand the difference between a courageous act and a foolhardy one. Similarly, you can't display the virtue of courage by doing an unjust deed, and you can't display the virtue of justice if you don't have the fortitude to stand up for what is right and the wisdom to know right from wrong.

These four cardinal virtues stood as fixed standards for centuries until they were supplemented by the three Christian virtues: *faith, hope,* and *love.* Here was a new dimension to the concept of the good life and goodness in a human being, for these Christian virtues speak to a spiritual side of human nature and how that spiritual nature broadens and deepens our understanding of what it means to live a virtuous life on Earth.

So, now we have a list of seven cardinal and Christian virtues, and they cover a lot of territory—too much, I think, to be really useful for our purposes. You see, the labels for these virtues are so broad that it is hard for us, and certainly for our children, to get a clear fix on the precise meaning of each. If children come to see *courage* merely as "heroism" or "bravery" and the kinds of deeds that make headlines or win medals, then the true meaning and the power of this virtue will have been lost upon them. Unless they understand that intellectual and moral courage are every bit as virtuous and as difficult as physical courage, unless they can identify the courage it takes to stand fast in hard places and to endure the tedious or difficult times in a job or a marriage, when giving up would be so easy and "sensible," they are not likely to admire that quiet courage in others or accept it as a noble goal for their own lives.

So let's break these categories down a little bit, and instead of seven virtues, let's make a list of words that all describe universal goods, but that may overlap each other at points along the way.

For example, William Bennett's best-seller *The Book of Virtues* [808.8 BEN] collects exemplary stories and poems under the following headings:

self-discipline	compassion
responsibility	friendship
courage	perseverance
honesty	loyalty
faith	work

These labels are not discrete, for surely *honesty, responsibility,* and *loyalty* cover some of the same territory, as do *courage* and *perseverance.* But that was not Bennett's purpose, and it should not be ours.

A national organization called the Character Counts! Coalition, which promotes ethical and moral behavior in both children and adults, focuses on "six pillars of character": *trustworthiness*, *respect*, *responsibility*, *fairness*, *caring*, and *citizenship*. (For information about Character Counts! programs and materials, write or call the Josephson Institute of Ethics, 4640 Admiralty Way, Suite 1001, Marian Del Rey, CA 90292–6610; phone 310–306–1868.)

We need to describe the virtues we hold dear so that we can be able to talk about them with our children. We could replace *self-discipline*, on Bennett's list, with "self-control," "temperance," or "patience"; we could substitute "honesty," "integrity," or "loyalty" for the *trustworthiness* pillar used by Character Counts! In fact, we could list every one of these words—it simply does not matter. What does matter is that we have a list at all, for with this list we are saying to our children that there **are** qualities and traits to admire in people, and to work to acquire for ourselves; there **are** universal principles for living a good life; there **are** "goods" in the world, and these are what they are.

Let me add a few more to those already mentioned, and we'll have a starter list, at least—one that you can add to and modify any way you wish.

charity	friendship	perseverance
honesty	respect for truth	courage
hope	responsibility	courtesy
integrity	self-control	duty
justice	self-discipline	empathy
love	temperance	faith
loyalty	wisdom	fortitude
patience	work	

Now we can whittle down this list to a manageable number—perhaps four or five, no more than ten—so that we can focus our attention and our children's attention on seeing examples of those virtues, or the absence of those virtues, in fictional and historical characters as well as in present day human beings. By dealing with just a few items at a time, children will find these virtues (and their names and meanings) more memorable and easier to discuss, which was just what the founders of the Boy Scouts of America intended when they selected twelve noble characteristics for all scouts to memorize in the Scout Law: "A Scout is *trustworthy*, *loyal*, *helpful*, *friendly*, *courteous*, *kind*, *obedient*, *cheerful*, *thrifty*, *brave*, *clean*, and *reverent*."

Virtues, not Values Clarification

In creating your own "short list," however, don't fall into the trap of trying to rank the virtues according to their order of importance. This is the logical fallacy that lies at the heart of the "values clarification" and "moral reasoning" programs that too many public schools substitute for true character development in their curricula. Each of the "moral dilemmas" used in these programs (for example, you see your friend steal an item from a store, and the security guard asks you if you saw the theft take place; which virtue is more important to you, *loyalty* to your friend or *honesty* in your reply?) pits one virtue against another, and always the dilemma occurs because of a failure to act virtuously in the first place (in this case, shoplifting). Is it any wonder that many students learn from these programs that moral behavior is "anybody's guess" or that any behavior can be judged right or wrong depending upon how well you argue the point, and some people are just better at arguing than others? "In short," says William Kilpatrick, Professor of Education at Boston College, in his book *Why Johnny Can't Tell Right from Wrong* [370.11 KIL], "it's a strange way to teach morality....Debunking moral values before they are learned is not good policy. Before students begin to think about the qualifications, exceptions, and fine points that surround difficult cases they will seldom or never face, they need to build the kind of character that will allow them to act well in the very clear-cut situations they face daily" (p. 88).

Perhaps the ultimate aim of these "dilemma-based" or "teacher as talk-show host" classrooms is to instill the one virtue that public schools unashamedly profess: tolerance. It follows naturally that, if moral reasoning and critical thinking demonstrate that nothing is unequivocally right or wrong for all people, at all times, and everywhere, then we should be tolerant and accepting of all beliefs and behaviors, and we should declare them to be just as moral and just as virtuous as our own. (Not the least of the problems with this strategy is the logic of the argument: If nothing is truly good or right, then how can we apply those labels to tolerance itself. If nothing has any universal value, then neither does tolerance.)

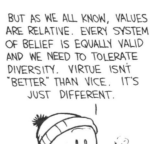

I did not include *tolerance* on the list of virtues I suggested earlier because it is different from the other items in one significant way: it is an "easy" virtue. Real virtues all have a price and are not acquired without giving something up or choosing the harder path. *Honesty, courage, charity, patience, perseverance*, all demand that you do the hard thing when the easy thing is quite readily available. *Tolerance*, on the other hand, demands little and costs you nothing. It **is** the easy road, and while we may think of tolerance as good and proper in certain circumstances, and intolerance as wrong and evil in various applications throughout history, unconditional tolerance itself makes a mockery of any list of virtues or any declaration that there are "goods" in the world to which we can all aspire.

Instead of ranking or comparing virtues as a means of reducing the list to a manageable few, think instead about making several short lists and replacing one with another after a few weeks or months. With a few virtues in hand to focus upon, then, you can begin to employ a teaching technique that has been used by the very best teachers and coaches for many years: catch them being good.

Praising Virtuous Behavior

It is so clear now that it has become a maxim in both the teaching of children and the training of adults: Far greater results are achieved through positive reinforcement than through punishment. By praising the demonstration of a specific behavior or skill when it first appears, and every time it appears thereafter, you dramatically increase the likelihood that that goal will be realized and displayed again in the future, and also internalized as a standard in the student's or employee's own mind. Coaches know how difficult it is to convey in words, or even in demonstrations, the precise physical maneuver they are trying to teach an athlete, and they know that just saying how the current level of performance is "wrong" or "unacceptable" doesn't help the athlete figure out what "right" feels like. But when coaches see the maneuver done correctly—even if it was done just by accident or chance—and when they praise that display right away, the athlete knows immediately what "right" feels like, and knows also that he or she is capable of performing the skill properly and that such performance results in praise.

The very best classroom teachers are coaches, too—instructors, yes, but especially keen observers who are constantly on the lookout for even the smallest indications of success, so that they can pounce on the moment with praise for the specific skill or behavior they want to see replicated or built upon.

This is why it is so important that in developing our children's character, we as parents know precisely what moral behaviors we are trying to encourage and that we have words we can use to describe and discuss those behaviors. We have to be vigilant observers, too, looking for displays of virtue or commendable behavior in our children, and be ready to pounce on those instances with praise.

Whenever a child struggles through a lengthy homework assignment, or diligently studies for an upcoming test, or continues to work hard in an athletic event even when the contest is already lost, or re-works a term paper until it can be submitted with pride—the virtue of *perseverance* (or *diligence* or *fortitude*) that the child exhibited must be pointed out and praised. That child must know that you respect and admire *perseverance,* and that you respect and admire your child for displaying that virtue, especially when he or she could have taken the easier path and maybe no one would have even noticed, and maybe no one else—except your child and you—would have even cared.

That's why we **must** praise the virtue rather than the result. The perseverance displayed is much more important and praiseworthy, at least from a character development standpoint, then the grade the child receives for his or her effort. First of all, the grade is not entirely within the child's control, and second, the grade may be some time in coming, but the perseverance needs to be praised right away.

"Catch them being good" is not only a way of encouraging in your children the virtues you think are important, it also impresses on them, over and over again, the idea that "virtue" and "morality" and "character" are more than just topics of intellectual musing and debate; they involve physical activities that we call "conduct." They describe and determine the words and actions we display every hour of every day in social situations—not just in big decisions or crises, but in "the little, nameless, unremembered acts" as well.

By praising their virtuous choices and their virtuous actions, we will be guarding against the all-too-common situation in which children come to see *good* associated with immobility and *evil* with activity; *not doing* something is good, but you must *do* something to do evil. Instead, we will be encouraging the idea of *doing* good and the idea that *not doing* can be evil.

Modeling Virtuous Behavior

Character development, just as all other areas of Family Learning, is best taught and learned when parents act as models for their children's behavior. Your children need to know that these same virtues you talk about with them are meaningful guides in your own life, every day. Most of all, they need to know that adhering to or aspiring to these virtues is a struggle for you, as well; that *patience* and *self-control* are often difficult to maintain in pressure-filled situations, and that sometimes you regret you didn't display the *compassion* or *courtesy* you could have when the opportunity was there to take the more difficult, but more virtuous, path. Character development, after all, is just like learning itself: a continuing, never-ending process. Just as your children need to see you continuing to learn, they need to see you continuing to develop your character, as well, continuing to strive to "be all that you can be."

So we have to keep ourselves attuned to all the opportunities and lessons that come along in our everyday lives and serve to test or develop our own character and strengthen or clarify our own vision of virtue. These lessons may come from wholly unexpected sources, as a story that Wayne Dosick, in his wonderful book *Golden Rules* [649.7 DOS], points out:

There was an old man who lived in his son's house. Life was very pleasant for him: he had his own room, with ample space for all his things; his son and daughter-in-law treated him well; there was a young grandson in whom he took great delight.

Every evening, the family gathered around a large round table for dinner. There, they shared good food and quiet conversation. The man was happy and content.

As the years went by, the old man's health began to fail. His hands began to shake, and, sometimes, because of his trembling hands, he would spill his tea or drop his plate.

With each spill, the son became more and more upset with his father.

One evening, as the family sat around the dinner table, the man accidentally hit his bowl with his soup spoon, and the bowl broke, spilling soup all over the table.

The man's son jumped up from his place and shouted at his father, "What's wrong with you? You are so clumsy. If you can't eat properly at our table, you will have to eat alone in your room. I'm tired of you spilling food and breaking our good dishes."

The next day, the son brought home a wooden bowl, and, from then on, the old man ate his dinner in his own room, out of his wooden bowl. He said nothing to his son or daughter-in-law, but being away from his family at dinnertime pained him very much.

One day, when the son came home from work, he found his young boy sitting at the workbench in the garage, quietly working on a project.

"What are you making?" he asked.

His young son proudly held up his work. "I am making a wooden bowl. I am carving it all by myself."

"A wooden bowl?" asked his father. "What will you use it for? We already have such beautiful dishes."

And the little boy answered, "I know, Dad, but I'm making this bowl for you, when you grow old like Grandpa, and come to live with me. When your hands begin to shake and you break my plates, I'll have this bowl ready for you to use in your room."

When the father heard this, he immediately ran to his own father and fell to his knees. "Father, my father, I am so sorry. Please, please forgive me for not showing you the respect and honor that is rightly yours."

And that night, the whole family sat together again at the big round dining room table. (pp. 19–21)

Both the father and his child in this story are unwitting teachers; neither intended to pass along a powerful lesson about proper behavior to the other. But they did, and each lesson made a deep impression.

Equality and Virtue

It has always been a wonder to me that the modern push for "equality" in public education—that is, the effort to make every student equal by discouraging individual excellence and encouraging uniform rewards for the group—has not created among today's education planners and theorists any enthusiasm for making character development part of the standard K–12 curriculum. I mean, as illogical, impossible, or even nefarious as the goal itself may appear to most parents and teachers (shouldn't the schools be in the business of helping every child achieve his or her maximum potential?), there is one and only one area of learning and training where equality among all students can actually be achieved: character development. Children are never going to be uniformly knowledgeable or skillful in mathematics or spelling or basketball (even if we give them the same grade for their efforts), *but all children can be as virtuous as the most virtuous child in school.* They can never be equally skilled in debating or philosophizing about virtue, but that's not what virtue is about anyway. Virtue, morality, ethics, and character development are entirely concerned with conduct and behavior.

So, here is the one area of learning and growing that affords every child an opportunity to be as accomplished at something as anyone in the entire school, yet this area we have declared to be off bounds for all children except those who are privileged enough to escape schools that have equality as their goal. It just gets curiouser and curiouser.

USEFUL FAMILY RESOURCES

The Book of Virtues, edited by William J. Bennett (New York: Simon & Schuster, 1993) [808.8 BOO].

The Children's Book of Virtues, edited by William J. Bennett (New York: Simon & Schuster, 1995) [J 808.8 CHI].

Golden Rules: The Ten Ethical Values Parents Need to Teach Their Children, by Wayne Dosick (San Francisco: HarperSanFrancisco, 1995) [649.7 DOS].

Helping Your Child Succeed in Public School, by Cheri Fuller (Colorado Springs, Colo.: Focus on the Family, 1993) [370.19 FUL].

Selling Out America's Children: How America Puts Profits Before Values—and What Parents Can Do, by David Walsh (Minneapolis: Deaconess Press, 1994) [305.23 WAL].

Teach Your Children Well, by Christine Allison (New York: Delacorte Press, 1993) [808.8 ALL].

Teaching Your Children Values, by Linda and Richard Eyre (New York: Fireside Books, 1993) [649.1 EYR].

20 Teachable Virtues: Practical Ways to Pass on Lessons of Virtue and Character to Your Children, by Barbara C. Unell and Jerry L. Wyckoff, Ph.D. (New York: Perigee, 1995) [370.11 UNE].

Why Johnny Can't Tell Right from Wrong, by William Kilpatrick (New York: Touchstone, 1992) [370.11 KIL].

Everybody Needs a Hero

Now that we have a list of virtues in hand, and we have pared it down so that we can focus on just a few at a time, we need to locate as many examples as we can find that show our children what these virtues look like when they are put into action. Unfortunately, we can't draw upon our own daily experiences or those of people we know for many of these examples because clear-cut instances of virtuous behavior are not abundant today, and have never been. Benedict de Spinoza hit the nail on the head when he said, in the very last line of his *Ethics,* "But all noble things are as difficult as they are rare." Indeed, it is precisely because they are difficult that they are also rare. Real virtues require taking the harder road when an easier, less demanding path is readily available.

Models from Literature

But examples of identifiable virtues in action are easily found in novels and short stories and even movies. In fact, most truly great stories are built around situations or instances in which a character must choose whether or not to behave in a virtuous way, and the consequences that arise because that character chose to act, or not to act, in a certain way. Authors William Kilpatrick, Gregory Wolfe, and Suzanne M. Wolfe put it this way in *Books That Build Character* (check the 372.6 or 808.8 sections of your library):

> Reread some of the great classics of literature and you will be surprised to find
> how often the plot revolves around simple moral failings on the one hand, and
> simple kindnesses on the other.... The great authors understand that people are
> brought low by common problems more often than by extraordinary ones. (p. 33)

So fictional tales offer us a world of experiences for our children to examine and imagine their own character being put to the test. What would I have done in the situation that character faced? More important, what **should** I have done? *Books That Build Character* is an excellent guide to the many fairy tales, myths, and novels that can be used for family read alouds or for children of any age to read on their own. Another resource that contains descriptions of character-building books and stories is *Why Johnny Can't Tell Right from Wrong*, by William Kilpatrick [370.11 KIL]. Collections of classic stories themselves include *Teach Your Children Well*, by Christine Allison [808.8 ALL]; *The Book of Virtues* [808.8 BOO] and *The Children's Book of Virtues* [J 808.8 CHI], edited by William Bennett; *Classics to Read Aloud to Your Children* [808.8 RUS] and *More Classics to Read Aloud to Your Children* [808.8 RUS], by William F. Russell.

When we hold up these stories and the actions of these characters against the backdrop of our list of virtues, what shines through is the image of a *hero*. Here we have the mechanism for identifying and judging both heroes and heroic acts, and our children can see exactly how a hero behaves and what it is about that behavior that makes it truly heroic.

Heroes or Celebrities?

This is no small feat, for most children today haven't a clear idea at all about what a hero is, nor do they have any notion about how to go about making such a judgment. Just look at the responses that *The World Almanac* received when it conducted a large-scale poll of students in grades 8 through 12 during the 1980's (the poll was discontinued shortly thereafter) titled "Heroes of Young America." The students were asked to "select those individuals in public life that you admire most"; their responses were then tabulated and reported as the "Top Ten Heroes" of each year. Nowhere among these heroes is the name of Abraham Lincoln, Martin Luther King, or Mother Teresa. But here are the names that received the most votes each year and achieved the status of "Top Hero":

1980 - Burt Reynolds	1981 - Burt Reynolds
1982 - Alan Alda	1983 - Sylvester Stallone
1984 - Michael Jackson	1985 - Eddie Murphy
1986 - Bill Cosby	1987 - Tom Cruise
1988 - Eddie Murphy	1989 - Michael Jordan

Without guidance and encouragement, our own children will also confuse *heroes* with *celebrities*. They will admire people for their fame instead of questioning whether the qualities and actions that produced that fame deserve to be admired. Many adults, too, admire someone for the wealth or power he or she has achieved, and that admiration is unencumbered by any consideration of how the wealth or power was created or the use to which it has been put.

What we need are some real-life examples of people who are living by and acting out the virtues that we hold up as defining "good character" in a person. We have to be vigilant in looking for these examples, and we have to understand that they are likely to appear only as sparks, and faint ones at that. Let me explain.

Unlike storybook characters, human beings are fallible; even the best men and women—real heroes—make mistakes and unwise choices from time to time. These errors and flaws do not mean that the humans who committed them are bad people, but rather, that they are people—just people.

Education professors and educational theorists in our universities today have made a business out of finding every possible character flaw and failing in the heroes of our nation's history, with their stated purpose being to make sure children understand that one person is no better than another: we **all** have flaws, so we **all** are equal. What a shame that these policy makers and opinion makers think it is part of the school's duty or mission to hold up the worst in human experience as examples for our children, instead of focusing on the best, the shining moments when some of our species have shown the rest of us the glorious heights that even humans can attain.

But that's the problem with the whole concept of "hero," for we quite easily fall into the trap of assuming that heroes are always heroic. We put a sports figure up on a pedestal for always coming through in clutch situations and then find our hero spitting on an umpire or being arrested for drug possession. Even fictional heroes at times behave in ways that are less than admirable; e.g., Lancelot and Guinevere committed adultery, and Odysseus tried to "dodge the draft" when his country needed him to fight in the Trojan War.

How much better it would be if we confined our admiration to "heroic acts" or "heroic qualities" or "examples of heroism" instead of using the term "hero" at all, at least as it applies to real human beings. Then we could focus our thoughts and our children's thoughts on the specific qualities that made a certain action or decision heroic. Then we can look at the lives of real human beings—past and present—and use their best actions as models for our own behavior, not their worst to excuse our own faults.

"Small Print" Heroes

Now, I said that these sparks of heroism may be faint ones, too, and by that I mean that we should not look for examples of virtuous human action only in splashy news events or situations of extreme duress. Instead of focusing on the headlines, says Dr. Steven Carr Reuben, Rabbi of Kehillath Isreal in Pacific Palisades, California, in his book *Raising Ethical Children* [649.7 REU], we need to help our children learn from "the small print of life."

> After all, opportunities for unusual heroism are rare, but opportunities for everyday heroism are just that, everyday opportunities for ethical greatness.
>
> Teach your children that greatness lies not in the splashy headlines of life, but in the small print—not just in coming through in the rare moments of extraordinary crisis, but in being there for others in the simple, ordinary moments of their everyday lives....
>
> Point out how they feel when a kindness is done to them. Point out how they feel when someone goes out of their way to help them with a difficult problem, or make them feel more comfortable in a new social situation....
>
> Studies of altruistic behavior during the Holocaust in Europe showed that those individuals who risked their own lives to protect others, who took children into their homes to hide them from the Nazis, or set up secret schools, or provided food and clothing for the oppressed, by and large never thought they were doing anything extraordinary at all. They consistently reported to those who studied such behavior that they simply couldn't imagine acting in any other way. To them, such behavior was the everyday, ordinary expression of what it means to be a human being in society with other human beings who have similar hopes, dreams, and needs. (pp. 184–86)

This is the type of quiet heroism that so often gets overlooked and goes unappreciated. Yet each of the virtues I listed in the previous section can be played out in small print as well as headline events. We and our children need to know that the quiet, small-print examples of these virtues all require the same moral choice—to take the harder path when the easy road is readily available—that makes the headline versions so newsworthy. Is returning a lost wallet that contains $1,000 *more* virtuous than returning one containing only $10? Of course not, just as the courage and fortitude that a champion athlete displays in winning a grueling event is not more admirable than the courage and fortitude of a father or mother who stays the course throughout the hard times that occur in any job or any marriage. It doesn't become more noble just because the athlete's achievement gets reported in a section of a newspaper that is devoted to such things, while no one cares to report or read about similar courage on the job or at home.

So this is what **we** must do—report about and read about and tell stories about the choices and commitments that define a person's life, so that our children will know that their lives, too, will be defined by the choices and commitments they make every day in the "small print" of their own lives.

For example, a story that never made the newspapers occurred several years ago in a large, teaching hospital in the Midwest. A surgical nurse who was in her last months of training assisted in a prolonged abdominal operation and was responsible for seeing to it that all the equipment used in the operation was accounted for when the incision was finally closed.

As the surgeon prepared to complete the operation and called for some suture to do so, this nurse-in-training, who knew she needed the recommendation of the surgeon who was operating that day, refused to allow the procedure to continue.

"We used twelve sponges in the operation," she said, "but I can find only eleven now, so one must still be in the body."

"I removed all the sponges," the surgeon replied in an angry tone, "so let's get on with this and close!"

"No," the nurse cried. "We **must** find that other sponge. We owe that responsibility to the patient."

"You're right; we do," the surgeon repeated, now revealing the missing sponge that was hidden beneath his foot. "I'm proud of you," he said as he tied off the last suture. "I hope you decide to work at this hospital, but I'll be happy to recommend you wherever you choose to go."

Our children need to hear stories like that to know that even though this kind of steadfast sense of responsibility and duty will never make the headlines and will never command extravagant rewards, those are not the reasons such virtue is ever displayed in the first place. As the old adage tells us, virtue really **is** its own reward; people act in virtuous ways during their everyday lives because doing so fills them with real self-esteem and a sense of real self-worth, while not doing so would have precisely the opposite effect.

Here's another example, a true story from the world of sports.

Roberto DeVicenzo was among the best professional golfers of his day, winning national championships not only in his native Argentina, but all over the world, including a victory in the prestigious British Open in 1967. But when he first joined the tour, he struggled, as almost all rookies do, just to make enough money to live from one tournament to the next.

After several weeks and months, he finished high enough on the leader board to have his first big payday as a golfer, and he received a check for what was to him a large sum of money.

As he walked to his car, he was approached by a disheveled young woman carrying a child in ragged clothes, and the woman said, "Oh, please, help me, sir. My child is very ill, and I have no money for medicine, not even for food."

DeVicenzo took out a pen and signed his entire prize check over to her on the spot and without hesitation.

A few days later, as he was hitting balls on the practice tee at the next stop on the tour, several of the veteran players made it a point to come over to him and inform him that the woman he had given his check to was a well-known con artist on the circuit, and that she had made a sucker out of him.

"You mean, she wasn't poor after all?" DeVicenzo asked.

"That's right, rookie," they laughed. "We see her pulling this scam at almost every course we play."

"You mean," DeVicenzo said through a growing smile, "the baby isn't sick or hungry or without hope? Well, thank you for telling me: That's the best news I've had all week!"

Now, can you imagine a child—a child whose parents instilled in him or her the idea that athletics required the type of character displayed by Roberto DeVicenzo—can you imagine that child ever choosing a self-centered, ill-mannered, amoral, but physically gifted millionaire athlete as a role model? Yet, if a child learns that winning and income and notoriety are the real measures for a sports hero instead, then such a choice would be quite natural and is, unfortunately, quite common as well.

The Role of Sports

It all depends on what you think the purpose of athletics is in the first place. Here's how I see it.

The real function of sports—all sports—is not to help us measure *how good* we are, but to teach us *who* we are. Sports compresses life's defining moments and events in such a way that we experience personal crises and crossroads many times during the course of every competition. Every weekend golfer has to decide over and over again such personal, moral issues as "Will I move the ball to give myself a better shot when no one is looking?" "Will I throw my club in anger after hitting a bad shot?" and "Will I find some excuse, no matter how flimsy, to rationalize and justify my own poor performance?" Tennis players have to decide for and by themselves whether winning the match is more important than making accurate line calls on their opponents' shots and whether losing an important point is cause enough to spout vocal vulgarities. Even in contests where there are referees and umpires who serve both as police officers and judges, competitors must choose whether or not to bend the rules until someone catches them.

All these same choices, or very similar ones at least, occur in daily life, too—on the job, in the classroom, in social situations of various kinds. But they don't occur with the frequency and the regularity that sports provides, and so while our struggles to decide whether we can justify cheating on a test, or cheating on our taxes, or cheating on our wives or husbands seem like momentous and special events in our lives, sports provide opportunities for us to prepare for these moral decisions over and over again before we ever have to make them.

Sports put our character to the test all the time, even before and after the event takes place. Preparing for a contest of any kind forces us to find out how able we are to endure the rigors of training and whether we can do so with a glad heart and an encouraging spirit. And when the contest concludes, we must choose every time how we are going to behave when we experience the thrill of victory or the agony of defeat. These choices, too, have their counterparts in our working life, our school life, and our family life.

So, just as we need to focus our children's attention on the heroic acts that appear in "the small print of life," we should show them our concern for those character-defining moments that occur in "the small print of sports," too. Let them see that it matters to you how professional and collegiate athletes behave both on and off the field. Let them know that when they participate in any contest, what matters most to you is not *how well* they do, but *what* they do and *who* they are.

Teaching and Learning Through Stories

Telling stories about the character and virtues of real heroes, both in the sporting world and the world at large, is one of the best ways to help your children know exactly what behaviors you admire and respect. They will remember these stories, and they'll think of you when they tell them to their own children.

You'll find many such stories in Wayne Dosick's wonderful book *Golden Rules* and in other works that are located in the 649.7 section of your local library. Also look through the many stories collected by Jack Canfield and Mark Victor Hansen in their series of books titled *Chicken Soup for the Soul* [158.12 CHI] for specific examples of the particular virtue you want to highlight for your children. There are some excellent character-developing stories as well in the pages of the *Reader's Digest,* especially in a feature titled "Heroes for Today," which chronicles recent acts of "small print" heroism.

The whole point of finding and telling stories that focus on character is to give your children something they can grasp and remember, and to give you a ready-made opportunity to affect their hearts and minds. All of us—children and adults—like to hear stories; stories have a special way of holding onto our attention, both during the telling and after. So, by using stories, parents can teach without seeming to teach and without encountering the initial reluctance that greets those who try to teach, whether in school or at home.

You see, "Here's a story I heard today; tell me what you think of it" doesn't sound like teaching at all, does it? And because stories can be told almost anywhere, any time, they can fit themselves to each family's needs or schedule. For example, little stories or anecdotes can be used at mealtime to introduce a prayer of thanks.

Before we begin, let me tell you a little story about a young couple who were very poor, but who were very much in love. As they sat down to share the little food that they could afford for dinner, the husband said in a hopeful but almost apologetic voice, "Some day, my dear, we will be rich." His wife smiled as she took his hand and looked deeply into his eyes. "Some day we may indeed have a lot of money, if that is God's will," she replied. "But, darling, we are already rich."

Lord, help us to realize how blessed we are in riches that money cannot buy, and to know that the love we share as a family is a precious, priceless gift from you. Amen.

Keep an eye out for little stories that deal with big ideas, stories that encourage your children to think—even for a minute—about who they are and how they look at life. Jot these stories down and collect them to use whenever an opportunity arises. And always save some room in the telling for your children to talk about what the story said to them, or to re-tell the story back to you in their own way. This is not "teaching" in the strictest sense, either, but it is—and always has been—the surest way for real learning to take place.

Identifying Virtues in Characters From History

There are, of course, countless stories about heroes and heroic acts that are part of our country's history and the history of other countries, as well. Even though these stories are disappearing from your children's textbooks and lessons in school, they are important for your children to hear just the same. They demonstrate for all of us a standard of excellence that, I grant you, we may never attain, but at least we'll always know what excellence is, and also what it is not. Alfred North Whitehead put it this way in his book *The Aims of Education:* "Moral education is impossible without the habitual vision of greatness."

This idea was the inspiration behind then-senator John F. Kennedy's Pulitizer Prize-winning *Profiles in Courage* [923.27 KEN]. In this book, Kennedy focused on eight U.S. senators—well-known figures such as John Quincy Adams and Daniel Webster, as well as less-celebrated names like Edmund G. Ross and George Norris—all of whom made decisions and took stances that put their popularity and their careers at risk. "This is a book," said Kennedy, "about that most admirable of human virtues—courage.…The stories of past courage can define that ingredient—they can teach, then can offer hope, they can provide inspiration" (pp. 1, 246).

The 920 section of both the adult and the juvenile collections in your library is very fertile ground to browse for character-building stories from history. Here you'll find such collections as *Heroes for Our Times*, by Will Yolen and Kenneth Seeman Giniger; *Famous American Women*, by Hope Stoddard; and a series of brief biographies titled *Great Lives* (I particularly like the books in this series on "Human Rights" and "Exploration").

Identifying Virtues in Characters From Movies

Movies are also a medium ripe with examples of character-defining behaviors that parents and children can explore together. *Chariots of Fire* (1981), for instance, is a wonderful illustration of how athletics—in this case the 1924 Olympics—is a vehicle for testing every competitor, but the test is about who they are, not just how well they perform. A basketball film called *Hoosiers* (1987) also shows how real-life virtues, and their absence, are evidenced in this sport as well.

Historical films that lift our spirits by showing us the principled and virtuous decisions and acts of real people include *A Man for All Seasons* (1962) and *A Night to Remember* (1958). You can find additional suggestions for worthwhile films to watch with your children on pages 305–13 in William Kilpatrick's *Books that Build Character*.

There are two movies, however, that deserve special mention here because they give us and our children a theme that we can all apply to our own lives: *It's a Wonderful Life*, a 1946 film starring Jimmy Stewart, and Charles Dickens' immortal *A Christmas Carol*. (I particularly like the 1984 version of *A Christmas Carol* in which George C. Scott plays Ebenezer Scrooge, but the 1951 film starring Alastair Sim is considered the "classic.") Both *It's a Wonderful Life* and *A Christmas Carol* appear often on television during the Christmas season, but both deserve to be enjoyed by families throughout the year because the themes they share are worth remembering all year long: Every life makes a difference, and each of us has the power to choose what that difference will be.

Neither George Bailey, in *It's a Wonderful Life*, nor Ebenezer Scrooge has the slightest inkling of the effect that his life has had upon other people. Indeed, neither character would ever acquire that knowledge or understand the difference his life has made in the world if it weren't for the supernatural intervention of George Bailey's guardian angel and the ghost of Scrooge's business partner, Jacob Marley.

We, the viewers, are privileged to see this revelation, and we are almost compelled to take stock of our own lives in a way that George Bailey and Scrooge could not do until they, themselves, were shown how.

It's a Wonderful Life shows us how far-reaching the effects of the most common, ordinary, work-a-day life can be, and how our virtuous acts—or their absence—can create wholly unforeseen and unforeseeable consequences long into the future. It is the story form of an old saying that hangs in needlepoint on many a grandparent's wall:

> "Life is like a field of newly fallen snow;
> Where I choose to walk, every step will show."

A Christmas Carol, on the other hand, offers us the additional insight that we can choose to create whatever kinds of footprints we want, regardless of our past behaviors that we now regret. Or, as another aphorism expresses it:

> "Today is the first day of the rest of your life."

We can choose to have a positive or a negative impact on the world, but two things are clear: We **will** have an impact one way or the other, and if we do not consciously choose and strive for the good, we can't expect to have that kind of impact on other people, including our children.

So now let's focus in on some of the ways that we can help our children see what striving for the good looks like in daily practice—activities that I hope will inspire you to create other ideas for modeling virtuous behavior and to share those ideas with other families, as well.

USEFUL FAMILY RESOURCES

Books that Build Character: A Guide to Teaching Your Child Moral Values through Stories, by William Kilpatrick and Gregory and Suzanne M. Wolfe (New York: Simon & Schuster, 1994) [J 028.52 KIL or 372.6 KIL or 808.8 KIL].

Chicken Soup for the Soul: 101 Stories to Open the Heart and Rekindle the Spirit, by Jack Canfield and Mark Victor Hansen (Deerfield Beach, Fla.: Health Communications, 1993) [158.12 CHI].

Family Classics: Films Ideally Suited for Family Viewing (Evanston, Ill.: Cinebooks, Inc., 1988) [791.4375 FAM].

Famous American Women, by Hope Stoddard (New York: Thomas Y. Crowell Company, 1970) [920.073 STO].

Great Lives: Exploration, by Milton Lomask (New York: Charles Scribner's Sons, 1988) [J 920 LOM].

Great Lives: Human Rights, by William Jay Jacobs (New York: Charles Scribner's Sons, 1990) [J 920 JAC].

Heroes for Our Times, by Will Yolen and Kenneth Seeman Giniger (Harrisburg, Pa.: Stackpole Books, 1968) [920 YOL].

Profiles in Courage, by John F. Kennedy (New York: Harper & Row, 1955) [923.27 KEN].

Teach Your Children Well, by Christine Allison (New York: Delacorte Press, 1993) [808.8 ALL].

Why Johnny Can't Tell Right from Wrong, by William Kilpatrick (New York: Touchstone, 1992) [370.11 KIL].

Random Acts of Virtue

So far, in this section on how Family Learning can encourage character development in both children and adults, I have suggested that parents create a list of virtues they want their children to emulate and that they look for examples of those virtues in other people—historic characters, fictional characters, and modern-day heroes. Now we look at some activities through which parents and children can see examples of these virtues in action by experiencing them first-hand.

The teaching tool we will employ for this purpose is *modeling*—that is, demonstrating to your children the virtue and the behavior you want them to adopt. While modeling is an important and useful teaching technique in all the other areas of learning (displaying that you value good spelling or proper English, for example), it is essential to the Family Learning of virtue because it establishes so clearly the idea that virtues are not just to be known, but lived, and that adults, as well as children, need to be constantly mindful that every day presents new and wonderful opportunities for their own self-improvement.

Certainly, children can be encouraged to develop such virtues as *perseverance* and *duty* by being assigned household chores to perform, and regular chores do, indeed, help children learn that cooperation is essential to living in a family or in a community. But assigning tasks does little to develop the person doing the assigning, and Family Learning is as much concerned with learning by parents as with learning by children. Modeling, however, carries with it the extra advantage of inducing the feeling and spirit of virtue in those who are doing the modeling—namely, parents—so that the feeling and spirit are transmitted to children along with the virtue.

Being a Role Model

Modeling virtuous behavior to and for our children requires a little departure from the way we usually think about performing good deeds. It would be hypocrisy, would it not, for us to do good just so that others will see it? Well, it surely is hypocrisy if your motivation is just to have others think well of you by such intentional displays of virtue. But the focus in modeling virtuous acts for our children is not on ourselves; our motivation is the betterment of our children, instead. So, creating situations for your children to, in effect, "catch you being good" is not deceitful, or prideful, or motivated by self-interest, and so it is not, I think, hypocritical at all.

Most of the modeling of virtue that we do as parents, however, is not designed or crafted for our children's benefit. It is, instead, simply the way we live and a demonstration of who we are. Our children see the way we behave in all kinds of situations, and they learn from those examples. As Dr. Steven Carr Reuben points out in his book *Children of Character* [649.7 REU]: "Being a role model for our children is not an option. It is a fact of life. We *are* a model for our children's behavior, day after day, every day, so we must be careful about what we model" (p. 53).

When a telephone solicitor calls during your family's mealtime together, the message and the tone you convey in your response to this interruption will be heard and felt by your children as well as by the solicitor. If you are harsh or sarcastic or, perhaps, even vulgar to this person whom you do not know, it will be very hard for your children to believe that *kindness* is on your list of personal virtues or that it should be on theirs. And if you excuse your gruff behavior by wondering aloud how anyone can be "so rude as to interrupt us during our dinner," your children will surely understand that unkind, unvirtuous actions can be justified by a similar lack of virtue in others.

We must all recognize that modeling is a very powerful teaching tool, but it works both ways. The models of *un*virtuous behavior we carelessly or unwittingly provide for our children will shape their character far more profoundly than any positive moral instruction can ever repair or equalize. And if there is a disparity between our words and our actions, children will detect the contradiction immediately and unfailingly. "Do as I say, not as I do" has never worked—not at school, not in the workplace, not at home—and it never will.

In *Raising Ethical Children* [649.7 REU], Dr. Reuben says this about the value that modeling has in encouraging virtuous behavior in children:

> Over the years I have worked with parents and teachers of all ages and back-grounds in workshops on values, ethics, and discipline in both the home and

school. I have often asked them to relate examples of how their own parents influenced their values.

I am sure it will come as no surprise for you to learn that, one hundred percent of the time, the most important way that adults felt their own parents passed on values to them, was simply by example. One hundred percent of the time, ethical adults—parents and teachers—could recount examples from the behavior of their own parents that illustrated the values they were trying to impart. (pp. 113–14)

It has often been said, and it has always been true: Children learn what they live.

While we may think we can predict the time that a solicitor is most likely to call—dinnertime—we can't possibly know the date, or even that the incident will occur at all. So this is one of those hundreds of ideal modeling situations that we cannot control or implement whenever we desire, but we can prepare ourselves to take maximum teaching advantage of them when they do occur. Here's another.

Would you like to model the virtue of honesty for your children so that they can witness you practicing this virtue in your daily life? Would you like them to see that you are willing—even eager—to make the kind of sacrifice that always attends the performing of any virtuous act? Well, consider some of the common family situations in which your personal honesty is suddenly and unexpectedly put to the test and becomes the sole determining factor for the actions you will take.

For example, you and your child are making a purchase at a grocery store or a department store, and the cashier mistakenly charges you *less* for an item than you believed the correct price to be. Do you question this mistake, this *under*charge, or do you only raise the issue when you feel you've been *over*charged? For your children's benefit (as well as your own), you should seize this opportunity to model the virtue of honesty in action, and consider whatever price you pay to be an educational bargain. Often it will cost you nothing at all because the correct price was actually lower than what you assumed it to be, but the modeling will have still taken place, and the lesson will still have been driven home.

This situation sometimes occurs in a restaurant, too, where your check does not show a dessert or a beverage that you or someone in your family actually ordered and consumed. Instead of considering yourself lucky and not mentioning the oversight, consider yourself **very** lucky for being presented a glorious opportunity to model honesty in action for your children, and gently point out the omission to the waiter or cashier.

Once again, we cannot predict when these opportunities for modeling honesty in the marketplace will occur, but we can prepare ourselves for them and be especially vigilant for them so that we can take full educational advantage of them whenever they come our way.

Family Activities That Develop Character

Now, there are modeling situations that we can control, and so we can not only plan for them and prepare for them, but we can also put them into action when we determine that the time is right and use them to help our children learn what they live. There are countless examples of family activities that promote character development in this way, and you should always be on the lookout for such ideas and opportunities in books, magazines, local newspapers, and in your talks with other parents.

For instance, your community may have a homeless shelter or a soup kitchen that serves meals to those in the area who are experiencing hard times and misfortunes that you hope your family will never know. These shelters rely upon the goods, and especially, the services donated by people in the community in order to maintain their operation and continue their mission. If you can help your local shelter by serving meals or washing dishes or sweeping floors for a few hours, why not let your child accompany you and experience the nobility of service and sacrifice first-hand?

It can be argued that the most important and essential of all the virtues is empathy, for if a child cannot and does not see the welfare and happiness of someone else as being a vital, personal concern, and at least as important as his or her own welfare and happiness, then what is the good or the use of being trustworthy or courteous or "doing unto others as you would have them do unto you"? Volunteering your time and effort to make life a little better for someone else would be utterly meaningless unless you cared enough for other people to think that their happiness was worth your sacrifice. So children learn to see not just how blessed they are, when they join you in serving at a shelter, but also how right and good it is to bring some comfort and perhaps even some joy into lives that have known little, if any, of either. Former U.S. senator Bob Dole has, for decades, spent his own birthday doing volunteer work at retirement centers in and around Washington, D.C., as an annual reminder to himself that his focus should be on others. Could an idea like this become a family tradition in your home, too?

Here is another example of a family activity that parents can use to encourage virtuous, ethical behavior in their children, this one from Wayne Dossick's book *Golden Rules* [649.7 DOS]. It is precisely this type of idea that we should keep looking for because it can be easily put into practice and can become a family tradition. Dossick himself instituted this particular activity with his own sons while they were still quite young.

Every time we went to the supermarket, we would buy one extra item of nonperishable food—a box of cereal, a can of tuna fish, a package of macaroni and cheese, a jar of peanut butter.

We put the food directly into a brown paper grocery bag that we kept in the trunk of the car. When the bag was full, we delivered it to one of the food pantries or soup kitchens that helps feed hungry people.

It was really a very simple way of giving because it took no extra time or effort, and it cost only a few dollars a week.

How proud and happy Scott and Seth were when the bag in the trunk was filled up, and they could carry the groceries in to the food pantry.

And what a powerful lesson it was! What a vivid, dramatic—and effective—way it was to teach young children the importance of giving and to infuse in them their personal responsibility to share—then and always. (pp. 88–89)

 We can also encourage our children to put a human face on their giving—that is, to realize that the old clothes and broken toys they contribute to organizations like Goodwill or AmVets are actually needed and are actually used by people, old and young, who have so little themselves that our surplus is their necessity. Our children need to see their giving as not being mere housecleaning, but, instead, a joyful act that improves the lot of the recipient in some way, and the life of the giver, as well. We can make sure that what we donate always includes at least one item from our wearable wardrobe, not just our discards. A good shirt, a good pair of socks, a warm sweater—items that we would feel good about wearing, but that make us feel even better knowing that they have brought a measure of joy to someone else. And our children, too, can always contribute one special item each time—it could be clothing or a favorite toy—that will make them feel good knowing that some other child is happier for the gift and happier still to have something of such quality and value.

"Pass It On"

While we should always be on the lookout for ways to model virtuous behavior for our children, we should look as well for ideas that help bring virtue into our own daily lives. Philosophers since Aristotle have stressed the need to develop good habits (in thinking, feeling, and acting) so that the virtuous deed becomes the normal, the automatic mode of behavior. And the more we can bring these habits of virtue into our lives, the better we will be and the better models we will be for our children.

Here's an example of just such an idea—one that is so easily imitated and adopted by others that it grew into a nationwide movement.

A woman pulled up to the tollbooth at a busy bridge crossing and handed the attendant a five-dollar bill. While waiting for her $4.50 in change, she was overcome by a sudden inspiration about how to use that money for the enjoyment of others. "Keep the change," she told the attendant. "I want to pay for the next nine cars behind me."

Then she said something that elevated this action from a simple gift to a truly inspired model for virtuous behavior: "Tell them to pass it on."

"Pass it on." What a powerful message that is. Three simple words, but they convey volumes of wisdom and philosophy. "Here," they say, "I have done this for you, and it has brought you joy or peace or made your life better in some way. And all I ask in return is that you do for someone else what I have done for you."

This is modeling at its finest. As a modeling activity, these three powerful words can be translated this way: "Watch this. I'll show you an example of the behavior that I want you to emulate; I won't just talk about it. And now that you have seen what it looks like, and now that you know how good it feels to be on the receiving end of such a gift, you also know exactly how to generate that feeling in someone else. Do it, and you'll experience also the joy that I have felt by being on the giving end. This joy I also give to you—pass it on."

Whether that incident at the tollbooth actually occurred or not, no one knows for sure, but the story of that incident has been so widely told and has struck such a responsive chord that it has generated a national following called the "Random Acts of Kindness Movement." People from all over the country have submitted suggestions for ways to make simple acts of kindness part of daily behavior (for example, letting someone go ahead of you in a checkout line, shoveling snow from the sidewalk of any elderly neighbor), and those ideas were collected in a book titled *Random Acts of Kindness* [177.7 RAN]. (To submit ideas for future collections or to receive a free packet on how you and your community, business, church, neighborhood, or family can participate in Random Acts of Kindness, write or call Conari Press, 2550 Ninth Street, Suite 101, Berkeley, CA 94710; phone 1–800–685–9595.)

Most of the ideas described in this book (and subsequent collections titled *More Random Acts of Kindness* and *The Practice of Kindness*), are, in fact, "random"; that is, they are not formalized, regularly occurring activities, but they pop up almost by chance or whim, just like the inspiration that occurred at the tollbooth. And they also have another similarity to the tollbooth incident: the element of anonymity. None of the nine motorists knew anything about the driver who had pre-paid their tolls, and so the only way they could repay the gift they had been given (if they wanted to do so) would be to "pass it on."

There is a special and wondrous beauty in an anonymous gift, for it is truly selfless, and no part of it is done as a way to reflect upon the giver. Think about the gold coins that began to appear in the Salvation Army's Christmas kettles during the mid-1980's and that now show up in these kettles every year in every part of the country. The coins are worth several hundred dollars, which could be claimed as a legal tax deduction by the donor. But, instead, these coins are given anonymously—dropped secretly into the sidewalk kettle of an unsuspecting bell-ringer, to be discovered only when all the donations are counted late that night. No name, no fame, no deduction. There's only one person who knows the donor's identity, but that's the only person whose respect the donor is seeking.

The seventeenth-century British preacher and writer, John Bunyan, put it this way: "You have not lived today until you have done something for someone who can never repay you." That's what the virtues of empathy and compassion and charity are all about—not the honor and praise that others bestow upon one who gives, but the inner glow of goodness and worth that rewards every selfless sacrifice.

(The project I have described and labeled "Community Learning" on pages 354–59 holds countless benefits for towns and school districts and states that choose to adopt it. But to me, no benefit outranks the possibility—indeed, the promise—that Community Learning will inspire parents, teachers, librarians, and grandparents to contribute character-building ideas and activities that they have read about, heard about, or practiced in their own families. Some of these ideas, I am sure, will contain the elements of anonymity and "pass it on" that made the tollbooth incident so inspirational, but we won't know those ideas or be able to share them with our children until there is a vehicle for collecting and disseminating them. That is what Community Learning is all about.)

The Gift of Encouragement

There is another experience that can also create the kind of joy that comes from spirit-filled giving, but this one doesn't require gold coins or qualify for a tax deduction. In fact, this activity involves giving up something that costs nothing at all. The truly priceless commodity I am referring to here is *encouragement*—a powerful gift that parents, especially, should practice giving every day.

All of us can remember some very special, perhaps critical, times in our lives when a parent, a teacher, a supervisor, or a close friend said, in effect, "Go for it! I know you can do it. I believe in you." Maybe what we remember is a time when we wanted, we needed, to hear those words, but they never came.

Encouragement costs absolutely nothing to give, but it is the most valuable and powerful motivational tool in the home, the school, or the workplace. It has been shown over and over again to be far more powerful than money or other rewards, both positively, when encouragement is given, and negatively, when it is withheld. It is the "home-field advantage" that sports teams are given by their fans, and it should also be the "home and family advantage" that we give to our children.

Eric Buehrer says, in a wonderful family resource titled *Creating a Positive Public School Experience* [371.01 BUE],

> We all need someone who believes in us, who sees our best, and who cheers us in our lives. When you do this with your children, they will feel more secure in sharing their fears, hurts, and failures with you. They will trust their fragile feelings with you more readily because you have repeatedly demonstrated your belief and confidence in them. (p. 74)

The Family Learning method for helping your children experience the benefits of encouragement and the joy that comes from encouraging others is similar to the practices I suggested for developing math, science, or other school skills. Just as we must create a "math attitude" and a "science attitude" in ourselves and in our children, so we must adopt an "encouraging attitude" that permeates our home and family life. And, just as we use math and science stories to help us demonstrate that these subjects are an unexceptional part of normal family life, so stories in which an encouraging word or deed produces exceptional performance and miraculous results can help us and our children remember that being an encourager throughout life is an unmistakable sign of character development. As Alan Loy McGinnis points out in *Bringing Out the Best in People* [153.8 MCG], "The biographies of the great are sprinkled with accounts of how some teacher or some kindly employer looked closely enough to see a spark no one else saw and for periods, at least, believed in their ability to perfect that gift when no one else did" (p. 53).

The 920, 658.4, and 248.4857 sections of your local library are ideal places to start looking for encouraging stories to tell at dinnertime, bedtime, any time. Also listen for and jot down especially good stories that you hear in speeches and sermons because if they are inspirational to you, that inspiration will come across when you tell them to your children. Here are a couple favorites of mine.

Dr. Norman Vincent Peale will always be remembered as a pioneer in developing human potential through positive self-imaging—a technique that today dominates training in all fields, from business management to professional sports. Indeed, his landmark book, *The Power of Positive Thinking,* has been printed in dozens of languages and has sold tens of millions of copies worldwide.

But when Dr. Peale wrote the manuscript for this book (while he was in his fifties), he felt only the repeated sting of rejection for his efforts. Publisher after publisher turned down the work criticizing it as being "far-fetched" and "unmarketable."

After receiving yet another letter of rejection from yet another publishing house, Dr. Peale declared it the last straw. He tossed the entire typewritten manuscript into the wastebasket next to his desk, and when his wife, Ruth, went to retrieve it, he said, "No, Ruth! We've wasted enough time on that project already. It is a failure, and now it resides where it belongs. I forbid you to take that thing out of the wastebasket."

And the whole story would have ended right there, except for one thing: Ruth Peale was an encourager. She believed in her husband, and she believed in his work. She believed so strongly, in fact, that the very next morning she went to the office of an editor at one of the few publishing houses that had not yet seen the now-discarded manuscript. On his desk she placed a very large, cumbersome, and awkwardly wrapped package, too large to be a manuscript of any kind, or so the editor thought.

What the editor found underneath the wrapping, of course, was a wastebasket, with the manuscript for *The Power of Positive Thinking* still inside. Ruth Peale had obeyed her husband's instructions to the letter, but she had also obeyed the voice of encouragement that was part of her own character. And it was only because of that voice that this particular editor ever got the chance to recommend that his company publish what would become one of the most influential books of the twentieth century and one of the largest-selling books of all time.

Here's another story about encouragement, this one from Robert Schuller's book *Power Thoughts* [248.4857 SCH]:

> A beggar sat across the street from an artist's studio. From his window, the artist sketched the face of the poor, defeated soul. After the sketch was complete, the artist began to add color to the sketch of the beggar's face. As the brilliant hues of the oil paint brushed across the canvas, the beggar's face began to change.
>
> Into the dull eyes the artist put the flashing glint of an inspired dreamer. He brightened the skin on the man's face to give him a look of iron will and fierce determination. He brushed the beggar's hair to give him a clean, regal look.
>
> When the painting was finished, the artist called the poor beggar in to see it. The beggar did not recognize himself. "Who is it?" he asked quietly. The artist smiled.

The beggar looked at the painting closer, with a deeper appreciation. "Is it me?" he finally asked. "Can it be me?"

"Yes," replied the artist. "That's how I see you."

The beggar squared his shoulders, stood up tall and proudly said, "If that's the person you see—that's the person I'll be!" (p. 193)

Adopting an attitude of encouragement is something that we can practice with our children and model for them at the same time. And we can do this without cost, yet get much in return. The great American essayist Ralph Waldo Emerson once wrote, "It is one of the most beautiful compensations of life that no man can sincerely try to help another without helping himself."

Once adopting the attitude of encouragement becomes a habit in our lives, we begin to see the good in other people more than their faults, and so we focus on the opportunities and the possibilities for a better world instead of all the daily evidence that points the other way.

Think about the difference between Ebenezer Scrooge and his nephew in Dickens' *A Christmas Carol*. "If I could work my will," Scrooge says, "every idiot who goes about with 'Merry Christmas' on his lips, should be boiled with his own pudding, and buried with a stake of holly through his heart."

But Scrooge's nephew had adopted a hopeful attitude and the habit of encouraging others. He saw only the good that the Christmas season and the Christmas spirit brought out in himself and in his fellow human beings. "And therefore, uncle, though it has never put a scrap of gold or silver in my pocket, I believe that Christmas *has* done me good, and *will* do me good; and I say God bless it!"

What Scrooge's nephew is also saying with each "Merry Christmas" is that phrase from the tollbooth: "Pass it on." When you encourage and uplift someone else, you demonstrate not only how it is done, but how easily it is done.

You can hope that your children adopt an attitude of encouragement throughout their school days and throughout the rest of their lives, but you can be assured that they **will** remember the encouragement you give them at home. So, just as in the other areas of Family Learning, your efforts to encourage your own child may well accrue benefits far into the future, for your children will want to "pass it on" and encourage their own children, and so on, and on.

That's what parents are for; that's what families were designed to do. Learning is a natural part of living together as a family, but we have a responsibility to see that what our children learn is worth passing on and on. Our teaching and our example will be living in our children when they are no longer children, and in their children, too. That is also by design.

Consider the words of Kahlil Gibran in *The Prophet* [892.3 GIB or 892.76 GIB]:

> You are the bows from which your children as living arrows are
> sent forth.
> The archer sees the mark upon the path of the infinite, and He bends
> you with His might that His arrows may go swift and far.
> Let your bending in the archer's hand be for gladness;
> For even as He loves the arrow that flies, so He loves also the bow
> that is stable.

USEFUL FAMILY RESOURCES

Bringing Out the Best in People: How to Enjoy Helping Others Excel, by Alan Loy McGinnis (Minneapolis: Augsburg Publishing House, 1985) [153.8 MCG].

Children of Character: A Parent's Guide, by Steven Carr Reuben (Santa Monica, Cal.: Canter & Associates, Inc., 1996) [649.7 REU].

Creating a Positive Public School Experience, by Eric Buehrer (Nashville, Tenn.: Thomas Nelson Publishers, 1994) [371.01 BUE].

Golden Rules: The Ten Ethical Values Parents Need To Teach Their Children, by Wayne Dossick (San Francisco, Cal.: HarperSanFrancisco, 1995) [649.7 DOS].

More Random Acts of Kindness, (Berkeley, Cal.: Conari Press, 1994) [177.7 MOR].

The Practice of Kindness: Meditations for Bringing More Peace, Love, and Compassion into Daily Life (Berkeley, Cal.: Conari Press, 1996) [177.7 PRA].

Raising Ethical Children: 10 Keys to Helping Your Children Become Moral and Caring, by Steven Carr Reuben (Rocklin, Cal.: Prima Publishing, 1994) [649.7 REU].

Random Acts of Kindness, (Berkeley, Cal.: Conari Press, 1993) [177.7 RAN].

A Vision for the Future:
Community Learning

Everybody knows something—some little insight or activity or technique that can make a certain piece of learning understandable or memorable or useful. These little learning aids help clear away the fog that so often blocks a child's understanding or curiosity, and all of a sudden, an idea or concept that was obscure or difficult or useless becomes knowable and clear and buoying to the spirit.

This *Family Learning* book is built around the dozens, perhaps hundreds, of little learning "tricks" and learning aids that I have acquired over the years from my father and mother, from some brilliant teachers I have had along the way, from friends and colleagues and acquaintances who know that I am always interested in hearing about their little insights into learning, as well as from general resources like books, magazines, and television programs. But this book doesn't even scratch the surface of the countless bits of wisdom and insight that are hiding in families and schools and workplaces all across the country, waiting to be tapped.

I cannot recall a single instance in which a speech or a workshop that I have given has failed to elicit at least one of these little learning aids from an audience member or participant. "You know," someone will say with obvious pride in the remembrance, "what you said made me think of a little trick my dad taught me a long time ago about how to...." Or they'll say, "Maybe you can add this to your collection; its a little memory aid that my students have found very useful in helping them to understand...."

You see, the problem is that, as valuable as these little keys to learning are to all the children and adults who need them, there is just no way to get these ideas and activities into the many homes and classrooms that could put them to use. None of the tricks and insights is big enough or important enough, by itself, to be a book or a magazine article or to be featured on a television show. And so all of these wonderful learning aids stay locked up, being passed on from parent to child, teacher to student, but never branching out to other families or other schools. Isn't that a shame?

What a waste—and all because we haven't appreciated the enormous value and potential of these seemingly insignificant insights and stories, nor have we figured out a way to share them among all the people who could benefit from them.

Well, here's a suggestion.

If you believe, as I do, that a program of Family Learning—that is, a program that encourages out-of-school learning of all kinds among learners of all ages—is beneficial not only to the families who practice it, but to their schools and their communities as well, then we will also agree that it is those school districts and those communities that should be promoting family-centered, out-of-school learning. Both school leaders and civic leaders should be advocating and encouraging "parent involvement in learning" (not just the usual parent involvement in *schooling*) because such involvement will help unite the community around a common belief—namely, that *everyone can learn*—and around a common theme that all its citizens can support: *Learning is valued in this community*. Just as learning can become a "family theme," so it can identify an entire community, as well. Communities that recognize and proclaim the value of learning for all citizens, young and old, become better places in which to live and work and raise families, too.

Community-wide Family Learning is what I call "Community Learning," a term that encompasses any and all community-supported programs that encourage families to take advantage of the countless learning opportunities that exist throughout the course of everyday family life in the community.

The theory and practice of Community Learning rest upon three vital institutions within every community: families, schools, and the public library. It is the public library that provides the link between families and schools, for it is the public library that contains the knowledge and the resources that parents need in order to feel comfortable and confident in their ability to share learning activities with their children.

Consider, if you will, the possibility of implementing one form of Community Learning right in your own city or school district—a program that would help link these three fundamental institutions and would build bridges between them for the benefit of the whole community. In this program, the public library would be the repository for all those little learning aids and insights that are known only to certain parents, teachers, and hobbyists in the community, and through the public library these ideas and activities would be disseminated to interested parents, teachers, and children throughout the area.

Imagine a three-ring binder marked "Community Learning Activities" lying on a table at your local library. Inside that binder are $8\frac{1}{2}$" x 11" cards that have been separated into sections marked "Language," "Science," "Mathematics," "Geography," and so on to cover all major subjects including "Character Development." Each card features a learning idea and a learning activity that parents can share with their children when the appropriate time for that particular piece of learning arises. Each card suggests a general age or grade for which the particular learning might best apply, as well as a specific topic label that will help parents match the card to their children's individual interests.

Each card contains enough background information on the topic to allow parents to feel confident in their ability to carry out the learning activity with their children, and each includes library resources that parents can employ to deepen and broaden their understanding of that particular topic. All a patron needs to do, then, is to select a particular card that matches his or her child's learning interest, photocopy that card, and take the copy home along with any listed library resources that will help both in understanding the topic and in sharing the activity.

On page 357 is an example of how one Community Learning card in the "Science" section might appear.

Every card in the collection would follow the same format:

Topic — identifies the area of study featured in the activity.

Calendar Connection — provides a link or "celebration" that parents can use to introduce topic at home.

Suggested Grade Level — a very general classification (primary, elementary, junior high, high school, and combinations).

Background Information — helps prepare parents to share the topic and activity with their children.

Activity — something that parents and children *do* together that helps reinforce or explain a particular piece of learning.

Resources — suggestions about how to get additional information on this topic or activity, including the Dewey numbers and page references of books in the local library's collection.

Learning Paths — suggestions to help parents build upon their child's interest in this topic or activity by branching out into other areas of learning.

Submitted by — possibly the most important section of all, for it is here that a parent or teacher or hobbyist gets recognition for developing the activity, or remembering the activity, or finding the idea in a book or magazine, and making it available to others.

356

Community Learning Project

Activity Card #SCI-23
Liquids Floating on Liquids

Topic: Learning about density is essential to knowing why things float.

Calendar Connection: March 24 — *Exxon Valdez* causes worst oil spill in U.S. history (1989)

Suggested Grade Level: junior high

Background Information: When tankers run aground or leak oil into the ocean, the oil forms a "slick" that floats on the surface of the water and eventually washes up on shore, polluting the land and beaches. Just as solid objects (like corks or stones) either float or sink in water, so too will some liquids (such as gasoline) float on top of water, while others (such as molasses) will sink to the bottom. It all depends upon their **density.**

Density tells us how heavy something is *for its size*; that is, it's weight per unit volume. If an object or a liquid weighs more than *the same volume* of water weighs, it will sink in the water. If its density is less than water's, it will float.

Activity: Fill a tall drinking glass or beaker half way with tap water and see if a fresh egg will float on the surface of the water. The egg sinks to the bottom because its density is greater than the density of fresh water.

Now remove the egg and stir several tablespoonfuls of salt into the water. Will the egg float in the salt water or sink as before?

The density of salt water is greater than the density of fresh water; it's even greater than the density of an egg. That is why the egg floats in the salt water. That is also why it is much easier for humans to float or swim in the salt water of an ocean than in the fresh water of a lake or swimming pool.

Now carefully pour in more tap water to fill the glass completely. Do you think the egg will rise with the water level or sink to the bottom? It may seem strange at first, but not only does the egg remain floating on the surface of the salt water, *the fresh water also floats on the salt water,* and so the egg stays between the two layers. The fresh tap water is less dense than salt water, and so until the salt mixes evenly throughout all the water in the glass, the less dense liquid will float on the more dense liquid.

Resources:

175 Science Experiments to Amuse and Amaze Your Friends, by Brenda Walpole (New York: Random House, 1988) [J 507.8 WAL], pp. 38-39.

Science Experiments with Water, by Sam Rosenfeld (New York: Harvey House, Inc., 1965) [J 500 ROS], pp. 29-44.

Learning Paths

Science: Archimedes' Principle (see card #SCI-17); Plimsoll Line (see card #SCI-39); What methods are used in cleaning up oil spills? See *How Do They Do That?* by Caroline Sutton [J 031.02 SUT].

Geography: Locate the sites of major oil spills around the world (see "Record Oil Spills" in *The World Almanac* [R 032.02 WOR]).

Submitted by: Kathryn J. Myers   **Local Public Library:** St. Charles, Illinois

Some of these cards will feature concepts and activities that are very simple; they will be designed for use with the youngest school-aged children. But these cards have the same purpose as all the others in the collection: to encourage learning on the part of parents, and then to show parents how to pass some of that new learning on to a son or daughter. So these most basic or primary cards can serve as inroads to adult education, as well, because parents whose own knowledge or schooling has been limited for whatever reason can use these cards, *and the motivation of helping their children learn*, to acquire basic skills and understandings that they may never have sought from other available resources and institutions.

Parents, of course, are not the only ones who can make use of these ideas and activities. Local teachers can use these cards as enrichment lessons for individual students, or they can adapt and modify the activities for in-class use. Librarians can direct school-age patrons who are researching various topics to the materials listed in the "Resources" section of cards in those subject areas.

You may be wondering why space is provided to list the name of the community along with the name of the person who submitted the idea. Well, once a "Community Learning Project" becomes a fixture in any school district or community, there is no reason that the learning ideas and activities generated there cannot be shared with other school districts and libraries throughout the state. In this way, a Sacramento teacher's insight about how to clearly convey a difficult math concept to her fifth-graders becomes immediately available to teachers and parents in Palo Alto, Bakersfield, and all other California towns that have a "Community Learning Project." Similarly, a flying club or even an airline company in Chicago could develop a learning card that gives parents some insights and activities to do on an airplane trip that will help them understand and explain the science or geography they can learn from looking out an airplane window. As soon as that card becomes part of the "Community Learning Project" in Chicago, it also appears in the three-ring binders at libraries in Peoria, Springfield, and St. Charles because all these Illinois towns, both large and small, have "Community Learning Projects," as well.

Now, a card submitted by the Historical Society of St. Charles, Illinois, that describes ways that parents can share the town's history with their children may not be very useful to parents in Chicago, Peoria, or Springfield, and so that particular card may appear only in the binder at the St. Charles Public Library. But whether a card remains only in the local library or is of such general interest that it appears in libraries throughout the state, that card proudly carries with it the name of the person or group that submitted it and the name of the community that encouraged them to do so.

You may wonder why that teacher's idea from Sacramento or Bakersfield in California can't be passed along to library patrons in Chicago and Peoria and other towns in Illinois. Well, there's no reason that it can't. The possibilities here are limitless, and if any of you who are reading this want to explore these possibilities by establishing a "Community Learning Project" in your own area, I'd be very interested in hearing about the project or helping you get started. Please drop me a note in care of First Word Learning Systems, Inc., Publishing Division, 37W222 Route 64, St. Charles, Illinois 60175-1000.

As George Bernard Shaw once said: "Some men look at things that are and ask, 'Why?' I dream things that have never been and ask, 'Why not?'"

Community Learning…why not?

CALENDAR OF

JANUARY

3: Birth of Victor Borge, p. 32

4 (GREGORIAN CALENDAR): Birth of Isaac
    Newton, p. 152

15: Birth of Martin Luther King, p. 310

20: Birth of Daniel Bernoulli, p. 166

26: Australia Day, p. 207

FEBRUARY

ENTIRE MONTH: Pronunciation, p. 83

Mardi Gras, p. 72

10: Birth of Samuel Plimsoll, p. 174

WEEK OF VALENTINE'S DAY: Random Acts of
    Kindness Week, p. 342

15: Birth of Sir Francis Galton, p. 293

18: Birth of Ernst Mach, p. 160

22: Birth of George Washington, p. 207

MARCH

1: "March" simile, p. 48

5: Birth of Gerardus Mercator, p. 194

9: Birth of Amerigo Vespucci, p. 207

20 (APPROX.): Spring equinox, p. 225

23: Patrick Henry's speech delivered, p. 310

24: Birth of Henry Houdini, p. 118

31: "March" simile, p. 48

APRIL

FIRST SUNDAY: Daylight Saving Time begins,
    p. 218

FIRST WEEK: Opening of baseball season,
    p. 310

APRIL (continued)

6: Peary and Henson arrive at the North Pole,
    p. 244

14: Lincoln's assassination, p. 254

14: Birth of Roberto DeVicenzo, p. 331

THIRD MONDAY: Boston Marathon, p. 271

18: San Francisco earthquake / Paul Revere's
    ride, p. 283

21: Birth of Friedrich Froebel, p. 302

23: Birth of William Shakespeare, p. 66

27: Death of Ferdinand Magellan, p. 207

30: Birth of Johann Karl Friedrich Gauss, p. 118

MAY

6: *Hindenburg* disaster, p. 66

20-21: Lindbergh's flight, p. 166

28: Birth of Dr. Joseph Guillotin, p. 59

TUESDAY AND WEDNESDAY AFTER MEMORIAL
    DAY: National Geography Bee finals, p.194

WEDNESDAY AND THURSDAY AFTER
    MEMORIAL DAY: National Spelling Bee
    finals, p. 76

JUNE

8: Birth of Frank Lloyd Wright, p. 302

9: Birth of John Gillespie Magee, Jr., p. 166

14: Flag Day, p. 271

15: Signing of the Magna Carta, p. 76

15: Benjamin Franklin's lightning experiment,
    p. 183

16: First helicopter flight, p. 166

21 (APPROX.): Summer solstice, p. 225

23: First typewriter patented, p. 42

25: Custer's last stand, p. 254

FAMILY LEARNING

JULY

1: Canada Day, p. 207
5: Birth of P. T. Barnum, p. 59
20: Neil Armstrong walks on the moon, p. 236
26: Birth of George Bernard Shaw, p. 76

AUGUST

NATIONAL AND WORLD SCRABBLE CHAMPI-
    ONSHIPS, p. 36
1: Birth of Jules Léotard, p. 59
7: First photo of Earth from space, p. 218
13: Left-handers Day, p.293
26: Birth of Antoine Lavoisier, p. 147

SEPTEMBER

NATIONAL AND WORLD SCRABBLE CHAMPI-
    ONSHIPS, p. 36
2: Calendar Adjustment Day, p. 283
9: Battle of Marathon, p. 271
11: Birth of O. Henry, p. 54
17: Signing of the Constitution, p. 276
22 (APPROX.): Autumn begins, p. 141 / Autumn
    equinox, p. 225
27: Matchbook patented, p. 276
28: Birth of Confucius / Teachers' Day, p. 48

OCTOBER

12: Columbus Day, p. 261, 266
14: Battle of Hastings, p. 72
LAST SUNDAY: Daylight Saving Time ends,
    p. 218
25: "Charge of the Light Brigade," p. 310
28: Statue of Liberty dedicated, p. 283
30: Birth of Richard Brinsley Sheridan, p. 42

NOVEMBER

3: Birth of the Earl of Sandwich, p. 59
SECOND WEEK: National Geographic
    Awareness Week, p. 194
18: Birth of William Gilbert, p. 135
19: Lincoln's "Gettysburg Address" delivered,
    p. 310
21: First untethered balloon flight, p. 166
FOURTH THURSDAY: Thanksgiving Day, p. 266
29: Birth of Christian Doppler, p. 160
30: Birth of Mark Twain, p. 54

DECEMBER

15: Ratification of the Bill of Rights, p. 276
17: Wright brothers' flight, p. 166
21 (APPROX.): Winter begins, p. 141 / Winter
    solstice, p. 225
21: Pilgrims land at Plymouth, p. 226
25: (JULIAN CALENDAR): Birth of Isaac Newton,
    p. 152
31: Edison's electric light demonstrated, p. 276

Index

Would you like to introduce
someone you know to the joys of
Family Learning?

See reverse for ordering instructions.

Order Form

FAX orders: Fax this order form to **(630) 377-7703**

TELEPHONE orders: Call our **Toll Free Order Line 1-888-414-8881**
(It's a palindrome! See pp. 42-43 for other numbers, words, and sentences that read the same backward and forward.)

POSTAL orders: Send this form with payment to
> **First Word Learning Systems, Inc**.
> **37W222 Route 64, Suite 203**
> **St. Charles, Illinois 60175-1000**

Ordering Instructions

Family Learning, by William F. Russell, Ed.D. (368 pp.)   **Price: $26.95**

Step 1 Indicate number of copies ordered _____ x $26.95......................$ _____

Step 2 Add 6.50 % sales tax for books shipped to Illinois addresses
($1.75 per book)...$_____

Step 3 Add shipping/handling (2-3 day delivery)
$5 for first book; $3 for each additional book ....$_____

Step 4 Total enclosed ....$_____

Step 5 Indicate method of payment:

☐ Personal or Business Check

☐ Visa ☐ MasterCard   Name on Card (print) _____

Card Number _____ Expiration Date _____/_____

Signature _____

Step 6 Send to (please print):

Name _____

Address _____

City _____ State_____ Zip_____ – _____

Telephone (_____) _____

Would you like to introduce
someone you know to the joys of
Family Learning?

See reverse for ordering instructions.

Order Form

FAX orders: Fax this order form to **(630) 377-7703**

TELEPHONE orders: Call our **Toll Free Order Line 1-888-414-8881**

(It's a palindrome! See pp. 42-43 for other numbers, words, and sentences that read the same backward and forward.)

POSTAL orders: Send this form with payment to
> **First Word Learning Systems, Inc.**
> **37W222 Route 64, Suite 203**
> **St. Charles, Illinois 60175-1000**

Ordering Instructions

Family Learning, by William F. Russell, Ed.D. (368 pp.)   **Price: $26.95**

Step 1 Indicate number of copies ordered _____ x $26.95......................$ _____

Step 2 Add 6.50 % sales tax for books shipped to Illinois addresses
($1.75 per book)...$_____

Step 3 Add shipping/handling (2-3 day delivery)
$5 for first book; $3 for each additional book ....$_____

Step 4 Total enclosed ....$_____

Step 5 Indicate method of payment:

☐ Personal or Business Check

☐ Visa ☐ MasterCard   Name on Card (print) _____

Card Number _____ Expiration Date _____/_____

Signature _____

Step 6 Send to (please print):

Name_____

Address _____

City _____ State_____ Zip_____ – _____

Telephone (_____) _____